THE POLITICAL ECONOMY OF HOUSING

Studies in Critical Social Sciences Book Series

Haymarket Books is proud to be working with Brill Academic Publishers (www.brill.nl) to republish the *Studies in Critical Social Sciences* book series in paperback editions. This peer-reviewed book series offers insights into our current reality by exploring the content and consequences of power relationships under capitalism, and by considering the spaces of opposition and resistance to these changes that have been defining our new age. Our full catalog of *SCSS* volumes can be viewed at https://www.haymarketbooks .org/series_collections/4-studies-in-critical-social-sciences.

Series Editor
David Fasenfest (York University)

New Scholarship in Political Economy Book Series

Series Editors
David Fasenfest (York University)
Alfredo Saad- Filho (King's College London)

Editorial Board
Kevin B. Anderson (University of California, Santa Barbara)
Tom Brass (formerly of SPS, University of Cambridge)
Raju Das (York University)
Ben Fine ((emeritus) SOAS University of London)
Jayati Ghosh (Jawaharlal Nehru University)
Elizabeth Hill (University of Sydney)
Dan Krier (Iowa State University)
Lauren Langman (Loyola University Chicago)
Valentine Moghadam (Northeastern University)
David N. Smith (University of Kansas)
Susanne Soederberg (Queen's University)
Aylin Topal (Middle East Technical University)
Fiona Tregenna (University of Johannesburg)
Matt Vidal (Loughborough University London)
Michelle Williams (University of the Witwatersrand)

THE POLITICAL ECONOMY OF HOUSING

The Case of Turkey

SILA DEMIRORS

Haymarket Books
Chicago, IL

First published in 2023 by Brill Academic Publishers, The Netherlands
© 2023 Koninklijke Brill NV, Leiden, The Netherlands

Published in paperback in 2024 by
Haymarket Books
P.O. Box 180165
Chicago, IL 60618
773-583-7884
www.haymarketbooks.org

ISBN: 979-8-88890-236-3

Distributed to the trade in the US through Consortium Book Sales and
Distribution (www.cbsd.com) and internationally through Ingram Publisher
Services International (www.ingramcontent.com).

This book was published with the generous support of Lannan Foundation,
Wallace Action Fund, and the Marguerite Casey Foundation.

Special discounts are available for bulk purchases by organizations and
institutions. Please call 773-583-7884 or email info@haymarketbooks.org for more
information.

Cover design by Jamie Kerry and Ragina Johnson.

Printed in the United States.

Library of Congress Cataloging-in-Publication data is available.

Contents

Acknowledgements   IX
List of Figures and Tables   X
Acronyms and Abbreviations   XII

1 General Introduction and Methodology   1
   1   What Is This Book About?   1
   2   Background   2
   3   Analytical Framework and Methodology   4
   4   An Intermediate (Operational) Methodology: from 'Structures of
       Housing Provision' to 'Systems of Provision'   8
       4.1   *Structures of Housing Provision Approach*   8
       4.2   *Systems of Provision Approach*   9
   5   Data Collection   12
   6   The Structure of the Book   13

2 Ground Rent and Housing   15
   1   Marx's Theory of Agricultural Rent   16
       1.1   *Differential Rent*   19
       1.2   *Absolute Rent*   21
       1.3   *Monopoly Rent*   22
   2   Ground Rent in Urban Land   23
   3   Ground Rent in Urban Residential Land   28
   4   Scarcity, Monopoly Rent and Housing   35
   5   Ground Rent and Housing Sub-markets   38
   6   Housing, Ground Rent and Capital Accumulation   42
       6.1   *Localised Monopoly Rent (Development Gains) vs. General
             Monopoly Rent*   49
   7   Conclusion   51

3 A Theoretical Investigation for Financialisation with a Focus on
   Financialisation of Housing Provision   54
   1   Financialisation: an Explanandum or Explanans?   55
       1.1   *Analytical: Understanding Financialisation through Marx's
             Theory of Money and Finance*   57
       1.2   *Historical: Thinking Financialisation within and through
             Neoliberalism*   64
       1.3   *Uneven and Combined Development of Financialisation*   67

2   Intensive and Extensive Expansion of Finance   70
    2.1   *Financialisation of Social Reproduction*   71
3   Financialisation of Housing   74
    3.1   *Housing Development Finance*   75
    3.2   *House Purchase Finance*   80
    3.3   *Social Housing*   88
4   Conclusion   93

4 **Neoliberal Transformation and Financialisation in Turkey through an Authoritarian Form of State**   95
    1   Capitalist State as the Condensation of Class Relationship   96
    2   The Transition to Neoliberalism and Financialisation in Turkey: from 1980 to 2001   102
    3   The Consolidation and Institutionalisation of Neoliberalism and Financialisation in Turkey: Post-2001 Period   113
    4   Conclusion   134

5 **Housing Provision in Turkey — a Historical Overview**   136
    1   1950–1980: Housing SoP under ISI   136
    2   1980–2001: Housing SoP in the Early Phase of Neoliberalism   141
    3   Conclusion   150

6 **State in Housing Provision**   151
    1   TOKI as a Particular Articulation of Political and Economic Intervention   151
    2   Land   154
    3   Planning   155
    4   Housing Provision: Is TOKI a Robin Hood or an Unrivalled Monopoly?   156
    5   Emlak Konut REIT   168
    6   Finance of TOKI   171
    7   Urban Transformation: from Slum Upgrading to Mass Regeneration   174
    8   Conclusion   183

7 **Consumption of Housing**   184
    1   Housing Purchase Finance and Mortgage Boom?   184
    2   Two Sides of the Same Coin: Financial Inclusion and Exclusion   197
    3   Alternative Searches for Further Financial Inclusion: a Shadow Banking-System in Turkey   200

4   Effective Demand in Housing   205
5   Residential Land and House Price Inflation   209
6   Housing as a Speculative Investment Tool: Consumption of Housing
     for the Appropriation of Monopoly Rents   213
7   Housing Inequality: Wealth Effect and Crisis of Social
     Reproduction   216
8   Conclusion   218

8 Production of Housing   221
1   A Bird's Eye Shot to the Housing Supply-Side Dynamics in the Post-
     2002 Era   222
2   Housing Developers and Housing Production Process   232
3   Housing Development Finance   249
4   The Volume of Housing Production and Housing Stock   257
5   Construction Move: a Political Project and a Macroeconomic
     Tool   260
6   Conclusion   262

9 Conclusion   263

   Appendix 1 Interview Schedule and Codes   273
   Appendix 2 Distribution of Non-institutional Population by Equivalised
   Household Disposable Median Income Groups and Housing Living
   Conditions Indicators (2006–2018)   276
   Appendix 3 Divergence between Construction Costs and House Prices in
   Turkey (June 2016–September 2018)   280
   Bibliography   281
   Index   322

Acknowledgements

I am grateful to many friends and colleagues at SOAS, University of London who have generously contributed to my understanding of the political economy of housing. I would like to express my special thanks to Galip Yalman, Thomas Marois, Ertuğrul Ahmet Tonak and Ali Rıza Güngen, who read drafts of this book and offered criticisms and encouragement. My greatest thanks go to Alfredo Saad-Filho. Without his support, guidance, encouragement, wisdom, intellectual passion and curiosity, I would not have been able to complete this work.

This book is for two special women, Aynur and Müberra, with love.

Figures and Tables

Figures

1   Number of interviews   12

2   Percentage of the banking sector in the financing of the government's domestic borrowing in Turkey (1987–2016)   119

3   Ratios of the public sector borrowing requirements (PSBR) and the central administration's budget deficits (CABD) to the GDP (%) in Turkey (1990–2018)   119

4   Capital inflows: The net FDI and net portfolio inflow — in US\$ million — and the annual GDP growth rate in Turkey (2002–2019)   120

5   Household consumer credits in US\$ (2000–2019)   121

6   GDP in US\$ billion and the ratio of the household debt to GDP (%) in Turkey (1990–2019)   121

7   Turkey's external debt stock divided by the public sector, banking sector, non-banking financial sector and non-financial corporations — in US\$ billion (1990–2019)   123

8   Changes in inflation (%), the CBRT interest rate and the USD/TL (2013–2019)   126

9   Total assets and the land and housing stock value (LHSV) of Emlak Konut REIT — in million TL (2003–2019)   169

10   Distribution of TOKI's net sales revenue — selected years (%)   173

11   Annual profit of TOKI — in billion TL (2005–2017)   173

12   The financial position of TOKI — in billion TL (2005–2018)   174

13   Share of the state-owned, private and foreign banks in overall mortgage lending (2003–2019)   189

14   The change in the ratio of mortgage loan rates (the end of each month — %) (2002–2019)   190

15   The total number of people using mortgage loans (million people) (1997–2019)   192

16   The volume of the outstanding mortgage loans (billion TL) and the ratio of mortgage loans in GDP (2002–2019)   193

17   The ratios of mortgage loans in total consumer loans and total assets of banks and the ratio of mortgage debt in total household liabilities   194

18   The number of mortgage loans extended, billion TL (1998–2019)   194

19   Shadow banking system in housing purchase finance   201

20   The ratio of mortgage-backed sales in total house sales (2009 and 2019)   202

21   The financial methods in the house sales in Turkey (2009 and 2019)   202

22   The financial methods in the luxury (branded) housing purchases — selected months   204

23   The relationship between the number of mortgage-backed sales and interest rates on mortgage loans   204

24   Foreign demand for housing in Turkey (2013–2018)   206

25   The ratio of the branded-housing sales to foreigners within total branded-housing sales   207

26   Nominal and Real House Price Index in Turkey, Istanbul, Ankara and Izmir (2010=100)   210

27   Real House Price Index (2007=100)   211

28   The first-hand and second-hand housing sales (2013–2020)   215

29   Housing price to rent ratio (2003=100) and residential investment gross yield rate (%)   216

30   Housing Affordability Index [for 10-year maturity]   218

31   Share of housing producer groups in annual housing starts (number of dwellings)   222

32   Distribution of GDP (by production approach) across construction and real estate activities (2000–2018)   229

33   Housing and construction (non-residential), percentage of total investment and GDP (2006–2014)   230

34   Number of REITs and total portfolio values — in US$ million (1998–2019)   251

35   Outstanding domestic debt of construction companies (billion TL)   253

36   Annual building permits and occupancy permits (number of dwelling units)   259

Tables

1   The foreign exchange (FX) position of the NFCs — in US$ billion   124

2   Payment schemes for affordable houses   159

3   TOKI's housing projects between 2003–2014 — selected cities   164

4   Total housing units provided by TOKI (2003–2018)   166

5   The current shareholder structure of Emlak Konut REIT   170

6   TOKI's capital gains from Emlak Konut's annual profits (2003–2019)   171

7   Mortgage-backed covered bonds in Turkey   186

8   The ratios of non-performing (NP) mortgage loans in total mortgage loans and total non-performing (NP) consumer loans   198

9   The external debt of the construction and real estate sectors and their percentage within the external debt of the NFCs (2004–2019)   255

10   Housing stock, number of dwelling units (NDU)   260

Acronyms and Abbreviations

ACC	Advanced-capitalist countries
AKP	*Adalet ve Kalkınma Partisi* (Justice and Development Party)
ANAP	*Anavatan Partisi* (Motherland Party)
AR	Absolute rent
BAT	Banks Association of Turkey (*Türkiye Bankalar Birliği,* TBB)
BIS	Bank for International Settlements
BIST	*Borsa Istanbul* (Istanbul Stock Exchange)
BRSA	Banking Regulation and Supervision Agency
CBRT	Central Bank of the Republic of Turkey
CCFCC	Commodification, commodity form and commodity calculation
CDOs	Collateralised debt obligations
CEECs	Central and Eastern European countries
CGF	Credit Guarantee Funds
CHP	*Cumhuriyet Halk Partisi* (Republican People's Party)
CMB	Capital Markets Board
CPI	Consumer Price Index
DFLs	Decrees having force of law
DR	Differential rent
EAP	Emergency Action Plan
EOI	Export-oriented industrialisation
EU	European Union
FDI	Foreign direct investment
FED	Federal Reserve of the USA
FX	Foreign exchange
GDP	Gross domestic product
GDS	Government debt securities
GFC	Global financial crisis
GYODER	*Gayrimenkul ve Gayrimenkul Yatırım Ortaklığı Derneği* (Real Estate and Real Estate Investment Trusts Association)
HDF	Housing development finance
HPI	House price index
IBC	Interest-bearing capital
IMF	International Monetary Fund
IMO	*İnşaat Mühendisleri Odası* (Chamber of Civil Engineers)
INTES	*İnşaat Sanayicileri İşveren Sendikası* (Turkish Employers Association of Construction Industries)
IPOs	Initial public offerings

IRAS	Independent regulatory agencies
ISI	Import substitution industrialisation
IT	Inflation targeting
KONUTDER	*Konut Geliştiricileri ve Yatırımcıları Derneği* (Association of Housing Developers and Investors)
LCCS	Late-capitalist countries
LMC	Loanable money capital
LTADR	Law on the Transformation of Areas under Disaster Risk
LTV	Labour theory of value
LTV	Loan-to-value
M&A	Mergers and acquisitions
MBS	Mortgage-backed securities
MCB	Mortgage-covered bonds
MDC	Money dealing capital
MENA	Middle East and North America
MHF	Mass Housing Fund
MPE	Marxist political economy
MR	Monopoly rent
MUSIAD	*Müstakil Sanayici ve İşadamları Derneği* (Independent Industrialists' and Businessmen's Association)
NFCS	Non-financial companies
NPLS	Non-performing loans
OCC	Organic composition of capital
PM	Prime Minister
PPA	Public Procurement Authority
PPI	Producer Price Index
PPL	Public Procurement Law
PPP	Public-private partnership
PRR	Price-to-rent ratio
PSBR	Public sector borrowing requirement
PWC	Post-Washington Consensus
QE	Quantitative easing
RAS	Relative autonomy of the state
REIFS	Real estate investment funds
REITS	Real estate investment trusts
RP	*Refah Partisi* (Welfare Party)
SDIF	Savings Deposit Insurance Fund
SEES	State economic enterprises
SFIS	Special Finance Institutions
SHP	Structures of Housing Provision

SIF   Social Insurance Fund
SMES   Small and medium-sized enterprises
SOES   State-owned enterprises
SoP   Systems of Provision
SSI   Social Security Institution
TCC   Technical composition of capital
TL   Turkish Lira
TMB   *Türkiye Müteahhitler Birliği* (Turkish Constructors Association)
TOKI   *Toplu Konut İdaresi Başkanlığı* (Mass Housing Administration)
TSEP   Transition to Strong Economy Program
TurkStat   Turkish Statistical Institute
TUSIAD   *Türk Sanayicileri ve İşadamları Derneği* (The Turkish Industrialists and Businessmen's Association)
VLP   Value of labour-power
WB   World Bank
WC   Washington Consensus

General Introduction and Methodology

1   What Is This Book About?

The world economy has experienced major developments over the past few decades driven by dramatic changes in the realm of finance and beyond. The role of housing in these changes has played a significant part in the related debates not least due to its central role in the global financial crisis of 2007–09. Housing studies have mushroomed since then, with a specific focus on the growing role of finance in housing provision. Nevertheless, most of the existing studies focusing on the relationship between finance and housing overlook some vital aspects such as the production and consumption of housing as a wage-good, the specific agents involved in the provision, the housebuilding industry and the role of land in the housing systems as a necessary condition for the production and consumption of housing. In contemporary capitalism, housing, which is a basic social need with its sheltering function, has an asset role due to the intervention of speculative finance into housing. Nevertheless, before understanding this intervention, it is important to understand how housing has been produced as a commodity in the current phase of the capitalist mode of production. For this, this book explores the analytical and historical process of how housing, a special use-value and social relation, which is crucial for the social reproduction of labour-power, becomes an instrument of speculative finance to feed itself.

Although there is a rich literature on the financialisation of housing, its variegated character and unevenness between countries make it harder to use 'financialisation' as a social phenomenon to understand its broad and varying impacts on housing provision systems of different countries. At this point, this book offers a Marxist methodology to housing studies by introducing the logical-analytical understanding of the core concepts, adopting historical-systemic consideration and then lowering the abstraction level for understanding the unevenness among housing systems across countries. Although the second part of the book explores the political economy of housing in Turkey, the first part of the book formulates a methodological and theoretical framework to provide a comprehensive approach for comparative housing research from a Marxist political economy perspective.

Furthermore, the global tendencies of capitalism, such as the neoliberalisation and financialisation of housing, not only have different degrees and forms in different countries but also exist together with the national processes of capital accumulation. Because housing is a social relation, the social relations of power attached to housing needs to be identified and analysed to understand a specific housing system in a country. The specific historical processes, peculiar institutional forms, different inter- and intra-class struggles co-exist with the financialisation of housing in different countries. Therefore, this book aims to discuss how the interaction between the global tendencies of capitalism and the national processes of capital accumulation affect the system of housing provision system in Turkey during the 2000s and 2010s.

2   Background

Turkey, which experienced a simultaneous mortgage and construction boom in the recent decades, provides an interesting laboratory to examine the impacts of financialisation of housing in a semi-peripheral country. Moreover, 2002 lay the foundations for the creation of a new mode of authoritarian state in Turkey alongside the increased role of financialisation in the housing sector, the years which followed consolidated this position and witnessed cycles of boom and bust within the housing market. For these reasons, this period was chosen as the focus on this book and is connected to the theoretical and empirical contributions of the book.

The process starting with the existing ruling party, *Adalet ve Kalkınma Partisi*'s (AKP), coming into power in 2002 was accompanied by an aggressive restructuring of the state and society in Turkey. This process, which will be discussed as the consolidation and institutionalisation of neoliberalism and financialisation, was realised through a new authoritarian state form in Turkey, which can be simply defined as the domination of the executive power over other branches and institutions of the state. The reconstruction of state capacity in a neoliberal authoritarian form paved the way for the formation of the Mass Housing Administration (Toplu Konut İdaresi Başkanlığı/TOKI). TOKI is a financially autonomous public agency equipped with private enterprise qualifications, extremely centralised (top-down) power and authorisations in land development, planning, social and private house-building, slum renewal and urban transformation. This book will argue that TOKI is a historical and institutional outcome of the new phase of capitalism (financialised neoliberalism) and a sign of the contemporary form of authoritarian statism in Turkey.

The book will also argue that TOKI became a crucial institutional agent in the commodification and privatisation of land and housing in the post-2002 era.

The post-2002 era was marked by the expanded and transformed presence of finance in the housing sphere and the heavy involvement of commercial banks to the mortgage market for the first time in Turkish history. For commercial banks housing loans became the most important component of their consumer loan portfolio taking nearly 50% share. During the same period, the institutional and legal infrastructure of both the primary and secondary mortgage markets was established which resulted in an unprecedented mortgage boom and household indebtedness in the country. This also created the surge in demand for owner-occupation, increased housing inequality, the co-existence of financial inclusion and financial exclusion mechanisms that will be discussed in the context of the financialisation of social reproduction.

The 2000s witnessed the increasing involvement of the private sector in housing production and differentiation within the sector. This differentiation was not only according to the size of the businesses but also business models, production techniques, financing methods (and their financialisation levels) and their engagement with other actors in the housing provision system, i.e., the state, landowners and financial institutions. The fractionalisation among housing developers was accompanied by a record level construction boom. The number of housing developers and real estate investment trusts (REITs) rapidly increased and the flow of capital from other sectors of the economy to the construction and real estate sectors became the subject of the most heated debate in the country in recent decades. Soaring house prices underpinned by the inflating land prices during the 2000s and 2010s not only created a novel incentive (for the housing developers, landowners, REITs, housing investors and the state) to appropriate capital gains attached to housing but also these agents' growing orientation to get capital gains on housing fed house price inflation in Turkey. Nevertheless, the construction companies and banking sector's heavy reliance on external funding created a strong link between the boom-bust cycles of the housing market and the financial cycles in general (monetary expansion-tightening phases of Turkey that are directly linked to the global liquidity conditions and foreign capital inflows).

Taking into consideration the aforementioned context this book explores how and to what extent was the production and consumption of housing in Turkey restructured by the expanded and transformed presence of finance and an authoritarian form of state in Turkey between 2002 and 2019.

3   Analytical Framework and Methodology

This book is grounded in Marxist political economy (MPE) in general and in Marx's labour theory of value (LTV) in particular. MPE offers a broad and consistent methodological and conceptual framework to explore housing as a unit of analysis with its historical, social, economic and political aspects. To analyse the concrete and complex social relations in a specific time and place, MPE combines abstract concepts and concrete forms in a unified framework (Ilyenkov, 1982). To do this, this book follows a road map that moves from higher to lower levels of abstraction with the ultimate aim of examining them for the contemporary housing provision in Turkey. This approach is similar to Marx who starts with establishing the nature of value and the production of surplus-value in Volume 1 before exhibiting (in an analytical order) the emergence of more complex concepts such as the price of production, rent and interest-bearing capital in Volume 3 of *Capital* — to theorise more exhaustive phenomena (such as the ground rent in housing and financialisation). LTV will be discussed ahead of identifying the levels of abstraction for this book as the concepts and theories which will be developed will correspond to the LTV.

What differentiates the LTV from classical political economist's value theories is that LTV is not a theory of price (albeit having an explanatory power for it — see Chapter 2) but "a theory of class, class relations, and exploitation in capitalism, with capitalism being understood as a mode of production, social reproduction and exploitation" (Saad-Filho, 2019: 4). Marx's LTV starts with commodities. By isolating the values from price formation, Marx first assumes that commodities exchange at their values to analyse the economic exploitation of the class of labour by the class of capitalists, who own and control the means of production. However, what is bought and sold is not the labour in capitalism (unlike slavery) but labour-power in return for a wage. Therefore, labour-power itself becomes a commodity in capitalism and becomes the source of values of all other commodities thanks to its unique use-value. All commodities, first and foremost, are use-values arising from either a social need or psychological needs and they are all the products of labour and the outcome of social relations between different concrete labours. Commodities also have exchange values that equivalise distinct use-values to each other "in terms of commanding a monetary equivalent" (ibid., 20). While concrete labours are producing specific use-values such as houses, automobiles, foods, etc., the commodities in their exchange values hide the concrete useful labour (and its social division) by generalising (homogenising/fetishizing) it as abstract labour. For Marx, abstract labour, which is historically specific to capitalism, is not an imaginary thing, since it exists in any commodity purchased by money. Hence, the exchange values of commodities quantify (monetise) abstract labours (through different magnitudes of labour-time to produce different commodities) by concealing the social relations of production and hence economic exploitation of labour by capital. Abstract labour, as a logically and historically derived concept from material reality, is the foundation of Marx's LTV that can explain many other aspects of material reality "at distinct levels of complexity including the capital relation, surplus-value, competition, the distribution of labour and its products, interest-bearing capital, and so on" (Saad-Filho, 2002: 12–13).

Based on Marx's initial assumption that commodities are exchanged at their values, the economic exploitation of labour is observed that labour-power is purchased by the capitalist at a value less than the performance of commodity-producing labour. This is both the source of surplus-value and the primary and qualitative dimension of LTV. After showing this, Marx explains how surplus-value is quantitatively appropriated by capitalists in the rest of Volume 1 discussed through the different methods of production with the proposition of the concepts of absolute and relative surplus-value (see Chapter 2). The necessary abstraction of values as prices in LTV then have the explanatory power for the contingent aspects (such as demand-supply conditions, monopolies, scarcities, etc.) of the formation of market prices, which is itself the main object of study of orthodox economics. Here, the important point for LTV is that the emergence of more complex categories in lower levels of abstraction does not displace value, abstract labour and surplus-value but rather reproduces them within the definite historical and social class relations. Moreover:

> the question is not whether the multiplicity of processes and determinants along the route from production to exchange invalidate the LTV or not, but how these take place and how they are to be reproduced in theory, something that cannot be proved by definition of labour value, but only by following the processes from production to exchange.
>
> FINE, 2012: 197

Hence, the logical links between the different categories of political economy of housing such as value and ground rent or money, credit and interest-bearing capital will be established by following the processes from production to exchange and to consumption (by considering each sphere as parts of a unity/whole) in this book. However, analysing value in the complex framework of economic and social reproduction attached to housing necessarily raises the question of methodology that is materialist dialectics in Marxist theory (a part of which was already shown above).

To examine the political economy of housing in more particular and concrete levels, the analysis will move from higher to lower-level abstraction. By looking to the most abstract, housing provision must be evaluated based on the general laws of capital accumulation in a social formation dominated by capitalist relations of production. Based on this, housing is a social relation having both analytical (logical) and historical (and hence systemic) character. While the first necessarily refers to the use and exchange values of housing as a product of labour, the second invites us to consider the provision system itself through the periodisation of capitalism. For the former, housing is a mode of shelter, but in capitalist societies, housing is mostly produced and consumed as a commodity. However, it is also a specific wage-good, which is essential for the social reproduction of labour-power and is exceptionally expensive. As a spatially fixed/immobile commodity, the access to land is a condition of the production of housing and it must be consumed on the same land, where production takes place. Hence, a house's inevitable dependence on landed property makes the rent theory an inextricable part of housing as a unit of analysis. The theorisation of the ground rent in the context of residential land will draw on Marx's theory of rent, grounded in his theories of value, prices of production and capital accumulation. Although the ground rent categories were developed mainly based on the social relations of production in agriculture, the logical-historical method of Marx in the theorisation of agricultural rent enables us to examine the same analytical categories in the system of landed property under which housing takes place. For this, instead of an automatic application of the readily agreed conclusions reached in the analysis of the intervention of the landed property into capitalist agriculture, the book will specify the social relations, processes and conditions for the creation and appropriation of values as rent in the context of capitalist housing production. The same level of abstraction, which Marx applied in Volume 3 of *Capital* and *Theories of Surplus-value*, is necessary for the examination of the logically-derived rent categories in the context of urban residential land before moving to more historically and concretely specific developments.

For lower-level abstraction, housing provision, as a part of both economic production and social reproduction, needs periodisation of capitalism, thus, must be examined through the different phases of capital accumulation. In reference to Bertell Ollman (2003), Marx's dialectics needs social phenomena to be understood as a dynamic process and relation. Therefore, abstraction helps to focus on the particular temporally-isolated moments or spatially-isolated forms of the social phenomenon in question. Housing provision in the period of financialisation that is attached to neoliberalism refers to a temporally-isolated moment of the housing provision and, establishes a level of generality. Financialisation of housing, first, will be investigated at this level of generality. However, before understanding the broad impacts and outcomes, tendencies and counter-tendencies of financialisation as a historically-specific phenomenon, financialisation itself needs to be located in an analytical framework from an MPE perspective — for which the book will discuss financialisation within Marx's theory of money and finance (and so LTV). Then, the spatially-isolated aspect of housing provision in the financialised-neoliberal period will be established for Turkey as a 'form' or 'determination' of the generality (ibid.).

Finally, the periodisation of housing provisions in relation to the different forms of state will be explored as another temporally-isolated moment. The production and consumption of housing is primarily a national relation and process and systems of housing provision in different social formations will have different historically and socially-specific class formations and institutional forms through which the dominant capitalist relations are managed, reproduced and realised. To shed light on the presence of diverse forms of the state and different relations between the state and the classes (and class fractions) taking place in housing provision in different times and places, there is a need for an additional analytical lens to understand the state itself. Instead of externally relating or dualistically conceptualising the state and the market (or society), MPE focuses on internal relations between economics and politics in capitalist societies. This book follows Nicos Poulantzas's (1975) relational approach in the theorisation of state and defines the capitalist state as the condensation of social class relationships. Based on this, the prevalence of an authoritarian state form in Turkey since the early 1980s (see Chapter 4) is considered as an outcome of the historically-specific institutionalisation of class relations and the balance of forces in Turkey in the neoliberal phase of capitalism. Therefore, the spatially-isolated form of the neoliberal state is operationalised for Turkey with the ultimate aim of understanding the peculiar institutional form in the housing sphere (i.e. TOKI) and the conflicts and alliances among the classes and class fractions attached to housing provision in Turkey.

The complex web of relations connected to the growth of mortgage lending, household indebtedness, increasing house prices, etc., that are 'real concrete' in the words of Ollman (2003), will be reconstituted as a 'thought (theorised) concrete' by employing the above-summarised logical and historical abstraction processes in this book. In consequence, this book is both highly abstract regarding the theoretical investigation and highly concrete and complex in terms of empirical study. Therefore, there is a need for a supplementary methodology for combining the theory with the empirical investigation.

4   An Intermediate (Operational) Methodology: from 'Structures of
     Housing Provision' to 'Systems of Provision'

The structures of housing provision (SHP) approach was developed by Michael
Ball (1983) with the aim of developing a method of analysis grasping the multiple dimensions across different housing systems. SHP was developed in the
1980s as a result of debates among Marxist housing researchers and it was then
ignored for decades under the shadow of neo-classical and post-modern housing studies. The succeeding approach, with the slightly altered name, 'systems
of provision' (SoP) was developed and extended by Ben Fine and was "heavily
influenced by the work on the housing systems by Michael Ball" (2013a: 219).
The SoP approach, which is broader in application than the SHP approach,
encompasses and develops the latter. Therefore, this book will combine both
approaches as a means of investigating the political economy of housing in
general and in Turkey in particular.

4.1   Structures of Housing Provision Approach

SHP is defined as "the product of particular, historically determined social
relations associated with the physical processes of land development, building production, the transfer of the completed dwelling to its final user and its
subsequent use" (Ball, 1983: 17). While the provision of housing is a physical
process of production, the allocation and consumption of housing as a commodity is a product of the particular social relations between the social agents
taking place in the provision process. For Ball (1986: 160), "what determines
the nature of a [SHP] is how the various social agents intervene in the physical process of provision". These agents are not only the ones who are located
in the relations of production (e.g. workers, landowners, housebuilders, plan-
ners) but also the others who are a part of the exchange and consumption (e.g.
financiers, investors, property owners, tenants). The SHP approach concerns
integrating the spheres of production, exchange and consumption so that
housing provision can be seen as a unified, continuous process.

Even if some particular aspects of an SHP are more dominant than others,
the understanding of this necessitates an analysis of interactions among the
agents involved in the total process of provision. Since these agents are not
static across time and space, housing provision must be located within the
broader social developments and struggles, which reformulate the interrela-
tions between them. Based on this, on the one hand, SHPs are "historical products and cannot be separated from their contemporary environment", on the
other hand, the peculiar internal dynamics and social struggles in each SHP
determine the nature of the provision itself (ibid., 163). This makes it necessary

to specify the social agents involved in a particular SHP and elaborate "power struggles that go on over its nature via economic and political processes" (ibid., 148). Because of this dynamic relation, SHPs are not permanent structures but social constructs of historical contingencies that vary across spaces. Therefore, an SHP is specific to a particular country. Although there are similarities between the SHPs in different countries in the same period due to the global tendencies of capitalism, each SHP must be explained through its particular form of interactions within a similar set of social relations. In comparative housing research, it is very important to understand that the global tendencies of capitalism are uneven across countries.

Therefore, the SHP approach was not designed as an across-the-board theory but an "intermediate or operational methodology", which must be combined with different theories. The approach itself is only useful and "can powerfully reveal causalities" when examined empirically and "when used in the appropriate combinations" with appropriate theories explaining these causalities (Ball and Harloe, 1993: 4).

However, the biggest criticism of the SHP approach became the underestimation of the state and the prioritisation of housing production over consumption, particularly in the research of Ball and his colleagues when applying the approach. According to Kemeny (1987: 253):

> While the Provision Thesis performs an extremely valuable pedagogical device to redress an imbalance which has undoubtedly existed between production and consumption issues, there is ... a severe danger that the pendulum will be swung too far in the opposite direction.

Although these criticisms may be right, the potential of the SHP approach cannot be disregarded and Fine's attempt to develop the approach is significant for overcoming the shortcomings of the approach.

4.2 Systems of Provision Approach

The SoP approach was originally developed by Fine and Leopold (1993) to understand private commodity consumption. The SoP approach presented an alternative perspective against the orthodox understanding of consumption in neoclassical utility theory in which the consumption paradigm is thought to be a result of the judgements of rational, self-seeking individuals. SoP was later extended to understand the role and impact of finance and financialisation in different sectors and the role of the state along specific commodity lines. Therefore, the identification of an SoP is not fixed but rather it hinges on the research question, that is the role of finance and the state in the system of housing provision in Turkey.

The starting point for Fine (1996: 7) is that:

> Each system of provision constitutes an integral structure, with a logic and dynamic of its own. It is structured by the different activities that take place from production through to final use, and incorporating finance, delivery, work organisation, etc. There is a different mix of public and private enterprise, and a different interaction with the rest of the economy (as in input-output linkages, for example) and with the society more broadly (as in the political and social significance of the provision concerned).

The SoP approach seeks to examine the consumption of a particular commodity by examining production processes and by investigating the full chain of provision in its concrete specificity. For the study of consumption, Fine adopts a vertical analytical structure in which consumption is "attached to distinct, and distinctly structured, systems that are commodity-specific" (Bayliss *et al.*, n.d., 1). Each SoP is required to be addressed regarding the material, social and cultural specificities shaping production, distribution, access and the nature of the conditions under which they come about (ibid.). Consumption is seen to be formed via a complex network of structures, agents, processes and relations changing across time and location. Therefore, each SoP is affected by broader social, political, economic and historical factors, i.e., the broader system of accumulation within which it is an integral part. Within each SoP different norms are established which is distinctive to a mode of provision "with corresponding incidence of levels and quality of consumption across different social groups" (Fine, 2009a: 5). Therefore, "the nature of the moral and historical element is different both within and between different items within the consumption bundle" (ibid., 5). Although these moral and historical elements depend on class struggle and the overall value of labour-power primarily, it cannot just be reduced to class conflict as each SoP is also influenced by the levels and incidence of norms for consumption. For Fine:

> whilst the value of labour-power is given at any moment as an abstract and simple determinant, as accumulation proceeds, so the reproduction and transformation of that value of labour-power is determined at the more complex level of differentially segmented and functioning labour markets and the differentiated systems of provision attached to differentiated standards of consumption.
>
> ibid., 5

Therefore, the material culture and meaning of a commodity to consumers and providers also have a strong effect both in shaping the SoP of this commodity and on consumption patterns. In other words, goods and services have "cultural significance associated with modes of provision" and "our relationship with [them] is culturally and socially dependent" (Bayliss *et al.*, n.d., 5) for example whether there is family solidarity in the access to the consumption of housing or not. Hence, the cultural perceptions and identities of the individuals (gender, class, nationality and age) are determinant in production and consumption processes in the SoP approach and the crucial point is that consumers "are not passive recipients but are active collaborators" (ibid., 6).

If the particular focus of an SoP is on financialisation it will be necessary to differentiate the presence of finance according to different SoPs in a country and the same SoP across countries. The reason for this is that the way and process in which finance intervenes in different sectors of the economy is contingent on the features of the commodities provided in these sectors. Moreover, the variegation is not only related to the sector-specific forms and impacts of financialisation but also to the ways in which the intervention of finance shapes the behaviour of other agents within an SoP. For instance, in a housing SoP, the interaction of finance with the state, landowners, house-buyers and constructors and the interaction and relation of these agents with each other varies across countries. The novelty of the approach in the investigation of the financialisation of housing SoP is its invitation to look at not only the financialisation of housing consumption but also the financialisation of housing production, landed property and the state (institutions in provision).

For government provision of goods and services, Fine (2002) also developed a public sector SoP (PSSoP) approach. Fine believes that a theory of social policy also involves many structural determinants and the complex interaction of agencies, processes, relations and institutions. Therefore, each PSSoP should be analysed by reference to not only structures, agencies, and processes but also power and conflicts emerging in the material provision. For this, the chain of activity must be evaluated as a whole (Fine, 2009b). Particularly, when the focus is the impact of financialisation in SoPs/PSSoP, it is possible to see, for instance, different degrees and forms of financialisation. Moreover, the extent of financialisation of public SoPs is also highly variegated through sectors and countries. Hence, SoPs/PSSoP are contextually driven rather than being simple projections of a blueprint. In summary, the SoP/PSSoP approach enables the incorporation of all the relevant elements in the provision processes, to view their interaction with each other and to locate them in a more general systemic context (Fine, 2013a). However, in this book, the housing SoP and PSSoP

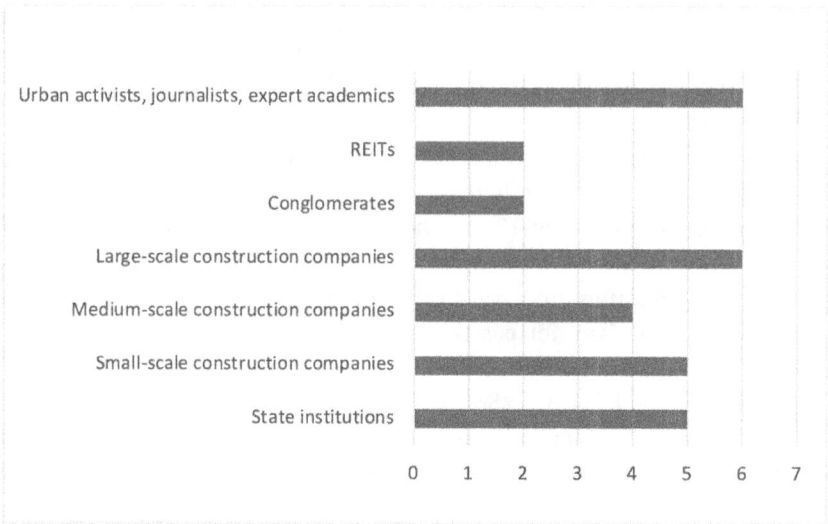

FIGURE 1   Number of interviews

will not be examined differently since these two systems are integral in the Turkish context.

Consequently, the operational research methodology, which is applied in this book, is the SoP approach with the backing of the SHP approach. It is a well-equipped, coherent method of analysis to examine a housing system as a whole rather than in a piecemeal fashion.

5   Data Collection

This book combines both qualitative and quantitative data collection techniques to analyse the agencies, processes and relations in the housing SoP in Turkey. Regarding the qualitative one, semi-structured interviews were conducted during fieldwork between June 2015 and January 2016 in Turkey. A total of 30 interviews were undertaken, as shown in Figure 1.

According to the legal code (No. 9617) on the classification of the small and medium-sized enterprises in Turkey, while the small-sized enterprises are the businesses employing less than 50 employees annually and whose annual net sales revenue or financial balance does not exceed TL25 million, the medium-sized enterprises are the businesses that employ less than 250 employees per year and whose annual net sales revenue or financial balance does not exceed TL125 million. The size of the small and medium-sized construction companies in my survey was determined according to these criteria. Also, the large-scale developers in the interviews employ more than 250 employees annually. As detailed in Appendix 1, the interviewees from the private companies are either owners or shareholders or managers of the companies, whose headquarters are in Istanbul or Ankara. The semi-structured interview data was mainly used in Chapter 8 discussing the production process of the housing SoP in Turkey.

The interviewees from the state institutions were the top-level bureaucrats in TOKI, Emlak Yapı[1] and the Metropolitan Municipality of Istanbul. These bureaucrats were in the critical positions of the institutions in question and hence they provided very important information on the policy formulation process and the central and local governments' role in the housing SoP in Turkey. Therefore, excluding the urban activists, journalists and expert academics, the field method of the book is based on the elite interviews that focus on the sphere of production and state.

However, the book also uses qualitative and quantitative methods of data collection for examining the consumption of the housing SoP in Turkey. For this, official governmental reports such as the annual reports from the Undersecretariat of Treasury, the Chamber of Accounts, the Central Bank and the Banks Association of Turkey, the sectoral journals, newspaper archives and media discussions and international sources were consulted in understanding the contemporary mode of housing consumption in Turkey.

6   The Structure of the Book

Following this introduction chapter explaining the methodology, the analytical framework of the book and the data collection techniques of the case study, Chapter 2 examines ground rent in housing following a theorisation of ground rent for urban land and residential land. This chapter analyses the intervention of landed property into the formation of the structure of capital accumulation in the housebuilding industry. Chapter 3 makes a theoretical investigation for financialisation in general and financialisation of housing provision in particular. Chapter 4 aims to answer the question of what the state actually is, from an MPE perspective, by adopting Poulantzas's theory of capitalist state. Although the chapter aims to bring the state into the analysis of neoliberal transformation and financialisation in Turkey, it does not examine the scholarly literature

---

1   At the time of the interview, Emlak Yapı was a subsidiary of TOKI and working together with Emlak Konut REIT, but currently it merged with Emlak Konut REIT.

on theories of the state and instead makes a concrete analysis of the role of the state in the formation and consolidation of neoliberalism and financialisation in Turkey. This historical overview aims to understand class fractions, the conflicts and alliances among classes and class fractions and state restructuring in Turkey with the ultimate aim of showing the reflections of these relations in the housing system of provision in the subsequent chapters. Chapter 5 provides the history of housing provision in the pre-2002 period in Turkey to be able to provide a brief historical context to the contemporary structure of the Turkish system of housing provision and to explain the evolution of Turkey's urbanisation, demographic changes, the emergence (and transformation) of the actors in housing and land markets and the changing modes of the Turkish state's intervention into housing. Chapters 6 (state), 7 (consumption) and 8 (production) are the core empirical chapters of the book and discuss the relations, processes and actors in housing provision in Turkey and investigate the impact of financialisation on the system of housing provision. The book's contributions are brought together in the conclusion chapter, which also discusses potential directions for further research.

CHAPTER 2

Ground Rent and Housing

This chapter will develop a theory of rent in the context of residential land through certain abstractions. It will be argued that the impact of landed property on housing can only be fully understood through a concrete analysis of how land is accessed, how houses are produced and consumed, the specific agents in the housing SoP and their relations with each other, the role (and form) of the state and national financial structures. The concrete discussion of the the-oretical investigation in this chapter will be made for Turkey in the empirical chapters of this book.

Housing is a spatially-fixed commodity and therefore access to land is essen-tial for the production of housing and the product (housing) must be consumed on the same land, where production takes place. Therefore, any work focusing on housing is inextricably linked to rent theory due to the inevitable depend-ence of houses on landed property. Moreover, for understanding why housing is exceptionally expensive vis-à-vis other commodities necessary for social repro-duction and why house prices massively inflated in the last two decades in sev-eral countries, the development of land rent theory in urban settings is crucial. The price of the land on which houses are produced is the major cost of the housebuilder and house prices differ based on this factor as other costs (within the same country) remain pretty much stable irrespective of location (or mini-mal regional variation in construction costs vis-à-vis large regional variation in house prices). This chapter will consider how and why ground rent is the most important factor for expensive house prices and variations across geographies.

This chapter draws on Marx's theory of rent starting with the theory of agri-cultural rent because ground rent categories were developed mainly on the basis of the social relations of production in agriculture. Certain abstractions will be made to analyse ground rent in an urban context and in a residential context.[1] It will be argued that monopoly rent (MR) is the main category to explain ground rent arising on urban residential land. This chapter aims to

---

1   There is a significant controversy among Marxist scholars working on urban ground rent (Tribe, 1977; Edel, 1976; Harvey, 1974; Haila, 1990; Christophers, 2010; Jäger, 2003; Krätke, 1992; Smyth, 1985; Bruegel, 1975; Markusen, 1978; Walker, 1974; Park 2011; Ward ve Aalbers 2016). For this book, the main reason for the disagreement and conceptual confusion among Marxist researchers is that the analytical concepts developed by Marx based on the social relations of production in agriculture are mechanically and partially transferred to the urban space with-out considering Marx's broader political economy, being an application of, and grounded

explain why most of the housing-rents derive from the circulation of revenues. The socially constructed scarcities and effective demand for housing will be discussed in order to understand the conditions for the generation and appropriation of MR on urban residential land. Following this, the theoretical findings will be evaluated in the context of housing submarkets and the chapter will be concluded with an analysis of the intervention of landed property into the formation of the structure of capital accumulation in the housebuilding industry.

1   Marx's Theory of Agricultural Rent

The aim of the chapter is to understand ground rent in the context of housing in line with Marx's theory of value rather than to clarify the divergence of Marx's rent theory vis-à-vis Ricardian, Malthusian and neoclassical theories of rent. However, it is worth mentioning that the neoclassical rent theories, inheriting the classical political economists' works on 'economic land rent', consider land only as a factor input (analogous with labour and capital) and rent as a flow of income or a monopoly price that arises from its contribution in production (Marshall, 1961; Mills, 1972; Jevons, 1970; Fallis, 1985). The common point in different neoclassical models is the attempt to measure rent based on the general theory of price. In other words, rent reflects a scarcity price of land, which is treated not as a specific property of land but as a general condition of any scarce commodity (Barnes, 1988). Hence, land rent becomes "the highest latent opportunity cost of land" (Gaffney, 1969: 141) as a consequence of the "competing demands between products for land usage" (Fine, 1983: 133). In these competing uses, the optimal (efficient) allocation of scarce resources (land in this case) is achieved through the intervention of land rent. Furthermore, the similarity in different neoclassical models is the over-emphasised utility function (thereby demand-side[2]) in the determination of land rent and the ignorance of the supply side since land is considered as fixed in supply (Gaffney, 1969; Alonso, 1964; Johansson, 1986; Muth, 1969). The neoclassical scholars' ahistorical and technical view of rent is the main reason why I prefer to follow Marx's

---

in, his value theory. Therefore, this chapter begins with an analysis of agricultural rent to understand the logical-historical method in which key concepts emerge.

2   In neoclassical economics, Malthusian understanding of the pressure of rapidly growing population on the limited land has been very widespread in rent theories (Marshall, 1961; Lipton, 1989).

theory of rent which sheds light on the historical and social relations associated with landed property.

Ricardian rent theory sees rent as a pre-condition of the production on land and as determined by the price of production (albeit not the reverse). Marx borrowed the rent categories from Ricardo and applied them to his own theoretical framework which resulted in Marxist rent theory being confused or associated with Ricardian theory (e.g., Tribe, 1977; Edel, 1976; Christophers, 2010). This is a misinterpretation of Marxist rent theory as will be discussed below (Fine, 1979). In the Ricardian theory, rent emerges from the differential quality of land and subsequent differential productivity, which is compared and determined according to the worst land in use, under perfect competition (Ricardo, 2001). For Ricardo, the worst marginal land establishes the market price and bears no rent and this no-rent bearing land determines the market price of agricultural products (ibid., 46–47). Based on this, rent in other land equals a residual (surplus) between production costs on land in question and that of the worst land in use. In addition to the Ricardian extensive margin, which establishes the market price by the worst land in use, his intensive margin (improvements arising from additional capital investments) leads him to consider rent to be paid for each additional capital invested — that also refers to diminishing returns due to the lesser productivity of successive capital investments to land in use. Moreover, Ricardo considers rent as a physical property of the soil and the existence of landed property as a factor determining merely who "bestows the right to revenue with no further effects" (Fine, 1994: 283). Therefore, for Ricardo, land rent basically becomes a static distributional competition on surplus profit (based on an identification of value and exchange value[3]) vis-à-vis Marx's priority on the dynamic relation between ground rent and capital accumulation upon the land.

Unlike neoclassical and Ricardian rent theories, Marxist rent theory is not a theory of soil but a theory of the historically-specific social relations of production attached to the soil. On the one hand, because surplus-value is produced and appropriated in the form of rent through the landed property, "the appropriation of rent [takes an] autonomous and specific economic form in which landed property is realised on the basis of the capitalist mode of production" (Marx, 1991: 753). On the other hand, the origin of rent in Marxist theory is the class property relations that are "contingent upon a historical element [and] social relations associated with landed property" instead of the physical

---

3   See Himmelweit and Mohun (1978) and Week (1997) for a critique of this.

properties of land and technology[4] (Fine, 1980: 327). Nevertheless, these social relations may have "endless variations and gradations" varying across time and society (Marx, 1991: 927). For this reason, neither there can be a general theory of rent (e.g., encompassing both feudal and capitalist ground rents) "nor can the conclusions reached for one instance in which a rent relation exists be automatically applied to others" (e.g., from agriculture to housing) (Fine, 1979: 248). From this point forth, rent must be investigated based on the specific social relations of production attached to the landed property concerned i.e., houses for the purpose of this study.

The main concern of Marx's rent theory is understanding "how the laws that apply to industrial capital in general [the 'normal' process of accumulation of industrial capital and value formation] are modified by the existence of landed property" in capitalist mode of production (ibid., 242). However, ground rent in Marx's theory is mainly analysed in the context of capitalist agriculture and the rent categories are developed on the basis of the social relations of production in agriculture. For the general concern of this chapter, these main theoretical concepts will be briefly introduced so that they can be discussed in the case of urban land.

The starting point of Marx's theory of rent is the existence of ground rent under capitalist relations of production:

> [Ground rent] is that form in which property in land is realised economically, that is, produces value. Here, then, we have all three classes — wage-labourers, industrial capitalists, and landowners constituting together, and in their mutual opposition, the framework of modern society.
>
> MARX, 1991: 1285

There are two prerequisites for the existence of ground rent: production of surplus profits (extra/surplus surplus-value) and the presence of a class of landed proprietors having the monopoly of private ownership in land and appropriating these surplus profits in the form of rent. The surplus profits produced take the form of differential rent (DR), absolute rent (AR) and MR. These analytical categories at the abstract level are important to understand the capital accumulation attached to the landed property in more concrete levels since these different forms of rent derive from different sources (Clarke and Ginsburg, 1976). The transformation of values into prices of production happens in a

---

4 Technical conditions of production are important for the determination of the level of rent but not for its existence.

two-stage process in Marxist theory in general and in rent theory in particular. In this regard, DR refers to competition within the same sector which establishes market values. In contrast, AR derives from competition between sectors that establishes the prices of production. This discussion theorised by Marx in Volume 3 of *Capital* (1991) concerns how surplus-value is distributed between capitals in competition and will be explored due to its relation with the development of rent theory.

Competition between capitals within a sector (intra-sectoral competition) establishes sectoral market value, which is determined by the average socially-necessary labour-time to produce commodities in this industry.[5] The sectoral market value is distinct from the individual capitalist values due to, for instance, the changing efficiency of technical equipment or the level of access to credit or more/less labour-time required for individual capitalists' production than the market value expresses (Marx, 1991: 279). However, with the formation of sectoral market value through the inter-sectoral competition at the level of production, the excess or surplus profits would be accrued to the individual capitals having below-market individual values (Marx, 1968: 208).

Marx argues that different industries may have different rates of profits determined by their organic composition of capital (OCC), which measures c/v – the ratio of total means of production used per production unit to the total wage goods – in value terms. As a logical tendency, the competition between different sectors (inter-sectoral competition) would lead to a switch of capital flow from the industries having a low OCC to the ones with a high OCC until to the point where the rates of profit become equalised to ensure that none of the capitals would have a lower-than-average rate of profit. As a logical tendency, through the competition between sectors, value (and surplus-value) is redistributed and the general rates of profits are equalised between sectors and prices of production are established (Marx, 1968: 208).

1.1   *Differential Rent*

In the case of agriculture, the difference between market value and individual values resulting from the productivity differences of capitals invested in different lands is the source of differential rent. The surplus profits arising from the competition within the agricultural sector is not itself the reason for the existence of ground rent in agriculture as if it was, it would exist in all other

---

5   However, as put by Fine (1979: 244) "Marx does not insist that the market value always equal the average value (III, p. 183). If either the most favourable or the least favourable technique is sufficiently weighty as compared with the average, then the technique concerned rather than the [arithmetic] average regulates the [sector's] market value."

industries. Rather it is the existence of the landowner who appropriates surplus profit "out of the pocket of the manufacturer and into his own" (Marx, 1991: 786). As a result of the competition within the agricultural sector, some capitalists produce commodities below the socially-necessary labour-time. This happens because surplus profits in agriculture change according to land quality, i.e., fertility differences, leading to the rise of differential rent 1 (DRI) and according to the size of capital invested leading to differential rent 2 (DRII). The analysis of DRI in Marx starts with the surplus profit arising as a result of the permanent fertility differences across lands, that cannot be eliminated by competition between capitalist farmers. Landed property puts a barrier on capitals investing in more fertile lands by appropriating (differential) surplus profits in the form of DRI — the investment of different sizes of capital is ignored here. In this case, although surplus-value in the form of DRI is created, the formation of market value in agriculture is distorted (Fine and Saad-Filho, 2010: 156). This distortion in market value stems from the existence of landed property. In other words, the presence of landed property alters the formation of market value in capitalist agriculture since the different qualities of land (the non-existence of lands with equal fertility) lead to the formation of market value not according to the sectorally-specific average/normal individual values but according to the production on the least fertile (worst) land in use. In this case, unlike Ricardian rent theory, "the determination of market value ... is based necessarily on the exchange-value of the product and not on the soil and the differences in its fertility" (Marx, 1991: 799).

In contrast, DRII derives from the appropriation of surplus profits by the productivity differences that emerge from the application of different sizes of capital to equal qualities of lands — the fertility differences are ignored here. The surplus profit appropriated by the landowner[6] in the form of DRII does not refer to more or less efficient methods of production but only to "the differences in the distribution of capital (ability to obtain credit) among [capitalist] farmers" (ibid., 815).

However, in agriculture, neither lands of equal fertility nor equal capitals exist generally. Here, both DRI and DRII have been demonstrated through certain abstractions regarding the distribution of capitals and fertilities since DRI and DRII are neither detachable nor additive in Marx; rather they interact with each other in more concrete analysis. Therefore, the formation of market value in agriculture is simultaneously determined by the co-existence of both DRI

---

6   The whole surplus profits in the form of DRII does not have to be appropriated by the landowner but a part of it may accrue to the capitalist tenant themself.

(worst land) and II (normal/average size of capital), although this determination is hard to make in such an abstract level (Fine, 1979: 254).

1.2   *Absolute Rent*

The formation of AR derives from the transformation of market values into prices of production. Although both AR and DR concern the appropriation of surplus profit in the form of rent and create obstacles to capital investment brought by landed property, they "are located at different levels of analysis and, therefore, their source is correspondingly different" (Fine and Saad-Filho, 2010: 161). Whereas productivity differences within agriculture are the source of DR, AR originates in the productivity differences between agriculture and other sectors in the economy.

As mentioned above, the inter-sectoral competition establishes the prices of production and regulates the capital flows between sectors. Nevertheless, the formation of market prices in agriculture in general and inter-sectoral capital movement into agriculture in particular face an obstacle posed by the landed property. In other words, capital flowing onto a new land in agriculture is charged by the landowner. This charge takes the form of AR, which is different from DRII, as in this case, the capital moves to a land, which is not used before. Marx (1991: 1555), unlike Ricardo, tried to show that even the worst land charges a rent, i.e., AR, as whenever land is private property:

> If all the land suitable for agriculture in a certain country were leased
> – assuming the capitalist mode of production and normal conditions to
> be general – there would not be any land not paying rent; but there might
> be some capitals, certain parts of capitals invested in land, that might not
> yield any rent. For as soon as the land has been rented, landed property
> ceases to act as an absolute barrier against the investment of necessary
> capital.

Here, capital flowing onto new land leads the capitalist tenant to sell the agricultural products at a price above their price of production and this surplus difference between the sale price and the price of production is captured by the landowner in the form of AR. Put it differently, AR as an extra (surplus-value) payment made to the landowner was added to the price of production of agricultural products, rather than being redistributed across the economy that would equalise the general rates of profits.

Therefore, the extensive cultivation of land and so the rise of AR leads to the rise of OCC in the agricultural industry at a slower pace than the social average. However, Marx analysed this tendency of lower OCC in agriculture together with its counter-tendency, which is the existence of the DRII, i.e. intensive cultivation of land. AR cannot rise above DRII, otherwise, capitalist farmers would make an intensive investment (by paying DRII) instead of extensive one (by paying AR). In this way, the OCC in agriculture, which decreases due to the rise of AR,[7] would increase by the intensive cultivation of land. As put by Fine (1979: 262):

> AR is limited by the difference between value and price of production in correspondence to the upper limit on the charge for extensive cultivation posed by the alternative application of capital to intensive cultivation (DRII).

The deeper discussion of AR in an agricultural setting is out of the scope of this chapter. Instead, AR would be re-evaluated in the context of urban land below.

1.3 Monopoly Rent

For Marx (1991: 898), monopoly price is "determined neither by the price of production of the commodities nor by their value, but rather by the demand of the purchasers and their ability to pay". MR derives from this genuine monopoly price as a temporary form of rent. Unlike DR and AR, the source of MR is in the circulation of revenues (wages and profits) rather than the circulation of capital (surplus-value produced on land) (Harvey, 1985; 1999). In other words, while DR and AR derive from the sphere of production, MR derives from the sphere of exchange following the appropriation and distribution of surplus profits in the economy. This is why if landowners charge MR from capitalists, the price of production of agricultural commodities can rise above their value. Among all the rent categories, MR is the only rent which derives from outside the social value produced in agriculture. However, the rise of MR needs the existence of natural or artificial monopolies on some agricultural products enabling the capitalist farmers to sell them above their values which are determined by the degree of willingness, ability and unsatisfied demand of the purchasers.

---

7 Marx also discussed the conditions though which AR would disappear: (i) "the average composition of capital [OCC] were equal to, or higher than that of average social capital" (Marx 1991: 892); (ii) if "all the land suitable for agricultural capital in a certain country were leased" (ibid: 899); (iii) if "conditions of production in intensive cultivation became the same as those prevailing on average in industry" (Marx 1968, ch XIII).

2   Ground Rent in Urban Land

Marx's theory of ground rent in *Capital* was developed with regard to agricultural land. Before going further, it is important to highlight some restrictions to transfer the rent categories to an urban context. Ball (1985a: 74) as one of the pioneers in the investigation of ground rent in the urban setting gives an important warning:

> The major problem faced by attempts to transfer the concepts of agricultural rent to the urban context is that the economic mechanism through which rent is appropriated are not the same. The basic points associated with the monopoly conferred by land ownership still hold but the conditions structuring the 'fortuitous circumstances' are different.

Because of this, the theory of rent in an urban setting cannot be same as in agriculture. At the abstract level, it is presumed above that in the agricultural sector the ground rent emerges through the relation between a class of landlords who has a monopoly in landed property and a class of capitalist tenant farmers who uses soil to produce extra surplus-value to pay to the landowner in exchange for their access to land. However, this relation is not reproduced in urban land. Rather there are different agents involved in the processes of production and exchange as stated below:

> Moreover, we are dealing with combinations of social relations in the urban context which are different from those in agriculture. There are a series of social structures of building provision into which landed property and land rent may intervene. Each is a historical product.
>
> BALL, 1985a: 515

Put it differently, "the existence of urban rent (that accrues to the owners of houses, factories, infrastructure and the like) is rooted in a specific social relationship, that is, the private ownership of land" (Swyngedouw, 2012: 311) and unlike agriculture, there are many different social relations of production in the urban sphere. More specifically, wide-range and diverse kinds of land use take place in urban spheres. In each of them, there are different social relations attached to the landed property changing according to the different uses of urban land. Therefore, the rest of this chapter will argue that the form of rent emerging in urban land depends on what the land is used for.

Ball (1985a: 75) notes that:

> the notion of a uniform commodity and a single market price cannot hold in the urban context. Ground rent is charged on buildings which by definition are all different, if for no other reason than their location. Selling prices for built structures vary considerably.

Ball compares the commodities produced in agricultural land and in urban land, i.e., corn and buildings respectively. According to Ball, unlike corn, buildings do not have any uniform market price and neither the determination of the relation between individual prices and market price nor the competition within the building industry corresponds to the agricultural situation. This investigation regarding the diverse kinds of urban land use and different types of building provision is very important. Although these warnings of Ball are indeed crucial and will be taken into consideration in the analysis of urban ground rent below, this book does not agree with the conclusion of Ball (1985a: 512–3) as follows:

> for Marx, rent is the payment of a revenue to landed property for the right to use a piece of land ... where no such payment takes place, rent does not exist ... The need to limit the category of rent to payments to landlords is very important for the urban context. Failure to conform rigidly to the definition can lead to endless confusion.

On the contrary, Marx (1991: 785) expressly discusses that in the waterfall example:

> Nothing is altered if the capitalist owns the waterfall himself. He still draws the surplus profit ... not as a capitalist, but as the owner of the waterfall; and for the precise reason that this excess arises not from his capital as such, but rather from his disposal over a natural force that is limited in scope, separable from his capital, and monopolizable, it is transformed into ground rent.

From this point forth, there are two hypotheses to argue: (i) even if the land is owned by the builder capitalist themself, instead of a landowner who charges rent from them, the ground rent can still emerge in the urban context; (ii) the presence of diverse kinds of land use, different types of production and different market structures do not obstruct the use of the rent concepts in an urban context since these concepts provide a fruitful methodology to carry the value analysis of ground rent to the urban setting. In other words, the sources of rent in Marx were developed in a logical level and supplemented with an analysis of the social relations of agricultural landed property rather than a mechanical application of the rent categories to agriculture. This enables us to examine and develop the same logical categories for different social relations of landed property.

Even though Marx's contribution regarding rent on buildings is limited to a few pages in chapter 46 of *Capital* 3, this material can be used as a start to lead the further analysis for ground rent in urban land:

> Wherever rent exists, differential rent always appears and always follows the same laws as it does in agriculture. Wherever natural forces can be monopolized and give the industrialist who makes use of them a surplus profit, whether a waterfall, a rich mine, fishing grounds or a well-situated building site, the person indicated as the owner of these natural objects, by virtue of his title to a portion of the earth, seizes this surplus profit from the functioning capital in the form of rent ... As far as land for building is concerned ... this rent is characterised first by the preponderant influence that location exerts here on the differential rent ... Secondly, by palpable and complete passivity displayed by the owner ... finally, the prevalence of a monopoly price in many cases ... a more fruitful source for house-rent.
>
> MARX, 1991: 908

As can be seen from the above quotation, for Marx, DR arising through different surplus profits produced on the landed property is also relevant in the context of buildings. However, Marx (1991: 908) says that "rent is characterised first by the preponderant influence that location exerts", indicating that the main parameter in the determination of the quality of land in urban areas is its location rather than fertility. Moreover, while the quality of land in agriculture, i.e. fertility, changes slowly, the quality of land in an urban context, i.e. location, is subject to continual changes as a result of dynamic economic, political, and social processes. Fertility "always implies an economic relation, a relation to the existing chemical and mechanical level of development in agriculture, and, therefore, changes with this level of development" (ibid., 651). This change within the soil in agriculture is slower compared to changes happening in urban land. Unlike fertility, location does not refer to the naturally given conditions of soil but rather historically, socially and economically created qualities. Harvey (1999: 341) states that "locational advantages for specific land parcels can be altered by human agency" as the urbanisation process creates "man-made changes" to the quality of land, that are "socially created qualities" (ibid.). The main reason for this is that whereas the ground rent in agriculture mainly depends on investment in a specific land parcel, the ground rent in urban space is affected not only by capital investment in a particular land on which production takes place but also by investments and changes in the built environment surrounding that land. In other words, because "the locational advantage is perpetually in the course of alteration through investment in transportation and the shifting geographical distribution of economic activity and population" (ibid., 354) in urban space, the productivity of urban land consistently changes according to its proximity to these shifting activities. The increase in land values generated by a location that is directly affected by the social and economic developments is called "development gain" (Ball, 1983). This will be discussed in depth below, but for now, it is sufficient to say that the generation and appropriation of development gain are very important in the context of residential land.

Marx stated that the "palpable and complete passivity displayed by the owner", Marx (1991: 908) which suggests that the creation and appropriation of ground rent are more than a simple distributional issue. Even in the complete passivity of the landowner, rent level can change according to the production and investment activities of a producer on land. This passivity might have been thought of by Marx as the passive role of the landowner with regard to the domination of labour and the consequent developments of capital accumulation. However, in the urban context, landowners do not refer to one of the three great classes in a capitalist society, instead, many class fractions and institutions are also landowners. Massey and Catelano (1978: 40) stated that in modern capitalism:

> Landed property no longer exists as unified and relatively homogenous class interest, but comprises motley and heterogeneous groups ranging all the way from ancient institutions (the Church, the Crown, large aristocratic estates), through financial institutions (banks, insurance companies and pension funds) to a wide range of individual and corporate owners (including workers who own their homes) and government agencies.

The creation and appropriation of development gains through landed property, therefore, contains much more complex relations than in agriculture. Marx did not investigate the social relations of production in urban land but rather in agriculture where the surplus-value produced on the agricultural land is shared between landlord and capitalist farmer. In contrast, much larger parts of society struggle for appropriating ground rent created in urban land. Therefore, this chapter advocates that landowners are not passive agents but rather very active in appropriating ground rent generated in urban land, especially in the current phase of capitalism.

Finally, Marx (1991: 908) notes that while MR (and monopoly pricing) is uncommon in the agricultural context, it is much more prevalent in the urban context. In the case of urban land, there is a wide scope for the creation of the underlying conditions for the emergence of MR. The pace and rhythm of social and economic reproduction create human-made scarcities on landed property through which MR arises. In other words, MR can be extracted if desirable land quality is in short supply (that cannot be easily replicated elsewhere) and the monopoly power of the owner who has control over such special quality of land enables her to link this desirable land together with certain kind of activities (Harvey, 1999). For MR, Marx (1991: 787) gives the example of the vineyard producing wine of extraordinary quality produced in small quantities and so empowering the wine-grower to realise abundant surplus profit out of monopoly price that is excess over both the value and production price of the commodity.

This makes MR quite different from DR and AR. Whereas the level of DR and AR are determined according to the competition within a sector and between sectors respectively, monopoly price in general is "determined only by the purchasers' eagerness to buy and ability to pay, independent of the price determined by the general price of production, as well as by the value of the products" for unique and non-replicable land uses (ibid., 910). From this point forth, landed properties that are undersupplied with respect to demand can be traded at a monopoly price. Here, it is important to bear in mind that the level of MR is strongly related to the broader conditions of economic and social reproduction which regulates and organises supply and demand conditions in the economy (Fine, 2012: 82). Furthermore, unlike DR and AR, MR is not directly linked to the production process (and the composition of capital in the industry concerned); but instead, it is extracted out of distribution process, i.e. the sphere of exchange, such as wages, taxes, interest and profits. Herein, the crucial point distinguishing Marx's MR from vulgar economists' rent theorisation is that although MR is not extracted from surplus profit produced on a particular land which rent is paid, all forms of revenue appropriated as MR constitute a part of surplus-value of other commodities that are produced elsewhere:

> [MR] ... must always indirectly form part of surplus-value. Even if it is not a part of the excess price over and above the production costs of the actual commodity of which it itself forms a component, as in the case of differential rent, or an excess part of the surplus-value in the commodity

of which it forms a component over and above its own portion of surplus-value as measured by the average profit (as in the case of absolute rent), it is still a part of the surplus-value of other commodities, i.e. those which are exchanged against this commodity with a monopoly price.

MARX, 1991: 971–972

However, in his brief contribution, Marx considered the ground rent on urban land in general regardless of their intended uses. Yet, in urban space, land is used for specific purposes such as industrial, commercial, financial, infrastructural, governmental and residential uses. These different purposes of land use are crucial to understanding whether the ground rent is appropriated out of the circulation of surplus-value or the circulation of revenues. Although landowners and producers are mostly unconscious of the sources of rent and whether this source of rent comes from revenues or surplus-value does not matter for them, this differentiation is important to understand the capital accumulation process in any industry using land as an element, condition or a site of production. For instance, housing production differs from the production of factories in that house prices alter seriously in different regions whereas industrial production develops a uniform market price for the sale of commodities like agricultural production. At that point, I suggest that MR is the primary category in order to understand huge price differences for houses. This does not mean that DR is not relevant in residential land but rather that in the current phase of capitalism, urban land in general and residential land in particular have been used for speculative purposes that trigger the creation and appropriation of MR. In the section below, the aim is to show the changing rent categories according to the land uses and the importance of MR in the context of the housing industry.

3   Ground Rent in Urban Residential Land

The previous section argued that property investment activities generate conditions for the creation and appropriation of values as rent, i.e. development gain, in that not only location of the land on which production takes place but also the built environment surrounding this particular land is simultaneously decisive. To understand development gain in urban land, one must look at the circulation of revenues as well as the circulation of capital in production and the different uses of land must be scrutinised.

For the sake of clarity of the arguments presented here, the relationship between location and urban ground rent can be discussed through two different uses of urban landed property: i) industrial production and ii) housing production. Supposing that two land parcels on which both industrial and housing productions take place have the equal qualities, i.e., the same locational advantage with respect to proximity to transport and social facilities, the theorisation of DRI in Marx would indicate that locational advantage allows the individual capitalist to produce below market value. Therefore, at first appearance, locational characteristics affect the costs of production and lead to the emergence of DR.

In the case of land for industrial production, the quality of land is relevant (within broad levels) in the productivity level in that the cost of production changes according to the proximity to the transportation networks and other facilities. In the case of locational advantage of this specific land parcel with respect to the amenities and services (compared to other lands on which same industrial production takes place), the cost of production falls below the industry average and above-normal surplus-value is created by the capitalist in the primary production. Therefore, some of the extra surplus-value produced on that land can be appropriated as DRI by the landowner.

In the case of land for the housebuilding industry, the same locational advantage of the production parcel with respect to the closeness to transportation, infrastructural services and other facilities may decrease the construction costs compared to the housebuilding activities on brownfield land. Therefore, DRI may arise in that situation. However, this surplus-value is not substantial in the housebuilding industry since the cost, i.e. rent, of greenfield land neither cheapens the production costs below the industry average (compared to the housebuilding activities on brownfield land) nor leads to gaining above-normal surplus-value by the capitalist. Instead, the construction costs of houses (with the same sizes, floors, the inputs with the same prices) are more or less the same in different locations within the same country or region (Clarke and Ginsburg, 1976; Robertson, 2014a; Knoll *et al.*, 2017; Ryan-Collins *et al.*, 2017). Therefore, it can be argued that the main source of the rent in the housebuilding industry does not come from these small differences in the cost of production, i.e. DR, but is derived from MR, which is appropriated out of the circulation of revenues. Especially with regards to the huge differences in the prices of houses, it is not possible to explain this varying (disproportionate) price difference with the locational advantage that cheapens production costs below the industry average. A fortiori, the scarcity of desirable land in vicinities that have such qualities (locational advantages regarding the proximity to, for instance, decent paid works, good schools, parks, metros, low crime rates, and other desired destinations) for residential production causes low supply in consideration effective demand and therefore creates lucrative opportunities to appropriate development gain in the form of MR (Harvey, 1985; Charles, 1977).

In summary, although in both industrial production and housebuilding industry, the corresponding rent is differentiated according to location, the dominant forms of rent become different. In industrial production, the locational advantage leads to the rise of DRI, which is paid through the production process, i.e., circulation of surplus profit. In contrast, in the residential production, the vast majority of housing rents does not derive from the production of housing, i.e., circulation of surplus profit, but the circulation of revenues in the form of MR. Therefore, in the case of industrial production, the quality of the land leading to the rise of DR does not affect the price of production (but individual capitalist values), whereas in the housebuilding industry, the favoured location creating MR directly affects the quality of product and the prices of houses.

By the same token, not only new residential production but also already-existing houses are subject to ground rent changes according to the quality of land. As discussed above, the quality of land in urban space, location, is not fixed (or slowly changing) as is the case in agriculture. Instead, it is perpetually altering with the developments in the built environment. Therefore, even if there is not any production on a piece of land, as there are already houses there, any additional locational advantages[8] will bring additional capital gain in the form of MR to the landowner. This time the landowner will be a house-owner instead of a capitalist builder. For instance, when or even before a new railway is built in an area, the quality of the surrounding land will increase. The owners of the existing houses in this area will get additional (potential) MR that can be realised in the situation of any future exchange like selling or renting. Here, as no production takes place, the source of rent is not attached to the locational characteristics determining costs but rather based on the scarcity conditions of premium land (Clarke and Ginsburg, 1976; Berry 2014). Therefore:

> For land used for residential purposes, the improved location will allow the houses to be rented or sold for more — because of the premium attached to location, residential units become a higher-quality product than they would be if they were in a different location ... this is a classic monopoly rent — the rent arises because houses near the station are

---

8 Similarly, any locational disadvantage will decrease the potential capital gain of the land-owner. For instance, "the quality of the housing experience and the market values of nearby houses decline when a freeway is carved through a neighbourhood" (Berry, 2014: 397).

more desirable than houses further away and because there is an enduring shortage of them.

ROBERTSON, 2014a: 120–1

Moreover, this improved quality of land thanks to the construction of the railway may attract capitalist housebuilders in pursuit of development gain. The
main motivation of the housebuilders is to exploit the opportunities of this
socially-constructed scarcity vis-á-vis growing demand and to sell houses at
monopoly prices. On the other hand, the incentive for the industrial capitalist
to make production on the land close to the railway would be having lower production costs than the industrial average. While in the former, the development
gain is received out of industrial capitalist's surplus-value without affecting
prices; in the latter, it is "extracted from the community out of the consumption process rather than out of the production process" (Harvey, 1985: 82).

Thus far, it has been argued that the source of the development gain generated from the quality of land in urban space changes according to what the
land is used for; and in the case of residential land, locational advantage triggers the creation and extraction of MR in most cases rather than DR. Similarly,
DRII encounters similar barriers to explain residential rent. Intensive capital
accumulation referring to DRII can be applicable for multi-storey buildings or
new or refurbished improvements such as central heating, ample room space,
etc. (Jager, 2003; Kratke, 1992). As discussed in the agricultural context, the base
of DRII is always DRI (Fine, 1979) and because MR in land used for residential
purposes is more significant than DRI, more intensive production methods in
housing can be accrued as additional MR "through an enhanced capacity to tap
the circulation of revenues" rather than DRII (Harvey, 1985: 102).

With regards to AR in land used for residential purposes,[9] there have been
heated debates amongst Marxists. Marx's (1991: 762) analysis of AR refers to
"the whole excess of value over the price of production" resulting from the
barrier imposed by landed property. Until landowners receive a return, which
would be covered by the production of additional surplus-value in agriculture,
they withhold their land from the movement of capital. At this point, Fine's
(1979: 258) caveat is important to mention:

---

9   In the urban rent literature, AR is (i) considered as identical with monopoly rent by Lipietz
    (1985); Harvey and Chatterjee (1974); Scott (1976); Howard & King (1985); Park (2011); Ward
    and Aalbers (2016) (ii) not accepted as a land rent by Jäger (2003) (iii) identified with new
    names such as 'political rent' by Economakis (2003); 'reservation price' by Walker (1974).

[The] basis for the formation of AR [which is the production of additional surplus-value and divergence between market values and prices of production] has been confused with a condition for its existence, [which is] the flow of capital onto new lands. ... AR depends then upon the flow of capital onto new lands. But, if this use of new lands is taken to be the basis of AR, then its existence is independent of the formation of surplus profits. It is simply an extra payment for the use of new land ... As such, it corresponds to an appropriation of surplus-value from the social 'pool' and does not have its origins in the production of surplus profit within agriculture. The resulting increase in market price is best categorised as a monopoly price.

Hence, the short-cut and static application of AR on the grounds of the flow of capital onto new lands would suggest that housebuilder capitalists may prefer to extend production onto new lands and pay AR. This is instead of making extra capital investment on the existing land in the form of DRII which also requires new technological development for increasing the productivity in the housebuilding sector. However, as the basis of the AR is the production of *additional surplus profits*, which necessitates the capitalist housebuilder to sell the dwelling units *at a price above their price of production* (limited by value), the eagerness and capacity of demand to buy these dwellings is involved into the process in that the conditions of MR interrupts to the process of the appropriation of AR.

There are two purely technical arguments for the formation of AR in the housebuilding industry in the literature: i) the low OCC in the housebuilding industry and ii) the effective barrier argument. Regarding the former, in the context of agriculture, it is generally assumed that AR arises due to the low OCC in agriculture (Harvey, 1999; Ball, 1985b; Walker, 1974; Edel, 1992). However, this chapter follows the argument of Ben Fine (1979) that the low OCC in agriculture is not a result of AR produced by landed property but rather a condition of it. Correspondingly, on the one hand, some of the applications of AR to the urban context carry similar assumptions that due to the existence of AR, construction sector inherently has a low OCC (Walker, 1974; Edel, 1992). On the other hand, some urban scholars argued that a lower OCC in the housebuilding industry, compared to the average for all industries, stems from the slower pace of development of new techniques and machinery, i.e. slower development in the technical composition of capital (TCC)[10] (Berry, 1981; Smyth, 1985; Lipietz, 1974). As stated by Ball (1978: 80):

---

10   TCC is the proportion between the mass of means of production used per production and the amount of value added by living labour, who will transform the total means of production to the final commodity.

With a relatively static labour process, however, accumulation in the industry will tend to take the form of a quantitative expansion of a given labour process rather than the form of revolutionising that process through changes in the [TCC].

This book agrees with the second interpretation of why the housebuilding industry has a low OCC, instead of the first one linking this with the existence of AR. However, two important caveats are needed here. Firstly, although "improvements in technical efficiency will not be a major source of surplus profits for individual capitals in building as it is in other industries" (ibid.), this does not mean that housebuilders have a lower-than-average rate of profit. Secondly, slower technological development, which has been observed,[11] is not considered as a permanent feature of the housebuilding industry since it is subject to historical changes and transformations.

Furthermore, if there is a relation between ground rent and the slower development of technological developments in the housebuilding industry, this is much more related to the appropriation of MR rather than AR. As argued by Robertson (2014a: 109), in her study on housing-rent in Britain, "the low OCC in the housebuilding industry often appears to be the result of housebuilders capturing rent rather than avoiding it". The potential in the housebuilding industry for appropriating enormous mass of revenue gains in the form of MR leads capitalist housebuilders "to underinvest in more efficient methods of production, hence giving rise to the lower OCC in housebuilding" (ibid.). As it will discussed in detail below, most housebuilders are speculators at the same time; since they bet on the future exchange prices of landed property and exploit the opportunities arising from the shortage of desirable residential land with respect to effective demand (Ball, 1988; Harvey, 1974). The prevalence of MR is the most important feature of the housebuilding industry that shapes the capital accumulation process and lead individual capitals to increase their

---

11   Although more industrialised building systems were developed through the introduction of prefabricated housing production technology which is based on an assembly operation of previously manufactured components, housebuilding is still site-based production system and uses considerable amounts of labour. There is a slow rate of technological change in the sector. However, this is not a typical feature of the construction sector where there is a much more technologically-sophisticated production system in the construction of large infrastructure projects. Moreover, the low TCC (and OCC) of the housebuilding industry is not shared by the building materials industry. Therefore, increases in productivity in the building materials industry reduces the value of constant capital used in housebuilding industry itself (Ball, 1978; 1983).

development gains instead of investing in more efficient technologies and machines.

While the first discussion about AR in the urban literature has been based on the investigation of AR by linking it to low OCC in the construction industry, the second has been built on the 'effective barrier' argument which highlights the existence of a landed class hampering capital flows onto new lands by appropriating AR (Edel, 1976; Bruegel, 1975; Markusen, 1978; Walker, 1974). For instance, Edel (1976: 114–15) gave some examples of the conditions through which AR emerges in urban land:

(1) ownership of large estates constraining suburban growth, (2) monopoly control over building land by transit authorities, (3) fragmentation of ownership acting as a barrier to concentrated development in suburban or renewal areas, (4) deliberate delaying of development by monopoly development interests to force up prices, (5) speculative holding of idle land, (6) state planning and zoning controls.

Although the above examples may lead the rise of AR in urban land in general by way of the extension of production towards underdeveloped lands on the edge of cities, it is not thought that these examples give rise to AR in the context of residential land. The monopoly features of land ownership blur the distinction between MR and AR in the literature (resulting from the application of the concepts without analysing their logical basis) and lead to confusion over (even ignorance of) whether the movement of capital is related with cheapening the cost of production or increasing development gains. The zoning and planning decisions or monopoly interests themselves may create the conditions of localised scarcities on the existing lands. In this case, on the one hand, capitalist housebuilders may prefer to appropriate higher MR by more intensive investment in urban centres, multi-storey buildings for instance, instead of low-rise housing forms. On the other hand, the conditions of localised scarcity on the existing lands may cause capital to flow onto new lands, which previously paid no rent. In that case, housebuilder makes an extensive investment, but high likely because they consider that there will be a demand for the housing units produced in brownfield areas — if not, there will be a realisation problem. In this case, the rent arising from this scarcity becomes MR instead of AR. Put it differently, monopoly features of landownership and land market regulations work as a mechanism triggering the creation of artificial scarcities of landed property, which, in turn, leads the rise of the levels of MR, rather than the rise of AR. Moreover, as noted before, the quality of land parcel on which housing production takes place directly depends on the quality of built environment surrounding that parcel and its quality is subject to rapid changes particularly with "ever-expanding range of activities associated with both economic and social reproduction that has marked the neo-liberal era" (Fine, 2009b: 4). Therefore, the quality of brownfield land is not a permanent feature of the landed property but the transformation of the brownfield land to a new greenfield land would create the opportunities to appropriate rent from the circulation of revenues, i.e. MR.

In summary, this section argues that the incentive of decreasing production costs in housing production (DR) is less significant compared to the motivation of housebuilders to appropriate development gain in the form of MR, notably when we consider that the industry has a slow pace of technological development. Following this, for a better understanding of the generation of MR from property development, one must take into consideration the rapidly changing conditions of the spatial configuration of cities. While discussing monopoly price, Marx (1991: 772) argued that the "price of things, not being subject to the law of value, may be determined by many 'fortuitous combinations'". However, the following section will suggest that the widespread existence of capital gains appropriated as MR from the property development indicates more systemic combinations rather than fortuitous combinations. Similarly, Harvey (1985: 64) argues that "if [MR]^{12} is a transfer payment to a scarce factor of production, then the urbanisation process has also multiplied the opportunities for realising [MR]". There are many reasons for scarcity to emerge in urban areas from public to private investments on urban land such as hospitals, shops, schools, means of transport and so on. Especially urban gentrification processes, spatial segregation and involvement of the state, finance, speculative builders and landowners in producing spatial configurations of urban land uses changes have become the main constituents of these systemic combinations.

4   Scarcity, Monopoly Rent and Housing

The discussion on scarcity has generally been avoided by Marxist scholars due to the fundamental role of scarcity in neoclassical economics in the explanation of the economic relations that is so-called unlimited human wants and needs in a world of limited resources. Marx did not directly write on the concept of scarcity but rather criticised the vulgar economists' understanding of

---

12   Harvey re-names MR as class-monopoly rent. This is neither necessary nor true conceptualisation. As mentioned above, unlike agriculture, it is not possible to talk about a specific class of owners in urban land because there are many different landowners.

scarce factors of production, i.e., land, capital and labour. Nevertheless, Marx (1991: 784) stressed the scarcity of land only in one passage in *Capital* Vol. 3 under the discussion of ground rent stating that "those manufacturers who own waterfalls exclude those who do not from using this natural force, because land, and particularly land endowed with water-power, is scarce". Unlike the neoclassical economists Marx does not refer to pre-given natural limits but rather monopoly-ownership of natural resources resulting from the historically specific set of relations and forces of production, exchange and consumption (Perelman, 1979; Scoones *et al.*, 2014).

Liodakis (2016: 227) emphasised that "the class-based access to the means to satisfy human needs" and therefore increasing scarcity in a given level of actual production as compared to potential production. Instead of seeing scarcity as an outcome of a mere distributional struggle, Liodakis analysed scarcity according to "what, and how much is produced, and by what techniques, as well as on the formation of social needs and the determination of scarcity" in capitalist societies (ibid., 232). This approach suggests that effective demand arises from unequal relations between social needs and productive potential in a given society subject to the logic of capital in the capitalist mode of production. Under capitalism, social needs are manipulated, artificially expanded and increasingly commodified by capital (Hampton, 2013; Liodakis, 2016). This, therefore, creates a continuously increasing scarcity of different commodities that are necessary for social reproduction. Liodakis' approach carries a danger of considering scarcity as a general tendency of capitalism and instead, scarcity (i.e., temporary shortfall of the supply of certain commodities or resources) can be evaluated as a consequence of different social, economic and political conditions and a contingency rather than a necessity of capitalism. In house-building, although effective demand vis-a-vis scarcity can be a general sectoral tendency due to the prevalence of MR (see below), the systemic increase of scarcity cannot be generalised to the capitalist mode of production. However, as a contingency, the "intensification of scarcity ... may go hand in hand with occasional abundance or purposive withdrawal and destruction in some sectors" (ibid., 233). Liodakis' work highlights that scarcity of desirable (high-quality) land and MR for housing do not emerge from the naturally limited land for residential production but from a class-based disequilibrium between the housing need and demand and productive potential. Moreover, effective demand comes not only from social need but also from the use of housing as an asset (investment tool) and the potential capture of capital gain in the form of MR.

Harvey stated that "urbanisation creates extensive man-made resource systems" such as offices, shops, transport links (1974: 249). The uneven distribution of these resource systems generates localised scarcities (human-made islands) on land for particular uses (Harvey, 1985: 79; Berry, 2014). While the valorisation of land is crucial for housebuilders, the actual (but temporary) limits on the amount of housing that can be close to urban services and resources prevent supply expanding to fully meet the demand in a short-term. Therefore:

> historically-geographically produced conditions place a specific location in a distinctive position vis-à-vis other places ... as the collective outcome of many successive rounds of capital investment in space and its associated uneven development.
>
> SWYNGEDOUW, 2012: 313

These conditions themselves create different (hierarchical) qualities between different urban land parcels and between housing sub-markets in which different levels of effective demand is generated and different amounts of development gain (MR) is appropriated.

The effective demand vis-a-vis the relative scarcity of the supply of desirably located land for residential usages (which paves way for different amounts of MR) can be created by various landed interests. Although in the agricultural case, the scarcity of land is thought to be the withdrawal of land from capital investment by a class of landowners; in an urban context, both of effective demand for housing and scarcity on high-quality residential land can be created by capitalist housebuilders through landholding; by the state through zoning, building and land-use regulations, land development and allocation activities and so on; or by the financial system, through housing development and purchase finance. For instance, housebuilding firms may store land for their future investments in expectation of the increase in land values and therefore increasing their chances of appropriating MR. Landholding, as an important part of housebuilding activity, stems from the fact that "the value of any parcel of land contains the values of all other parcels at the present time as well as the expectations of future values" (Harvey, 1973: 186). Moreover, as potential uses of a particular land depend on the surrounding neighbourhood effect which is subject to rapid alterations in contemporary urban environments, new scarcities for residential uses have been continuously reproduced.

In summary, this section has argued that residential land is not naturally limited or equally scarce, rather different qualities of urban residential land are artificially (on purpose) created according to their closeness to human-made resource systems. Similarly, effective demand does not merely refer to a social need for sheltering but also manipulation and artificially expansion of housing wants and demands and production of new modes of consumption.

The next step is to discuss the distinctive meanings of scarcity for different classes. While for upper classes, the scarcity refers to the prestigious houses in the more central, accessible or desirable locations of cities with most developed urban services, for the lower classes, affordable housing with the accessibility to other use-values which are necessary for their social reproduction becomes scarce. This is strongly related to the uneven development/allocation of urban facilities and the resulting sub-markets for housing.

5   Ground Rent and Housing Sub-markets

The literature argues that geographical differentiation, racial, ethnic and class segregation, price differences, dwelling type, legal and illegal housing, household income levels, social status, the rental and sales markets and many other factors may cause the housing market to be divided into a series of sub-markets (Edel, 1976; Smith, 1986; Lipietz, 1985; King, 1989; Haila, 1991; Lim, 1987; Butcher, 2020; Zangger, 2021). Among these, the most commonly mentioned factor is the income levels of households. Although "housing production ... .is itself highly differentiated in income groups" (Lipietz, 1985: 196), it is important to exercise caution when identifying housing submarkets strictly according to income levels, since this can cause a static Weberian categorisation of class rather than a dynamic Marxist class analysis (Berry, 1986). For instance, different fractions of working classes that are in the same income range can have access to different sub-markets in that political/ideological mechanisms may be determinant.[13] However, what I want to show here is the interdependence of housing submarkets rather than arriving at "a theoretical rigorous classification of housing submarkets" which are affected not only by income levels but also many other factors (King, 1989: 866). Therefore, varying processes of ground rent extraction in different submarkets coexist and interact within the same spatial formation and that gives an opportunity to analyse these submarkets as a part of the SoP in a given social formation. The analysis begins with the proposal that MR arising in one housing sub-market is realised elsewhere due to the injection of new effective demand into the circuit of exchange. As exemplified by Harvey (1974: 250):

---

13   See Jesus (2016) for the selective inclusion of working classes into an affordable housing
        programme in Brazil.

Suppose, for example, that there is a speculative boom in the inner city through which new sub-markets are formed out of existing neighbourhoods and that the old residents of these neighbourhoods are forced to seek housing opportunities in suburbia. Then, the greater the [class-] monopoly rent earned by the inner-city speculator, the greater the opportunity to realise rent on the suburban fringe.

Harvey's example is otherwise known as gentrification and is a common way of appropriating MR in inner cities. Increased inner-city land values due to gentrification lead to high levels of MR in the existing houses, newly built houses and commercial spaces in that area. It is much easy to theorise monopoly price in the case of upper-class housing that has prestige and status locations in cities. However, the question to understand is whether the intra-metropolitan locational differences of different submarkets, such as working-class housing, can be considered as MR. MR is constitutively determined by the "buyer's needs and ability to pay" (Marx, 1991: 756), but this is a broad statement that changes according to many factors such as prestige, tastes, wages, transportation costs, the level of employment, the access to mortgages etc. Therefore, the use-value of housing and the creation of demand must be examined in terms of job locations (spatially concentrated) and access to jobs, schools, nurseries etc. for the working classes. Several scholars have theorised the relations between these reproduction costs and housing locations as DR (Alcaly, 1976; Feldman, 1977; Park, 2011). Their main argument is that the differences in commuting time of labour-power cause the generation of an extra surplus on land which is closer to transportation facilities and therefore appropriation of this surplus as DR. Although housing is crucial for the reproduction of labour-power and therefore an important component of the value of labour-power, this does not affect the production of surplus-value on residential land of which differences give rise to DR. Instead, the ground rent appropriated from housing having a better location in term of job access (and therefore having lower transport costs) is paid out of the wages of working classes. From this point forth, the highest demand and inherently the highest scarcity for housing concentrates on the residential locations that are close to transportation and other urban facilities. The uneven capital investment in the built environment may lead to the creation of MR for 'affordable houses'[14] as well.

---

14   The term 'affordable housing' will be used for the privatised social housing programme in Turkey.

The formal housing market in many countries has a scarcity of housing with such conditions for lower-income groups. Lower-income groups are left with the choice of either informal and unauthorised housing provisions e.g. slums or to become a legal homeowner/tenant in the formal housing market provided by capitalist housebuilders that are generally densely populated and located in the outskirts of metropolitan cities with a lower quality of infrastructure and services. The former scenario will not be analysed with regards to ground rent since in this case there is a non-market[15] (or informal) way of access to housing rather than fully capitalist housing production. Regarding the latter, there is a formal landowner and capitalist housebuilder that is similar to the one for the provision of housing for upper classes.

There might be individual capitals specialised in the lower-income group housing sub-market (local, small-scale builders) or large housebuilding firms might find it attractive to operate in this sub-market if there is effective demand here. The most important difference between the upper- and lower-class sub-markets is affordability and for capitalist housebuilders producing for the lower classes, the cost of production must be cheap. Although housebuilders have some strategies to decrease the cost of production, like the use of cheaper building materials and minimising the size of the flats, the most important reduction in costs would come from the choice of land having lower prices and lower ground rent that are generally located in less developed areas of cities.

As discussed above, the quality of land, i.e., location, for housebuilding activity is not a factor determining production costs substantially but a factor determining product quality and consequently prices. Therefore, DR is not the primary rent category to explain the capital accumulation process in the housing sector, though this does not imply that DR does not exist in residential land. From this follows the appropriation of a large portion of ground rent out of revenues within general circulation processes rather than the production of extra surplus profits in the context of housing production for the lower classes as well. At this point, by following Robertson (2014a: 122), this book proposes to call the differences in the housing ground rent between these sub-markets as the "differentiated monopoly rent" that leads to the different rates of profits in these submarkets. Here, the differentiated MR derives from different monopoly prices generated via different (hierarchical) qualities of land for residential production and different levels of effective demand for housing in different (but interconnected) sub-markets. Therefore, differentiated

---

15   Sometimes there may be the co-existence of the formal (market-based) and informal (non-market) forms of housing production (see chapter 5).

MR on housing regulates housing submarkets and determines the location of social classes. Moreover, housing sub-markets are necessary for the creation of new scarcities in different localities which will prevent local oversupplies. That is to say, localised MR arising in one housing sub-market has knock-on effects on others. Nevertheless, the level of MR appropriated in these submarkets will differ according to the size of capital applied and the quality of sub-markets with higher quality sub-markets bringing a higher development gain for the building-capitalist (Ball, 2003) and the contingent imbalance between demand and supply.

Moreover, a systematic increase in general MR through, for example, government policies, may lead the movement of capital into hitherto underdeveloped, marginal lands (in the most deprived areas of the cities) and the appropriation of AR by making land prices prohibitive. However, this is not a widespread phenomenon in the formal housing market because (i) due to a lack of amenities and employment opportunities these marginal lands are not in high demand (unless they are peasants or farmers or it is an industrial area which can create employment opportunities); (ii) housebuilders might have to compete with the informal housing (and land) market; (iii) housebuilders might not prefer to gain low development gain against high production cost in such brown-field areas; (iv) there might be a realisation problem for housebuilders in the case of lack of effective demand. Therefore, once again, AR is not the main mechanism to explain the operation of rent in the context of residential land and the housing industry.

Although demand-side factors, i.e. the eagerness and capacity of payment of demand, are definitely important in the determination of the differential advantages of different locations (differentiated MR) in these sub-markets, there is a danger of a "spatial myopia [which] goes hand in hand with reifying the limited effective choices open to most house purchasers into a theory of demand-determined residential location" (Ball, 1985b: 521). Put it differently, the demand and supply factors leading to the emergence of effective demand on housing sub-markets are a consequence of a set of historical, institutional, social and economic configurations in a given society. That is to say, they do not occur through fortuitous and chaotic market conditions but a range of interventions of state and finance that attract capital to (or not to) flow onto housing sub-markets. These configurations themselves create differentiated (hierarchical) qualities of land and relative scarcity, i.e., supply shortage of housing and differentiated social and economic motivations of consumers. Therefore, demand and supply of housing do not follow the neoclassical equilibrium scheme, as capitalist market and non-market mechanisms always feed these chronic shortages and artificial scarcities. Even if equilibrated in one market, there are always new markets, i.e., the formation of housing submarkets, feeding this circulation. The resulting differentiated structure between submarkets, then, contributes the realisation of MR since uneven development between differentiated submarkets has a role in channelling capital into urban development (Harvey, 1974; 1985; King, 1989).

6   Housing, Ground Rent and Capital Accumulation

The effect of ground rent on capital accumulation in different industries using landed property as an element/condition/means of production (such as mining, oil and natural gas, diamond fishing, housing and real estate) has long been examined by many scholars (Scott, 1980; Bina, 2006; Campling and Havice, 2014; Fine, 1994; Saito, 2017; Basu, 2018.). The impact of ground rent on accumulation is contingent on the peculiarities of each industry's own capital accumulation processes (Fine, 1985). Therefore, there cannot be one uniform impact of ground rent on accumulation (ibid.). So far, this chapter has argued that MR is the main rent category in urban residential land. The determination of this is crucial in understanding the pace, periodicity and direction of capital accumulation in the housebuilding industry. However, for a better understanding of capital accumulation in the housebuilding industry and the importance of MR within this process, this section will start with an analysis of the production process of housing.

Based on the LTV, the motive force of the production of housing is the production of surplus-value through the conventional cycle of capital $M - C$ $... P ... C' - M'$ (M' = M + ΔM, with ΔM being the surplus value). In its most abstract scheme, the capitalist housing producer[16] spends money (M) to buy commodities (C), i.e., labour-power and means of production, to produce the final commodity (C'), housing in this case. Housing as a final commodity (C') embodies added (surplus) value which is realised after being sold for M'. The capitalist housebuilder can consume entire surplus-value or reinvest some of it to repeat the circuit of capital. Similar to all other commodities, the value

---

16   As rightly put by Berry (2014: 399), "there are many different capitals that come into contact during the housing provision process. Developers, builders, materials suppliers, estate agents, surveyors, valuers, solicitors and financiers ... From a Marxist viewpoint, only those capitalists producing the dwelling and the infrastructure embedded in the land appropriate surplus value ... Thus, exchange professionals and financial capital profit from their role in realizing the value in housing produced; without their intervention the circulation and accumulation of capital through the housing system would stall."

of housing is determined by the socially-necessary labour-time to produce them. This requires both constant capital as the machinery and technical equipment and variable capital as the amount of value-added by the workers and ground rent, which differs housing from other commodities. Moreover, the surplus-value and the rate of exploitation in the housebuilding industry can be increased by the production of either absolute surplus-value or relative surplus-value.[17] Although in modern capitalism, the production of relative surplus-value prevails, the widespread existence of the abstract surplus-value in the construction industry has been observed in many countries, especially in the global South.[18] In this context self-employed, informal, seasonal migrant and unskilled manual workers enable capitalist housebuilders to employ workers through the systems of the piecework, subcontracting paying below minimum-wages and demanding long working hours. The production of relative surplus-value in the housebuilding industry depends on the decrease in the labour-time to produce housing via new technological developments and inclusion of new machinery which is relatively slow in this sector. Therefore, the housebuilding industry tends to be a more labour-intensive sector rather than capital-intensive (Smyth, 1985; Ball, 1988; 2003) and the production of housing as a commodity needs a large amount of labour-time. This slower technological development and labour-intensive nature of the housebuilding industry leads that the value of housing does not fall "the same extent as many of the commodities contributing to the reproduction of labour-power" such as food, water, clothing, etc. (Ball, 1978: 79). In a similar line, in the housebuilding industry, the transformation of capital from its commodity form (C') to

---

17   Absolute surplus value can be produced through the extension of the working day or "a change either in the productiveness or in the intensity of the labour" (Marx, 1990: 646). However, the production of relative surplus value, "revolutionises out the technical processes of labour … therefore presupposes a specific mode, the capitalist mode of production, a mode which, along with its methods, means, and conditions, arises and develops itself spontaneously on the foundation afforded by the formal subjection of labour to capital" (ibid., 645). Therefore, the production of relative surplus value refers to the developed stage of capitalism as the innovations, scientific developments and mechanization decrease the value of labour power and increase the productivity and productivity gains of capitalist producers.

18   See Chang (2008) for South-East Asia; Ngai and Huilin (2010) for China; Srivastava and Jha (2016) for India; Cho (2004) for Korea; and Wells and Jason (2010) for Africa. However, in the countries with restrictive labour laws such as France, Germany and Sweden, this is not relevant despite there are still some practices of subcontracting, flexible hiring in the industry (Ball, 2003; Duncan, 1986). The prevalence of subcontracting, flexibility, informality, etc. may be considered as a coping strategy of the housebuilding industry against uncertain demand and unsteady production rates (Ball, 2003).

its money form (M') generally needs a long period of time and this is another reason why housing is not to be cheapened in the same extent as other commodities (Pickvance, 1976; Boddy 1976; Harvey, 2012).

Houses, like all other commodities, have values as well as prices and the value determined by labour-time does not correspond directly to the market price of housing that is the direct cost faced by consumers. The transformation of the value of housing into its market price is determined by "the capital–labour ratios, scarcities, skills, monopolies, tastes and by more or less accidental variations in supply and demand" in general (Fine and Saad-Filho, 2010: 21) and by "land costs, monopoly pricing and by the structure of housing finance" in particular (Ball, 1978: 78). Nevertheless, although land is the most important cost for the housebuilder, it is also the main principle determining the profit of capitalist housebuilder: "the builder makes very little profit out of the building themselves; he makes the principal part of the profit out of the improved ground rents" (Marx, 1991: 909) i.e. MR and "speculative anticipation of the demand for houses", (Marx, 1992: 312) i.e. effective demand.[19]

Creating the conditions for the realisation of these rents has been the foremost way of providing rapid capital accumulation out of residential use of land. However, land is both a cost and a speculative asset for the housebuilder. Therefore, the level of development gain which will be appropriated in the form of MR depends on the level of capital gain which will be appropriated by the landowner. This point needs a closer analysis since this is the most important competition among capitalist builders.

All housebuilders are industrial capitalists due to their function within the circuit of capital. However, speculative housebuilders,[20] in addition to their building activities as industrial capital, are also mercantile capitalists, buying cheap and selling dear and getting the highest possible profit (Ball, 1983; 1988; Massey and Catalano, 1978). Although, at first sight, they are no different from any capitalist industrialist in the sense that all have to advance constant and variable capitals necessary for production and to sell the commodity at the end; what makes speculative builders different from other productive

---

19   However, the exact division of the surplus value from the building activity and the ground rent from the landed property within the total profit of the housebuilder cannot be done at such an abstract level.

20   There are different kinds of housebuilders and some build to individual's specifications with predetermined prices. Although this method is preferred by high-income groups, it constitutes only a small part of the industry. In some other cases, builders can be the contractors of larger building firms or state. In this section, our main focus will be speculative builders, which build for a general housing market instead of a specific client since speculative housebuilding prevails in Turkey.

capital and gives them a specific mercantile character is, first, the necessity of the purchase of land, second subsequent to the production, the capacity of appropriating development gain in the form of MR. This derives from the change in land values between the acquisition of land from landowners to the sale of landed property to the consumer. However, this two-fold character of speculative building brings a conflictual accumulation process to the building industry.

On the one hand, producers try to minimise the conversion of their potential development gain into ground rent which is paid to the landowner. At that point, speculative builders are very similar to capitalist tenant farmers in that both have to pay a fee to access to the land; but, due to different market and rent mechanisms, their resistance is also different (Ball, 1985a). Housebuilders generally buy land rather than renting it. Landowners extract rent in one go and therefore the struggle, i.e., bargaining, between landowner and housebuilder on capturing a larger amount of capital gain, starts at the time of land purchase. The main profit for both sides comes from the successful manipulation of land exchange, i.e. paying as little as possible for builders and vice versa for landowners. However, there are two layers of the competition for MR appropriation. The first competition takes place between developers for buying land and getting development permission in the best locations (or in areas expected to have this potential in the future). The scale and intensity of this competition between developers for development gain also determine the second competition which is between a speculative builder and landowner. Here, landowners by no means take a passive stance in the appropriation of ground rent (Harvey, 1999). On the contrary, the extent of developer's ability to leave landowner ignorant about the potentialities of the piece of land or of landowner's knowledge regarding the land market in a broad sense and her own land's potential (current or future value) in a narrow sense is decisive in the distribution of capital gains (Lipietz, 1985). Ball points out that:

> although housing development gain is divided into the builder's development profit and the landowner's land price, the exact division between the two components is theoretically indeterminate as it depends on the contemporary balance of power between builder and landowner.
>
> 1983: 144

It is important to emphasise the impossibility of categorising urban landowners as a class in itself due to the diversity of land ownership in the urban context and due to the transfer of ownership rights through land trading, speculative housebuilders can be thought as speculative landowners at the same time. For breaking down the possibility of any absolute monopolistic control of landowners and increasing their chance of appropriating MR from further investments, large speculative housebuilders commonly hold land banks.[21] In the composition of these land banks, correctly predicting the development potential of a locality and optimal timing for the purchase of land are crucial for the success of housebuilders as mercantile capitalists (ibid.). This is the highest risk activity for speculative housebuilders since the land bank may accumulate or lose value over time and housebuilders should forecast against the uncertain demand in certain vicinities and future monopoly prices for their spatially-fixed products (ibid.). However long land is kept in stock as a part of a land bank, there must be an actual industrial production process for the realisation of development gain for speculative builders rather than only holding an appreciating financial asset (land) since "the profits from accumulated capital gains [land appreciation] are only notional until they are realised through sale" of the finished product (Robertson, 2014a: 175; Duncan, 1986). Again, here, the timing of production is as crucial as the timing of land purchase for profit margins of housebuilders in the sense that the subsequent marketing and sale processes are expected to accompany with the heightened effective demand which must be again correctly predicted by speculative builders (Harvey, 1974; 2012). The existence of the effective demand for housing units in a specific vicinity does not guarantee the development gain of the builder even if they already acquired land and started to production there, because the construction process is relatively long and there is a time gap between the purchase of the land and the sale of the housing units on that land. For this, the speculative capitalist builder has to calculate when to acquire land, when to start production and when to put the completed units to the market. Because of this time gap between the decision of production and the circulation of housing in the market, the biggest risk in the industry is not being ready in the boom phases in which effective demand heightens and credit is abundant and available (Charles 1977). The profit margins of the speculative builders, which is determined by the realisation of MR, also depend on the speed of response of the builder to the circulation of revenues in the economy (Ball, 2003). In the meantime, if effective demand is curtailed, via for instance, with the financial deleveraging or altered market expectations, builders may have to cut the prices by decreasing the amount of development gain significantly or can stay with the

---

21   In some countries there may be landholding taxes dissuading speculative builders to hoard land for a long time such as in Sweden and France (Barlow and King, 1992).

unsold housing units.[22] As can be seen from this, the mercantile character of speculative housebuilding industry takes place before and after production, that is land purchase and house sales respectively.

On the other hand, this potential of appropriating MR through land-focused strategies of capitalist housebuilders may lead a precedence of mercantile activities over productive activities that in return creates a contradictory accumulation process in the housebuilding industry. Ball (1988: 46) addresses this, by saying that:

> Within the overall circuit of capital the requirements of production are subordinated to the needs of the speculative timing of purchases and sales. The subordination arises because the turnover of capital for a speculative builder does not depend on steady production rates but on the successful manipulation of land purchases, development programmes and building sales.

Therefore, success in the land market becomes primary for speculative housebuilders and competition occurs at the point of accessing to land, rather than at the level of production (Barker, 2004). The speculative activities of capitalist builders for increasing their profits have impacts on the productive activity itself. Because effective demand for the product (housing) is mainly determined by location, speculative housebuilders may prefer to increase their profits through investing in land rather than fixed capital and therefore may "minimise the capital tied up in production" (Ball, 1983: 160; White 1986). This specific relation to land in the housebuilding industry, different from other industries, causes a unique means of accumulation in which the competitive advantage among firms in the industry is not gained by technological innovations. From this point of view, it can be suggested that the tendency of minimising capital investment attached to production and technical innovation in housebuilding industry (lowering OCC) stems from the land-focused activities of speculative builders aiming to appropriate MR.

Therefore, the capacity of appropriating MR and the potential of having high-profit margins brings along a contradictory process for the accumulation of capital in the industry. This contradiction was best stated by the question of Harvey (1985: 101): "how much rental appropriation is appropriate to

---

22   Rapid changes in effective demand and MR may be thought as the most important reason of the fast entry and exit of capital from the housebuilding industry, though it may be harder for larger firms. Moreover, the relatively less fixed-capital tied up to the production makes the entry and exit easier compared to other industries (Charles, 1977; Ball, 2003).

sustain the accumulation of capital?" Although whether the profit comes from productive or unproductive capital investment, i.e., the ratio of MR in total return, is not important for individual capitalist, this distinction matters for the sustainability of investment to housebuilding industry. The answer to the question of Harvey should be given firstly by considering the source of MR. As highlighted before, the primary distinctive feature of MR is the independence of the level of rent from the production of surplus-value on land, unlike DR and AR. Whereas DR could not exceed the surplus-value produced on a particular piece of land; and AR could not exceed the level of DRII (otherwise the capitalist would prefer the intensive investment instead of the extensive investment); MR is appropriated from the circulation of revenues that comes from the total surplus-value which is produced elsewhere in the society. As it derives from "the circulation of the (surplus) value produced across the economy" (Saad-Filho, 2019: 101), ultimately it depends on (and is limited by) the level of the productive activities in the economy. This is the reason why its level is constrained by the level of real productive activity in a broader sense as "if all capital chases rent and no capital goes into production, then no value will be produced out of which the transfer payment that rent represents can come" (Harvey, 1985: 64). However, for the individual capitalist, these general determinants of the sustainability of capital accumulation are mostly over-shadowed by the profitability calculation of their speculative activities.

The investment activities of housebuilders also alter according to the distribution of MR between landowners and developers. Producers weigh to make intensive investment against extensive investment according to the level of rent demanded by the landowner. In a parcel of land whose owner demands high MR due to its desirability, the housebuilder may also try to appropriate high MR by making an intensive investment (increasing the number of residential units, for instance); but in that case, the revenue paid to landowner should not exceed the development gain appropriated by the builder. If it does, they would prefer to make an extensive investment to decrease the cost of production by moving onto less advantageous land that will also decrease the development gain in the form of MR (or no MR). Nevertheless, MR arising from the scarcity and effective demand in a specific locality is in no way permanent. The pressure of rising MR on both producers and consumers and shifting geographical patterns in the circulation of both capital and revenues leads to urban and residential developments to spread to new hubs on cheaper lands. In other words, the barrier put on capital and labour by too high MR in one submarket pave the way for new (differentiated) monopoly rents in new submarkets. Here, the role of the state and finance in creating favourable circumstances for the generation and appropriation of MR is crucial.

6.1 Localised Monopoly Rent (Development Gains) vs. General Monopoly Rent

Because the payment capacity of any buyer relies on the levels of wealth, savings, wages and the availability of credit, the creation of effective demand is also crucially connected with the general economic conditions and the structure of the system of accumulation more generally (e.g., the degree and form of financialisation). Therefore, MR needs to be considered not only in the context of local determinants but also with national and global economic, social and political conditions. Regarding the former, localised MR (development gain) arises on a particular residential land in a desirable vicinity since there is a localised scarcity (due to the limited number of houses that can be built) against people demanding to live in that area. Regarding the latter, "general monopoly rent"[23] for housing arises "from the differences in the relative speeds of the circuit of production and the circuit of revenue" in an economy in abstract terms (Robertson, 2014a: 125). In less abstract terms, general MR may increase at a systemic level for any enduring reason which creates a general scarcity vis-a-vis existing effective demand in the national context, i.e. the general housing shortage against the demand, which may increase due to the population growth, new household formation, changing class structure and distribution of income, the increase in multiple homeownership (thanks to its increasing asset role), the deterioration of the existing stock of buildings, shortages caused by dramatic events such as war, earthquake and so on; or it may decrease due to de-commodified provision of housing (for instance by state), increase in interest rates, the collapse of the credit system, the depression of wage rates, economic recession, etc. (Fine and Harris, 1979). Nevertheless, these changes in the level of general MR are "differentially realised by location" as a result of "the regional distribution of economic activity and local neighbourhood factors" (Robertson, 2014a: 127).

From a similar perspective, housebuilding industry is considered as a cyclical industry in which output and profits arising from the circulation of revenues also expand/shrink according to periods of economic downturn and contraction (Ball, 2003; Tibaijuka, 2009; Charles, 1977; Byrne, 2019; Agnello and Schuknecht, 2011; Berry 2014). The absence of the "steady production rates" and the change in housing supply according to boom-bust phases, i.e. property market cycles, is considered as an indication of this cyclicality (Ball, 1985a: 127; Barras, 1994; Barlow and King, 1992; Topalov, 1985). This cyclical fluctuation

---

23   In her work on the UK, Robertson (2014a) focused on the role of finance in the creation the general monopoly rent, which she defined as the gap between demand (excess demand) and supply (undersupply) in housing provision at a systemic level in a country.

in the housebuilding industry is strongly related to the volatile nature of MR (thanks to MR's revenue character and relative elasticity of revenue vis-à-vis production). Logically, it can be expected that in the boom phases, in which general effective demand and MR increases, housebuilders rate of production increases. Nevertheless, this also depends on the struggle between landowners and capitalist builders on capturing larger amounts of MR. Moreover, in the boom phases, the scope of the industry has a tendency to expand; and in the following bust phases, the number of active firms decreases; bankrupt companies, which do not have strong balance sheets to resist against the market downturn, may be taken over by the larger and older ones (Barlow and King, 1992; Ball, 2003). Nevertheless, the increase in supply, i.e. turnover of capital for speculative builders, depends on their belief and expectations on getting adequate returns, which is determined by the favourable macroeconomic and institutional configurations, which is organised in line with the pace and rhythm of the economic and social reproduction of capitalism.

However, because speculative housebuilders are not only industrial capitalist but also merchant capitalists; in the downswing phases of the market, they may increase their mercantile activities, for instance, by investing in their land banks as a surviving strategy (White, 1986). A land bank strategy may become significant for not only success but also the survival of the housebuilders. On the one hand, in the boom phases, if housebuilders have a land bank, they can put the stocked land into production and realise MR as fast as possible and therefore; they can better catch up the increase in effective demand and have substantial development gain by appropriating as much MR as possible by skipping the land purchase stage and accompanying harsh negotiations with landowners (who are probably better informed with the increasing market value of their land and keen to capture a greater part of the MR) before this favourable economic and political atmosphere, in which consumers are willing and able to pay, ended. On the other hand, in the bust phases, the land bank again becomes significant for the survival of housebuilders, albeit generally for the larger ones (Ball, 1988; 2010; 2013; White, 1986, Rydin, 1983; Wellings, 2006). The uncertainty of effective demand and MR in the housebuilding industry and the difficulty in estimating how long the boom-bust phases will last[24] lead larger housebuilders to invest in land banks.

However, whether the prevalence of the speculative activities in the housebuilding industry encourages or discourages accumulation changes according

---

24   It is not easy to forecast how long the effective demand will last since this is strongly related broader state of affairs of national and global political economy.

to the dynamics of different phases of capital accumulation, different forms of state and different conditions of economic and social reproduction since the own limits, pace and rhythm of capital accumulation is contingent upon how landed property interacts with capitalist development in a specific time and in a specific social formation (Fine and Saad-Filho, 2010). The following chapter will discuss whether the financialised-neoliberal phase of capitalism has created favourable conditions for speculative activities and landed property valorisation and, the uneven impacts of neoliberalism and financialisation on the relationship between the ground rent and landed property. The differences in the development of capitalist relations of production, different class structures, particular societal relations and power struggles and peculiar political and ideological relations within each country are all determinant in the generation of ground rent and capital accumulation upon landed property in the housing SoPs of these countries. For instance, Robertson (2014a) discusses that the restrictive planning system in the UK discourages housebuilders to expand the housing supply. However, as will be shown for Turkey, the desire of capturing more MR as profit encourages housebuilders to make more investment in building activity thanks to the authoritarian planning system which unprecedently centralised the land use planning and zoning decisions and created favourable conditions for an enhanced flow of capital into housebuilding industry. Based on this, the conditions for the existence and appropriation of MR are not just dependent on the fortuitous circumstances of changing demand and supply but also creative acts of capital and state (Berry, 2014). Therefore, speculative housebuilding activities occur not only through the efforts of builders but also beyond (but by including) them with the involvement of state and financial instruments. Housebuilders, landowners, the working classes, the state and finance are all involved in the appropriation of MR. For understanding political and economic interests and strategies for rent appropriation of these agents, it is crucial to understand the role and location of these agents in the housing SoP in question and the dynamics of this housing SoP itself, that will be examined in the context of Turkey.

7   Conclusion

The formation of value and price of production in housing is shaped by the intervention of landed property and this makes housing inseparably linked to ground rent. This chapter argued that Marx's theory of ground rent on agriculture, rooted in his value theory, provides a useful method for tracking the relation between ground rent and housing and the form of urban ground rent can be understood based on what is it used for. Regarding the residential use of urban land, this chapter argued that development gain arising out of location, which is the main determinant of land quality and price, mostly takes the form of MR in the housing industry. However, the quality of housing arising out of location has a strong neighbourhood effect in that the quality of a specific land parcel (on which housing production takes place) is directly determined by its proximity to other urban resources and amenities. The actual (but temporary) limits on the amount of housing that can be close to urban activities, services and resources prevent supply expanding to fully meet the demand in a short-term that creates the conditions of the generation and appropriation of MR. The locational advantages/disadvantages determining the quality and price of the residential land (and thereby houses) is subject to dynamic changes in the urban development process. This is strongly related to the pace and rhythm of economic and social reproduction and consequent urban division of space.

It has been also argued that speculative element in the urban land ownership and housebuilding industry is an integral part of the creation of both effective demand and MR. Therefore, it is argued that a large portion of the profit of speculative housebuilders derive from the circulation of revenues and betting on the future value of land parcels. Because residential land has differential qualities and different housing markets have different artificial scarcities vis-a-vis effective demand, the monopoly rents are differentiated according to housing markets and sub-markets. This affects not only the development gain of speculative housebuilders but also the capital gain of landowners that ultimately depend on the balance of power between the actors in a specific housing SoP and social and institutional configurations shaping the system of land ownership, property relations, planning system, land use and building regulations.

Moreover, it has also been argued the revenue character of MR makes the production and distribution of housing very sensitive to not only local and neighbourhood effects but also broader national and global dynamics. Although it is mainly a domestic industry, this unique feature of the housebuilding industry coming with the MR appropriation makes it one of the industries whose boom and bust cycles have been strongly influenced by the macroeconomic expansion and downturn due to the volatile nature of the MR and effective demand. Based on this, the next chapter will discuss that both boom-bust cycles of the housebuilding industry and macroeconomic expansion and downturn phases in economies have been accelerated with the financialisation of economic and social reproduction.

Finally, this chapter argues that the impact of landed property on housing can only be fully understood through an empirical analysis of the interaction of relevant agents in a specific land regime and housing provision system since the determination of MR as the dominant form of rent in the housebuilding industry is not for orthodoxy. Instead, the analysis of the role of ground rent in housing in this chapter is developed based on the historically-specific social relations of production attached to housing through certain abstractions. It has been discussed that the prevalence of MR in the housebuilding industry as a (current) general sectoral tendency is contingent upon the widespread existence of speculative landowners and speculative housebuilders in commodified housing provision systems which was assisted by a range of interventions of state and finance. Nevertheless, at a more complex and concrete level of analysis, the current sectoral tendencies, which are themselves subject to historical changes and transformations, may exist with its counter-tendencies and contingencies such as collective, decommodified forms of housing provision.

CHAPTER 3

A Theoretical Investigation for Financialisation with a Focus on Financialisation of Housing Provision

The world economy has witnessed the hegemonic role of finance since the collapse of the post-war boom. Although the role of finance has always been important for the accumulation of capital, the last three decades were marked by an unprecedented expansion of speculative finance into almost all spheres of economic and social life coupled with the massive rise of global financial revenues. But it was not long ago when mainstream economics started to acknowledge this rapid expansion of financial activities vis-à-vis productive activities. Even so, the hesitation of mainstream economics and its media and political organisations to use financialisation as both a concept and a phenomenon is still valid. This hesitation is rooted in the lack of a methodology capable of addressing such a systemic and historically dynamic concept. Therefore, it is not surprising that the term financialisation emerged from critical political economy and has been used and analysed by Marxist, Keynesian and Post-Keynesian scholars, using different understandings and analytical frameworks.

Nevertheless, the widespread use of the term among the heterodox literature does not make it unproblematic. On the contrary, its extensive and frequent use without a systematically-developed analytical and theoretical base has made it a polysemantic concept. Although I believe, as discussed below, that financialisation is a multi-dimensional phenomenon with its various forms and impacts on economic, social and cultural spheres, the different aspects of it represent neither the definition nor the explanation of the concept. Some critical scholars reject the use of financialisation "as a project of intellectual inquiry" (Michell and Toporowski, 2014: 80) due to the "different meanings according to the context and the individual using the term" (ibid., 68) or "the study of the effects of finance rather than the study of finance per se" (Christophers, 2015: 230) in the financialisation literature. I agree with the critics in the sense that the usage of the concept without a theoretical and analytical accuracy prompts to "speculatively linking up incidents in how business is done today" (ibid., 80). However, this does not apply to the entire financialisation literature; hence, the notion should not be abandoned. I believe that the concept of financialisation is not only well-equipped but also a necessary analytical tool for analysing the structural transformation of capitalism in general and housing provision in particular in recent decades.

This chapter is divided into two sections. In the first section, financialisation will be analysed by locating the concept logically/theoretically and historically/systemically. The ultimate aim is to understand the analytical and historical backbone of the concept from a Marxist perspective and then to address the heterogeneity of the phenomenon. The second section of the chapter will investigate the general dynamics of financialisation of housing by analysing the intervention of finance into housing production and consumption, respectively. The chapter will be concluded with the general impacts of financialisation on social housing provision based on the relevant literature.

1 Financialisation: an Explanandum or Explanans?

Although the works of Marxist and other heterodox scholars on financialisation are vast and complement each other, there is a remarkable disagreement over how to define financialisation. The simple and broad definition of financialisation by Epstein (2005: 3) is widely accepted and used as an introduction in financialisation surveys; he defines the concept as: "the increasing role of financial motives, financial markets, financial actors and financial institutions in the operation of the domestic and international economies". Similarly, Foster (2007: 1), in line with the earlier works of the Monthly Review School (MRS) define financialisation as "the shift in gravity of economic activity from production to finance" because for the MRS, within monopoly capitalism, the replacement of the smaller firms of the competitive capitalism by the giant monopolistic corporations created a tendency of the increase in the production of economic surplus and this swelling economic surplus cannot be absorbed in the sphere of production due to the lack of profitable investment outlets. Therefore, the 'stagnation of production' is the main reason for the 'financial explosion' in this new era (ibid.).

For Arrighi (2004: 536), "finance capitalism was no new-born child" because "financialisation has always been the predominant response to the overaccumulation problem of the established organising centres of the system of accumulation". Therefore, for him, financial expansion (i.e. the maturity of a particular capitalist development in which accumulated capital of capitalist centres is transferred from trade and production to financial speculation) is a recurrent world systemic tendency as part of the long systemic cycles of accumulation.

For the Regulation School, because it aims to periodise capitalism according to the corresponding regime of accumulation, and to document the rise and the renewal of growth regimes, financialisation refers to the crisis of the Fordist regime of accumulation, which was mainly based on the productive accumulation, economic growth and labour-capital compromises in the post-war era. Aglietta (1998), Boyer (2000; 2001) and Chesnais (2001) searched for a possible new regime of accumulations which will substitute the former one. However, unlike a singular regime of accumulation like the Fordist regime, financialisation as the current dominance and importance of financial capital and stock market over economic growth is named 'post-Fordist regime[s] of accumulation' and defined by "labour-market flexibility, developing high-tech sectors, booming stock market and credit to sustain the rapid growth of consumption and permanent optimism of expectations in firms" (Boyer, 2000: 116).

The Critical Accountants, unlike the literature investigating financialisation based on their traditional theories, synthesised different theoretical approaches in their works: liberal collectivist theory of the 1920s and 1930s, agency theory of the 1980s and 1990s, the political economy from the 1990s onwards, and cultural economy from 2000 onwards (Ertürk *et al.*, 2008). Based on the combination of these different theoretical stances, 'a bricolage' in their saying, they defined financialisation as 'coupon pool' capitalism, which is "a new generic type where the pool of new and issued coupons becomes a regulator of firm and household behaviour and a regulator of macro-economic trajectory" (Froud *et al.*, 2002: 275).

Lapavitsas and dos Santos define financialisation as a systemic transformation of financial relations and capital accumulation process based on the altering behaviours and inter-relationships of three fundamental agents: non-financial corporations (NFCs), banks and workers (Lapavitsas, 2009a; 2009b; Dos Santos, 2009; Lapavitsas and Powell, 2013). They argued that (i) large NFCs have diminished their dependence on bank loans and have integrated into global financial markets through gaining financial skills in independent financial trading, seeking profits in the sphere of circulation; (ii) banks have been restructured and their activities have been transformed from investment banking activities to mediating activities in financial markets and lending to households, whose revenues have become the greatest source of profit for banks; (iii) financial transactions have penetrated the household revenues, and households have increasingly involved in financial activities by being both debtors and asset holders.

There are several other important contributions to financialisation literature which are impossible to cover here because of the limited space. The survey on the financialisation of housing in the second part of this chapter largely benefits from the rich and comprehensive literature within the context of financialisation as explanans. However, the increasing popularity of financialisation harmed its analytic base. As Aalbers points out, "sometimes financialisation is the explanandum (the phenomenon to be explained), sometimes the explanans (the thing that explains), and at other times it is not even clear which of the two it is" (2019: 3). Hence, the priority while investigating financialisation is to differentiate between explanandum and explanans. For the explanandum aspect, there is a need to define financialisation from an MPE perspective, to trace the phenomenon from its abstract and simple form to concrete and more complex form. In this regard, Fine (2013b) sees financialisation as the intensive and extensive accumulation (expansion) of interest-bearing capital. Furthermore, the road map drawn by Fine (2013b) and Fine and Saad-Filho (2018) to analyse financialisation systemically, opens a discussion on financialisation within Marx's theory of money and finance in pursuit of a logical-analytical understanding of financialisation. The next section introduces the core concepts with reference to Volume 3 of *Capital* focusing on conceptualising interest-bearing capital and other monetary forms in Marx with the aim to trace their relations around financialisation. The subsequent section locates financialisation within a Marxist periodisation of capitalism, for its historical-systemic consideration.

1.1 Analytical: Understanding Financialisation through Marx's Theory of Money and Finance

The theory of interest-bearing capital (IBC) in Marx which is developed in the third volume of *Capital* lies on the general circuit of industrial capital, illustrated as $M - C ... P ... C' - M'$ (M + ΔM). During this circuit, industrial capital goes through three stages: i) industrial capital appears money capital that buys labour-power and means of production $(M–C)$; ii) it takes the form of productive capital through the consumption of these inputs for the production of commodities, and iii) the sale of produced commodities in the form of commodity-capital in the market $(C'– M')$. The industrial capitalist enters this circuit to receive more than the initial amount of money and generate surplus-value or M' = M + ΔM. Under the capitalist relations of production, surplus-value constitutes the source of all other forms (profit, rent, interest, etc.). Moreover, the transformation of money into capital is a defining feature of capital accumulation through the re-investment of (some or all of) the acquired surplus-value into production as well as constituting the starting point of finance in Marx.

From this point forth, Marx uses money in two ways in his analysis: as money per se and as capital, based on the role of money within economic reproduction as a whole. While his analysis of merchant's capital is based on the role of money as money, the analysis of IBC is predicated upon the role of money as capital. Regarding the former, the function of selling the produced commodity within capitalism "has been taken over from the producer by the merchant and transformed into his special business" (Marx, 1991: 382). In other words, merchant capital operates as a means of commodity exchange and, therefore, helps to realise the surplus-value within the exchange. Although merchant capital does not produce either value or surplus-value (as it does not produce any commodities but simply facilitates their movement), its profit consists of a deduction from the surplus-value produced by the industrial capital as a whole.

Marx also distinguishes between commercial capital and money dealing capital (MDC), within the scope of merchant capital. Broadly speaking, this separation can be thought of as the trading merchant capital (commercial capital), and non-trading merchant capital (MDC). Indeed, this social division of labour is a result of the specialisation of particular fractions of capital for certain activities with the development of capitalism. While commercial capital buys commodities and sells them at a higher value, enabling the exchange of commodities, MDC specialises in controlling and managing money which is required for economic reproduction as a part of the circulation. However, with the development of capitalist credit system, "banks tend to appropriate the functions of MDC, leading to the disappearance of the latter as an independent form of capital" (Itoh and Lapavitsas, 1999: 70), so MDC can be thought of as part of banking capital today.

Moreover, the function of money as a "means of hoarding and means of payment" forms a basis for the capitalist credit system (Mavroudeas and Lapavitsas, 1999: 4). The first form of hoarding appears in the phase of $M–C$ as part of the functioning money capital since capitalists have to hoard enough money to buy labour-power and means of production to enter into production and to hoard precautionary idle reserves. Also, money hoarding appears in the process of capital accumulation as capitalists save and accumulate a part of their profits (ΔM) for reinvestment. These profits are accrued until being sufficient for starting to a new circuit and form latent money capital (still money as money). For both, the accumulation of money is associated with the development of merchant's capital since "the hoard itself has to be looked after, which is again a special operation" (Marx, 1991: 432). The formation of money reserves constitutes the first necessary step of the capitalist credit system since it is created regularly but spontaneously throughout the capital turnover to ensure the continuity of the economic reproduction process (Brunhoff and Foley, 2006).

In the context of the development of capitalism, "this spontaneous basis for the credit system is expanded, generalized and elaborated [in that] money now functions only as means of payment, i.e., commodities are not sold for money, but for a written promise to pay at a certain date" (Marx, 1991: 525). These promises to pay (bills of exchange or certificates of debt), which are circulated as means of payment, form the commercial credit or credit money, in the hands of merchant capitalists. With this particular form of credit, "the commodity is alienated first and its value realized only later" (ibid., 492). At this point, credit money still functions as money by assisting the aggregate demand, although the metallic substance of money is replaced by the circulation of debt certificates.

Consequently, in an advanced credit system, "hoards and savings [regularly created in the course of economic reproduction] are collected and centralised in the financial institutions and transformed into potential money capital available to industrial capital" (Fine and Saad-Filho, 2010: 143). In other words, the capitalist credit system, through banks, serves to collect and concentrate the temporarily unoccupied money of all social classes, and to reserve funds of the business community, and make these 'social funds' available to be loaned out and function as IBC (Marx, 1991: 528).

From this point forth, credit relations in the capitalist mode of production need to be analysed not only as a credit in general but also as a particular type of credit where money can be used both as money, which is part of merchant's capital, and as capital (i.e. IBC). This calls special attention to the other side of the credit system in Marx's analysis since "on the whole, [IBC] under the modern credit system is adapted to the conditions of the capitalist mode of production" (1991: 704). This other side of the credit system, (i.e., the management of IBC via borrowing and lending money), appears as an intermediary between facilitating (industrial and merchant) capitalists as borrowers, on the one hand, and money capitalists as lenders, on the other hand. Within the context of this particular form of borrowing and lending relations, money as capital is a commodity which should not be confused with the functions of industrial capital in the circulation process as commodity-capital (C) and money-capital (M). The use-value of this special commodity (i.e., IBC) to the borrower is "its ability to be transformed into productive capital which alone can be used in the production process where surplus value is generated" (Harris, 1976: 147). Therefore, the peculiarity of IBC does not consist in the act of borrowing and lending itself but rather the use of this borrowed money to make more money. Specifically, IBC uses credit relations to expand accumulation, aiming to appropriate a certain quantity of unpaid labour as surplus-value (Brunhoff, 1976).

Although the actual transformation of money into capital only occurs in the hands of industrial capitalists (going through the movement $M – C– M'$), in both departure and return points of the circulation of IBC, the money takes the form of a commodity as capital for the owner of the money. Broadly speaking, money (M), which is advanced as IBC (a potential money capital), returns to the owner as "realised capital (M + ΔM), where ΔM represents the interest" (Marx, 1991: 461). Here, what makes IBC a commodity as capital is its capacity of self-expansion not only for money capitalists but also for industrial (or merchant) capitalists simultaneously. Therefore, the movement of IBC is represented as $M – M – C – M' – M'$. If we look at this representation closer, when money capital is transferred to industrial capitalist by money capitalist, it already starts its function as capital (i.e., money is given out as capital), as self-valorising value, from the start. Nevertheless, when the functioning of industrial capital ends, the money flows back to the money capitalist, as repayment. Therefore, considering the entire reproduction process, IBC has a special character in that "money breeds money" $(M – M')$ (ibid., 466). Simply, money capitalists neither sell nor buy, they only lend and advance money as capital. This is why "this lending is the appropriate form for its alienation as capital, instead of as money or commodity" (Marx, 1991: 471).

There are two crucial points here. First, the reflux of IBC, which is a definite sum of value, to its real possessor (i.e. the money capitalist) is not equivalent with the money capital (M) given out at the beginning of the circuit but it must increase its value (i.e. valorise itself) as M + 1/X M. Hence, "this sum of value plus the surplus-value or profit is withdrawn from the circulation sphere" (ibid., 467). The IBC is lent out as capital and returns as such, so there is no qualitative change at this point but a quantitative one $(M – M')$. Second, regarding the qualitative change that occurs only when valorised and realised as capital, there must be a division of profit into interest and profit of industrial capitalist. In this way, "the merely quantitative division becomes a qualitative one" (ibid., 499). As a logical consequence, the whole profit as realised capital cannot belong to the industrial capitalist, so she must pay the value (M) plus interest (surplus value,1/X M) to the real possessor. Here, Marx emphasises that the double existence of the same sum of money as capital for both the borrower and the lender does not double the profit (M') because profit is created only by the industrial or merchant capitalist via the use of the borrowed money (IBC) and divided into surplus-value and interest. Therefore, interest, which becomes the 'price' of the borrowed IBC, is a superficial and fetishised form of return for Marx.

There is a caveat at this point in that the period of reflux of IBC to the money capitalist is not determined by the production process of the industrial capitalist, but it depends on the legal transaction between the lender and the borrower. Therefore, there can be neither a natural rate of interest nor natural limits to the interest rate due to the independent characteristics of IBC and resulting autonomy of interest regarding profit. Unlike the MDC and commercial capital, whose returns, as part of industrial profits, are subject to a rate of profit equalisation, the return of IBC is independent of the general rate of profit because "competition in money markets does not bring about the tendency to settle the rate of interest at some technically determined rate" (Fine, 2013b: 52). Marx (1991: 489) argues that:

> [Although] IBC becomes a commodity sui generis with interest as its price, and this price, just like the market price of an ordinary commodity, is fixed at any given time by demand and supply, ... [the] process of fixing the rate by supply and demand [for IBC] does not apply to the equalization that produces the general rate of profit.

Therefore, the rate of interest is socially determined, at any given time, by the competitive relations between borrowing and lending capitalists and the relative social power between them, the money flows in and out of the money markets, the role of state, the technological change, the exploitation rate, the dynamics of accumulation, among other factors (Harvey, 1999; Fine and Saad-Filho, 2010).

Quantitatively, the interest rate is unrelated to facilitating capitalists or the distribution of surplus value between industrial and merchant capitals but to money capital as a palpable and empirically given quantity (Marx, 1991: 500). At this point, the money capitalist demands the payment of her return, according to the proportion on the loan contract, independently from the profit of the industrial capitalist, though (Brunhoff and Foley, 2006). For the money capitalist, the origin of her surplus-value in the form of interest, is obscured in the narrowed formula $(M – M')$, which does not change the fact that interest is ultimately derived from the production of surplus-value and may not be produced by this borrower but by the overall economy (Brunhoff, 1976), analogous to the monopoly rent shown before.

Overall, IBC has important roles in the development of capitalist production. By using the credit system, IBC i) advances money capital for the appropriation of surplus-value in the form of interest; ii) regulates the flows of money in and out of the money markets iii) standardises the loan contracts among facilitating capitalists; iv) "speeds up commodity circulation and reduces turnover times" (Saad-Filho, 2015: 5); v) "directly funds investment, employment and expanded reproduction" (ibid., 4); vi) lifts the general rate of profit (Fine, 2013b), and vii) accelerates competition between other capitalists in capital accumulation, although it is not subject to this competition (Weeks, 2010). Alongside these coordinating tasks, its accumulation is at the expense of both industrial and commercial capitals in that IBC takes "its share of the surplus before the remaining surplus is distributed to the other capitals as profit" (Fine, 2013b: 53).

Nevertheless, in modern capitalism, the distinction between money as money and money as capital is not directly observable in practice because of the existence of the hybrid forms between IBC, merchant and industrial capitals. Especially with the development of the credit system, some of the funds in the hands of financial institutions, performing the functions of MDC, are also part of IBC. At first appearance, money has the same form for all borrowers and lenders on the money market. Money, whether originates from productive capital or individual hoards and savings, whether it is used as IBC or not, constitutes the money market as a whole in that both have the same effect on the interest rate. For Marx, this pool of money represents loanable money capital (LMC) because neither its source nor its application is pre-determined. Instead, within the credit system, money capital appears "as a concentrated and organized mass" (Marx, 1991: 490). Therefore, what matters for the theoretical investigation is not "whether IBC and MDC are empirically separable or not", since there are hybrids, as the capitalist corporations can operate in different activities at the same time, but "how corresponding capitals are situated within the accumulation and circulation of capital as a whole" (Fine, 2010: 111, 112).

Due to the development and organisation of credit system in general, and of IBC in particular, the same capital in circulation seems to be duplicated in different hands, in different forms and with different uses, at the same time. Despite this multiplication, this sum of money exists in its metallic form only at one point. For the rest, Marx (1991: 601) argues that "the greater part of this 'money capital' is purely fictitious". For instance, if government bonds, corporate debts, investment trusts, and consumer debts, such as mortgages, or shares are sold as securities, they become capital only for the person who buys them, even though their capital value is just an illusion.[1] Therefore, these securities are not genuine capital but the creditor's paper legal claims to a share of the future surplus-value, i.e., a mere title to real capital.

Marx (1991: 597) argues that fictitious capital is formed through capitalisation based on the monetary interest rate:

---

1 Sometimes they may represent a real capital such as in the case of national debts.

Any regular periodic income can be capitalized by reckoning it up, on the basis of the average rate of interest, as the sum that a capital lent out at this interest rate would yield [in that] the annual interest is taken as the capital value of the legal ownership title to the annual [income].

Most importantly for the real economy, the market values of these titles act independently from the actual money capital they represent. Namely, the future promises on fictitious capital are not guaranteed *ex ante,* subject to speculations, anticipations and emerging beliefs among the market actors. Instead, the price of these titles depends on the rate of capitalisation and "the potential to find an outlet on secondary markets" (Milios and Sotiropoulos, 2009: 178). This is why the monetary value of fictitious capital is not limited to (may or may not match up) the underlying surplus-value production or the nominal value of the asset which it is attached to (Brunhoff, 1998).

Here, the accumulation of fictitious capital goes hand in hand with the accumulation of IBC since fictitious capital is nothing more than "the independent circulation of IBC in paper form" (Fine, 2013b: 50) or what Marx (1991: 594) calls "interest-bearing paper circulat[ing] as money capital on the stock exchange". There is a mutual relationship between IBC which has a tendency to fictitiously capitalise and trade every stream of revenue and fictitious capital which becomes a means of IBC since it "can serve as the basis for further exchange as IBC" (ibid., 55). This last point is crucial for the definition of financialisation because the capacity of IBC to overcome the limits of surplus-value production and its domination over all other forms of capital expands in the financialised capitalism.

Before going further, it is important to emphasise that this book defends neither a separation between fictitious capital and IBC[2] nor a definition of financialisation based on fictitious capital. This book argues that fictitious capital refers to a probability of the fictitious value of the financial claims upon an asset; yet it does not mean that the market value necessarily differs from the underlying value of the asset. Thus, fictitious capital does not refer to a complete separation from the real value but a relatively autonomous character. Moreover, the outcomes of the circulations of different forms of capital within the financial system are not pre-determined in that "the expansion of money as money may allow for the successful realization of fictitious capital as real accumulation and, vice versa, the expansion of fictitious capital may lead to no real accumulation at all but merely the expansion of credit" (Fine,

---

2   IBC is "always being the mother of every insane form" (Marx, 1991: 596).

2013b: 50). Therefore, whether the circulation of capital corresponds to a real or fictitious accumulation is not contingent upon the capital but the movement of capital, institutional frameworks and other aspects of the economy (Saad-Filho, 2015). Lastly, in line with Marx, this book argues that sources of all financial earnings ultimately arise from the surplus value produced in the entire society, i.e., the transfer of a certain sum of unpaid labour to the rentier sectors of the economy.

To summarise, "the financial system feeds on its own circulation" (Brunhoff, 1998: 96) and this "parasitical character of finance [IBC] is inseparable from its functional role", which is mainly financing the capitalist reproduction (ibid.). Specifically, the functional roles of the credit system and IBC, within the capitalist accumulation, are ignored when finance is illustrated as purely parasitic. Nevertheless, within financialised capitalism, this contradiction condenses and the tendency of finance to breed itself takes precedence over its functional role, like the monopolistic role of IBC in all spheres of the economy, including production, circulation and distribution. This becomes the main reason of the instabilities and crises of contemporary capitalism, e.g., the Global Financial Crisis (GFC) of 2008.

Based on this analytical foundation, this book adopts the definition of financialisation, in terms of IBC, as per Fine *et al.* (2016: 13):

> [Financialisation refers to] the intensive and extensive accumulation of [IBC], intensive in what are longstanding if inventively proliferating financial markets, and extensive by the incorporation of new domains, especially those related to social reproduction.

This approach defines financialisation using Marx's method, in contrast to the theorisation of financialisation with the presence of more finance. Therefore, defining financialisation narrowly, as IBC or explanandum, allows the investigation of the broader, diverse and complex impacts of financialisation on different sections of the economic and social reproduction, as explanans.

1.2   *Historical: Thinking Financialisation within and through Neoliberalism*

Complementary to the analytical understanding of financialisation based on Marx's theory of finance, the second step for a systemic examination of financialisation must be locating the concept within a historical context. This way, the logical understanding of financialisation can be integrated within the "historically-systemic analyses attached to" MPE (Fine and Saad-Filho, 2018: 348). This section argues that since financialisation has occurred in a particular period of the capitalist mode of production and cannot be identified with capitalism as such, it is necessary to locate the concept on a periodisation of capitalism. Therefore, this section aims to understand financialisation through neoliberalism since it is accepted that neoliberalism refers to the current stage of capitalism.

Capital is a social relation; hence, historical, structural and institutional forms in which value relations have been (re-)organised alter according to different phases of capital accumulation. Similarly, capitalism as a mode of production has been reproduced and had structural transformations since the beginning of the industrial revolution. This dynamism is shown within the Marxist tradition, where any effort for periodisation means "classifying events and/or processes in terms of their internal affinities and external differences in order to identify successive periods of relative invariance and the transitions between them" (Jessop, 2001: 1). Nevertheless, there are different criteria in periodising capitalism among Marxists which focus on different but interrelated points. For instance, some studies focus on different forms of state with changing class patterns and power relations (Poulantzas, 1975; Jessop, 2001; 2014) or on different forms of capital (Baran and Sweezy, 1966; Mandel, 1975; Itoh, 2001; Lapavitsas, 2011) while others focus on agencies (Bieler et al., 2010), economic and social reproductions (Fine and Harris, 1979; Fine, 2013b) or technology, labour productivity and distribution (Duménil and Lévy, 2001a). Despite the different methodologies, focus and labels, there is some consensus regarding the stages of capitalism that arise from the structural crisis of the preceding ones: competitive capitalism (laissez-faire), monopoly capitalism (imperialism, managerial capitalism), state-monopoly capitalism (Keynesianism, Fordism) and neoliberalism respectively. Although these stages refer to successive historical periods, Marxian effort for periodisation should not be understood as a chronology (Jessop, 2001). The details of the differentiation between these stages are beyond the limit of the chapter. Our main concern is financialisation in the context of neoliberalism.

The milestone of the rise of neoliberalism was the 1978–79 dollar crisis arising from the collapse of the stock market and the high inflation pressure on the US economy and the accompanying political transformations starting with the election of Margaret Thatcher in the UK and Ronald Reagan in the USA[3] (Duménil and Lévy, 2004). Therefore, anti-labour policies and harsh austerity

---

3   Although neoliberal policies became emblematic with the successive elections of Thatcher and Reagan governments in the Global North, Chilean military junta under the leadership of Augusto Pinochet became an earlier laboratory for the neoliberal project (Albo and Fanelli, 2014).

measures in the Anglo-Saxon world, such as the attack against the welfare state, and in the rest of the world through the replacement of the import-substitution industrialisation (ISI) with the export-oriented industrialisation (EOI) are coupled with the shock therapy applied by the FED (Panitch and Gindin, 2011). Under the leadership of Paul Volcker, the FED increased the interest rate to stabilise the dollar and fight against inflation, a historical move for the increasing power of financial capital (Aglietta, 1998). In the fight against inflation, a set of measures were beneficial for financial capital, including the newly introduced floating exchange rate, the high interest rates which increased the interest returns of creditors and stockholders, and the decreasing inflation which saved the investments of financial capital (Duménil and Lévy, 2001b; 2004). Nevertheless, neoliberalism as a system of accumulation is much more than these economic measures:

> [It] has four distinguishing features: the financialisation of production, ideology and the state; the international integration of production ('globalisation'); a prominent role for foreign capital for globally integrated production and the stabilisation of the balance of payments, and a macroeconomic policy mix based on contractionary fiscal and monetary policies and inflation targeting, with the manipulation of interest rates becoming the main policy tool.
>
> SAAD-FILHO and MORAIS, 2018: 56

While neoliberalism provided a favourable atmosphere for the restoration of stagflation and decreasing profit rates, especially in the Global North thanks to the capital-friendly policies (Guttmann, 2016), for the Global South, the process moved top-down under the supervision of the Bretton Woods institutions. The neoliberal policy prescription for the Global South were guided by the neoclassical economic theory and institutionalised under the name of the Washington Consensus (WC)[4] (Saad-Filho, 2005; Soederberg, 2005; Lapavitsas, 2009b). However, at the end of almost two decades, in the 1990s, the outcomes of the neoliberal doctrine in the Global South were below the expectations of the advocates. Therefore, the rising dissatisfaction from the mainstream academia made way for new policy framework under the name

---

4   The WC primarily targeted the neoliberal transition of post-Soviet countries, the termination of the ISI policies in the developing countries and the opening these countries into short-term flows of foreign capital through a set of measures such as the flexibilization of labour market, fiscal discipline, liberalization of interest rates, competitive exchange rates, privatization of SOEs.

of new institutional economics. Joseph Stiglitz, as the newly appointed economist in the World Bank (WB), introduced revised policy suggestions, known as the post-Washington Consensus (PWC). By focusing on more social issues of the Global South, which were ignored for two decades, the PWC brought urbanisation, civil society institutions, anti-corruption, and a market-friendly state into the development agenda.

While both the WC and the PWC have the same methodology and conservative fiscal and monetary program, with an emphasis on financial deregulation, privatisation and liberalisation, the major difference between them is "[their] speed, depth and method of reform" and the revision of the idea of the withdrawal of the state from the market (Saad-Filho, 2005: 118). Specifically, both constitute different phases of the same neoliberal project. This is also why this second phase of neoliberalism has been crucial for the consolidation of the expanded role of finance on economic and social reproduction (Fine, 2009b). In other words, neoliberalism, as the current stage of capitalism, has materialised the conditions in which financialisation has occurred by creating the affirmative regulatory and ideological conditions and strengthening the role of finance at political, societal and cultural levels (Albo *et al.*, 2010; Chesnais, 2002). Although financialisation underpins neoliberalism as its economic core, neoliberalism cannot be reduced to financialisation (Fine and Saad-Filho, 2018). In this book, financialisation is not considered a pre-requisite of neoliberalism but an expected outcome of it (Pereira, 2017). By encompassing all the spheres of social, political and economic life, the neoliberal reforms enable the internationalisation of production and finance, open new ways for the commodification of social reproduction and, therefore, facilitate the expansion of IBC to ever more areas of economic and social reproduction. Therefore, this book argues that financialisation rises through neoliberalism but not vice versa.

1.3   *Uneven and Combined Development of Financialisation*

As discussed in the previous section, financialisation refers to the neoliberal phase of capitalism. However, the heterogeneity among countries increased the complexity of both. Regarding neoliberalism, Jessop (2002: 460) argues that:

> Ideal types [do not] represent some normative ideal or other. They are theoretical constructs formed by the one-sided accentuation of empirically observable features of social reality to produce logically coherent and objectively feasible configurations of social relations [which] are never found in pure form. Each has contrasting implications for economic and social policy.

Therefore, when moving from abstract to concrete, these "logically coherent and objectively feasible configurations" clash and the general may depart from the particular or, in other saying, the incidences, forms and effects of the dominant system of accumulation can be different in different social formations. This is equally applicable for both neoliberalism and financialisation. The discrepancy between the rhetoric of neoliberalism and of its impact on financialisation are the indication of this heterogeneity and unevenness at the concrete level. While in most Latin American countries, a neo-developmentalist model was integrated into the neoliberal economic programme (Ebenau, 2014), at the ideological and organisational levels, neoliberal regimes can take communitarian, statist, corporatist and authoritarian forms (Jessop, 2002). Several factors such as historical, institutional and political variations between countries, balance of classes and differences in the integration of countries into the global capitalism determine the changing forms of neoliberalism as well as the different degrees, forms and outcomes of financialisation. Therefore, although "finance alone does not, and cannot, account for national diversity", thanks to the financialisation of global capitalism, "finance has become an increasingly important determinant, exacerbating combined and uneven development ... across the global economy" (Ashman and Fine, 2013: 145). The differences in the national financial systems of countries, in their locations in the global capitalism and in their integration with the international circuit of capital are clearly influential on this unevenness. However, this should not let one to fall into the trap of methodological nationalism since "the redistribution of surplus in the form of interest is internationally organized in ways that cut across financial systems that are supposedly national but in fact provide the basis for advantage (and disadvantage) in the workings of international finance" as a whole (Fine, 2013b: 56).

Nevertheless, three problems can be identified in the literature, including the focus on the financialisation of advanced capitalist countries by ignoring the rest of the world and the search for the same outcomes of Anglo-Saxon and European countries in the developing countries. In the Anglo-Saxon space, the US is the birthplace of financialisation, thanks to its advanced financial markets and the domination of the US dollar in the international transactions, although financialisation is international through its impacts and outcomes. Also, the third problem is a reaction to the other two issues and is the description of financialisation of the Global South as "subordinated financialization" (Powell, 2013; 2018; Bortz and Kaltenbrunner, 2017; Choi, 2018). The subordinated financialization literature interprets the time difference between financialization in the Global North and Global South in a way that financialization is "embroiled/exported" to the latter by the former (Lapavitsas, 2009b; Bonizzi,

2017). Financialisaton in the Global South is shaped by the imperial relations within the international monetary system, the holding of massive amounts of reserve currencies, the economies' greater reliance on short-term capital inflows and the peripheral location in the world economy. Hence, financialisation in the Global South has different forms, processes, impacts and outcomes than the Global North and the above-mentioned features are the common way of the late-capitalist countries' integration in the global finance, as seen in the case of Turkey (Chapter 4).

However, defining financialisaton in the Global South as subordinated financialisation brings financialisaton theories to a new Third Worldist approach through which imperial relations between the advanced-capitalist countries (ACCs) and the late-capitalist countries (LCCs) take precedence over the genuine dynamics of capitalism and capital accumulation processes.[5] From this perspective, neoliberalism in LCCs can be analysed as subordinated neoliberalism and even capitalism in LCCs as subordinated capitalism. This leads to neglect the different impacts of financialisaton on domestic political economies such as "social relations of power and class specific to different phases of capitalism as underlying causal factors" (Marois, 2011: 176). The mode of integration with global finance and the positions of countries within world capitalism is significant, although the over-emphasis on the level of integration, as seen in the subordinated financialisaton literature, fails to understand "the integrated nature of the financial system with specific systems of accumulation, where the nature of this integration is context-specific and determined by historical, institutional and social factors" (Waeyenberge and Bargawi, 2015: 11). Therefore, the diverse impacts and outcomes of financialisaton in both LCCs and ACCs should be understood in the context of combined and uneven development of capitalism in which development and underdevelopment are not only "mutually determining processes" but also "a necessary outcome of the unfolding laws of motion of capitalism itself" (Mandel, 1975: 85).

Hence, financialisaton in a specific country needs to be understood within the context of the country's system of accumulation. Each system of accumulation composes of a juxtaposition of the global tendencies of the current phase of capitalism and "specific historical and institutional trajectories of national processes of capital accumulation" (Kaltenbrunner and Karaçimen, 2016: 288). Nevertheless, the unevenness of financialisaton goes beyond the

---

5 Nevertheless, the subordinated financialization literature is empirically very rich and fills a very important gap in the literature. Despite the theoretical divergence, our arguments for Turkey do not challenge the findings of the subordinated financialisation literature on developing countries.

national differences since varying forms and impacts of financialisation can be observed not only at national level but also at regional, urban and sectoral levels.

As discussed in the introduction chapter of the book, each country is composed of many commodity-specific systems and the presence, development and evolution of finance in these sectors differ due to the sector or commodity-specific particularities. Specifically, finance must be located within the chain of activity that provides the commodity in question (Robertson, 2014b) because the intervention of finance into each SoP is different through the ways, extents and consequences of financialisation in different provision systems which cannot be generalised from the country-level factors. Therefore, commodity and sector-specific dynamics must be considered since generalisations such as the household indebtedness or the growing role of consumer lending in a country is not sufficient to understand how financialisation affects the consumption patterns for a specific commodity in the country in question. For instance, not only the role of finance and the impact of financialisation on housing SoPs are different between Turkey and Brazil but also the role of finance and the impact of financialisation on housing SoP and infrastructure SoP (Fine, 2009b). This heterogeneity is related to the extent and influence of financialisation and the interaction of finance with other agents within a SoP. The intervention of finance, for instance, into housing production and housing consumption has different impacts and processes of financialisation on housebuilding firms, housing consumers, and different degrees of commodification of housing provision. Therefore, in each industry, the specific characteristics of the produced commodity and industry-specific challenges rising from the transformation of the economy or the sectoral integration within the global value chains become important for understanding how finance is embedded into the industry.

2   Intensive and Extensive Expansion of Finance

For tracking more complex forms and investigating the impacts of financialisation on the different sections of the economic and social reproduction, this book adopts the narrow definition of financialisation as the intensive and extensive expansion of IBC in neoliberalism (Fine, 2009a; 2010; 2013b).

However, in neoliberalism, the activities attached to IBC expand to a great extent. A wide range of activities under the umbrella of IBC, varying from the household credit relations to the financial operations of capitalist firms, suggest tracking the positions of corresponding capitals within the circulation of capital and how all other forms of capital interact with the hegemony of IBC in financialised capitalism. While financialisation paves the way for further penetration of IBC in some sectors of the economy like banks and NFCs, the recent decades are marked by the integration of IBC into the areas which are considered non-economic.

2.1 Financialisation of Social Reproduction

The extensive expansion of IBC in economic and social reproduction is complementary to the intensive expansion of IBC. This means the attachment of IBC "to new activities from which it was previously absent or even absented by virtue of regulation or a form of provision" (Fine, 2013b: 55). Specifically, financialisation has transformed the organisation of social and economic reproduction such that IBC expanded not only to the operations of merchant and industrial capital but also to the spheres of health, pensions, housing, education, energy, etc. through its capability of drawing all resources (LMC) from the economy. This includes all potential revenue streams or bundles of contractual claims to properties as soon as they are capitalised and traded (Marx, 1991). Therefore, financial actors including banks, investors and speculative funds are involved in the areas which they are not interested in or did not have a chance to access before. In the literature, a large set of domains and areas have been documented empirically within the scope of financialisation. Although the definition of financialisation depends on the quantitative expansion of IBC, there are indirect impacts of financialisation on social reproduction, for instance, through "the broader impact of neoliberalism upon social reproduction" (Fine and Saad-Filho, 2010: 157). This suggests reconsidering the relations and borders between economic reproduction and social reproduction, which is considered the realm of political and ideological superstructure (Althusser, 2010). The boundaries between social and economic reproduction have become more complex and ambiguous in the financialised capitalism since the relatively decommodified activities within social reproduction have shifted to economic reproduction, as an indication of the extensive expansion of IBC.

The financialisation literature argues that social reproduction has been privatised, commodified and individualised through the associated changes in value of labour-power, meaning that the provision of goods and services necessary for the reproduction of labour-power has been provided through the capitalist market at the expense of public and other non-commodified ways of provision. This is strongly related to neoliberalism as this shift has changed with the neoliberal capitalism since the late 1970s. As argued above, neoliberalism has created a favourable atmosphere for the promotion of financial capital and helped financialisation become a historical-systemic tendency with its counter-tendencies and hybrid forms. As argued by Fine (2013b: 55):

> Financialization depends upon how such expansion of financial activity straddles the boundaries between IBC and other forms of capital in exchange: is it merely an expansion of credit or does it involve a requirement of surplus production and appropriation beyond what would be expected of "normal" commercial activity.

Therefore, the question is if the boundaries between IBC and other forms of capital have increasingly become blurry, how we can determine whether a SoP is financialised or not. Considering that the analysis of financialisation of social reproduction is equivalent to the analysis of the processes of commodification in terms of shifting norms and modalities and the changing interests within the provision, changing institutional structures and the new financial intermediations in the household reproduction, the answer to this question becomes more complex.

Although commodification is the main tendency in the financialisation of social reproduction, it does not always lead to the ultimate extinction of decommodification since it depends on the existence of class struggles and social resistance. Therefore, what is crucial here is to recognise and analyse the coexistence of financialised and non-financialised forms of social reproduction and hybrid forms. Also, commodification and privatisation are much older and broader than financialisation and are direct indications of neoliberalism. However, this is not the case of financialisation since not all forms of commodification and privatisation result in the expansion of IBC. To analyse the relationship between financialisation and privatisation and commercialisation, Fine (2020: 212–3) identified three analytical but not hierarchical levels of commodification, including commodification, commodity form and commodity calculation (CCFCC) which corresponds to fully-established capitalist production, the presence of revenue streams not necessarily through privatised capital, and the incorporation of market logic or substitutes.

At a closer look, the initial condition of the commodification of the social product is to maximise profit with the abstraction of labour. Commodification directly creates the opportunities for financialisation since it creates the opportunities for the increased deployment of IBC by securitising and trading revenue streams in financial markets. As argued by Albritton (2012: 67), a complete commodification including a "completely commodified labour market" is not possible in practice but in a theoretically-idealised laissez-faire capitalism with "no trade unions, no oligopoly, and competitive economic sectors". This is why, even a fully-established private capitalist production is regulated, to support commodification ideologically, legally and politically. Because of this, the commodification and privatisation of social reproduction leads to financialisation provided that income streams and potential interest payments are securitised.

In addition, financialisation occurs when there is no direct capitalist commodity production but a 'commodity form' (CF), which refers to monetary payments on an asset or a debt instrument, such as mortgages, pensions, and social security. Although these are modern forms of CF, CF is much older than capitalism and includes bribery and usury. Marx (1990: 165) argued that "the commodity-form [rises with] absolutely no connection with the physical nature of the commodity and the material relations arising out of this [as] the fantastic form of a relation between things". Even there can be a "dematerialisation of the commodity form, where the act of exchange centres upon those [experimental] commodities which are time rather than substance based" (Lee, 1993: 135). While capitalism accelerated the tendency for the creation of CF, financialised-capitalism not only intensively and extensively expands this tendency but also facilitates the dematerialisation of CF. For instance, Perelman (2003) and Rotta and Teixeira (2018) consider copyrights, patents, and intellectual property as CF. Another tendency in capitalism is the transformation of CF into commodification (e.g., labour-power). Therefore, in the case of CF, any regular payment (e.g., interest payments, fees, user charges), independent from its source, can be capitalised as an asset and speculatively traded as IBC (Fine and Saad-Filho, 2018). When the CF becomes an asset, its exchange becomes independent from the underlying need such as a home, retirement, health and thus social reproduction is financialised. So even the expansion of simple consumer loans, e.g., mortgage loans without securitisation, might contribute indirectly to financialisation through assetisation, i.e., the transformation of recurring revenue streams into tradable assets, as will be shown for Turkey. Here, independently from the intention of lender, money as money can be realised as money as capital or IBC.

Moreover, commodity calculation refers to the situations with no revenue streams, monetary payments, exchange or any kind of monetisation but the presence of monetary criteria, practices, narratives and financial rationales in the decision-making processes (Bayliss *et al.*, 2017). This is not financialisation since there is no commerce or monetised, securitised and traded income flows. Commodity calculation takes place in the majority of the activities today, varying from the increasing self-responsibility and individual risk management to entrepreneurial citizenship, from financial inclusion to financial literacy campaigns (Martin, 2002; 2014; Langley, 2008). Therefore, this book considers it as the indirect impact of financialisation but not financialisation itself. Fine (2017) also highlights that financialisation strongly accelerates the transformation of commodity calculation to commodification.

Consequently, extensive expansion of IBC, which covers a broad set of topics varying from wealth effect to household indebtedness, from macroeconomic policy to social policy, will be empirically examined based on CCFCC both in the remainder of the chapter and in the case chapters of the book. The next section discusses the general tendencies of financialisation of housing, although these are subject to the variegated and uneven outcomes across countries, as seen for Turkey.

3   Financialisation of Housing

As argued in Chapter 2, because housing is a landed property, the provision of housing is first and foremost related to the land on which production takes place. This makes housing different from other commodities. The form of ground rent, which is the economic form of landed property, is determined by the production on the land in question. In the context of residential land, monopoly rent (MR) is the main rent rising from the housing production and, unlike other forms of rent, it derives from monopoly pricing. The amount of MR in the context of housing is determined by the degrees of human-made scarcity of desirable land for residential production and effective demand, namely the willingness and payment capacity of demand. Therefore, as put by Marx (1992: 312), "the profit on the actual construction is extremely slight; the main source of profit of house-builders comes from raising the [MR], from the clever selection and exploitation of the building land [and] speculative anticipation of the demand for houses". Hence, the profits of speculative housebuilders ultimately depend on the changes in land values between the purchase of the land and the sale of the housing units on that land. Both the value of any land parcel and housing are subject to dynamic changes in the course of urban development and the dynamics of economic and social reproduction affect both scarcity of residential land with desirable (or needed) qualifications and effective demand for housing. Nevertheless, during the provision of housing, MR is appropriated by many landed interests including builders, landowners, state and finance.

Henceforth, looking at the role of finance in the provision of housing, we can observe two main points where finance steps in: (i) to finance land purchase and housing production for builders and (ii) to finance the purchase of housing for consumers. The first one will be discussed as the housing development finance (HDF) and the second as the house purchase finance (mortgages). The impacts of financialisation on HDF and mortgages will be examined respectively. Following this, the next section analyses the financialisation of social housing.

3.1   *Housing Development Finance*

The role of IBC is crucial in the production of housing through the general characteristics of the industry, the transformation of capital from its commodity form (C') to its money form (M') which needs a long period of time, due not only to long housing production lead times but also to longer times for the realisation and the sale of the completed housing units. Thus, housebuilders mostly need credit to finance land purchase, which is the most expensive input of production. In this case, IBC directly accelerates the turnover of capital in the production process and indirectly accelerates the appropriation of MR in the industry since the amount of MR appropriated by the builders depends on the acquisition of land and the sale of completed housing units as quickly as possible when there is high effective demand (Harvey, 2012). Moreover, because finance has the power to "manipulate and control both supply and demand" (ibid., 46), the intensive expansion of finance brought important quantitative and qualitative changes to the housebuilding industry. In this sense, there are three main changes that financialisation brought to the housebuilding industry which have been approached as general tendencies, based on a survey on different countries' building industries, while the heterogeneity of this process has been ignored.

The first change is the raising of capital via domestic and international private equity funds, promoting initial public offerings (IPOs) on the stock exchange or issuing stocks and corporate bonds which became widespread funding arrangements for large housing-developers. Capital markets not only gave house-builders more availability to finance their activities but also provided cheaper and longer-term financing opportunities to boost their growth through short-term bank credits (Romainville, 2017; Ball, 2010; Sanfelici and Halbert, 2015; Shimbo, 2019; Wissoker, 2016). Moreover, by issuing debt and equity, housing developers attracted pensions, mutual funds, insurance companies and investment banks and led them to "collect huge amounts of capital, of their own and from third parties [and] invest in real estate projects" (David and Halbert, 2010: 105). Debts and equities of housebuilders hereby provide a stream of revenue for the secondary market. By acquiring stocks, financial investors become shareholders of housing development companies in return of future interest, dividends, or capital gains. However, sometimes, these institutional investors directly acquire land and real estate as an asset by pushing housebuilders out (Aalbers, 2019; D'Lima & Schultz, 2019). At this point, the role of REITs is crucial thanks to the novelties they bring into the sector. REITs represent "a profound institutional transformation in which the real estate sector has come to resemble an economic sector composed of finance markets and instruments rather than a sector defined by producer markets" (Gotham, 2009: 357). By combining a variety of activities[6] such as carrying out housing projects, securitising and trading land and real estate in capital markets, leasing real estate from house-builders and renting in return of capital gains, REITs embody the finance-real estate complex (Erol and Tırtıroğlu, 2011; Aalbers and Haila, 2018; Waldron 2018).

Here, when the ground rent is capitalised through trading land on capital markets or when real estate is securitised by housing-developers or REITs, the relationship between MR (and all other forms of rent) and IBC becomes blurred. Because the underlying sources of both MR and IBC derive from the circulation of revenues, it is not possible to find the exact division between them. At a closer look, "the money laid out by the buyer of land [or real estate] is equivalent to an interest-bearing investment", i.e., claims on future value (Harvey, 1985: 367). Therefore, the circulation of IBC in the form of fictitious capital expands the limits of circulation of revenues through the capitalisation of land values (ground rent) in general and through the securitisation of real estate and MR in particular. Indeed, land and housing become financial assets as part of the financial investment portfolios of the owners which are "in principle no different from stocks and shares, government bonds, etc. (although it has certain qualities of security, illiquidity, etc.)" (Harvey, 1989: 96) and their values are "set in anticipation of either some future stream of revenue or some future state of scarcity" (2014: 240). Financial institutions put pressure[7] on maximising their capital gains in the short-term, either through direct ownership or shareholding of building firms, and hereby reinforce the MR appropriation. Here, capital gains of financial institutions, at least in part, derive from MR

---

6   Since REITs are subject to national regulations, the scope of activity of REITs varies from country to country. See chapter 8 for Turkey.

7   Regarding the 'shareholder value orientation' of housebuilding firms, because the housebuilding is a nationally-surrounded industry, which is liable to domestic regulations such as legal authorizations, property rights, national land regimes, country-level sectoral stimuluses or restraints, local authorities' planning permissions, consumers' traditional expectations and tastes, etc., the national and local political relations are substantially important and decisive in the housebuilding industry. This creates country-specific peculiar forms of 'shareholder ideology' in the housebuilding firms of different countries (see Rafferty and Toner (2019) for Australia; Sanfelici and Halbert (2015) and Halbert and Attuyer (2016) for Brazil; Hirayama (2017) for Japan; Romainville (2017) for Brussels; Srivastava and Jha (2016) for India; Wissoker (2016) for the USA).

attached to the land and housing. This is also the case for housing-developers and REITs, when they capitalise land and real estate or when they raise capital in debt and equity markets, the division of their profit coming from the MR appropriation and IBC cannot be determined, since financialisation makes the relationship between rent and interest much more intimate and interwoven.

Secondly, financial investors' increasing investments to housing and land markets to receive high returns of capital gains thanks to role of MR in the housebuilding industry, does not merely stem from the supply-side factors. As already argued, the level of MR, accrued to development gains of builders and capital gains of financial institutions and landowners, depends on the level of effective demand in an economy which is directly related with mortgage finance. The determination of effective demand and MR and, therefore, the profit margins in the industry, which is crucial for the financial investors, cannot be separated from the households' demand for houses. This demand made the housing sector attractive for speculative finance, developers and landowners. The creation of effective demand for housing is directly related the payment capacity of buyers which is ultimately connected to the broader economic, social and political conditions and, therefore, to the degree of expansion of mortgage finance. Consequently, the "general monopoly rent" for housing in an economy, differently from localised MR, arises "from the differences in the relative speeds of the circuit of production and the circuit of revenue" in the economy (Robertson, 2014a: 125). This suggests that financialisation created the favourable conditions not only for the localised MR which can be captured via individual productive activities but also the general monopoly rent by expanding the speed and scale of the circuit of revenue vis-á-vis the production circuit. Housebuilding industry is cyclical showing strong boom-bust cycles in which output and profits vary based on periods of economic expansion and downturn. As mentioned in Chapter 2, this cyclical fluctuation in the housebuilding industry is strongly linked with the volatile nature of MR and effective demand. However, financialisation strengthened the pace and volume of the boom phases of the housing industries of many economies in an unprecedented manner (Byrne, 2019; Van Gunten and Navot, 2018). Indeed, an ever-increasing amount of IBC flowing to mortgage finance, land and residential markets inflated land and house prices in many economies since the early 1990s.[8] House price inflation, driven by the tremendous amount of finance flowing onto mortgages, and land price inflation, stemming from the

---

8 See the link for global house price index: https://www.economist.com/graphic-detail/2019/06/27/global-house-price-index?date=1980-03&index=real_price&places=AUS&places=USA.

speculative land-based activities of house-builders and landowners, encouraged further speculative finance flow into housing and land markets and further inflated the prices (Rolnik, 2019; Evans and Herr, 2016; Ryan-Collins *et al.*, 2017). House-price inflation induced many developers, landowners and financial investors to gain substantial profits (Bernt *et al.*, 2017; Fields, 2017; Aalbers, 2017, Kitzmann, 2017).

However, there is a dual process here. On the one hand, the demand stimulated by the expansion of finance does not necessarily increase supply; it may merely inflate prices. If the supply does not respond to this demand in a country,[9] the effective demand regarding unmet scarcity feed by far the house price inflation.[10] On the other hand, the increase in effective demand may lead to both construction boom and house price inflation, which is expected to be less compared to the former case, in another country.[11] This duality stems from the country-specific and institutional factors. Namely, the level of the house price inflation and housing supply varied by country during the last three decades, according to differences in land regimes, availability of developable land, the role of state and housing policies, planning regulations, housing finance structures, development of mortgage finance, the amount of the revenues circulated in the economy, the degree of financialisation of housing, pre-existing housing stocks, population growth, beliefs and expectations of domestic and international market actors.

Moreover, while financialisation accelerated capital inflows to housing and the booming mortgage finance significantly expanded the limits of effective demand, hence of inflated land and housing prices, the bust phase brought by the crisis of financialisation[12] caused a deep shock for housing-developers and

---

9   For the Netherlands see OECD (2011); for the UK, see Ball 2013 and Robertson 2014; Kendall
      and Tulip (2018) for Australia, see. They argue that the restrictive planning systems cause
      housing-developers not to respond to the increasing effective demand sufficiently and
      therefore feeds a chronic under-supply.

10   House price volatility, i.e. inflation and deflation, also show regional differences in a coun-
      try according to the locational reflection of general MR.

11   For the USA, see Taylor (2007) and OECD (2011); for Spain, see Coq-Huelva (2013); García
      (2010) and for Ireland and Spain, see Norris and Byrne (2015). Nevertheless, the experi-
      ences of Spain and Ireland show that increasing housing supply does not prevent price
      bubbles due to the capacity of (mortgage) finance to move faster than housing produc-
      tion (Ryan-Collins 2021). Despite its different volume and intensity, a similar situation is
      also valid for Turkey (Chapters 7 and 8).

12   The impacts of the US-origin global crisis did not occur in all countries concurrently and
      with the same intensity. Especially for the LCCs, the deeper impacts of the crisis can be
      observed after 2014 following the economic contraction in Eurozone region and capital
      outflows after the announcement of tapering QE policies by FED (Akçay and Güngen,
      2016). Therefore, both the late-coming impact of the crisis that is underpinned by the

financial actors. The abundant fictitious capital flowing into the housing made housing-developers and stock market actors to rely on the expectation of ever-increasing real estate prices in many countries, notably the US. The bust phase of housing cycle becomes the indication of the lack of sustainability of the difference between fictitious values of MR and real values produced in an economy. Since only a part of the fictitious capital flowing into housing finance ends up in new housing production, the value-creation through production becomes insufficient to sustain the expansion of the flows of fictitious capital (Harvey, 2012). The most severe case was the USA in 2008 through the sudden devaluation of mortgage-backed securities (MBSs), collateralised debt obligations (CDOs) and other mortgage-backed financial derivative products and later in some other European countries such as Spain and Ireland (Fernandez and Aalbers, 2016). However, the end of the boom phase of the housebuilding industry need not come with an economic crisis.[13] The cuts in resources feeding effective demand, such as mortgage finance, state policies, and other factors leading the reversal of the favourable conditions for housing developers such as the withdrawal of supportive sectoral policies or a general economic recession may bring a bust phase for the housebuilding industry.

For the housing-developers, when the boom phase ends, there is a huge risk of overaccumulation of capital, which is not realised due to the unsold dwellings and the substantial amounts of capital locked up in land banks. This was the case of many countries, namely when the economic conditions changed, construction firms either went bankrupt and had to exit industry with huge debts or took over by the larger firms or 'too big to fail' companies were saved by the specialised real estate departments of banks, real estate funds, sovereign wealth funds and the state (Rolnik, 2019; Schwartz and Seabrooke, 2009; Pollard, 2009; Fainstein, 2016; Aalbers, 2019; Santoro and Rolnik, 2017; Fields et al., 2016; Halbert and Attuyer, 2016). Therefore, although financialisation accelerated the size and volume of both localised and general MR by expanding the effective demand and brought lucrative opportunities for huge capital gains for developers, landowners and financial investors, the expansion of speculative finance made all agents in the housing SoPs vulnerable to economic shocks and huge losses.

---

changes in the global liquidity and counter-cyclical state policies change the time and intensity of the bust phase of housing cyclicality in each country.

13   See Karwowski and Stockhammer (2017) for the house price volatility in emerging market economies (EMEs) since 2008, that is compared with the Anglo-Saxon markets. Their data shows that house price volatility in EMEs was much stronger than the ones in the Anglo-Saxon markets (ibid., 73).

Thirdly, housebuilding industry is traditionally developed out of small-scale, family-oriented and regionally-based capital groups with a strong specialisation of housing sub-markets (Türel 2015; Ball 2003; Coiacetto 2006; 2009; Fix 2011; Gotham 2009). Alongside the significance of local information on land and residential market, this stems from the cyclicality of housebuilding industry and the rapid changes in effective demand and MR. However, financialisation caused many firms to switch from local to multiregional strategies and even international strategies and competition standards. Therefore, the capitalisation of the firms, IPOs, increasing mergers and acquisitions (M&A) and the pressure of shareholders created a tendency of concentration in the housebuilding industry (Sanfelici and Halbert, 2015; Charney, 2001; Ball, 2013; David, 2012; David and Halbert, 2010; Guironnet and Halbert, 2014; Wissoker 2016; Rafferty and Toner, 2019). Although the potential of having extraordinary gains by maximising MR appropriation from inflated land and housing prices (thanks to the expansion of IBC) led new capital flows onto the sector, the pressure of stock market communities on listed firms to grow and to increase share prices contributed to the formation of large, specialised and oligopolistic firms. The expansion strategies through diversifying geographical operations and market segments, the takeover of small firms by larger and more competitive ones and increasing merging of financialised large firms with small local firms accelerated the concentration in the industry in some countries such as Brazil and the UK (Cardoso and Aragão, 2012; Robertson, 2014b).

3.2   *House Purchase Finance*

Since the transformation of capital from its commodity form (C') to its money form (M') generally needs a long period of time, housing has a higher cost than other wage goods. Therefore, housing is not usually sold to the consumer in a direct one-go payment. The realisation of surplus-value in the house-building industry, therefore, requires "some institutional and financial arrangements that will support the payment capacity of the workers" (Berry, 1981: 3). To this purpose, credit relations and mortgages are crucial for the demand in housing SoP.

Apart from economic reproduction, housing is crucial for the social reproduction of labour-power. From a Marxist perspective, financialisation of housing consumption is located within the financialisation of social reproduction as the extensive expansion of IBC in a narrow sense, being subject to processes of CCFCC in a broad sense (Fine, 2017).

Before proceeding to evaluate how financialisation affects housing consumption, it is important to briefly mention the influence of housing on the value of labour-power (VLP). VLP concerns "the material standard of living" including the minimum requirements for the reproduction of labour-power that is socially determined and change from one commodity to another (Fine 2009a: 3). Housing is a component of the VLP with its sheltering function and an important portion of wage bundle of labour. However, the use value of housing "depends crucially on its location" with the accessibility to other use values such as electricity, water, hospital, school and transportation (Berry, 1981: 3). Also, VLP "does not depend solely upon a wage but is engaged in activity outside the place of employment, thereby involving the state, the household and other social relations, structures and processes more generally" (Fine, 2002: 9). Therefore, the role of housing on the VLP ultimately depends on the broader capitalist and non-capitalist relations including the role of state and family in the access to the housing. However, because these broader relations change according to different phases of capitalism, VLP is differently formed throughout historical development of capitalist relations according to "the conditions of absolute or relative the impoverishment [of] the different segments of the working-class" (Kowarick, 1979: 59). Therefore, in contemporary capitalism, the consumption of housing and transformation of VLP attached to it, has been shaped through the withdrawal of de-commodified forms of housing provision, retraction of state subsidies, and decreasing wage bundles, which is compensated with increasing mortgage finance. The quantitative and qualitative changes happening in mortgage finance in the recent decades led a transformation of the consumption standards of housing by increasingly attaching the VLP to IBC.

Thanks to the abundant global liquidity, low interest rates and low inflation level in macroeconomic environment driven by financial deregulation and liberalisation since the 1980s, which are the consequences of financialisation itself, the increasing amount of capital was channelled to housing purchase finance (Aalbers, 2008; Lapavitsas, 2009b; Fernandez and Aalbers, 2016). The re-regulation of mortgage markets caused not only the quantitative growth of housing credits, through the removal of credit constraints, but also the qualitative changes through several financial innovations, which ended up with "the integration of the housing finance markets within general circuits of finance" (Rolnik, 2013: 1063). Housing finance was historically provided by local specialised institutions such as national housing banks, credit unions, building societies, local savings banks and housing loans generally had below-market interest rates (Green & Wachter, 2010). However, in the last decades, with the restructuring of previous impeding regulations, mortgages have been increasingly funded by capital markets and commercial banks or in some cases, old specialised institutions were integrated with financial institutions through M&A (Aalbers, 2017). Henceforth, the new market structure was well equipped to support securitisation of mortgage funds and other mortgage products. Although mortgage-backed securities (MBS) originated in the USA in the early 1980s, securitisation was implemented in several countries including the UK, Netherlands, Australia, New Zealand, Canada, Spain, Italy, Portugal, Turkey, Mexico, Brazil, South Africa, South Korea, Malaysia and Kazakhstan, albeit to different extents and intensities (Aalbers, 2019; Rolnik, 2013; Soederberg 2014; Buchanan, 2017).

Through securitisation, mortgages, which are illiquid housing debts, were converted into liquid financial assets, traded in international capital markets and purchased by global investors. This way, banks not only transferred the risk of housing loans to investors but also expanded balance sheets that enabled them further lending. Put it differently, banks created portfolios of housing loans by packaging them with other assets and sold them to the financial investors via capital markets. The invention of CDOs was especially important for expanding the size of the mortgage markets and including different risk-level mortgage loans through the inclusion of less creditworthy households. The transfer of risk through derivative products and thus the expansion of mortgage lending, which increased effective demand and MR, inflated house prices and made the mortgage lending a more lucrative investment area. As put by Harvey (2012: 45–6),

> [this is] where fictitious capital comes in. Money is lent to purchasers who presumably have the ability to pay out of their revenues (wages or profits), which are capitalized as an interest flow on the capital lent out. ... [This is also relevant for] financial trading on existing housing. ... Even more tempting is to invest in [CDOs] made up of tranches of mortgages gathered together in some spuriously highly rated investment vehicle (supposedly "as safe as houses") in which the flow of interest from home-owners provides a steady income (no matter whether the homeowners are creditworthy or not).

This is exactly what makes mortgages financialised in a narrow sense. In contrast to the historical credit relations based on borrowing and lending money to purchase a house, through the sale and trade of a pool of mortgage debts, interest payments and rental streams together with other assets, IBC, in the form of fictitious capital, is appropriated by the investors. Here, potentially, a part of capital gains accrued to financial investors derives from MR. In other words, "by securitizing mortgage debt, finance has given global liquidity to class-monopoly rents" (Bryan and Rafferty, 2014: 408).

Nevertheless, the developments in house purchase finance in general and securitisation of mortgages in particular have been a result of the mutual steps of nation-state policies and global market forces. Therefore, apart from being uneven, the general tendencies of financialisation of house purchase finance has taken country-specific forms in which the new structures of housing finance were heavily influenced by the historically-specific structures (Green and Wachter, 2010; Aalbers, 2016; Cerutti et al., 2017; Van Gunten and Navot 2018). Moreover, although the institutional and market structures under-pinning mortgage securitisation were legally and technically established in almost all countries, in practice, securitisation has not been used as a source of funding in a widespread manner in most of the countries, apart from some ACCS and few oil-rich ones (Green and Wachter, 2010; Rolnik, 2013; Aalbers, 2017; Cerutti et al., 2017). Even for the ACCS such as the UK, the use of secu-ritisation for mortgage funding was relatively limited when compared to the pre-crisis USA (Green and Wachter, 2010). Rather, the major mortgage lenders have been commercial banks. The growth of mortgage markets and increas-ing ratio of mortgage debt to GDP have been noted almost everywhere since mortgage lending to households have become a lucrative area for both foreign and domestic banks in the 2000s (Ryan-Collins et al., 2017; dos Santos, 2013; Pósfai et al., 2018; Gagyi and Vigvary, 2018). However, in contrast to the securi-tisation and trade of mortgages in capital markets, such quantitative and qual-itative changes in house purchase finance are not financialisation in a narrow sense by its definition as IBC. Rather, the revolutionary expansion of mortgage markets and accompanying changes in the VLP attached to housing refer to financialisation in a broad sense. That is to say, the financial novelties directly affecting housing consumption transform the monetary payments on housing to a 'commodity form' because streams of revenues flowing into financial com-panies and banks (due to the housing-related debts) lead a greater integration of IBC into housing consumption and offer the scope for securitisation, which may or may not be allowed to take place (Fine et al., 2016). Yet, even if there is no securitisation, growing mortgage loans feed house prices and, in turn, cre-ate more space for further lending. Increasing amounts of MR coming from the inflated land and house prices are also partly and potentially accrued to capital gains of banks and other lenders. This way, increasing capital gains make lend-ing an attractive operation for financial institutions.

Furthermore, due to the increasing marginalisation and retreat of non-market forms of housing provision and the fill of this affordability gap with the tremendous expansion of mortgage finance, households became depend-ent on financial markets to access housing. The qualitative and quantitative changes making finance more accessible to a larger number of people caused the owner-occupation to be the main tenure form of financialised capitalism (EMF Hypostat, 2019; Rolnik, 2019; Gagyi and Vigvári, 2018; Ronald and Elsinga 2012). This is a consequence of an interdependent process: while the precondition of the flow of finance onto mortgage market is the increase in the demand for housing, the flow of finance in a larger amount and scope, accompanied by low interest rates, encouraged more people to own houses. The higher demand caused revenues to be packaged and traded in secondary markets and led more scope for financial profits for lenders. Therefore, the domination of mortgage-funded owner-occupation over all other tenure forms becomes critical for financialisation of housing in general.

Also, the literature argues that financialisation of housing consumption also signifies a greater inclusion of people from different classes and income groups who were historically excluded from accessing the mortgage market (Dymski, 2009; Aalbers *et al.*, 2017; Ronald and Elsinga 2012; Aalbers, 2011; 2019). Financialisation blurred the relationship between different classes and tenure categories and the access to homeownership increasingly moved away from being an opportunity for higher classes, at least presented as such. For this, the US subprime market became emblematic. For the US, what made the higher-risk mortgages available and profitable for lenders was the absorption of riskier mortgages as collateralised loans by securities-markets (Dymski, 2009). However, the securitisation of subprime loans as in the US is an exception rather than a widespread practice that was achieved by a few ACCs. Even in the countries with more mature secondary mortgage markets, the subprime market grew far less compared to the US (see Robertson, 2014b for the UK; Ben-Shahar *et al.*, 2019 for Denmark and Blackwell and Kohl 2018 for the OECD). Rather, it has been widely noted that both mortgage markets and housing loans have been driven by high- and middle-income households (Bayliss *et al.*, 2016; Freire *et al.*, 2007; Choi, 2018; Aalbers *et al.*, 2017; Isaacs, 2016). Therefore, the 'democratisation of household finance' agenda (Shiller, 2012) or 'credit socialisation' movement via greater financial inclusion was sustainable only to the point where fictitious values of high house prices continue to soar (see Garcia-Lamarca & Kaika, 2016 for Spain).

Moreover, the financialisation literature argues that through the emergence of housing asset-based welfare systems (Cook *et al.*, 2009; Crouch, 2009; Doling and Ronald, 2010; Smith *et al.*, 2008; Watson, 2009), homeownership can be used as collateral for social welfare, in a context of decreasing wages and the retreat of state-welfare forms, since increasing market values of housing creates a wealth instrument which can be saved and invested into. In this financialised welfare system, mortgage debtors may withdraw part of values of their houses or re-mortgage to pay for their other needs of social reproduction, such as education and retirement. As Smith and Searle (2010: 229) argue, "treat[ing] home equity like a savings account [becomes] something stored up for a rainy day and — when required — released cheaply and easily". The crucial issue becomes the house price inflation, which compensates insufficient wage shares for consumption. Accordingly, increases in house prices are accrued to the wealth of households, who trade up or purchase houses, in the form of capital gains that can be accumulated for future generations or as security and insurance for older people or spent on current welfare. Put it differently, as soon as house prices continue to soar and become higher than debt of mortgagers, households, who are fortunate enough to access to mortgage markets, do not only become only debtors but also wealth-accumulators.

There is a mutual relationship between the wealth effect and mortgage finance in that it is crucial that more people apply for mortgage loans for the sustainability of such volume and scope of mortgage loans and house price inflation. However, the only way for households' continuity of consumption by using housing as collateral is the persistence of rising house prices. As long as prices kept rising, the growing danger of mortgage lending and the risk of default are ignored, as seen in the US subprime crisis. Therefore, the sustainability of such wealth system ultimately depends on the sustainability of fictitious values of houses, which increasingly deviated from the real surplus-values created in the economy. Furthermore, there have been two direct consequences of this process. One is that "continuously rising prices eventually put considerable stress on new buyers. As interest rates reset on these mortgages, buyers found themselves unable to make payments" (Schwartz and Seabrooke, 2009: 220). The other one is the subsequent correction in housing prices following the burst which leads to credit contraction, high levels of personal debt, negative equity and collapse of consumption and loss of homes for households instead of accumulated wealth (Rolnik, 2019; Byrne, 2020).[14]

Nevertheless, the use of housing as collateral and home equity withdrawal are far from becoming a global phenomenon but remain limited to few ACCs. Even in these countries, it has been widely noted that household wealth attached to the use of housing as collateral is unequally distributed across

---

14   A recent body of literature shows that after mortgage defaults and foreclosures in the USA, Spain, Ireland and Germany, these distressed properties were bought by institutional investors such as REITs, private equity firms and hedge funds (Immergluck and Law, 2014; Fields and Uffer, 2016; Fields, 2018; Wijburg & Aalbers, 2017). Although limited in some ACCs, these corporate landlords pursue to extract augmented ground rents through a strategy of buying the foreclosed dwellings cheap and selling dear or leasing them in the private rental sector.

different income-groups, genders and ages, a fortiori, favoured middle- and upper-income older households who already own their homes (Dorling *et al.*, 2005; Berry, 2010; Broome, 2009; Forrest and Yip, 2011; Ryan-Collins *et al.*, 2017; Costa-Font *et al.*, 2010; Raviv, 2021).

Instead, what has been a common global phenomenon is the wealthier households' increasing investment in housing, without equity withdrawal schemes. Commodification of housing provision leads more people to appropriate capital gains by investing in housing, for instance, via the purchase of second homes. Those with higher incomes or access to mortgage credit, may appropriate capital gains in the form of MR through homeownership. For the realisation of this capital gain, homeowners have to sell, trade or lease their houses instead of living there. Especially in the context of house price inflation, investing in one or more houses and appropriating capital gains through an exploitation of (possible) MR increases become profitable investment for some middle- and upper-class households in many countries (García-Lamarca and Kaika, 2016; Kyung-Sup, 2016; Choi, 2018; Smart and Lee, 2003; Montgomerie and Büdenbender, 2015). However, commodification of housing provision excludes many people from this form of wealth accumulation (Lazzarato, 2012; Rolnik, 2019). In other words, the pursuit of capital gains through multiple homeownerships prevents others from accessing decent affordable housing (chapter 7). As Edwards (2016: 35) argues, "the 'housing ladder' is really more like snakes and ladders since there are losers as well as winners- and for the winners it is less a ladder than an escalator, continuously carrying property owners up the wealth scale". Therefore, as a consequence of financialisation, the house price inflation not only conceals the unequal and uneven distribution of wealth among households but also reproduces class inequality causing the already-disadvantaged groups to have the heaviest burden as 'debt-encumbered homeowners' against increasing MR (Fernandez and Aalbers, 2017; Ronald and Elsinga, 2012).

Lastly, financialisation in the broad sense created an ideology of homeownership (Soederberg, 2014; Leyshon and Thrift, 2007; Schwartz and Seabrooke, 2009). Although strongly related, the ideology of homeownership is broader than the transformation of consumption finance and privatisation of former welfare provisions. Rather, as part of the neoliberal consumption culture, which is constructed, shaped and strengthened by a variety of channels such as financial literacy campaigns, state policies, advertising and discourses, it becomes "a strong and persuasive ideological reorientation idealising the homeownership society" (Fernandez and Aalbers, 2017: 35). Based on this, the ideology of homeownership refers to a commodity calculation in which monetary criteria, financial practices and norms such as individualised responsibility for social reproduction and entrepreneur-citizenship capable of individual risk management increasingly prevail against collective capabilities, other tenure forms and decommodified forms of provision (Lazzarato, 2012). However, how this ideology of home-ownership society affects beliefs and behaviours of households is ultimately attached to the different housing SoPs since housing "constitutes and reflects social relations, processes, structures and agencies" interacted with each other and traditional cultures (Fine, 2013a: 223). Therefore, the ideological orientation towards the attitudes of financial calculation such as treating home as an asset, clashes and contradicts pre-existing cultures, values and norms of housing consumption in different countries. The already-existing discrepancy between house as a home — containing protection, privacy, ontological security and comfort — and house as an asset — wealth accumulation strategy, a welfare instrument — has different degrees and intensities in different SoPs.

Regarding the macroeconomic importance of housing finance and housebuilding sector, the use of housing as a macroeconomic policy tool to reinvigorate or stabilise the economy is a well-known practice, which has been applied in many countries in different periods of the history of capitalism (Rostow, 1949; Kuznet, 1952; Strassmann, 1970; Florida and Feldman, 1988; Doling and Ronald, 2014). In recent decades, the use of housing as a macroeconomic vitalisation mechanism has been integrated with the intensive and extensive expansion of IBC to housing. While in some countries this has been directly used for accelerating financialisation, in others macroeconomic measures, such as managing general inflation and limiting the devaluation of debt, attached to housing, has been taken against the crisis of financialisation. Firstly, thanks to the neoliberal housing policies supporting private housing provision, mortgage lending and household borrowing became the primary means of supporting aggregate demand (dos Santos, 2013; Crouch, 2009). The growing home-ownership, increasing mortgage indebtedness and housing-based wealth accumulation helped to boost demand-led GDP growth[15] in several countries, such as the USA, the UK, the Netherlands, Spain, Ireland, Turkey, South Korea (Watson, 2010; Brenner, 2006; Prasad, 2013; Fernandez and Aalbers, 2016; López and Rodríguez, 2011). These policies aimed to "replace the role of public sector deficits with private deficits in macroeconomic stabilization" in a context of stagnant wages and conservative

---

15   This macroeconomic growth model is unsustainable in a long-term since "it would eventually become impossible to service rising debts with stagnant household incomes — especially if interest rates had to rise in order to prick asset bubbles or keep inflation low" (Saad-Filho, 2010: 247–48).

fiscal policies (Saad-Filho, 2019: 307). However, the mortgage-demand-based growth, known as house price Keynesianism, has been a "welcomed side effect" of financialisation rather than an intentional one, at least in the US and the UK (Bayliss *et al.*, 2016: 10). Moreover, although it is essentially a demand-side growth model, in some countries such as Spain, Ireland, the US, Portugal and Turkey, the mortgage boom was accompanied with a construction boom (Norris and Byrne, 2015; Evans and Herr, 2016; Pollard, 2009). Here, wider real estate market, including housebuilding industry and its backward and forward linkages such as infrastructure sector, cement sector, other sectors of construction inputs, became a key catalyst for supporting capital accumulation through mainly MR creation and the employment of significant numbers of people in the construction sector (Tibaijuka, 2009).

Following the GFC, the "proliferation of demand side housing measures serv[ing] to keep house prices high" became intentional compared to the pre-crisis period in some countries such as Turkey, China, Brazil, Malaysia, South Korea, Japan, Trinidad and Tobago (Bayliss *et al.*, 2016a: 10; Rolnik, 2013; Tsai and Chiang, 2019; Choi, 2018; Hirayama 2012; Giang and Pheng, 2011). This is an indication of the continuity of financialised policies following the GFC, instead of its retreat, albeit in different forms and with a more active role of state which has been involved in realising the growth of owner-occupation and revitalisation of the decline in domestic effective demand, by encouraging commercial banks to extend their mortgage loans to low-income borrowers as seen in Malaysia, Brazil and China (dos Santos, 2013; Tsai and Chiang, 2019; Wu *et al.*, 2020; Aalbers and Haila, 2018).

3.3   *Social Housing*

Privatisation and commodification are the pre-requisites of financialisation of any housing provision. However, as argued above, not all forms of privatisation and commodification resulted in financialisation in narrow terms. Still, the qualitative and quantitative changes around housing is considered a part of financialisation in a broad sense, linked to the CCFCC. Therefore, this section argues that these broader impacts of financialisation also prevail in social housing.

The systems of state-provided housing provision, which generally identify with the Keynesian period, were withdrawn in the neoliberal period. However, Keynesian welfare state and its social housing policies were not a global phenomenon but limited to some Anglo-Saxon and European countries. Plus, the restructuring of housing policies in neoliberalism is not the inverse reflection of Keynesian-style housing policies. On the contrary, neoliberalism refers "to the systematic use of state power under the ideological guise of 'non-intervention', to impose a hegemonic project of recomposition of rule of capital" at different levels (Saad-Filho, 2019: 7). In neoliberalism, the state itself has been financialised and has been an important driver of financialisation of both economic and social reproduction. Therefore, in neoliberalism and in its financialised forms, the role of the state has been transformed but not annihilated. Also, countries and their housing systems have been differently integrated into neoliberalism and financialisation, similarly to the state-monopoly capitalism. In housing, "the role of the [neoliberal] state cannot be reduced to the question of whether the state provides some housing directly or not but also concerns how the state shapes land use, both development and house purchase finance, private production and other alternatives, and the tax, subsidy and benefit regimes that underpin consumption decisions" (Fine *et al.*, 2015: 13).

The promotion of ownership, the growth of mortgage markets, market-based access to housing, increasing commodification of land and urban resources have been the main pillars of housing policy in the contemporary capitalism. Nevertheless, how (and to what extent) these policies were achieved and how state intervened, managed and realised them show significant varieties across countries and programmes. Although the expansion of IBC in different housing SoPs has been increasingly prominent, the commodification and privatisation of social housing took many different forms. Moreover, the transformation of social housing, namely the paradigm shift towards financialised-neoliberal structures of provision, does not happen through an extinction of the existing structures of housing provision but often through the interaction with each other in specific cases.

As a consequence of financialisation, the role and importance of housing in the social reproduction of people have been overshadowed by the increasing importance in the economic reproduction, not least through its asset role. However, the social aspects of housing did not disappear but have increasingly intertwined, especially in the new forms of social housing provision. Also, the commodified and de-commodified forms of housing provision can co-exist in the same countries, even in the same programmes (Chapter 5). Of major importance here is "how the tensions between them are resolved" and who benefits from this at the expense of whom (Fine, 2014: 28). Although neoliberalism and financialisation affect the housing SoPs in all countries to different extents and intensities, they are also historical and institutional constructs reflecting different national and local political and ideological objectives, different class interests, different coalitions and conflicts shaped by the inner class dynamics and power balances that are specific to each country. Therefore, the interaction of financialisation with such country-specific factors is crucial for understanding a housing SoP.

The rest of this section examines three aspects of social housing that have been transformed with the intervention of neoliberalism and financialisation, including land, finance and housebuilding.

Land is the most important aspect of social housing in any country, therefore, financialisation of social housing happens primarily via "the application of a commercial rationality to land use" (Fine *et al.*, 2015: 27). While in some countries the private ownership of land is already high, in others a significant proportion of land is owned by the local or national governments. The literature discusses three main tendencies in the use of public land: i) increasing privatisation of state-owned land through its sale or transfer to private companies and financial investors; ii) the use of public land for speculative purposes by central/local states themselves at the expense of its non-profit uses as a part of social commons that were previously allocated to community-based organisations, workers' unions, housing movements, etc. and iii) the allocation of worst-quality land for social housing projects (if there are) that are located in extended urban peripheries far from public facilities (Fernandes, 2007; Haila, 2016; Rajack and Lall, 2009; Aalbers, 2019; Christophers, 2017; Rolnik, 2019; Soaderberg 2021).

However, there is also a third group of countries in the Global South, mostly in Latin America and Africa, which have informal land markets without well-established property rights (land-titling). Informal land parcels are generally invaded or informally purchased for self-built settlements, known as slums, by low-income families (Pearce-Oroz, 2007; Freire *et al.*, 2007; Durand-Lasserve and Selod, 2009; Ferguson, 2007). Because informal land market distorts the development of the market-oriented housing systems, a neoliberal prescription was presented by the WB in 1993 in a housing policy paper known as 'the enabling-markets approach'. The primary target for governments was identified as the formalisation of tradable property rights, legal registration of land and properties. LCCs are considered a substantial sum of 'dead capital' and unlocking these under-utilised assets through the establishment of property rights was thought both to stimulate economic development and make informal tenure an asset rich (De Soto, 2001).

In the last three decades, many countries have formalised their informal land market. However, international case studies have shown that, rather than alleviating poverty by giving full legal tide to low-income families who expect to use their properties as an economic asset, these reforms lead to the domination of owner-occupation over other forms of tenure and "the commodification of land and housing, often raising prices and excluding the poor" (Freire *et al.*, 2007: 35; Durand-Lasserve, 2007; Payne *et al.*, 2009; Henderson, 2009; Rolnik, 2019). While some owners of regularised land parcels make capital gains by capturing ground rent, the formalisation of property rights and informal tenure causes a greater part of slum-settlers to dispossess (Durand-Lasserve and Selod, 2009; Nielsen 2022). This is because the owners of formalised land are not necessarily the settlers or the former slum-occupants are evicted from regularised land and they become vulnerable in formal housing markets since they "are usually the poorest of the urban poor, may be unable to pay the higher rents that follow formalization and may be bid away to other informal locations" (ibid., 108). Moreover, the security attracts land speculators and feeds the land prices, in turn making the land less affordable for the poor. As argued by Durand-Lasserve and Selod (ibid.), "individual titling may then divide the population into two groups: households with land rights and those without".

Secondly, the privatisation of social housing took many different forms across countries. The main principle was established on the promotion of owner-occupation in almost all countries (Rolnik, 2013). In some countries with high public housing stocks, the rented public houses were sold to the sitting tenants, through right-to-buy policies as in the UK or massive privatisation of state-owned houses in former communist countries (Kitzmann, 2017; Lis, 2015; Stephens *et al.*, 2016). In some others, public budgets for rental subsidies were severely cut (see Byrne and Norris, 2019 for Ireland). However, rather than a complete destruction of social housing, the evolution of finance and housing governance led financialisation of social housing itself in many places. For the European countries, apart from a direct privatisation, housing cooperative associations merged with the financial corporations or turned to market-based funding (see Larsen and Hansen, 2015 for Denmark; Evans and Herr, 2016 for the UK; Van Loon *et al.*, 2018 for the Netherlands; Lima and Xerez, 2022 for Portugal and Ireland). The literature argues that the cuts in state funding for housing cooperatives and associations led them to turn onto capital markets to rise cheaper finance by investing and trading collective savings of the tenants in secondary markets, by issuing real estate bonds (using the social commons as collateral), or by engaging in derivative-based carry-trade activities (Aalbers *et al.*, 2017).

In the case of the LCCs, some social housing providers and financiers, such as the national mortgage companies and state housing institutions, have used securitisation for raising capital for their operations (see Rethel and Sinclair, 2014 for Malaysia; Soederberg 2014 for Mexico and Chapter 6 for Turkey). Therefore, the adoption of speculative accumulation strategies by the housing associations or by the state institutions not only brings new commodified criteria and ideology but triggers the financialisation of social housing via the expansion of IBC. Following a similar logic, Rolnik (2019: 214, 222) argues that microfinance, which has been given to "the economically active poor people" by the international institutions, commercial banks and NGOs to finance home repairs, extensions or self-built houses, recently turned to "the new subprime frontier for capitalism" due to the securitisation of microfinance portfolios.

However, increasing land and house prices with diminishing social housing provisions created an affordability crisis for the market-excluded ones in many countries (Rolnik, 2013; Čada, 2018; Romainville, 2017). Although the neoliberal discourse of the WC favoured the retreat of state from all aspects of housing except leading up to the legal environment for well-defined property rights and efficiently-working mortgage markets, the neoliberal housing SoPs were built with strong state intervention and, where necessary, governments continued to utilise "mortgage subsidies to expand the section of the population covered by mortgage markets [and] facilitate homeownership" (Fine *et al.*, 2015: 14). In line with PWC, the enabling-markets approach of the WB (1993) brought new criteria for demand-side subsidies: subsidies must be rationalized "ensuring that subsidy programs are of an appropriate and affordable scale, well-targeted, measurable, and transparent, and avoid distorting housing markets" (p. 4) and "governments should see subsidies as either transitional or as a last resort" (p. 40). Therefore, housing subsidies were rationalised not only *de facto* but also *de jure* in a policy level of neoliberalism, as soon as the ultimate target is the facilitation of the growth of demand and the extension of the home-purchase to the poorest. By transforming the social dimension of public housing policy into an affordability concern, states have authorised demand-side vouchers and subsidies to low-income families as part of different housing programs in many countries (Gagyi and Vigvary, 2018; Tibaijuka, 2009; Isaacs, 2016; Ram and Needham, 2016). The literature argues that the program enabled the middle-income households to buy houses rather than the most needy ones (Tibaijuka, 2009; Rolnik, 2019). Based on this, the capital subsidies-saving nexus can be considered within the scope of extensive financialisation as a commodity form.

Lastly, the general hallmark of the social housing programmes in the neoliberal era have been the changing the role of the state from a direct provider of houses to a rather regulator and facilitator (Halbert and Attuyer, 2016; Murray and Clapham, 2015; Bajunid and Ghazali, 2012; Copello, 2007; Shimbo, 2019). Therefore, the key principle has been the private sector participation in the provision of new buildings. From the perspective of neoliberal states, organising large-scale housing production was expected to kill two birds with one stone: i) delivering a solution to the affordability crisis for the market-excluded families and incorporating them to the formal housing markets and financial mechanisms; ii) improving the construction sector performance by creating a new housing sub-market and stimulating land and residential markets.

Therefore, the new social housing programmes are better to be analysed as an industrial policy which strongly tie up the aspects of social and economic reproduction. It is not a coincidence that affordable housing programmes were put into action in the face of GFC as a counter-cycle measure in several countries such as Brazil, Mexico, India, China and South Korea (Wu, 2015; Ram and Needham, 2016; Soederberg, 2014; Sengupta, 2019). For promoting house-building capitalists to enter to this affordable market, the main incentive of the state became land-use regulations and tax exemptions.

While in some cases, the local or central states provide land parcels for affordable housing production, either from public land or purchasing cheap, underutilised lands, in peripheral areas, in some other cases, large construction firms put their idle land banks to the project thanks to the states' promoting planning permissions, such as the accretion of rural land into urban borders, and provision of infrastructural services and other facilities (Rajack and Lall, 2009; Rolnik, 2019; Shimbo, 2019). Although profit margins become lower compared to the speculative practices of housebuilding capitalists, it can be suggested that following the GFC, against the decrease in the effective demand, the state-led commodification of low-income housing market works as a stabiliser against the market downturn and future uncertainty for the development firms. Furthermore, the state's capital subsidies to low-income families within the scope of these affordable housing projects are indirectly accrued to housebuilders' development gains.

To sum up, the transformation of social housing programmes through including the private actors and financial markets, commodifying public lands, even using decommodified methods (e.g. state subsidies) for expanding commodified conduits on behalf of private capital in general and financial capital in particular are considered as the financialisation of social housing in the broad sense, in the reading of this book. However, the general tendencies of financialisation of housing, reviewed in this chapter, remains descriptive unless distinct historical, institutional, social and ideological country- and programme-specific features, together with the counter-tendencies, are analysed at an empirical level.

4   Conclusion

This chapter argued that the literature is rich and comprehensive for understanding financialisation as a phenomenon. However, the broad and contradictory use of financialisation as a concept makes it harder how to analyse the changes in economic and social reproduction attached to financialisation.

Therefore, I suggested that there is a need for differentiating financialisation as explanans and explanandum to trace the phenomenon from abstract to concrete and from simple to complex. For this, the chapter first located financialisation, in a logical level based on the Marx's theory of finance. After defining financialisation based on the intensive and extensive expansion of IBC, I discussed the concept within a historical-systemic consideration. In this regard, I argued that financialisation rises through and within neoliberalism, which is the contemporary mode of capitalism. Following this, the diverse and complex impacts of financialisation among countries are argued as a reflection of combined and uneven development of capitalism. In this, not only financialisation has peculiar forms in different countries but also different SoPs and sectors are unevenly integrated with financialisation.

Based on the accumulated knowledge in the literature, which is used as complementary to our analytical definition, the second part of the chapter reviewed the intensive and extensive expansion of IBC to housing since the 1980s. While the first part argued that housebuilding sector has been financialised through a greater reliance on funding from capital markets, the use of complex financial methods and instruments and through shareholder pressure, the second part focused on financialisation of housing consumption through the quantitative and qualitative changes in house purchase finance. The chapter concluded with an investigation of financialisation of social housing through three aspects of public provision, i.e., land, finance and building.

This chapter analysed the general tendencies of the financialisation of housing in recent decades on the basis of a logical-historical definition of financialisation, based on Marx's theory of money. However, the increasing intervention of IBC into land and housing markets (by expanding the limits of effective demand and MR) does not follow a simple logic. On the one hand, the form and intensity of this intervention differs between countries. On the other hand, the structural transformation in housing SOPs (from the marginalisation or withdrawal of non-market ways for access to housing to the presentation of the homeownership as the most desirable tenure form) has been realised through a wide range of social, political and ideological mediations of nation-states. Despite the global character of IBC, housing, as a locally and nationally embedded wage-good, is still subject to domestic regulations. Therefore, the social relations of power and the inter- and intra-class conflicts around the housing provision system, that are specific to each country, need to be identified for understanding how the finance shapes the production and consumption of housing and interacts with other agents in the SOP in question.

CHAPTER 4

Neoliberal Transformation and Financialisation in Turkey through an Authoritarian Form of State

As discussed in the previous chapter, the process of neoliberalism and financialisation did not signify a suppression of national states but a transformation of the state and reconfiguration of its role in different countries. Despite the global character of accumulation, the reproduction of the necessary conditions for the expanded reproduction of the dominant social relations has a national character since "every process of internationalization is affected under the dominance of the capital of a definite country" (Poulantzas, 1975: 73). Moreover, the state is not only a facilitator of the consolidation of neoliberalism and financialisation ideologically, politically and economically but also a subject of financialisation itself not least through its restructuring.

Nevertheless, the state is a highly contested concept and an examination of the role of the state in a housing SoP requires an additional analytical lens. As discussed in the former chapter, the main pillars of housing policy in contemporary capitalism, such as promoting owner-occupation, the commodification of land and urban resources, the growth of mortgage markets, market-based access to housing, also depend on how the state intervened, managed and realised these policies that vary across countries and programmes. Moreover, not only the relationships of the state with other agents in the housing SoP but the appearance of different state institutions in the housing sphere can only be analysed by examining the state in a specific time and place. Since neither the history nor the current (neoliberal) mode of state interventionism into housing is homogeneously covering all the social formations, there cannot be a general theorisation of the state and housing.

The role of the state in Turkish housing SoP will be discussed in Chapters 5 and 6. This chapter shows that both the transition to neoliberalism and financialisation (1980–2001) and the consolidation and institutionalisation of neoliberalism and financialisation in the post-2001 era was realised through an authoritarian state form in Turkey. This chapter argues that the post-2001 era under AKP governments does not signify a rupture in the state form but a continuity of the authoritarian statism, despite different qualifications both in terms of capital accumulation and functions of the state. This historical overview is important to understand the conflicts and alliances among classes and class fractions, and state restructuring during the first and second phases of

neoliberalism and financialisation in Turkey with the ultimate aim of showing the reflections of these relations in the housing SoP in the subsequent
chapters.

The chapter starts by defining the state from an MPE perspective, by adopting Poulantzas's theory of capitalist state and his conceptual tools of social
classes, power bloc, forms of the capitalist state and authoritarian statism.
Although the chapter aims to bring the state back in the analysis of neoliberal
transformation and financialisation in Turkey, it does not examine the scholarly literature on theories of the state. Instead, based on Poulantzas's understanding of the authoritarian state form, this chapter analyses the role of the
state in the formation and consolidation of neoliberalism and financialisation
in Turkey.

1   Capitalist State as the Condensation of Class Relationship

Most Marxist scholars working on the theorisation of state focus on explaining the institutional separation of the state from the capital and civil society
by questioning the separation of economic and political. In this investigation,
the first conclusion becomes that there cannot be a general theory of state
for all modes of production, including slavery, feudalism, capitalism, but the
state must be theorised according to the modes of production, such as feudal state and capitalist state (Hirsch, 1978; Wood, 2003; Clarke, 1992; Bonefeld,
1992; Poulantzas, 1975). Capitalism itself, unlike other modes of production,
is constructed upon the separation between political and economic. As Marx
(1997: 45) argues:

> The character of [feudalism] was directly political — the elements of
> civil life, for example, property, or the family, or the mode of labor, were
> raised to the level of elements of political life in the form of seigniory,
> estates, and corporations. In this form, they determined the relation of
> the individual to the state as a whole — i.e., his political relation.

However, unlike the direct coercive mechanisms within the appropriation
process of surplus-value by feudal lords or religious authorities, in capitalism, the process of appropriation of surplus-value is mediated by anonymous
"economic (market) imperatives distinct and apart from direct political coercion" (Wood, 2002: 177). Hence, in capitalism, "exploitation is characterized
by a division of labour between the 'economic' moment of appropriation and
the 'extra-economic' or 'political' moment of coercion" (ibid.) and the latter is

undertaken by the state, which now has an institutional separation from the economy.

Nevertheless, the separation between economic and political in capitalism takes a fetishised form in that the state is considered an autonomous entity on its own (Mann, 1993; Skocpol, 1985; Evans, 1995; Polanyi, 2001). Holloway and Picciotto (1991: 79) argued that giving the state autonomy is a combination of reality and illusion which resembles it to a form of fetishism; reality depends on the ruling class while illusion consists in the complex social relation. However, the autonomisation is necessary for capital accumulation and requires separate political institutions.

In a parallel, the analytical separation of economic and political in capitalism creates an 'idea of free market', which does not exist and cannot survive in its "own inherently anarchic laws" without extra-economic interventions of the state (Wood, 2002: 178). The question then becomes how to analyse this separation without thinking of the political and economic fields as external to each other. For this, I apply Poulantzas's definition of the capitalist state as the material condensation of the class forces, and his methodology.

Firstly, Poulantzas (2014) rejects the exteriority between political and economic relations and considers 'political' internal to the establishment and reproduction of the relations of production. Although the existence of the state cannot be reduced to political domination, "the political field of the State (as well as the sphere of ideology) has always been present in the constitution and reproduction of the relations of production" (ibid., 17). Specifically, the intervention of the state into the economy does not happen from outside because the political and ideological relations already exist within the relations of production. While one instance of the state intervention and the relative separation of the state from the relations of production signify the necessity of legitimisation of capitalism itself, the other is the organisation of specific institutions for enhancing capital accumulation, the social division of labour, the reproduction of labour-power in capitalism (ibid., 50). Therefore, in capitalism, the state has a dual task as "promoting capital accumulation and the legitimating capitalist domination of the social order" (Panitch, 2002: 100), although this dual function becomes the source of the contradictions.

Secondly, by defining the state as the condensation of class relations, Poulantzas (2014) suggests that class contradictions in a capitalist society directly exists within the internal structure of the state itself. In contrast with the consideration of the class struggles only within civil society, the capitalist state becomes a moment of the class conflict. Therefore, the state is neither a thing, meaning a passive, neutral agency controlled by the bourgeoisie, nor a subject, an absolute entity with its own rational will, but a social relation, as the materialisation and reproduction of the class power and class-relevant social struggles in society. That is to say, power relations in society are materialised and condensed through the institutional materiality of the state.

Moreover, for Poulantzas (1973), social classes and class fractions are determined by the relations of production, such as productive labour and unproductive labour and commercial capital and financial capital. However, following this 'principal' determination, he discusses that this "is not sufficient to determine social classes" (ibid., 31). Instead, for him, the structural determination of classes requires the definition of a social class "by its place in the ensemble of social practices, i.e., by its place in the ensemble of the division of labour which includes political and ideological relations" (ibid., 27). In the determination and location of classes and class fractions, economic criteria are not sufficient, but it must be considered together with political and ideological criteria in particular social formations. Hence, the historically-specific and contextually-dependent processes of the formation of class and class fractions must be employed together with the location of classes at the level of the circuit of capital.

Furthermore, for Poulantzas (2014), the major role of the capitalist state is organising the dominant classes and dividing popular masses since the bourgeoisie cannot attain a political unity of its own. He argues that the capitalist state represents and organises the long-term political interest of a power bloc, which "is composed of several bourgeois class fractions" and represents an alliance characterised by "unstable equilibrium of compromise" (ibid., 127).

For Poulantzas, unlike Lenin, the state is not simply the dictatorship of one unified capitalist class but the relationship of forces among classes and class fractions. The institutional materiality of the state, which reflects the struggles of classes and class fractions, represents a strategic field, "a favourable terrain for political manoeuvre by the hegemonic fraction" (Jessop, 1985: 124). Although several fractions of the bourgeoisie "enjoy a political domination as part of the power bloc", albeit unequally, "the capitalist state must be a given fraction of the power bloc in order to assume its role as political organizer of the general interest of the bourgeoisie under the hegemony of one of its fractions" (Poulantzas, 2008: 307). However, the organisation of a power bloc by the state under a hegemonic fraction is always conflictual because of two main reasons. First, by defining the state as a condensation of the class struggles, Poulantzas rejects the idea of different classes and fractions as equal entities or the take-over of the state simply by a dominant class fraction. Instead, the political organisation of the power bloc and the state's internal organisation changes in line with the changing balance of class forces in a concrete social formation. Second, the state's dual functions in the organisation of the power bloc, including to ensure capital accumulation for the general interests of the bourgeoisie and guaranteeing social cohesion in the society (the presentation of the capitalist interests as the general interests of the nation) not only makes the power bloc inherently crisis-ridden but constitutes the internal contradictions of the state.

Here, the key concept becomes the relative autonomy of the state (RAS) concerning dominant classes and fractions which is the "the relative "separation" of the political and the economic that is specific to capitalism" (Poulantzas, 1975: 98). RAS is "the necessary condition for the role of the capitalist state in class representation and in the political organization of hegemony" (ibid., 132). Specifically, RAS reflects the contradictory functions of the state — promoting accumulation and legitimisation (e.g., the formation of the welfare institutions of the state). Hence, the political organisation of the power bloc by the state is not only necessary for the political unity of the bourgeoisie but also ensuring capital accumulation without leading a political (hegemonic) crisis in the society, although this is not a guaranteed outcome due to the very existence of the class struggles within the capitalist state. Regarding the RAS, the famous question of Miliband to Poulantzas is key: How relative is relative autonomy? Poulantzas (1976: 72) replies:

> the degree, the extent, the forms, etc. (how relative, and how is it relative) of the relative autonomy of the State can only be examined ... with reference to a given capitalist State, and to the precise conjuncture of the corresponding class struggle (the specific configuration of the power bloc, the degree of hegemony within this bloc, the relations between the bourgeoisie and its different fractions on the one hand and the working classes and supporting classes on the other hand, etc).

Although RAS can be considered vague, it does provide an empirically open methodology for tracking the historical and social particularities of the class power and state power in specific social formations. Besides, the degree, forms and extent of RAS depend on the different stages of capitalism, although even in the same phase of the capitalism RAS varies from country to country.

In addition, the class contradictions intrinsically exist within the state's apparatus as intra-state contradictions. The state as an institution organising conflictual unity in the power bloc cannot be considered a monolithic entity since "state's different apparatuses, sections, and levels serve as power centres for different classes and fractions centres of resistance for different elements among the popular masses" (Jessop, 1985: 125). The fragmentation between institutions, such as executive and parliament, the army, the judiciary, various ministries, regional, municipal and central apparatuses, establishes balances between both capital fractions and capital and labour. Such a formal separation of power between the executive, the legislative and the judiciary enables the state to effectively mediate between the different factions in the capitalist class. However, apart from this, there may be "internal contradictions between the diverse branches and apparatuses of the state" as the manifestation of the class contradictions within the power bloc as well as certain state institutions "having a privileged representative of a particular interest of the power bloc" (Poulantzas, 2008: 309).

Lastly, for Poulantzas, the RAS and the formation of the power blocs differ according to the phases of capitalism. In other words, "structural modifications in the relations of production and the processes and social division of labour" not only directly impact the relations and power balances between capitalist classes, like the industrial bourgeoisie and the financial bourgeoisie, but also the form of the capitalist state (2014: 204). Hence, different phases of capitalism lead the re-organisation of the power blocs under the leadership of one of the dominant factions that signify "shifts in hegemony from one class or fraction to another" (ibid., 159). Therefore, the forms of the capitalist state must be considered within the re-articulation of the political and economic instances in specific phases of capitalism. In Poulantzas's words (2014: 25), the capitalist state includes various stages such as the liberal state of competitive capitalism, interventionist state of imperialist-monopoly capitalism, and the present-day authoritarian statism. The difference between these lies in the exceptional forms of state (fascism, military dictatorship, Bonapartism) and the character of the regimes (e.g., presidential regime, parliamentarianism).

Unlike the exceptional forms in which democratic institutions, rule of law, and competitive elections are suspended, in the normal forms of the capitalist state, such as interventionist, liberal democratic and authoritarian, there are representative democratic institutions with competing political parties and hegemonic class leadership. While in the liberal democratic state the social class forces are organised through political parties and represented in the legislature organ, in the authoritarian form of state, different class fractions are represented in the executive organ, which becomes the main site of the class struggle in the power bloc. For Poulantzas, the authoritarian form of state refers to the crisis of political representation and the crisis of the state that results from the failure of dominant class fractions to organise their hegemony in the political sphere against growing inter- and intra-class contradictions. Namely, the authoritarian state is strongly related with a political crisis arising from the sharpening contradictions within the power bloc and accompanying difficulties to establish the hegemony of dominant classes. However, unlike military dictatorship or fascism, resulting from an extraordinary response given to the rising working-class movements and to the co-existence of economic and political crises of capitalism, the authoritarian state is more than a response of the dominant fractions forming the power bloc to the conflict created by a rising working-class movement or mass politicisation. Instead, it corresponds to a transformation prevents the emergence of such mobilisations. Hence, it derives primarily from the necessity to deal with the increasing contradictions within the power bloc.

Therefore, the hegemony of the power bloc and its political domination is established under the authority of the Executive rather than political parties. The general characteristics of authoritarian statism can be listed as such: i) the strengthening of the Executive; ii) the decline of Parliament; iii) the retreat of democratic liberties and greater exclusion of masses from decision-making and participation schemes; iv) particularistic legal regulations in significant (economic) areas through the extensive use of decree-laws; v) intensified concentration and centralisation of power within central state apparatuses (regarding the decreasing power of local and regional governments); vi) the growing economic role of the state; and the establishment of specialised economic apparatuses (that are directly attached to the executive organ) to represent and realise the interests of the hegemonic capital fractions. Although the parliament may continue "to occupy a specific place in the legitimating process by allowing the representatives of the popular masses to give a certain expression to their interests within the State", the executive and the administration "monopolize the role of organizing and directing the State with regard to the power bloc as a whole" (ibid., 222).

Besides, in the authoritarian state, there is a strong "tendency of power to be personalized in the man at the top of the executive — what we may term a personalized presidential system" (ibid., 228). Although this personalised presidential system may have some Bonapartist characters ("truly despotic and insulated power"), authoritarian statism cannot be linked to Bonapartism, not least because of the existence of representative democratic institutions and political parties despite their decreasing power (ibid., 228). Nonetheless, while the above-mentioned characteristics refer to the general tendencies of authoritarian statism, for Poulantzas, the authoritarian statism "can take extremely different forms" due to pre-existing institutional configurations, and country-specific dynamics in the class relations (2008: 398).

Although Poulantzas considered the authoritarian state form as a dominant tendency of the contemporary phase of capitalism arising from the internationalisation of capital, the increasing tensions between global capital accumulation and national character of the state and the heightened intra-class struggles in the power bloc, this book considers authoritarian statism as a contingency rather than a necessity of the form of the state in the neoliberal era. In other words, the organisation of the capitalist state in an authoritarian form is rather an outcome of the "historically-specific institutionalizations of class power struggles" and country-specific condensation of the balance of forces "that are malleable but also momentarily fixed and formative" (Marois, 2014: 311). Therefore, as shown below, authoritarian statism became the founding element in both Turkey's transition to neoliberalism in the 1980s and in the deepening of the neoliberalism in the 2000s. Therefore, the authoritarian statism becomes the key concept to understand the Turkish state's contemporary role in economic and social reproduction in general and housing in particular.

2   The Transition to Neoliberalism and Financialisation in Turkey: from 1980 to 2001

Similar to other LCCs, the post-war era in Turkey witnessed the employment of the ISI strategy under the interventionist form of the state and with a hegemonic ideology of national developmentalism. As a typical pattern of the ISI process, the productive capital focused on the production of the intermediate goods and consumption goods for that "technology, capital goods and inputs were imported" (Gülalp, 1985: 337; Kazgan, 1999). The main economic role of the state was allocating basic inputs and resources to productive capital mostly through financing capital investments in relevant sectors and establishing a domestic market protected from foreign competition (Boratav, 2003). Hence, as a late industrialisation story, the ISI period signified the formation of the big industrial bourgeoisie in Turkey under the shelter of protectionism. Again, in the context of late development where there was limited competition for entering into new fields of accumulation, the first-mover capital groups had monopoly in many fields of the protected domestic market by transferring the extra profits gained from one sector to other unoccupied sectors (Keyder, 1987; Öztürk, 2015). Therefore, in nearly a decade between 1960 and 1970, a limited number of large industrial monopolies operating in many different sectors emerged and they entered almost all sectors collectively (Öztürk, 2015). Moreover, highly diversified economic activities of these business groups made them organise in the form of conglomerates.

While these holding groups, which form the traditional bourgeoisie of Turkey, were both the hegemonic class fraction in the power bloc of the ISI period and the main beneficiaries of the state economic support in the form of various incentives and resource allocations, the other capitalist class fraction was composed of the several rural-based, small-scale industrial firms, which produced mostly intermediate inputs for the big monopoly industrialists (Keyder, 1987). These Anatolian-based small industrialists, which could not benefit from the state economic incentives and supports due to their sizes, were economically dependent on the development of the big bourgeoisie, as they were producing basic inputs for the latter (Gülalp, 1993; Karahanoğulları, 2009). Moreover, the big industrial monopolies organised as conglomerates "that grew through the [ISI] started to gain control over commercial and money-capital through the ownership of banks" from the 1960s on (Ercan and Oğuz, 2015: 120). Therefore, "they effectively blocked the growing potential of smaller capitalists" (Öztürk, 2015: 124). Consequently, the ISI strategy in Turkey resulted in the consolidation of the hegemony of big bourgeoisie organised as holding companies. Moreover, the rise of the bourgeoisie as a class for itself can be started with the establishment of TUSIAD (The Turkish Industrialists and Businessmen's Association) in 1971 which enabled Istanbul-based holding groups to express their common interests and become a very strong actor in the power blocs (Yalman, 2009).

At the point where the capital accumulation through ISI was no longer sustainable, TUSIAD became the main power determining the basic framework of the transition to export-oriented accumulation (Ercan, 2002). When the easier stage of ISI ended in the 1970s, the contradictions of the accumulation through ISI intensified, since the big bourgeoisie had already gained monopoly control over the domestic circuit of capital and "absorbed the potential of inward-oriented accumulation" in that the production of domestic consumer goods and low-value-added sectors reached its limits in terms of profitability, productivity level and the domestic demand (Ercan and Oğuz, 2015: 120; Yeldan, 1995; Keyder, 1987; Boratav and Yeldan, 2006). Moreover, import-dependency of industrial production and low export rates limited to primary goods such as agricultural products and the construction sector's investments in MENA region[1] "resulted in a large capital account deficit, while growing state expenditures intensified the fiscal crisis of the state" showing itself as a severe balance of payments crisis in the late 1970s when particularly the rapid rise in oil prices had aggravated Turkey's external debt burden (Hoşgör, 2016: 119; Köse and Öncü, 2000).

However, the late 1970s were market not only by the ISI crisis but also a hegemonic crisis, since the power bloc failed to establish a social coherence

---

1   The leading sector in the export was the construction sector in the 1970s. The biggest capital groups in the construction sector today such as STFA, Enka and Tekfen became giant companies in this period.

in the society in the face of organised working-class movements. While one instant of the ISI was the formation of the industrial capital in the country, the other was the development of the working-class as a strong principal force in the Turkish social formation. The establishment of revolutionary trade unions having strong links with social movements increasingly intensified working-class militancy from the 1960s and gradually turned into a serious obstacle to the reproduction of capital in the late 1970s. Boratav (2003: 146) says that:

> The number of working days lost by the strikes increased by two and a half times in 1977–80 compared to 1973–76. Therefore, the big capital circles started to openly call for "to stop this rambling movement", to discipline the unions, to create the necessary confidence environment for capital since 1979.

Under these conditions, by the end of the 1970s, the bourgeoisie began to concretise their proposals for the new economic program through their representative association, TUSIAD. In several of their reports, they openly called out the need to follow outward-oriented economic policy, suppressing real wages, facilitating the required conditions for increasing exports, liberalising the trade and foreign capital inflow (Topal, 2002). Consequently, the stabilisation-cum-structural adjustment policies, known as the 24th January Decisions in Turkey,[2] were immediately adopted by a mutual consensus among the Bretton Woods institutions and the big bourgeoisie (TUSIAD) in that two main strategic targets were market liberalization and strengthening capital against labour. The main economic functions of the state were determined as ensuring trade liberalisation, export promotion and the removal of "the dominance of the state in key industries [particularly in manufacturing] and in banking" (Taymaz and Yılmaz, 2008). However, the strong resistance of the organised working-class and radical leftist organisations and the hegemonic crisis in the state apparatus enabled the implementation of the 24th January decisions only with the coup d'état on the September 12th, 1980.

However, the restructuring of the state in an exceptional form between 1980 and 1983 cannot be reduced to enable the county to implement this neoliberal program. The transformation of the crisis into a hegemonic crisis made the military intervention a crucial way to re-establish class domination (Yalman, 2002). The violent defeat of the radical left, the discipline of the organised

---

2 A stand-by agreement was made with the IMF in January of 1980 and the WB provided the structural agreement loans for the period between 1980 and 1984.

working-class and the drastic suppression of the wages under the military regime also led all fractions of the capitalist class to give strong support to the regime and the new Constitution in 1982, which constituted the institutional framework of the authoritarian statism under the following civilian regimes in Turkey (ibid.).

Hence, the process of the establishment of the new neoliberal order initiated by the military regime was further deepened under the rule of the civilian government, ANAP, led by Turgut Özal, who was the neoliberal technocrat active in the preparation of the 24th January decisions before the coup; then the Ministry of Economy of the military regime and the leader of the ANAP serving as the as Prime Minister (PM) between 1983 and 1989 and then as the President of Turkey from 1989 until his death in 1993. Thus, Özal became the key political actor in the start-up phase of neoliberalism in Turkey, and the restructuring of the state in an authoritarian form. The implementation of the neoliberal programme without meeting any resistance or opposition from popular masses signified the restructuring of the state's economic and political functions (Boratav, 1994). In this period, the authoritarian statism manifested through the centralisation of decision-making, the increasing power of the executive regarding the legislature and judiciary and the changing "internal hierarchy of the executive branch through the creation of a specialized economic apparatus that worked in direct relationship with the Prime Ministry" (Oğuz, 2008: 159).

The primary way for the domination of the executive branch over legislative and judiciary branches became the widespread use of the decrees having the force of law (DFLs) that is used as an instrument to expand Executive's authority to make rules and to passivise the parliament and its legislation authority. The main aim of the widespread application of the DFLs became the rapid implementation of the market-oriented reforms without any bureaucratic obstacles and the restructuring of the internal organisation of the state (Yalman, 2009; Öniş, 2004). The use of the DFLs in ANAP period was instrumental in the creation of a new bureaucracy working directly attached to the PM. The contradictions between the old bureaucracy, which was powerful in the implementation of the national development program of the ISI period, and the new bureaucracy, known as Özal's princes, who were charged with implementing neoliberal market reforms, became the main manifestation of the intra-state conflict during the neoliberal restructuring of the state in the 1980s (Oğuz, 2008). Hence for facilitating the neoliberalisation process and the EOI, the neoliberal technocrats, who were working under the PM, were appointed into the critical branches of the state such as Central Bank, SOEs and state-owned banks "to work on the IMF structural reforms, and to neutralize any social or political resistance to neoliberalism" (Marois, 2012: 101; Agartan, 2017; Sönmez, 2011). It was also in this period that TOKI was established as an institution operating out of the conventional bureaucratic structure and as a relatively autonomous agency that is directly connected to the PM to execute mass housing projects (Chapter 5).

Another important manifestation of the authoritarian statism was the elimination of the budget right, which is approved and supervised by the legislative branch, as the most important achievement in the history of representative democracy (Karahanoğulları and Türk, 2018). Instead, extra-budgetary funds in the form of a shadow budget were created "through the diversion of tax resources from the parliament-controlled consolidated budget" which were directly disbursed under the control of the executive, without any permission and control of the parliament (Buğra, 1994: 145). These extra-budgetary funds were often used for financing the "neoliberal administrative structures and policies" (Oğuz, 2008: 164); and "creat[ing] and transfer[ring] funds to favoured sectors and/or firms and/or individuals" (Yalman, 2019: 64). The Mass Housing Fund under the control of TOKI became one of the most important examples of these extra-budgetary funds used as a tool transferring financial resources to the construction sector.

The first phase of the neoliberal integration to global markets (1980–1989) happened via commodity trade liberalisation for the domestic industry that significantly increased the import dependency for the production of the final commodities to be exported. Although the 1980s witnessed an export boom — exports increased nearly by 20% annually (in dollar terms) from 1980 to 1987 — the transition to ISI to EOI happened rather as a gradual process under substantial state support (Yalman, 2009). While the leading export sector and the basis of the export-oriented growth was the manufacturing sector, its low performance in the gross fixed investment[3] (nearly 2% per annum) showed that "industrial growth during the 1980s owes much to increased rates of capacity use following the very high levels of excess capacity reached during the crisis of the late 1970s" (Boratav, 1994; Şenses, 1989; Baysan and Blitzer, 1991). In other words, the unutilised productive capacity in manufacturing under the crisis conditions of the late 1970s was only realised in the 1980s through exporting. Therefore, despite the main economic target of the state was vitalising the capital accumulation by increasing the productive capacity of industry and promoting the realisation of the created surplus-value in international

---

3   The biggest component of the gross fixed investment between 1984 and 1988 became the housebuilding sector with its 24.5% share (annual average) thanks to the establishment of TOKI in 1984 and the formation of the extra-budgetary fund (chapter 5).

markets, the outward-oriented accumulation story of Turkey witnessed rather the reduction in manufacturing investments (Baysan and Blitzer, 1991; Celasun, 1991; Boratav and Yeldan, 2006).

In this context, the export-based growth was sustained via significant state incentives such as tax exemptions, price incentives, export subsidies, premiums, exceptions, tax rebates and the use of the state-controlled floating exchange rate system to moderate real devaluations (Sönmez, 1992; Baysan and Blitzer, 1991). Nevertheless, socialisation of the costs of the EOI by the state in this period led to pressure on public expenditures and resultant significant fiscal deficits, especially in the context of increasing "costs of export subsidization together with revaluation of foreign debt in domestic currency due to continued real depreciation" (Boratav *et al.*, 2000: 4–5). Hence, this period witnessed a dependency relationship between rising export revenues of private capital and the significant foreign debt accumulation of the state, manifesting via expanding fiscal gap, especially after the termination of the international creditors' and donors' debt reliefs, aids and loans from the mid-1980s. Such a transfer of the financial resources to the private capital became the main fragility of the capital accumulation system in this period.

However, the state's export incentives to capital groups happened according to their international competitiveness and export capacity. As the power bloc during the ANAP governments was established under the hegemony of the Istanbul-based large conglomerates, this hegemonic capital fraction had the biggest share in the state export incentives (Sönmez, 1992; Demir *et al.*, 2004; Karahanoğulları, 2009). Moreover, thanks to liberalisation and deregulation of the banking sector in the 1980s, these big business groups had a large control on the circulation of money capital in the country by establishing their banks as part of their conglomerates that "resulted in the exclusion of the SMEs from the credit system" (Öztürk, 2015: 129). This way, the hegemonic positions of these holding groups over production and merchant activities expanded to the financial activities by their control on money capital that had already started in the 1960s but accelerated from 1980 on.

However, as a semi-peripheral country, Turkey's export growth in the 1980s came from the export of low-quality, labour-intensive commodities instead of the production and export of technologically-sophisticated commodities that had important implications on the changing balance of class forces between Istanbul-based holding groups and small Anatolian firms. Although the latter did not benefit from the above-mentioned export incentives of the state (Boratav, 2003); the trade liberalisation and deregulation of the banking sector indirectly caused the rise of the Anatolian SMEs in this period thanks to the novel transnational connections developed by them. Firstly, the state support for these groups became via the construction of organised industrial zones for the development of SMEs. The construction of organised industrial zones in certain Anatolian cities led the establishment of more than 500,000 SMEs, which mostly specialised in the production of labour-intensive manufactures, from 1983 to 2000 (Hoşgör, 2011: 345; Gülalp, 2001).

Two additional factors are important to mention to understand the rise of class power of Anatolian capital in this period. Firstly, the ANAP government enacted a DFL in 1983 to enable the formation of the Special Finance Institutions (SFIS) that works as interest-free banks according to Islamic principles, operating based on Profit-Loss Sharing. The main purpose behind the formation of the SFIS was to encourage the international Islamic financial capital (particularly Saudi capital) to invest in Turkey "at the time of a petrodollar glut" (Öztürk, 2015: 129). The SFIS, which were mostly in the form of Turkish–Saudi joint ventures in the 1980s, became the major channels of financing of the productive activities of the Anatolian SMEs against the oligopolistic control of big holding groups on the banking sector. On the one hand, SFIS mobilised the savings of religious people who do not use the conventional banks and hence channelled new funds to the system (Demir *et al.*, 2004). On the other hand, "they provided constant flow of capital for these expanded or new companies [Anatolian SMEs], thereby encouraging their further expansion" (Hoşgör, 2011: 345).

The second financing mechanism for the Anatolian capital was the use of informal religious community networks in that the (FX) savings and remittances of the religious migrant workers in Europe were channelled to the SMEs as these migrant people became the informal shareholders of these firms. Hence, thanks to the SFIS and the migrant workers' remittances, the Anatolian SMEs expanded their production capacity and exporting power (Doğan, 2006; Demir *et al.*, 2004). Such a religious network and structure led them to be named as Islamic capital although "not all of these petty-entrepreneurs are necessarily Islamist, the Islamist segment of the business class comes primarily from among this sector" (Gülalp, 2001: 438; Akça, 2014).

While SFIS were important for the rise of the Islamic capital during the 1980s, it was rather the religious community members' mobilised idle capital (by becoming the shareholders of enterprises) that led them to grow rapidly in this early neoliberal phase (Öztürk, 2015; Hoşgör, 2011). This informal religious economic network also enabled some Islamic capital to diversify their business portfolio and to organise as big holding companies particularly in the 1990s that were generally called as Anatolian holding companies having thousands of shareholders unlike the family-business structure of the Istanbul-based holding groups (Adaş, 2009; Demir *et al.*, 2004; Özcan and Çokgezen,

2003). Moreover, the 1990s witnessed not only increasing diversification in the business sizes, geographical locations and sectors among the Anatolian/ Islamic capital but also political-ideological heterogeneity among these groups (Öztürk, 2015). For instance, there were some "hybrid holding groups", such as Çalık, Albayrak, Boydak that would become the most privileged groups, especially in construction and energy sectors during the AKP era having close relations with both religious-conservative networks and the Istanbul-based big business groups (TUSIAD) (ibid.).

However, while the intra-class conflicts between the big business groups and Anatolian SMEs were largely managed by the ANAP governments during the 1980s, the unprecedented rise of Anatolian capital made it much harder to establish a power bloc to represent the political unity of the bourgeoisie during the 1990s (Akça, 2014). Hence the 1990s were characterised rather by a political representation crisis arising from the increasing contradictions within the power bloc. With the dissolution of the uninterrupted rule of ANAP in 1991, the political scene in Turkey marked by the successive coalition governments from the centre-right and centre-left parties, although none of which achieved to re-establish the political unity of capital during these years. Nonetheless, the achievement of the Islamic Welfare Party (RP), representing the Anatolian/ Islamic capital, to win the local elections in 1994 and to come to the rule of the two biggest metropolitan municipalities of Turkey created important opportunities for the Islamic capital (Savran, 2002; Demir *et al.*, 2004). Hence, the local governments became the strategic fields for the Islamic capital to realise their economic interests. Especially in the construction sector, Islamic companies grew rapidly by being "awarded with contracts to provide local services", especially infrastructural facilities (Demir *et al.*, 2004: 171; Keyder and Öncü, 1994).

Moreover, particularly after RP, the predecessor of AKP, came into power through a coalition government in 1996, the rise of the political Islam and the gradual division of the society based on identity politics started to create a large discontent among the Istanbul-based big business groups and the military and finally the rising concern about the growth of Islamic fundamentalism in the country resulted in the military intervention on February 28, 1997 (Demir *et al.*, 2004; Dinç, 2018.). After this intervention, the RP was closed down "for violating the secularism principles of the Constitution by the Constitutional Court in 1998" (Atacan, 2005: 193). After the RP was closed down, the Islamic Anatolian holding companies, which were against the use of interest-based banking system, could not "survive under globalized accumulation" since "their [illegal] deposit collection methods eventually [led to their] downfall" (Öztürk, 2015: 131). The AKP as the reformist and moderate wing of the RP was

established in 2001 and strongly backed by the "rapidly growing and interna-
tionalizing sections of Anatolian capital" (Oğuz, 2008: 142).

Moreover, the capital accumulation process during the 1990s signifies the
first phase of the financialisation in Turkey. The market liberalisation process
in the early phase of neoliberalism can be periodised as two sequential processes: i) 1980–1989: the trade liberalisation, internal financial liberalization
and resultant export-oriented accumulation strategy backed by strong state
subsidies and a managed flexible exchange rate system; ii) 1989–2001: capital account liberalisation, external financial liberalisation and the accumulation based on speculative short-term capital inflows. The dynamics behind
the transition from one accumulation system to another is strongly related to
the fragilities (failure to some extent) in the EOI during the 1980s. The initial
export boom in the early 1980s gradually decelerated during the decade in
the context of the failure in the creation of new productive capacity, limited
technological upgrading and over-reliance on the import-dependent labour-
intensive manufactures (Boratav, 2003; Türel, 1998; Boratav and Yeldan, 2006).
Especially by 1988, this export-led system of accumulation reached its limits
not only economically but also politically due to a new wave of organised
labour protests (Boratav et al., 2000). In an environment where ANAP significantly lost its power to represent a political unity among the bourgeoisie and
to repress organised labour, the government unwillingly responded to the
revived trade-union activism and protest movements by a substantial increase
in wage incomes (ibid.). The drastic increases in real wages (reaching to 142%
in nominal terms) became one of the most important reasons behind coming
to an end of the export-based accumulation system, which was indeed based
on the regressive suppression on labour income (Boratav and Orhangazi, 2022;
Yeldan, 2001; Akyüz and Boratav, 2003).

The main policy response of the state to the increased wage costs, which cli-
maxed the fiscal deficit and public sector borrowing requirement (PSBR), was
the liberalization of the capital account in 1989 and the realisation of the full
convertibility of Turkish Lira (TL) in foreign exchange markets in 1990. Hence,
the complete liberalisation of financial markets paved the way for a massive
liquidity injection to the domestic economy in the form of short-term capital
flows (Boratav et al., 2000; Cizre and Yeldan, 2005). While the capital inflows
enabled to finance fiscal deficits and provided a short-term relief on both
PSBR and "inflationary pressures by cheapening import costs", they made the
economy dependent on short-term foreign finance and subject to the exposure of speculative cycles of capital movements (Boratav et al., 2000: 6). With
"the eradication of the government's ability to use independent monetary,

exchange rate and interest rate policies", the export promotion policy of the state through the real effective depreciation of the domestic currency came to an end; and the combination of high-interest rates and appreciated domestic currency became the main pillars of the economy to attract speculative short-term capital (Voyvoda, 2006: 130).

Based on this, the basic mechanism of the first phase of the financialised accumulation in Turkey (during the 1990s) was as such: the bank-owner holding groups borrowed cheap external loans (at low interest-rates) from the international financial markets and invested on the GDS which promised high capital gains (in the form of fictitious capital) in the context of skyrocketing public sector deficit. Hence, while the PBRS was completely financed by the GDS issuance in the domestic market, a new system of accumulation became prevalent for the hegemonic fraction of the bourgeoisie in this period — that is "advancing IBC [by them] in exchange for new fictitious capital" (Saad-Filho, 2015: 11). There is a broad consensus in the literature regarding financial liberalisation and debt relationship of the state with private domestic capital after 1989 which worked as a resource transfer mechanism to big capital groups thanks to the prevalence of the holding bank-ownership among the big capital groups (Boratav, 2003; Bahçe *et al*, 2015; Yalman, 2019).

Therefore, the main beneficiaries of the financial liberalisation became the bank-owner holding groups, which have greatly increased their profits by receiving high returns on financial assets during the 1990s, albeit becoming "extremely vulnerable to exchange rate risks and to sudden changes in the inflation rate" (Boratav and Yeldan, 2006: 417). Although the bank-ownership by holding groups had already started in the 1960s, and then gained speed in the 1980s, the 1990s witnessed a fierce competition among the industrial companies to own banks directly or via foreign partners and transform themselves to holding companies, a significant proportion was formed by construction companies (Gültekin-Karakaş, 2009; Ergüneş, 2009; Sönmez, 2011). Therefore, some of the hybrid business groups having close connections with both Islamic capital and Istanbul-centred business groups also took part in this GDS trade process. Nevertheless, the source of the intra-capitalist class conflict in this period became the capital groups that own banks and the ones that do not (Oğuz, 2008; Boratav, 1994). Hence, it is not surprising that "the most vocal critics [to financial liberalisation] belong to large specialised and influential (i.e., textile) industrial companies which do not have their own banking extensions" high likely due to the Islamic prohibition of charging interest (Boratav, 1994).

While the financialisation of the accumulation of the big capital groups manifested as the substantial increase in their non-operating incomes[4] in the 1990s, their savings and funds increasingly moved away from fixed capital investments towards holding speculative financial assets, particularly GDS (Balkan and Yeldan, 2002; Boratav and Yeldan, 2006; Ercan and Oguz, 2015). Although the financial liberalisation and the macroeconomic policies based on attracting the flow of international money-capital were profitable for individual capitals in the short term, they caused serious declines in production capacity, in the long run, leading to a blockage of the capital accumulation process and successive crises (Ercan, 2002). Hence, this first phase of financialisation, in the form of intensive expansion of IBC (the expansion of IBC to the operations of merchant and industrial capital), in Turkey resulted in the recurrent financial crises from 1994 to 2001.

Similar to other LCCs, the capital account liberalisation in 1989 culminated with the fragility of the accumulation system starting with the structural adjustment and liberalisation policies in 1980. Consequently, the increased exposure of the economy to the fluctuations of capital movements and the vagaries of the international financial markets became the decisive factor in the permanent financial instability and crises throughout the second half of the 1990s. Under a macroeconomic atmosphere "trapped with high real interest rates, appreciated currency and persistent balance of payment difficulties" (Voyvoda, 2006: 130), the debt turnover effort of the state through raising new debt in the domestic market turned to a fiscal crisis of the state in 1994 especially with the rising burden of excessively high-interest rates payments on GDS and "the sudden drainage of short-term funds in the beginning of January 1994" (Boratav et al., 2000: 7).

After a certain point, public debt turnover became the only goal of fiscal policy, and it was implemented with the primary budget surplus targets of the IMF-supervised programs, especially after 1999. Consequently, a new stand-by agreement was signed with the IMF in December 1999 that launched second-generation structural reforms in Turkey. While this program "utterly relied on a nominally pegged exchange rate system for disinflation and a targeted set of austerity measures and structural reforms to restore fiscal balance" (Voyvoda, 2006: 132), it collapsed with major outflows of capital that was followed by massive shocks and collapses in the foreign exchange markets and the banking system in 2000/2001.

---

4 55% of the earnings of Turkey's largest 500 industrial enterprises in this period were non-operating incomes (Karahanoğulları, 2009).

3   The Consolidation and Institutionalisation of Neoliberalism and
      Financialisation in Turkey: Post-2001 Period

The transition to the 2000s in Turkey occurred under an intense political and economic turmoil with a long period of weak minority governments failing to establish a unified power bloc, the loss of credibility of people to the existing political parties, long-standing high inflation and negative real interest rates, and the coalition governments' incapability to implement the new standby agreement signed with the IMF in 1999 and finally the devastating 2000–2001 crisis. Although the crisis started as a simultaneous banking sector-currency crisis, which was the outcome of the post-1980s' neoliberal economic programme, particularly financial liberalisation, and the reflection of the chain crises starting from East Asia spreading to the periphery of the world economy (Boratav, 2018), it expanded to other sectors at short notice, leading many firms to go bankrupt, collapsing the labour market and leading to economic shrinkage of 5.7% in 2001 (IMF, 2011).

Nevertheless, the 2001 crisis also signified "the crisis in neoliberalism", albeit not "the crisis of neoliberalism" in Turkey (Saad-Filho, 2010). It can be argued that the crisis in (early) neoliberalism created a suitable atmosphere for the restructuring/institutionalisation of neoliberalism. The establishment of the mature neoliberalism in the post-2001 era was accompanied by an aggressive restructuring of state and society in Turkey. The state was restructured through the re-articulation of its political and economic functions to reassert the hegemony of the dominant classes and to facilitate the financialisation of economic and social reproduction. This "process of re-building state capacity in line with the requirements of a [financialised] market economy" was marked by the reproduction of the authoritarian form of the state under the AKP governments in Turkey (Öniş, 2009: 429). Hence, as put by Bedirhanoğlu and Yalman (2010: 110), the AKP "represents more continuity than radical change in terms of the authoritarian form of the state [but] as an example of how the political Islam adjusted to neoliberal restructuring project" within the process of financialisation. Nevertheless, the reproduction of neoliberal authoritarianism through an Islamic-conservative model signified a significant rupture of the AKP governments from the radical Islamism of its predecessor RP, which had a strong anti-west discourse. While this rupture (self-described as conservative democracy) was largely welcomed by the Bretton Woods institutions, the big bourgeoise cautiously supported the rise of the AKP to power. However, the AKP's unexpected victory in the 2002 general elections, "a development which was arguably the outcome of the extraordinary post-2001 crisis atmosphere" turned to implicit support of different fractions of Turkish capital thanks to their full commitment to IMF-guided second-wave neoliberal program (ibid., 111).

Backed by the economic and political support of the IMF for undertaking the post-crisis economic recovery program and the legitimacy of the EU accession process — that was celebrated by the big bourgeoisie, liberal intelligentsia and foreign investors as a move towards the formation of democratic governance — the AKP established a new power bloc by successfully organising political unity of the bourgeoisie under the hegemonic fraction for the first time since ANAP. As widely agreed, the power bloc during the early AKP period was based on an alliance between "the economically dominant and politically hegemonic sector" comprising of the Istanbul-based big bourgeoisie which organised TUSIAD, and "the economically improving but politically subordinated faction" comprising of large and diverse group of enterprises, predominantly but not exclusively MUSIAD[5] members (Özden et al., 2017: 193).

On the one hand, AKP successfully managed to articulate the demands of the SMEs and the big bourgeoisie with a promise of revitalising economic growth between 2002 and 2008, almost all fractions of capital substantially increased their total assets and some managed to leap to the 'global player' scale thanks to the extremely favourable global economic climate of the early 2000s with global liquidity abundance, massive FDI inflows, and AKP's pursuit of massive privatizations and strict austerity policies at the expense of labouring classes (Öztürk, 2010). On the other hand, AKP gained the consent of the certain sections of the popular masses (particularly the urban poor) by combining the neoliberal social policy regime with Islamic charity networks (Bedirhanoğlu, 2009; Buğra and Savaşkan, 2014). While the austerity policies were followed, nearly all spheres of social reproduction were privatised and financialised and unprecedented flexibility was brought to the labour market; the neoliberal anti-poverty strategies and social assistance programs, such as the Green Card and conditional cash transfers, have matched with the AKP's religious grassroots charity works, that was inherent from the 1990s' local government practices, to win the support of the poor (Akça, 2014; Buğra, 2007; Eder, 2010; Yıldırım, 2009).

However, for a better understanding of the mature phase of neoliberalism and financialisation in Turkey, it is important to briefly discuss the IMF-supervised post-crisis recovery programme, named the 'Transition to Strong Economy Program' (TSEP). TSEP, which was also guided by a new three-year

---

5 MUSIAD is the most well-known business association of the conservative business groups established in 1990 to represent SMEs having Islamic orientation.

stand-by agreement signed with the IMF in 2005, principally aimed at maintaining a primary surplus through fiscal discipline and an exchange-rate-based macroeconomic stabilisation underpinned by structural reforms, including privatisations, social security reform, restructuring of banking and financial sectors, taxation and public finance reform (Ergüneş, 2009: 7; Cizre and Yeldan, 2005; Voyvoda, 2006). Alongside the ambitious steps taken for fiscal austerity, the program also adopted other monetary policies including the implementation of the flexible exchange rate, central bank independence, inflation targeting and reserve accumulation by the central bank. The full shift to the IT regime happened in 2006, and the inflation rate, which "had run persistently around 80–120% annually for about three decades between early 1970s and early 2000s, has stabilized within a band of 15–20%" (Erol and Tırtıroğlu, 2011: 176).

While this first phase of AKP rule in the 2000s was shaped by a de-politicised technocratic crisis-management logic under the IMF supervision, the "'stability' rhetoric played a prominent role in the AKP's hegemonic appeal [by helping] the government to speed up the pace of regulatory reforms and implement fiscal discipline without major opposition" thanks to portraying these structural reforms as a scientific remedy to achieve macroeconomic stability (Hoşgör, 2015: 205). Nevertheless, the depoliticisation of the second-wave structural adjustment policies and the reduction of the neoliberal economic management into a technocratic issue in the early period of the AKP rule led them the state to be organised in the form of technocratic authoritarianism (Akçay, 2013). While the strong executive power was crucial to the rapid implementation of the structural adjustment program, the executive also increasingly followed the requirements of technocratic rationality of the IMF program, not least through the prominence of specialised economic apparatuses within the executive power. In this sense, the independent regulatory agencies (IRAS) as specialised economic apparatuses, which were established in certain sectors of the economy as a condition of the IMF's structural adjustment package, have undertaken important functions in ensuring the technicization (depoliticisation) of the policy-making processes in this early phase (ibid.). The main logic behind the formation of IRAS was minimising the state in these economic spheres and reducing the state capacity into coordination and control. In the early years of the AKP, the relative autonomy of IRAS served to insulate the Central Bank and Banking Regulation and Supervision Agency "from popular democratic influence and working-class priorities" (Yalman *et al.*, 2019: 12). However, the technocratic appearance of the state as a neutral guarantor of the growth and macroeconomic stability by no means implies that the intra-class relations and the relations between the AKP government and Bretton Woods Institutions were always conciliatory and cooperative in the early 2000s.

The establishment of the Public Procurement Authority (PPA) as an IRA to manage and regulate the government's purchase of goods, services and works from the private sector through public tenders and auctions; and the enactment of the Public Procurement Law (PPL) can be given as an important example to track the intra-capitalist class contradictions and the AKP's particular strategies to control strategic state capacities vis-à-vis Bretton Woods Institutions during the early 2000s. While the establishment of the PPA and the restructuring of the public procurement policies with the purpose of 'increasing the efficiency of public expenditures' and 'preventing corruption and cronyism' were a conditionality of IMF loans and WB credits (WB, 2001), the amendment of the PPL in line with the EU Tender Directives was put forward as one of the conditions for Turkey's EU admission. At the bottom, the main rationality behind the restructuring of the public procurement was opening up "national public procurement markets to international competition" and particularly to European construction capital groups for the EU (Ercan and Oğuz, 2006: 650; Bayramoğlu, 2005; Gürakar, 2016). The determination of the scope and scale of the PPL by the AKP government, which happened through the fierce negotiations with the international institutions, were critical in the management of the contradictory demands of both foreign capital and domestic capital. While the large-internationalised groups of domestic capital largely supported a new procurement law that would bring the scale to the global level and lead them to merge with foreign capital groups, they also wanted to take advantage of the old regulations protecting domestic tenderers against foreign capital groups (Gürakar, 2016; Ercan and Oğuz, 2006). On the other hand, public procurement was also attractive for medium-sized capital groups that rapidly grew in the recent decade and, they wanted to continue to benefit from the domestic capital-oriented public procurement system (Ercan and Oğuz, 2006; Hoşgör, 2015).

However, the PPL enacted in 2002 largely favoured foreign capital groups and included the conditions lifting all the legal barriers to their access to public procurements and; none of the privilege demands of the domestic capital groups was involved in the law (Ercan and Oğuz, 2006). Especially the medium-scale capital groups that had largely benefitted from the Islamic local governments' contracts in the provision of local services during the 1990s were the ones having the most vocal critics of the new PPL. The PM Erdoğan started to a long negotiation process with the IMF, WB and EU to change the PPL in favour of domestic capital groups (particularly the SMEs that formed AKP's electoral support basis) in the public procurements. Although AKP "attempted to change 40 of the 60 articles in the original law within 2 years", in the face of strong opposition from (surveillance of) international institutions, they only succeeded in making a few critical changes in the law[6] (ibid., 652). These changes were in the form of exemptions from the PPL in some sectors like energy, water, transportation and communication sectors. Two important exemptions from the PPL were related to the housing sector and the privatisation of the state economic enterprises (SEEs) in terms of creating a strategic space for favouring domestic capital groups. While the exclusion of the housing works from the PPL served as a crucial mechanism for giving procurement of mass housing projects to the domestic construction capitalists that are politically close to the government and asymmetrically favouring them through TOKI (Chapter 8); the exclusion of the privatisation of the SEEs from the scope of the law led the government to sell them "below-specified values" and through the division of the big procurement purchases into small parts that enable the growing SMEs to access into the aggressive privatisation process (Ercan and Oğuz, 2006: 653; Buğra and Savaşkan, 2012; 2014).

The IMF-inspired TSEP also paved the way for the restructuring of the state apparatus through public sector reforms and restructuring of the banking sector that was also crucial in the restructuring of the housing SoP in the 2000s. Firstly, regarding the public administration reforms, the first AKP government (2002–2007) aimed at "institutionally separate the economic from the political ... that is, to internalize market imperatives into policy formation, depoliticize the process, and ensure that the needs of capital trump popular concerns" (Marois, 2019: 110). Therefore, fiscal discipline and transparency became the focus of TSEP in the reorganisation of the public sphere. In this regard, the Public Administration Law (No. 5227) was enacted in 2004 that was instrumental in "imposing neoliberal discipline on both institutional and fiscal designs of the state apparatus" (Özden *et al.*, 2017: 193). In this, the state is financialised not only in the broad sense through "concentrating political and economic power around state financial agencies such as the treasury, the central bank, banking regulators, and the ministry of finance and the economy" (Yalman *et al.*, 2019: 12), but also in the narrow sense, through the allowance of the public institutions to raise funds in capital markets against the cuts in the budgetary funds. In the Turkish case, the most distinguishing feature of the restructuring of the state (the organisational structures and functions of the various state institutions) was the extensive use of DFLs and omnibus

---

6 When the stand-by agreement ended in 2008, successive AKP governments changed the PPL more than 29 times (Buğra and Savaşkan, 2014).

bills that increasingly passivised the parliament and its legislative authority by empowering the Council of Ministers (similar to the ANAP period but in a much more discretionary and systemic way).

Secondly, the banking sector was reorganised under TSEP, which was crucial not only for the financialisation of Turkish economy in general but for social reproduction and housing in the post-2001 era. Although the banking reform already started with the foundation of the autonomous Banking Regulation and Supervision Agency (BRSA) in 1999 under which the Savings Deposit Insurance Fund (SDIF) operated by incorporating the insolvent banks into its own body, it accelerated with the rescues of state banks in the early 2000s. Also, the state-owned banks were not immediately privatised in accord with the IMF suggestions, they were aggressively commercialised in the sense that they completely adopted the practices of commercial banks (Marois and Güngen, 2019). Consequently, the extensive merging of SDIF banks, together with the rapid increase in the private commercial and foreign banks in Turkey thanks to "the growth in cross-border mergers and acquisitions in the banking sector since 2005" resulted in the elimination of the weaker ones and the increasing strengthening and concentration in the Turkish banking system (Marois and Güngen, 2019: 148; Bakır and Öniş, 2010). This paved the way for the strengthening of Turkey's bank-based financial system and the financialisation of banks. Although the financialisation of banks through their purchase of GDS continued during the 2000s as seen in Figure 2, their financial returns from these transactions shrank compared to the 1990s as a result of the reduction in public sector deficit and borrowing requirements (see Figure 3) thanks to the post-2001 fiscal discipline measurements.

The most important consequence of the decrease in the capital gains of the Turkish banks from financing public deficits became the diversification of financial products by the banks and their unprecedented involvement in consumer lending thanks to lucrative returns from the state-backed "large spreads between their borrowing and lending rates of interest" (Marois and Güngen, 2019: 140). However, the financial mechanism encouraging banks to finance household consumption cannot only be attributed to the restructuring of the banking sector through TSEP. As mentioned before, "highly accommodating monetary policies [in the ACCs] and the rapid expansion of liquidity in international financial markets, notably the US" triggered massive international capital inflows to all LCCs in search of profitable markets since the early 2000s (Akyüz, 2018: 10; Karwowski and Stockhammer, 2017; Kaltenbrunner, 2015). Similarly, Turkey had a significant surge in the capital inflows mainly in the form of FDI and portfolio flows until the GFC and later in 2010 and 2011 (see Figure 4) thanks to the continuity in the expansionary monetary policies in

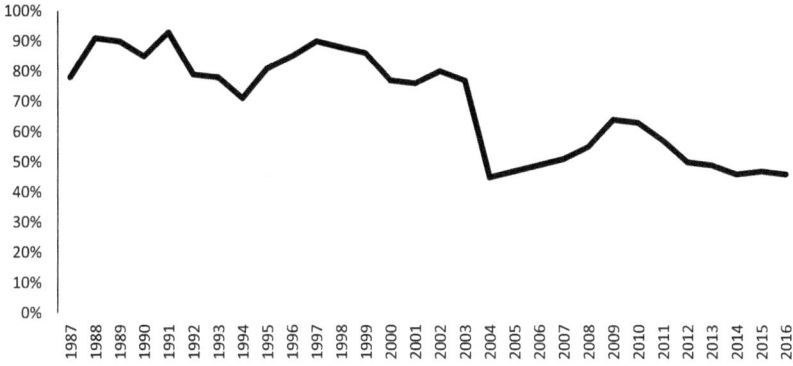

FIGURE 2   Percentage of the banking sector in the financing of the government's domestic
            borrowing in Turkey (1987–2016)
            SOURCE: THE AUTHOR'S CALCULATIONS BASED ON THE UNDERSECRETARIAT
            OF TREASURY'S DATA SET HTTPS://EN.HMB.GOV.TR/GOVERNMENT-FINA
            NCE-STATISTICS

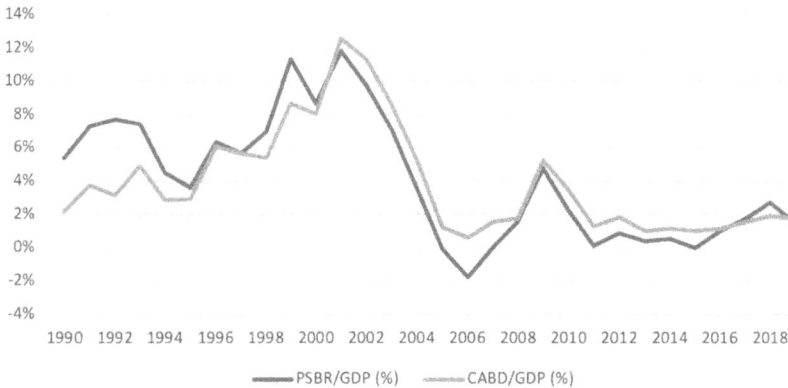

FIGURE 3   Ratios of the public sector borrowing requirements (PSBR) and the central
            administration's budget deficits (CABD) to the GDP (%) in Turkey (1990–2018)
            SOURCE: PREPARED BASED ON THE DATA SET OF THE PRESIDENCY OF
            STRATEGY AND BUDGET HTTP://WWW.SBB.GOV.TR/TEMEL-EKONOMIK-GOST
            ERGELER/

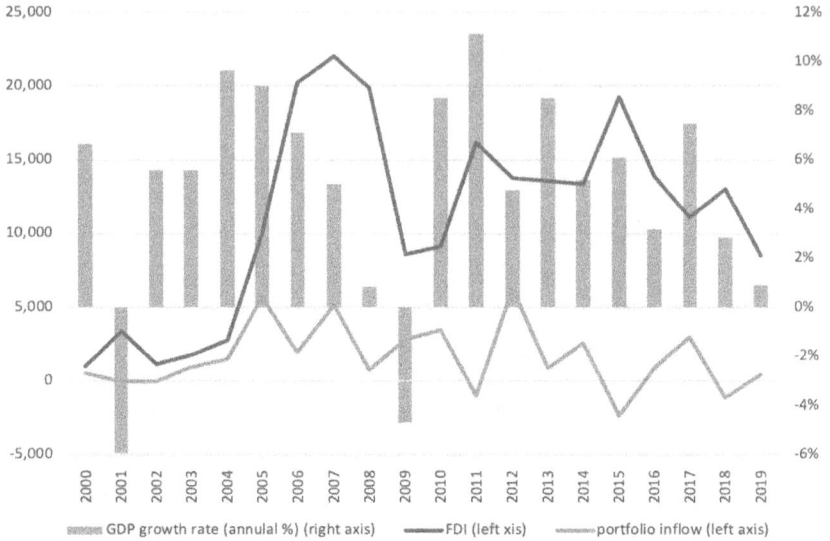

FIGURE 4   Capital inflows: The net FDI and net portfolio inflow — in US$ million — and the annual GDP growth rate in Turkey (2002–2019)
SOURCE: HTTPS://DATA.WORLDBANK.ORG/INDICATOR/BX.KLT.DINV.WD.GD.ZS?LOCATIONS=TR

the ACCs via quantitative easing (QE) following the GFC. This surge in capital inflows not only contributed to the high growth rates in Turkey but also significantly lowered the domestic interest rates that in turn accelerated consumer credits by stimulating domestic demand (Orhangazi and Özgür, 2015; Güngen, 2019).

As seen in Figure 5, from 2002 to 2014, household consumer credit increased by nearly 7,000%. Although such a boom in the consumer credits is not considered the financialisation in the narrow sense, it is accepted as financialisation of social reproduction in the broad sense through the expansion of CF since a large segment of the Turkish society started to take consumer loans for their social reproduction in the face of decreasing real wages. Moreover, the expansion of domestic credit market and debt-based private consumption have been used as an important macroeconomic tool to sustain aggregate demand and so stimulate economic growth (Bahçe *et al.*, 2015). As seen in Figure 6, the ratio of household debt to GDP rose from 2.96% in 2003 to 20% in 2013.

Moreover, the restructuring of the banking sector through TSEP was also momentous for the big business groups and their capital accumulation strategies. As discussed, in the former decade, it was very common for the industrial

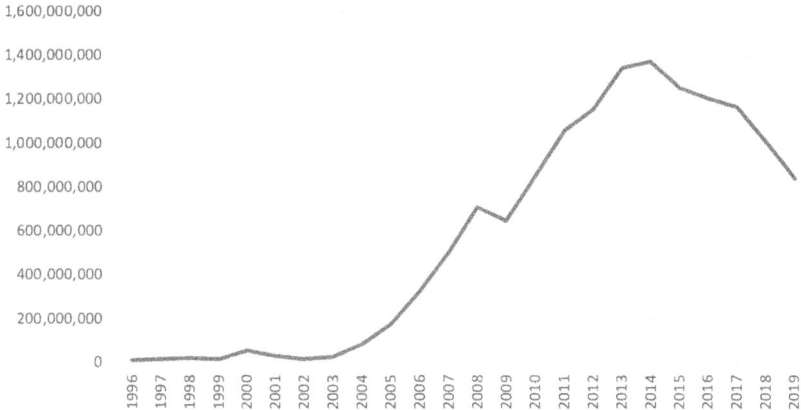

FIGURE 5   Household consumer credits in US$ (2000–2019)
             SOURCE: CBRT HTTPS://EVDS2.TCMB.GOV.TR/

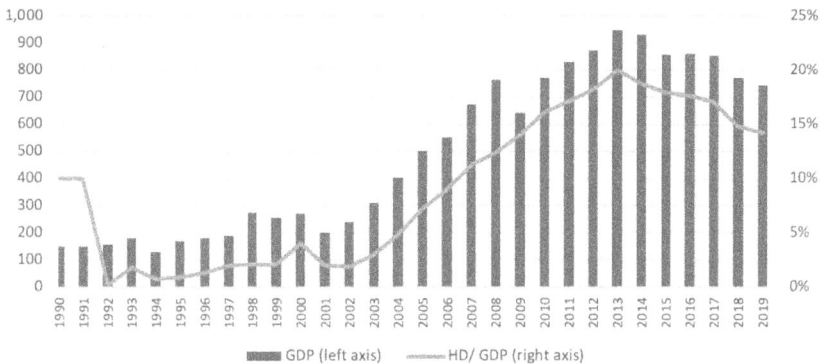

FIGURE 6   GDP in US$ billion and the ratio of the household debt to GDP (%) in Turkey
             (1990–2019)
             SOURCE: WB AND BIS HTTPS://DATA.WORLDBANK.ORG/INDICATOR/NY.GDP
             .MKTP.CD?END=2018&LOCATIONS=TR&START=1999; HTTPS://STATS.BIS.ORG
             /STATX/SRS/TABLE/F3.1

and merchant capital to be organised as holding companies and the bank-ownership was providing advantage not only for supplying IBC for their productive activities but also having astronomical capital gains (in the form of fictitious capital) from the GDS trade. Nevertheless, the re-regulation of the banking system eliminated some of these holding groups from the banking system. While some bankrupt banks, which were affiliated with holding companies, were transferred to the SDIF following the 1994, 1999 and 2001 crises, the

BRSA brought some criteria for bank-ownership such as limiting non-financial shareholding by 15% of the net worth of banks and higher ratios of leverage, liquidity and capital adequacy (BRSA, 2002). Although this process was not without tensions and struggles among business groups, it has been argued that it was necessary for a consolidated banking sector with large strong and trustable banks that would attract foreign capital (Gültekin-Karakaş, 2007; 2009).

Consequently, the post-2001 regulations ended the hegemony of the holding companies in the banking sector even though this does not mean the elimination of the large Turkish conglomerates from either Turkey's business structure or the construction sector. Instead, the Turkish NFCs increasingly turned to foreign funding opportunities in the 2000s, in the context of appreciation of the TL, thanks to cheap foreign currency loans and favourable global economic environment (Akyüz, 2015). Similarly, increasing global liquidity as a consequence of the QE policies in the ACCs and the resultant surge in the capital inflows in 2010 and 2011 led to further expansion of credit market, further appreciation of the TL, and made foreign borrowing attractive to the NFCs that resulted in the dollarization of the liabilities of the NFCs and the construction firms (Orhangazi, 2019; Bahçe *et al.*, 2015).

As seen in Figure 7, the 2000s and 2010s witnessed the striking rise in the foreign currency borrowing of the private sector, including banks, non-banking firms and NFCs. While the FX-denominated liabilities (particularly in US$) of the private banking sector increased from US$10 billion in 2003 to US$144 billion in 2015, the corporate sector's external debt rose from US$30 billion in 2000 to US$160 billion in 2019.

Moreover, as can be seen from the net FX position of the NFCs in Table 1, the NFC's external indebtedness has been remarkable in the 2000s and 2010s. Table 1 also shows that a significant part of the FX loans of the NFCs has been taken from the domestic banks. This indicates that domestic banks are still an important component of the NFCs' financing source in Turkey. Moreover, although the ratio of consumer loans within the banks' balance sheets strikingly increased since 2001, nearly 60% of total loans were loaned to the NFCs.

Regarding the financialisation of the NFCs, while large NFCs' primary funding methods have been borrowing from international financial markets and retained earnings (Demir, 2008; Özmen *et al.*, 2012; Demiröz and Erdem, 2019), the private sector's issuing of debt instruments did not show a dramatic growth but remained in the band of 15 to 25% of total securities. Moreover, this slowly growing corporate bond market "is dominated by relatively few corporations" (Güngen, 2019: 172). In the case of the stock market, there has been a slow but continuous increase in the number of traded corporations on Borsa Istanbul that rose from 288 in 2002 to 414 in 2018 (www.cmb.gov.tr). However,

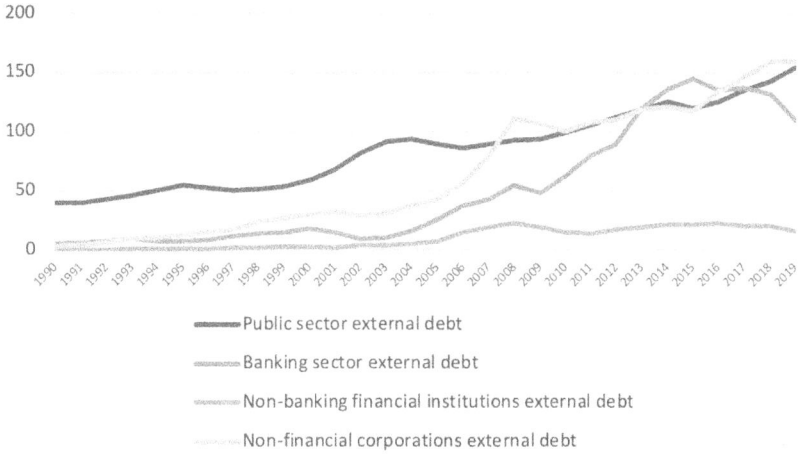

FIGURE 7   Turkey's external debt stock divided by the public sector, banking sector, non-banking financial sector and non-financial corporations — in US$ billion (1990–2019)

SOURCE: MINISTRY OF TREASURY AND FINANCE (HTTPS://WWW.HMB.GOV.TR /KAMU-FINANSMANI-ISTATISTIKLERI#)

the capitalisation rates of the companies were quite volatile during the 2000s and 2010s (ibid.).

At this point, there is a need for further clarification of the unprecedented acceleration in financial intermediation and financial depth in the Turkish banking system and the change in the integration of Turkey in the international financial system. These developments are directly connected to the housing SoP of Turkey in the 2000s and 2010s due to three reasons: i) housing loans composes nearly half of the consumer loans given by the commercial banks since 2005 (Chapter 7); ii) the construction and real estate sectors are one of the most (externally) indebted sectors in Turkey (Chapter 8); and iii) housebuilding industry is a cyclical industry having strong boom-bust cycles in accord with the periods of macroeconomic expansion and downturn due to the volatile nature of the monopoly rent and effective demand that has been accelerated with the financialisation of economic and social reproduction. For this, I will examine the post-2001 era briefly by dividing into five periods.

In the post-2001 crisis recovery period, Turkey had a modest growth between 2002 and 2008 thanks to IMF-inspired TSEP — the restructuring and strengthening of the banking sector, monetary stability, fiscal discipline measures, decline in the public debt, increase in exports, lower inflation and interest rates — and the extremely favourable global economic climate of

TABLE 1   The foreign exchange (FX) position of the NFCs — in US$ billion

Years	Net FX position	Domestic FX loans	Total FX liabilities
2002	-6,538	600	31,638
2003	-18,432	18,158	48,634
2004	-18,959	20,458	56,630
2005	-22,266	26,429	67,118
2006	-28,150	34,804	90,809
2007	-53,254	46,323	129,386
2008	-69,856	48,066	150,321
2009	-66,065	50,333	146,450
2010	-88,173	81,887	175,552
2011	-117,645	102,292	199,824
2012	-136,108	121,842	225,475
2013	-172,881	155,164	267,013
2014	-180,162	171,705	282,709
2015	-188,547	173,910	288,719
2016	-203,994	178,081	303,574
2017	-211,215	183,491	327,081
2018	-207,109	171,408	319,765
2019	-179,793	152,995	304,203

SOURCE: CBRT HTTPS://EVDS2.TCMB.GOV.TR/

the early 2000s — global liquidity, abundant foreign exchange and massive foreign capital flow in the form of both FDI and portfolio investments and therefore resultant credit expansion, increase in domestic demand, asset price inflation and debt-based private consumption (Boratav, 2014; Onaran, 2006; Bahçe *et al.,* 2015).

Moreover, the GFC did not result in the reversal of this favourable global economic picture for Turkey, except for a short recession in 2008 and 2009.[7]

---

7 Here, for understanding why Turkey like other LCCs did not have a severe negative influence of the GFC in this period, the uneven and combined development of financialisation would be worth to re-mention. The expansion of the US-led crisis to the rest of the world occurred based on the extent of the development of financial sectors of countries; their integration with US financial market and their economies' dependence on foreign trade (and the extent of integration in mercantile partnership with the US) (Lapavitsas, 2009b; Akçay and Güngen,

This stems from the policy response of the central banks of the ACCs to the GFC by decreasing their interest rates for increasing the money supply and stimulating the lending and investment in their domestic markets, that paved the way for a new wave of hot money flows from ACCs to LCCs due to their high-profit expectations from the increasing interest rate differentials between LCCs and ACCs (Barroso *et al.*, 2016; Painceira, 2012; Akyüz 2014). Moreover, within this abundant global liquidity environment underpinned by strong capital inflows, the Central Bank of Turkey (CBRT) was able to decrease domestic interest rates from 2010 to 2013 that spurred the household consumption and the housing effective demand (see Figure 8).

Three important consequences of this new wave of capital inflows in Turkey include the expansion in consumer credits and increasing role of the household debt in the Turkish economy's growth strategy, the increasing dollar-dominated indebtedness of the NFCs thanks to cheapening foreign borrowing, and the increase in current account deficits due to the dependency of Turkey's EOI to the imported intermediate goods, i.e., "the import-dependent nature of production" (Orhangazi and Özgür, 2015: 6). Indeed, these three main developments are directly related to the financialisation of the Turkish economy starting with the capital account liberalisation in 1989 and continuing with deeper integration of the Turkish economy within global capital markets. The process starting with the post-2001 crisis recovery program resulted in the financialisation of social and economic reproduction differently from the early neoliberalism and financialisation in Turkey, which was more based on the trade of GDS.

However, the increasing household indebtedness and dollar-denominated indebtedness of the NFCs became not only the main axis of the capital accumulation strategy of the AKP governments but also the source of the vulnerability. Specifically, while the increasing dollar liabilities of the NFCs made them directly and seriously vulnerable to foreign exchange risks, the Turkish domestic financial markets and private sector became "very sensitive to movements of foreign financial flows" that is itself dependent on the global financial conditions and the global liquidity (Bahçe *et al.,* 2015: 276). Moreover, because a significant part of this FX loans was taken from the commercial banks in Turkey and Turkish banks also largely borrowed from foreign financial markets to finance households and NFCs, Turkish banks also became directly vulnerable to increases in the foreign currencies and the changes in the interest rates in the ACCs, notably the US. Therefore, this capital inflow-dependent and

2016). Therefore, toxic debt instruments and derivative products of the US were not financed by the Turkish financial institutions, unlike the Eurozone countries that had a more severe effect of the GFC.

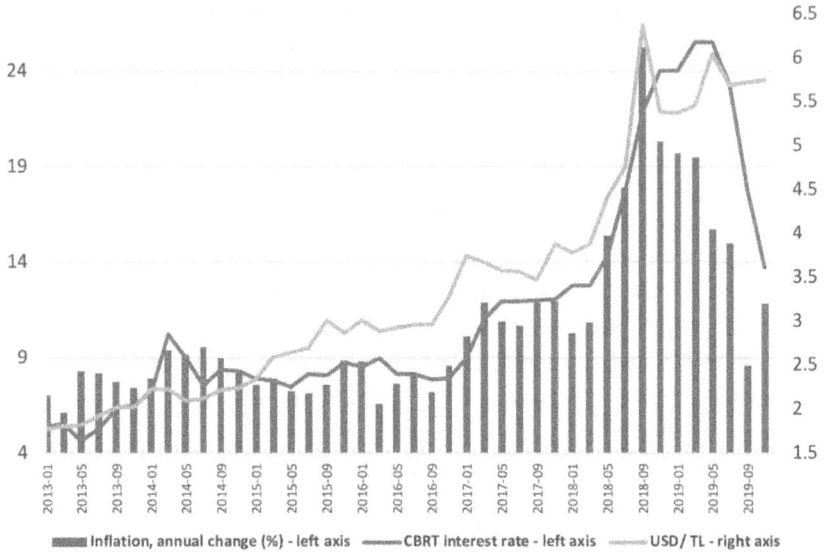

FIGURE 8   Changes in inflation (%), the CBRT interest rate and the USD/TL (2013–2019)
             SOURCE: CBRT HTTPS://EVDS2.TCMB.GOV.TR/INDEX.PHP; *THE WEIGHTED
             AVERAGE FUNDING COST

debt-led economic growth system in Turkey not only made the economy vulnerable to a debt crisis of NFCs but also a banking crisis in the case of insolvency of the NFCs. Especially sectors such as housebuilding industry which produces for the domestic market and therefore gains their revenues in TL became prone to insolvency (Chapter 8).

At a closer look, the year 2013, when the FED announced the tapering of QE policies in May, the expectations for high-interest rates in the US led some foreign investors in Turkey to turn towards the US bonds, following the depreciation of the TL and increase in inflation, as shown in Figure 8. This became the first time when Turkey was faced with the danger of the reversal of capital inflows and against this danger and the CBRT responded by increasing interest rate[8] sharply at an emergency meeting in January 2014.

Additionally, as a macroprudential measurement against the further depreciation of TL and widening current account deficits, the CBRT and BRSA brought some restrictions to the expansion of domestic consumer credit

8   As argued by Saad-Filho and Morais (2018: 56), "the manipulation of interest rates" is a common monetary policy of central banks in the neoliberal phase of capitalism and financialised system of accumulation.

market such as "raising consumer credit risk weightings and adjusting credit lines with income" (Vural, 2019: 272). Although the direct impact of this temporary restriction became the decrease in the growth rates of the economy, the continuity in the QE in the EU, Japan and the persisting negative interest rates in the US contrary to its tapering announcement, and the revitalisation of the capital inflows led the Turkish economy to defer this shock. However, because the vulnerability was structural which is the financialisation of the Turkish economy, the depreciation of TL, "amounted to 23% [only] in the first nine months of 2015" and the seriously indebted private sector became inherent to the economy (Marois and Güngen, 2019: 152).

Moreover, following the coup attempt in Turkey in 2016 (see below), AKP not only "attempted to convert stocks into liquid assets by founding the Turkey Wealth Fund"⁹ against a threat of economic slump but also lifted the limitations on consumer loans and credit cards; increased the minimum wages; raised the public expenditures (particularly in the construction sector), brought tax exemption in the purchase of luxury housing, decreased the number of down-payments in the housing sales, raised the credit card instalments by using state-owned banks and therefore turned back to the strategy of the economic growth based on the domestic credit expansion, household consumption and the resultant asset price inflation, especially in the face of deteriorating export rates (Yalman *et al.*, 2019: 16; Orhangazi and Özgür, 2015). This, however, was significant not only for the debt-based growth strategy of the AKP governments but also for not losing the support of the working classes by guaranteeing the continuity in their social and financial inclusion. Similarly, two other steps were taken by the AKP for getting the consent of the capital fractions in the power bloc. Firstly, for preventing the sudden currency depreciation and capital outflow, the CBRT increased interest rates sharply at the end of 2016 as the second time after 2013, as can be seen in Figure 8. On the one hand, because the increasing interest rates would increase the cost of domestic borrowing, this seems contradictory to the former measure of credit expansion and debt-based household consumption. On the other hand, this contradiction arises from the structural features of the financialisation of economic and social reproduction in Turkey through the co-existence of foreign-currency indebtedness of the NFCs and the debt-based welfare of households. In other words, the measures taken inevitably bring contradictions in an open

---

9   Following the establishment of the Sovereign Wealth Fund Management Incorporation as a sovereign investment fund in 2016, which is directly tied to the Presidency of the Republic and subject to the private law due to its joint-stock company structure, most of the largest SOEs and state-owned banks were transferred to the Fund.

and financialised economy, the decisions of central banks to control domestic markets and to decrease interest rates to fuel the economic growth via household consumption cannot be given independently without taking the developments in the global capitalism, the speculative anticipations of the international investors and therefore the direction of capital flows. Particularly in Turkey, because the productive-capital is mostly dependent on the imported intermediate goods, interest rate decrease decisions of the CBRT not only foster the depreciation of the domestic currency but also lead to the increases in inflation (Orhangazi and Özgür, 2015).

Furthermore, despite the interest rate hike by the CBRT, the domestic currency continued to depreciate strikingly until the mid-2018, as can be seen in Figure 8. The reason of the significant value lost in TL can be considered as continuing "balance of payments risk and portfolio outflows, as well as the state of emergency" [following the coup attempt] (Güngen, 2019: 174). Under these circumstances, the second measure of the AKP became the Treasury-sponsored commercial credit provision to the SMEs via the use of the Credit Guarantee Fund that was put into practice just before the Turkish constitutional referendum in 2017 despite "the risking to increase the budget deficit, leading to a major crisis in the public finances" (Topal, 2019: 239). Therefore, these short-term counter-cyclical measures resulted in the deferral of economic crisis and high growth rates (7.5%) in 2017, albeit increasing external indebtedness of the private sector, widening current account deficit and increasing inflation.

Finally, the short-term deferral of these accumulated fragilities in 2016–17 brought the country to the edge of a serious currency and debt crisis (accompanied with excessive current account deficit, exploded inflation and increasing unemployment) in 2018, that was resulted in rising NFC loan defaults and several concordat declarations. The first response became the third sharp interest rate increase by the CBRT to prevent further depreciation of TL as can be seen in Figure 8, and then followed another "state-sponsored credit expansion periods to make debtfarism work once again, which would for the AKP cadres serve keeping the political power" similar to 2016 (Güngen, 2019b). Therefore, the AKP government aimed to overcome the crisis through a co-existence of the expansionary fiscal and monetary policies (Boratav, 2019). For this, firstly the new Credit Guarantee Funds that had already reached to TL5.3 billion as of 2018 have been provided to the SMEs to revitalise investment from early 2018, then a massive debt restructuring process was started for the large NFCs and holding companies, most of which are in construction and energy sectors, having debt TL100 million or more and the SMEs having less than TL25 million debt via a "loan restructuring framework agreement" signed by Turkish banks and financial institutions in September 2018 (Daily Sabah,

2019). Consequently, as of October 2019, more than TL100 billion debt of the private sector has been restructured (ibid.). However, the recent (and biggest) interest rate hike response of the CBRT deeply accelerated the decrease in the household consumption and the ratio of household debt to GDP in the face of an unprecedented degree of unemployment rate (13.7% in 2019) and the highest rate of inflation since 2004.[10] Against this, AKP started to use state-owned banks to boost the household consumption, in that banks not only started to offer consumer loans in affordable interest rates but also restructured the credit card debts by offering private loans with long maturities and low-interest rates (Güngen, 2019). This was followed by the increase in minimum wages in 2019, gradual decreases in the interest rate from the second half of 2019, and government-declared price reduction campaigns, despite successive family suicides due to the excessive indebtedness and unemployment which had wide media coverage during 2019 (Telegraph, 2019).

Therefore, the situation in Turkey went beyond the debt-restructuring of the SMEs and reached to the stage of the too big to fail saving process similar to what happened after the bankruptcy of the Lehman Brothers in 2008. This debt-restructuring and the socialisation of the losses of the private sector inevitably brings the risk of the spread of the private sector debt to the public sector similar to the Eurozone region (Orhangazi, 2019). However, AKP continues to take some top-down measures against this danger through a direct order of President Erdoğan, thanks to the turn of the further consolidation of the authoritarian state with a transition to the presidential system in 2018, such as a reserve fund transfer from the CBRT to the Ministry of Treasury and Finance (Ant and Koc, 2019) and injection of a massive amount of money from the sovereign wealth fund to the state-owned banks to strengthen their capital position and lending capacities ($3.7 billion in 2019 and further $3 billion in 2020) (Ersoy and Kozok, 2020). Moreover, in the Turkish case, the issue of which business groups will be prioritised in the saving programs in the future is not easy to foresee when the political importance of the SMEs in the support of the power bloc[11] is taken into consideration. It is highly likely that this will fuel the conflict between different fractions of capital in the power bloc, especially regarding the direction of the economic policies: whether the heterodox

---

10   https://data.tuik.gov.tr/Bulten/Index?p=Labour-Force-Statistics-August-2020-33792 &dil=2 (Accessed 18 Feb 2023).

11   "AKP's policies towards the SMEs can be interpreted better in relation to the party's strategic politico-electoral choices as SMEs in Turkey account for 73.5% of total employment. Therefore, their importance lies in their action's direct effects on the lives of the poor labouring masses, who constitute the AKP's main electoral base" (Bedirhanoğlu, 2020: 59).

economic measures will continue or the IMF-backed TSEP program will be brought back to the agenda. As construction capital composes the most significant segment of the dominant capital fractions within the power bloc since 2002, AKP will likely give priority to them in the future, especially when it is taken into consideration that at the end of 2019, Turkey Wealth Fund borrowed a treasury-guaranteed loan of €1 billion from international financial markets to rescue three large construction companies, which had undertaken the construction of the commercial towers, shopping malls, hotels and luxury residences within the framework of the project of the Istanbul Finance Centre.[12] However, in the last instance, the future of the development of the debt and currency crisis in Turkey will be reformulated according to the changes in the future of the global capitalism, financial markets and global liquidity.

From this point forth, the rest of the chapter will examine the changing balance of class forces in the power bloc and the consolidation of the authoritarian form of the state in the post-GFC (the post-IMF) period with an ultimate aim of understanding the reflections of these relations in the housing SoP in the 2000s. As discussed so far, the early years of the AKP witnessed a relatively successful hegemony building through a contingent alliance between different capital fractions in the power bloc, "which was very much dependent on maintaining rapid economic growth" (Özden *et al.*, 2017: 200). The GFC became an important moment of the transformation of the relations within the power bloc, which primarily manifested itself by the different positions of the capital fractions on the renewing of the IMF standby agreement in 2009. While the TUSIAD continuously called for signing a new precautionary IMF agreement regarding the narrowing export markets and the hot money outflows, the SMEs sought main support after the crisis in public expenditures with measures such as tax reductions and SSI premium amnesties (Sönmez, 2010: 73,78). For the latter, a stand-by agreement with the IMF would prevent such support, as it would include conditions such as the autonomisation of tax control and the reduction of public spending. Therefore, this fraction organised through different business associations largely lobbied against a new agreement with the IMF (ibid.). For managing the contradictory demands of these two fractions of capital, AKP kept the stand-by agreement with the IMF on the agenda in line with the demands of the big bourgeoisie and it delayed the agreement that would prevent from transferring resources to the capital fractions that form its

---

12   The project aimed to build an international finance centre in Istanbul bigger than the
      ones in New York, London and Dubai and make Istanbul the headquarter of the global
      finance alongside developing new capital market instruments to attract capital in the
      Global North and the Gulf-based investors and Islamic finance.

support base. Consequently, the government made a statement in 2009 that the IMF's demands, particularly the autonomy of the Revenue Administration and the termination of the resource transfer from the central government budget to the municipalities, blocked the progress of the negotiations (Oğuz, 2011: 3). The refusal of signing a new agreement with the IMF was followed by the AKP's adoption of a new hegemonic discourse emphasising 'the transforming crisis into an opportunity' (ibid.). Indeed, the QE in the ACCs and the restoration of capital inflows realised a new short-lived economic boom in 2010 and 2011, as shown above.

Nevertheless, as the main uniting element in the power bloc has been the continuation of the economic growth, the declining growth tempo particularly after 2013, when TL started to depreciate and the external debt of the private sector became harder to manage; it became much difficult to maintain a unified power bloc. It can be argued that the "weakening ability [of AKP] to represent the economic-corporate interests of all constituents of the power bloc" resulted in both an increasing distributive injustice among the dominant classes and "a systematized authoritarianism at the politico-ideological realm — both in the domestic arena and external relations" (Özden et al., 2017: 201; Hoşgör, 2015: 216). The former has manifested itself particularly in the increasing orientation of the government to invest in big public sector projects in the 2010s. At the financialised stage of capitalism, where almost everything is commodified, the social reproduction areas have increasingly opened up to private capital as new venues of accumulation that has been lucrative for all fractions of the bourgeoisie since the early 2000s. However, as clearly observed in some sectors such as construction, tourism, health, education and energy sectors, AKP governments have used the public projects as a resource transfer to certain fractions of capital in various forms of political/legal interventions such as selective granting of permits and licenses, tax incentives, subsidies, privatisation of natural monopolies, and the allocation of public bids and investments (Sönmez, 2011; 2015; Buğra and Savaşkan, 2012). The most evident area of the distributional injustice (and clientelistic networks) favouring the bourgeois fraction, which has organic ties to the political power, was the construction sector. Indeed, the construction sector was already a prominent area of favouritism for this segment via local governments in the 1990s. However, the 2000s witnessed the realisation of major public investments in the national scale and those bourgeois fractions became the main beneficiaries of the discretionary treatment in public tenders (Sönmez, 2011; Karatepe, 2013). On the one hand, "AKP's preferential treatment of some bourgeois sections" in the distribution of public tenders "led to a whole series of hegemonic dislocations in the power bloc" (Hoşgör, 2015: 127). On the other hand, this was accompanied with an authoritarian configuration of certain state institutions (as a strategic field for political manoeuvre) to enable "a privileged representative of a particular interest of the power bloc", as I will show in the case of TOKI (Poulantzas, 2008: 309). However, as I will also show in the case chapters, the privileged representation of some class fractions' economic interests on certain state institutions, via administrative centralisation in Turkish context as a clear indication of authoritarianism, is an outcome of the complex and multifaceted relations of the state with different bourgeois fractions as a reflection of the intensifying intra-class conflicts in the power bloc.

The fractional cleavages within the Turkish bourgeoisie in the AKP period have been a prominent issue for scholarly debates. However, as argued by Hoşgör (2015: 203), the current studies "are mostly concerned with cultural habitus, ideological engagement, and/or personal attributes of actors (groups or camps) in question". Although the ideological linkages between the government and the newly empowered capital fraction, referred to as Islamic/Anatolian capital, have been a non-negligible networking source in the development trajectory of the latter, the reduction of class fractions to merely ideological characteristics of capital groups creates a significant theoretical problem concerning "class-theoretical account of the power bloc [that offers] to explain multiple (and contradictory) power relationships" (ibid.).

The most commonly cited categorisation of different fractions of the capitalist class in Turkey is based on their membership to various business associations, particularly through TUSIAD, which represents namely the Istanbul-centred big capital groups as the early participants in the accumulation process, and MUSIAD, which represents namely Anatolian-based SMEs as late participants in the accumulation process. However, such fractional categorisation, which had an explanatory power to some extent during the 1980s and 1990s, does not reflect the structural dynamics of accumulation and the relations of class forces in the post-2002 era. This is because it is not possible to generalise the Islamic/conservative capital groups as they do not constitute "a homogenous mass" with regards to neither scale nor geographical locations of production, nor ideological positions (Öztürk, 2015: 120). As shown many scholars, there are several Islamic-influenced capital groups which can be considered as a part of the big bourgeoisie (Öztürk, 2015; Yeşilbağ, 2016). Similarly, the matching of the SMEs with Anatolian/Islamic capital (through MUSIAD) was already challenged by several scholars (Hoşgör, 2011; Bekmen, 2014; Öztürk, 2015; Buğra and Savaşkan, 2012). Based on this, going beyond a crude secular versus Islamic or Istanbul versus Anatolian bourgeoisie, I follow the differentiation of capital fractions as "first-generation bourgeoisie" which refers to the capital fraction being grown in the 1960s and 1970s during ISI, i.e., early participants in the accumulation process, and "second-generation bour-geoisie" which includes not only SMEs but also financialised large-scale capital groups as of late participants in the accumulation process (Bozkurt, 2013).

Although the big financialised business segment within the second-generation bourgeoisie became a politically dominant capital fraction in Turkey during the 2010s, a general shift in the hegemony from the first-generation bourgeoisie to the second-generation bourgeoisie in the power bloc is a highly contested issue and its examination exceeds the scope of this book. Rather, as shown in Chapter 8, the housing policies of the AKP government during the 2010s aimed to ensure capital accumulation for both factions of the bourgeoisie, through various measures such as lifting the legal barriers on the commodification of land and housing, the creation of effective demand via several legal regulations, keeping labour costs low thanks to the precedence of subcontracting/outsourcing in the housebuilding industry, albeit quite asymmetrically in the allocation of public resources and the distribution of monopoly rents.

Secondly, from a Poulantzasian perspective, in its relationships with different fractions of capital, the state is not an external guarantor of the conditions of capitalist reproduction, but a moment of the process of reproduction. That is to say, the state-form fully internalises the inter and intra-class relationships, antagonism and specific crisis dynamics. Hence, the permanent political crisis of the state in the post-GFC period arising from the increasing contradictions within the power bloc resulted in the further concentration of neoliberal authoritarianism in the state form in Turkey. In other words, the long-term impacts of the GFC in the power bloc "implied a shift in the predominant authoritarian technique from a rule-based/technocratic strategy to a more discretionary one, such as rule by presidential decrees, almost completely bypassing parliamentary mechanisms" (Bozkurt-Güngen, 2018: 229).

Moreover, this authoritarian consolidation process starting with the gradual replacement of the military tutelage with a police and judiciary-centred one continued with an unprecedented domination of the executive branch in the management of capitalist contradictions, through the widespread use of the presidential decrees initially and then the gradual introduction of a new authoritarian constitution legalising *de-facto* control of the executive on high judicial organs (Akça, 2014; Özden *et al.*, 2017; Yılmaz, 2020; Atikcan and Öge, 2012). Plus, the employment of an ever-increasing arbitrary exercise of the state's coercive and repressive power on popular masses, the "reorganization of political support on the basis of an antagonistic division of the nation" and the management of this antagonism through faithful employment of a financialised regime of social reproduction in that the political reflex of popular masses has been increasingly shaped under the burden (and disciplining power) of financial indebtedness, precarious working conditions in the labour market, the risk of unemployment and the economic uncertainty marked the 2010s (Hoşgör, 2015: 215).

Lastly, the authoritarian consolidation of the state in Turkey reached its peak with the transition from the parliamentary system to the presidential system in 2017 following the failed coup in Turkey. Although a *de facto* presidential system was already in force thanks to the personalisation of the authoritarian state form in Turkey via a strong leader, it can be argued that the failed coup created "an important opportunity ('the gift of God' in the words of President Erdoğan) to prepare the ground for the transition from parliamentarian to a plebiscitary presidential regime" not least via a long-standing state of emergency rule (Yılmaz, 2020: 269). The subsequent evolution of the political regime through near erosion of the separation of powers, excessive personalisation of the rule of law and over-centralisation of political power led the scholarly literature to discuss that the authoritarian form of the Turkish state evolved into an exceptional state form particularly after 2015 (Oğuz, 2016; Özden *et al.*, 2017; Yılmaz, 2020; Kaygusuz, 2018). However, a discussion of this exceeds the limits of the book. Rather this book confines itself with an examination of the reflections of the authoritarian state form in the housing SoP.

4   Conclusion

The historical overview in this chapter aimed to show the class fractions, the conflicts and alliances among classes and class fractions, and state restructuring during the first and second phases of neoliberalism and financialisation in Turkish case with the aim to understand the reflections of these relations in the housing SoP in the subsequent chapters. The chapter discussed that both the transition to neoliberalism and financialisation and the consolidation and institutionalisation of neoliberalism and financialisation in the post-2001 era was realised through an authoritarian state despite different qualifications in terms of both capital accumulation and functions of the state.

By adopting Poulantzas's theory of the capitalist state and his conceptual tools, I analysed the neoliberal transformation and financialisation in Turkey in that the authoritarian statism became the founding element in both Turkey's transition to neoliberalism in the 1980s and the deepening of the neoliberalism and financialisation in the 2000s. Hence the authoritarian statism becomes the key concept to understand the Turkish state's contemporary role in economic and social reproduction in general and housing in particular. Moreover, the changing balance of class forces in the power bloc and the consolidation of the authoritarian form of state in the face of declining growth tempo in the post-GFC led to hegemonic dislocations in the power bloc that was under-pinned the distributional injustice between the first and second-generation bourgeoisie, in that the latter had a privileged representation in certain state institutions, notably TOKI.

The chapter also discussed that the process starting with trade liberalisa-tion in the 1980s and continuing with the capital account liberalisation in the 1990s took a new form of a neoliberal-financialised system of accumulation in the post-2001 period. The system of accumulation based on the intensive expansion of IBC (based on the GDS trade) in the 1990s evolved into the finan-cialisation of economic and social reproduction in the post-2001 period. The most distinguishing features of the system of accumulation in this mature phase have been an expansion in consumer credits and increasing role of the household debt in the Turkish economy's growth strategy, increasing dollar-dominated indebtedness of the NFCs and increase in current account deficits. While this capital inflow-dependent and the debt-led system became the main pillars of the financialised system of accumulation in Turkey in the contem-porary era, they also became the sources of the vulnerability as showed in this chapter. The new mode of integration of Turkey with the international finan-cial system directly impacts the organisation of the housing SoP in Turkey in the 2000s and 2010s. The subsequent chapters will discuss these relations and processes based on the housing SoP in the 2000s.

CHAPTER 5

Housing Provision in Turkey — a Historical Overview

This chapter discusses the history of housing provision in the pre-AKP period in Turkey to provide a brief historical context to the current structure of the Turkish housing SoP and a background on Turkey's urbanisation, demographic changes, the emergence and transformation of the actors in housing and land markets and the changing modes of the Turkish state's intervention in the housing market, in line with the periodisation of capitalism and the class and capital formation. The timeframe of the analysis starts with the late 1950s to late 1970s, when the ISI strategies led to the rapid expansion of informal housing, a novel pattern in capital formation and a particular form of speculative housebuilding in Turkey. The second phase, from 1980 to 2001, was marked by a neoliberal shift in the housing SoP in Turkey in that not only the state capacity in housing was reorganised and a formal housing market was established for the first time but the different fractions of construction capital also manifested a renewed interest in housing. Based on this periodisation, this chapter presents the historical overview before the AKP era.

1   1950–1980: Housing SoP under ISI

Since the establishment of the Republic of Turkey in 1923, housing has become one of the most important problems in the country due to rapid population growth, fast and unplanned urbanisation, the absence of social housing and public rental accommodation, despite the implication of the state in the land market thanks to the high proportion of state-owned land inherited from the Ottoman Empire (Tekeli, 1998; Türel and Koç, 2015). The housing SoP in Turkey was founded on a dual market structure stemming from the co-existence of formal and informal housing systems without well-established property rights, like land-titling (Türk and Altes, 2010). The roots of this dual structure can be found in the post-war era, when Turkey adopted the ISI policies based on the increasing investments of productive-capital and the expansion of the domestic market. The millions of rural people migrating to the major industrial cities not only formed the urban proletarian masses but led to unprecedented

growth of the urban population[1] in Turkey. The outcome was an extreme housing deficit in the industrial centres (Keleş, 2006). As the state resources were
allocated to support the industrial bourgeoisie and the required infrastructural construction, the state ignored the working-class housing issue and left
it to the informal market preceding the 1980s. In this context, from the 1950s
onward, the overwhelming sheltering need was met by the squatter (gecekondu[2]) settlements primarily on idle land near new factories on the edges
of the industrial cities. As part of Turkey's specific land regime and ownership
structure, these idle land parcels mostly belonged to the state and municipalities (Keyder, 2005).

Two stages of the gecekondu development process can be identified. The
first stage took place in the early years of the ISI period which witnessed the
first-generation labour migration. These rural-origin migrants appropriated
land without the infrastructural facilities and built small single-storey gecekondu through the labour-power of family members and fellow villagers
(Buğra, 1998). This first stage of gecekondu development was an immediate
response to the sheltering needs of the migrant families. The state's allowance to these illegal settlements can be thought as indirect subsidisation of
the reproduction of labour-power, which benefited "industrial capital since it
meant that a labour force could be built up without these new workers making
'excessive' wage demands" (Gough and Gündoğdu, 2009: 17). Therefore, in the
absence of state-provided housing provision, gecekondu inhabitants became
de facto property owners; hence, a large informal land market appeared, characterised by illegal renting and selling activities (Öncü, 1988).

The second stage of gecekondu development from the subsequent amnesty
laws appeared in the mid-1960s through which gecekondu were granted with
property rights and, therefore, *de facto* property ownership status of these illegal structures turned into *de jure* titles (Buğra, 1998). Moreover, most of the
gecekondu started to receive infrastructure and services including electricity,
water, and transportation. Therefore, they "evolved into substantial serviced
suburbs" (Lovering and Türkmen, 2011: 76). In the post-war era, with the transition from the single-party system to the multi-party regime, the popular support of gecekondu dwellers became increasingly critical in local and national

---

1 "The post-war period had witnessed a dramatic change in demographic patterns, culminat-
   ing in an increase in the population from 20 million in 1950 to 48 million in 1980 [and] the
   urban population increased from 30% of the total in 1960 to 37% in 1970 and 45% in 1980."
   (Keyder, 1987: 153).
2 Gecekondu means "placed/built overnight" in Turkish referring to illegal land seizures and
   settlements.

politics. The state's implicit support for gecekondu in the form of populist distribution policies in this context signified not only the need for cheap labour
force for the accelerating industrialisation in the country but also the search
for the legitimisation of the economic functions of the state which is articu-
lated with the political and ideological role, including electoral success and
social cohesion (Boratav, 2003).

In the second phase of the gecekondu development from the early 1970s,
"gecekondu brokers and speculators, informal yet organised interest groups in
the gecekondu market" occurred (Erman, 1997: 93). Land speculators and some
of the early gecekondu owners got involved in the land subdivision process
in that they either sold these invaded parcels to new-comers or built as many
gecekondu[3] as they can and started to rent them to the continuously increasing rural immigrants (Tekeli, 1982). Consequently, two new tenure forms
emerged including owner-occupation and private rental from squatted land.
This was the replacement of the solidarity network among the countrymen
fellows with the commercialised practices and widening inequality between
gecekondu dwellers (Gough and Gündoğdu, 2009). Therefore, while some of
the early-comers got rental returns by leasing their newly titled gecekondu
to new rural immigrants, gecekondu speculators bought peripheral land or
invaded new public land parcels with the hope of future legalisation of their
ownership rights and turned to slumlords (Yönder, 1987; Işık and Pınarcıoğlu,
2001). Therefore, the new and bigger wave of immigrants[4] arriving after the
mid-1970s had to pay huge amount of rents[5] for their gecekondu which had
been built on the already-invaded or purchased peripheral land (Erman, 1997;
Öncü, 1988).

Moreover, this second phase was important for the emergence of small capitalist housebuilders (yapsatçı[6]) and a new organisational form of housing SoP
based on a coalition between yapsatçıs and gecekondu owners, thanks to the
enactment of the Condominium Ownership law in 1965. The law permitted

---

3   They were still illegal, having titles but no construction permits.
4   "In the first half of the 1960s 59% of the population in Ankara, 45% in Istanbul and 33% in
    Izmir lived in irregular settlements. In the 1980s, these percentages were, respectively, 55%,
    70% and 50%" (Buğra, 1998: 307).
5   Because "tenancy agreements were informal, not based on formal contracts ... this informal-
    ity also made renters more vulnerable to evictions" (Yönder 1987: 218). According to the State
    Planning Organisation report (1991: 108), the percentage of the private tenants within total
    gecekondu population was 32.67% for Istanbul, 28.50% for Ankara and 27.70% for Izmir.
6   Literally, *yapsatçı* means 'build-and-sell' in Turkish. They are traditional housebuilders in
    Turkey that refer to small-scale, local-based, one-man construction firms having informal
    relations with slumlords and local authorities that helped them to skip construction permits.

joint ownership on land and built structures, such as apartment-flat-ownership with separate title deeds and facilitated the replacement of single-storey gecekondu houses, mostly in more central areas, with multi-storey apartment blocks and correspondingly created a speculative urban land market (Erman, 1997; Öncü, 1988; Türkün, 2014). In this process, yapsatçıs, which is a form of speculative housebuilding in the Turkish context, became the main agents not only for the commercialised gecekondu but also for the formal housing market serving a large section of the middle-class.[7]

Yapsatçıs had two methods of production including buying land and receiving an agreed share of the completed housing units. The first method included single-storey gecekondu from the newly-titled landowners which were replaced with multi-storey apartments and sold the housing units in the market. In the second method, the land-for-flat agreement had one flat for the landowner and 4 flats for the builder if the agreement is 20%, for instance. In this land-for-flat method, which is an equity-sharing agreement, yapsatçıs did not pay for land in advance, instead delivered the agreed number of flats to the landowner and extracted development gain by selling the rest of the flats in the market. In this model, the ground rent is not appropriated directly by the landowner but realised after the sale of the new housing units in the market similar to the capitalist builders and the amount of capital gain of the landowner depends on the bargaining between yapsatçıs and landowner at the beginning of the project. Prior the 1980s, the overwhelming majority of the yapsatçı production happened through the equity-sharing model since the hoards and savings of these small local-based capitalist builders were not sufficient enough to purchase land and they did not prefer to use commercial credits (possibly due to the high interest rates) (Öncü, 1988). The rapid turnover of the housing units was crucial for yapsatçıs as the development gain of the finished apartment block was used for the building costs of the next equity-sharing project.

To summarise, the housing SoP in pre-1980s was based on the gecekondu development and yapsatçı model that first emerged as a quick response to fast and unplanned urbanisation and labour migration but later evolved into a redistributive state policy for the organised working-class movement, supported with the legislative regulations and infrastructural services in the absence of alternative forms of housing provision (Keleş, 1990; Aslan, 2004). Starting with the 1970s, this redistributive strategy of the state resulted in the

---

7 "The possibility of joint-ownership in apartment blocks made high-rise residential developments the typical pattern of middle-class expansion in the 1960s and 1970s" (Öncü, 1988: 50).

commercialisation of gecekondu, the emergence of new housing submarkets and the rise of ground rent which was appropriated by landlords and yapsatçıs thanks to the expansion of cities' borders and the provision of infrastructure and services to the previously idle land. In the case of the apartment blocks built by yapsatçıs, the target population was the expanding middle-classes. Although yapsatçı firms were not the only construction firms in this period, the middle-scale or large technologically-advanced construction firms, some of which were the subsidiaries of big conglomerates, did not prefer to enter the housing sector due to the informal networks and the lack of well-established property rights in the land market. Other reasons include "the absence of large housing projects supported by the state or local government", the exclusion of the housebuilding industry from the state-provided concessionary credits, which were the loans given to priority sectors [notably manufacturing] with preferential interest rates, and how lucrative is the "state financed public works investments such as cement mills, irrigation projects, dams, power plants" (Öncu, 1988: 52–53).

Other attempts of the state to regulate, formalise and subsidise the housing market in the ISI era, even though relatively negligible, included housing cooperatives, which are non-profit private entities, were established for providing the owner-occupied dwellings for their members[8] and they were supported by local governments through provision of land at below-market value and public loans at below-market interest rate (Türel and Koç, 2015; Erol 2019a). However, prior to the 1980s, housing provision by cooperatives remained limited to the upper-middle classes since the formal employment with regular income was necessary for the membership in a cooperative (Türk and Altes, 2010). Secondly, two institutional housing finance institutions, namely the Emlak Bank and the Social Insurance Fund (SIF), were established to provide housing loans when commercial banks could not legally provide housing loans since the commercial credits were allocated to industrial capital (Baharoğlu, 1996). Emlak Bank provided housing loans at a highly privileged rate to civil servants who had state guaranteed salaries, financed house production and involved in housebuilding directly or via joint ventures, albeit at a negligible share within the total residential production (Erol and Patel, 2004). The SIF, operating between 1950 and 1984, awarded credits to workers who had been covered by social security and to cooperatives for housing production at a 4–5% fixed annual

---

8 In the Turkish housing cooperative system, cooperative members come together to buy a piece of land and then make an agreement with a contractor for the building work. The members "acquire dwellings in freehold ownership status after construction is finished, and then the cooperative is dissolved" (Bedirhanoğlu et al., 2013: 306).

interest rate and, consequently, funded the construction of 233,000 housing units during these years (Türel and Koç, 2015). However, state-provided housing construction, including subsidised cooperatives, through Emlak Bank and SIF constituted less than 10% of the total dwellings produced in the formal housing market (ibid.). In the context of such a limited formal housing finance system serving only a tiny part of the upper-middle classes, the widespread method of house purchase was "using existing assets and inheritance-savings" (Sarıoglu-Erdogdu, 2014: 159). Therefore, prior to the 1980s, while affordable housing was limited to the upper middle-class, the dominant forms of housing SoP became gecekondu and yapsatçı apartments, both supported by the state regulations.

2   1980–2001: Housing SoP in the Early Phase of Neoliberalism

In the 1980s, the country's increasingly continuing labour migration intensified the issue of the urban housing need.[9] Moreover, the housing SoP in Turkey suffered significant transformation in line with the neoliberal transformation of the country, the first phase of the authoritarian neoliberal restructuring of the state and the reorganisation of state-market relationship. As argued, Turkey's transition to neoliberalism began with the coup d'état of 1980 and further intensified during the ANAP government. The authoritarian measures taken by the military junta and later by civilian governments were vital in both ending the labour militancy and socialist movements and implementing the structural adjustment programme which would establish EOI and the new model of the global integration of the economy. Correspondingly, this early phase was significant for the establishment of the neoliberal principles in housing SoP, including the commercialisation of land and housing, the formation of a capitalist housing market and the foundation of legal and institutional basis of these policies.

At a closer look, it is possible to observe the increasing role of the state in housing SoP, starting with the military government through the first Mass Housing Law (No. 2487) implemented in 1981. Through this law, the military junta aimed at regulating and formalising the housing sector and subsidising the production of affordable mass houses for low and middle-income households since the housing problem had become an urgent issue at the turn of

---

9 The share of urban population within total population increased from 25% in 1950 to 43.9% in 1980, 59% in 1990 and 64.9% in 2000 (TurkStat).

the decade. A public fund, the Mass Housing Fund (MHF), was constituted to provide cheap loans for affordable housing production at the national level. According to the law, 80% of the fund would be allocated to beneficiaries that had no house and within the limit of 100 m² gross area[10] (Baharoğlu, 1996). Although the target was low and middle-income homeownership via a formal market, the loans would be accessible only to middle and high-income households because the obligatory down payments could not be covered by the urban poor and "the recommended minimum monthly income for participation in 1981 was TL59,000 (about US$600), which exceeded the salary of many civil servants" (ibid., 50). On the supply side, the mass housing institutions which would benefit from the MHF were determined as housing cooperatives, cooperative unions and social security organisations while in practice, small amounts of credit were given to some cooperatives (Türel, 2015). This law, which remained in force only for two years, failed for three reasons. Firstly, although the law required the allocation of at least 5% of the national expenditure budget for the housing finance, this promised amount was not received by the MHF and the rest remained far behind the demand. Secondly, the law had contradictions regarding the beneficiaries. Lastly, as the law did not include private construction firms for mass housing production, it received reactions from all fractions of capital, including large scale building firms and yapsatçıs. For instance, the dissatisfaction of Turkish builders with the law was organised and expressed by the Construction Sector Investors Organisation, which incorporated most firms in the sector at that time (Öymen, 1985).

Therefore, both the builders and their spokesmen constantly called for a comprehensive approach to the housing sector which paved the way for the new Mass Housing Law (No. 2985) in 1984 by the first civilian government after the military regime, namely ANAP (1983–1988). Hence, a new MHF was created and in the same year, TOKI was established (Law No. 2983). The law charged TOKI with supporting the fulfilment of the housing need and encouraging urban housing production, managing the MHF and providing cheap loans to both house-purchasers and builders to support housebuilding industry, taking promotive measures for the participation of banks to housing finance and, therefore, developing the housing finance system. Here, although the political-economic programme of ANAP under the leadership of Özal was based on the rigorous implementation of the structural adjustment policies and maintenance of the neoliberal principles, the ANAP government brought a more

---

10   The law defined the low-cost houses that are smaller than 100 m² as social housing (TOKI, 2011: 40).

comprehensive and sector-focused approach to housing policies. Firstly, ANAP aimed at developing a capitalist housing market based on formal tenure system, tradable property rights, technological development in building industry and large-scale housing production in which TOKI was the main instrument. Therefore, in the mid-1980s, the Mass Housing Law and TOKI represented a centralised state institution which would primarily subsidise house-purchase and private housing production and create effective demand in urban land (Işık, 1991). Secondly, TOKI was attached to the Prime Ministry, and hence directly accountable to the prime minister's office, which triggers the elimination of the intermediary ministries following "the idea of reforming the public bureaucracy, diminishing the extensive entanglements of the state in the economy, and making the state apparatus smaller but more efficient" (Kalaycıoğlu, 2002: 46). Here, the specialisation and centralisation of the decision-making process through the increasing power of the executive organ has been important for the implementation of neoliberal policies in Turkey not only in the 1980s but in the 2000s. Accordingly, TOKI was established as the main agency of the intervention of the state into the housing sector, thanks to its institutional arrangement reflecting the strong executive power. Consequently, the relative autonomy of TOKI as a crystallisation of the increasing importance of housing (as a sector more than a shelter) indicated the changing form of the state's intervention to housing in the early phase of neoliberalism. Notably, its extra-budgetary funds (MHF) not only enabled TOKI to operate fast but made it autonomous "from the parliament-controlled consolidated budget, allowing the government to disburse these funds without parliamentary authorization" (Buğra and Savaşkan, 2014: 51). This meant the strengthening of the executive and the authoritarian structuring of the state but also made TOKI biggest housing finance institution of the 1980s.

Firstly, MHF was independent of the general budget and comprised tax revenues applied to the consumption of several imported goods and services equipped with the qualifications of a national mortgage bank under the management of TOKI.[11] Secondly, TOKI operated through "its three loan originator banks from the mid-1980s to the 1990s" that were Emlak Bank, Vakıf Bank (state-owned banks) and Pamuk Bank (a private commercial bank) (Erol, 2019a: 251). In other words, the tax incomes of MHF were lent by the banking system to both house producers and purchasers. In the case of housing development finance, the beneficiaries were housing co-operatives, co-operative

---

[11]   MHF and TOKI would be used identically in this section as they worked as twin institutions (Topal *et al.*, 2015).

associations, joint venture construction businesses and private housebuilding firms involved in mass housing projects, which were "directly reimbursed in full by the MHF upon completion of building" (Keyder and Öncü, 1994: 410). The financial support to private builders was the most important novelty in this period since cheap credits in the form of "implicit interest rate subsidies" were their long-expected aspiration from the state (Bedirhanoğlu *et al.*, 2013: 308). Thereupon, more than 500,000 dwellings "that were financed by TOKI [from 1984 to the mid-1990s] enjoyed substantial amounts of unintended interest subsidies" (Erol, 2019a: 251). This way, the share of the real estate credits within the total private housing investments increased from 12% in 1983 to 32% in 1986 (Türel, 2015).

Similarly, on the demand side, TOKI's support to households consisted of implicit interest rate subsidies[12] during 1984–1989. In this system, 10 to 40% of the cost of the dwelling unit was drawn as a down-payment and the rest of the household debt was paid as monthly instalments with long maturities (75–240 months) (Akın, 2008: 10). Consequently, TOKI funded over 250,000 long-term mortgage loans through the banks from 1984 to the mid-1990s (Erol, 2019a: 250). Moreover, the MHF loan criteria were changed so that no income level was determined for beneficiaries, the former 100 m^2 gross area limit was replaced with 150 m^2 per unit and the condition of no-previous home-ownership was removed (Topal *et al.*, 2015: 26). Therefore, as it can be seen from these new regulations, the ones enjoying the demand-side financial incentives of the state in this period became the middle and upper-income households, "the so-called fixed income groups-mainly employees or retired personnel of assorted bureaucracies and state enterprises" living in the biggest cities of Turkey (Keyder and Öncü, 1994: 404).

While TOKI promoted the private capital investment in housebuilding industry and the increase in effective demand, which contributed to a construction boom lasting until the end of the 1980s,[13] the housing shortage which affected low and middle-income households increased during this period (ibid.). This led TOKI to produce affordable houses on public land for these groups, albeit at a negligibly small amount of 0.6% within total housing construction between 1984 and 2002 (see Figure 31).

---

12   "Fixed mortgage interest rates were set at 15, 20, and 25%, depending on the size of the dwelling unit, while inflation rates varied between 29 and 69%" (Türel and Koç, 2015: 57).

13   Between 1982 and 1988, construction activities composed 7% of total GDP. While public investments focused on infrastructural production, the housebuilding was completely left to the private sector and cooperatives. 58% of the total residential stock in 2001 was completed between 1980 and 2000 (Balaban, 2008: 105).

While the ANAP government centralised the housing policies and the housing finance system through TOKI, land development and planning system was
decentralised through the increasing power of local governments. The municipalities taken over by ANAP as the result of the 1984 local elections became
influential in the empowerment of local governments (Boratav, 2003: 169).
These were financially supported by an increase in their share of tax revenues
(Keyder and Öncü, 1994). Secondly, a two tier-system formed by the greater city
municipalities and district-level municipalities was established in three biggest cities of Turkey (Istanbul, Ankara, Izmir). This was "designed to centralize
major metropolis-wide functions and place them under direct authority of the
metropolitan mayor" (ibid., 404). While the greater city municipalities were
charged with the metropolitan-level planning and cadastral work, the district
municipalities did the same for their territories. The increasing financial and
command powers of municipalities paved the way for the use of high-quality
agricultural and forestry land (in the favourable locations of metropolitan
peripheries) for commercial and residential development and, established
the legal and institutional basis for the provision of infrastructural services
for these new settlement areas by using public funds (Purkis, 2014; Gough and
Gündoğdu, 2009). Therefore, the central government and municipalities had
a more active ('enabling' in the WB terminology) role in the housing and land
markets and, for the first time, the Turkish state implicitly and legally facilitated land development for speculative aims.

There were three housing producers in this period. First, housing cooperatives became the most important housing suppliers in the early neoliberal
era as they were the main beneficiaries of the TOKI funds with almost 90%
of TOKI funds given to the cooperatives in 1984–2005 (Türel, 2015). These
incentives triggered the establishment of many housing cooperatives[14] from
the mid-1980s to the late 1990s. Although cooperatives were initially formulated as non-profit social housing organisations, they rapidly turned to the primary channel for homeownership of the urban middle classes in this period.
There were two groups organising housing cooperatives. The first one was
occupational groups such as teachers, doctors, policemen, civil servants, and
bank employers (Buğra, 1998) and the second one was the private developer
firms which were organised as cooperatives to take advantage of the above-
mentioned incentives lacking the control[15] of the state. Therefore, the share

---

14   "While 140 housing co-operatives were established yearly prior to the Law [MHF in 1984],
      2700 housing cooperatives have been established yearly since" (Türk and Altes, 2010: 28).
15   "63.4% of the cooperatives were not controlled by officials" in this period (Özdemir,
      2010: 1103).

of housing production by cooperatives within total production increased from 7.41% in 1980 to 30% in 1988 and continued around 20% annually until 2000 (Figure 31).

Secondly, the dominant housing producers of the pre-1980s were still active but since the interest groups chasing ground rent appropriation varied in this period, the only space left for their operation was the conversion of gecekondu to multi-storey apartments through equity-sharing agreements. In the 1980s, however, it was still "only a small proportion of [people living in gecekondu] had received full title to their land" but rather most of them were paying rent for their gecekondu (Yönder, 1987: 215). Also, a more "systematic legal basis for 'ownership' of gecekondu land" was established by the ANAP government with new amnesty laws which enabled land-titling and the conversion of gece-kondu to legal apartment blocks were put into action (Atasoy, 2016: 11).

There were two political and economic motivations behind this law, which legally enabled yapsatçıs and squatters to share the resultant ground rent. Firstly, the articulation of the squatters to the formal housing market was sig-nificant as gecekondu were seen as the core for labour militancy and social-ist movements and the formal homeownership was expected to hamper the radicalisation of the urban poor (Boratav, 2003). Besides, the defeat of the organised labour-power and the subsequent structural adjustment policies rigorously implemented by the ANAP government which declined real wages and increased unemployment contribute to the legalisation of rent appropri-ation by the squatters (ibid.). However, when considering that "one third of the households in gecekondu dwellings were renters", policy strengthened the commercialisation trend rather than solving the sheltering problem of the urban poor[16] (Pamuk, 1996: 108).

Moreover, the development gains of yapsatçıs started to decrease at the end of 1970s because "the supply of serviced land near or in the city centres [had] been depleted" and the landowners, who had such quality land, claimed greater returns (up to 50%) (Öncü, 1988: 54). Plus, yapsatçıs had neither sufficient capital nor technological development to compete with the cooperatives and large-scale constructors. In this context, their increasing pressures on the state can be considered as another reason for the amnesty laws enacted by ANAP government. Also, the 1980s witnessed the move of the large construction cap-ital into the housebuilding sector for the first time. With "the drop in the vol-ume of work in the Middle East" notably due to the decrease in oil prices in the

---

16   By 1996, nearly half of the total urban population lived in *gecekondu* settlements (Baharoğlu and Leitman, 1998: 116).

1980s, they started to "become interested in expanding their local operations" (ibid., 53). This is why the establishment of TOKI which would facilitate mass housing projects and increase housing demand by providing cheap loans to the middle and upper-middle classes was crucial. Therefore, the ANAP government prepared the legal and institutional basis for making the housing market a lucrative investment space for them. TOKI credits were given for the ones who would undertake mass housing projects and large-scale house-producers established housing cooperatives to benefit from the tax exemptions and land allocations at below-market prices by the local governments. Besides, local governments carried infrastructural services to the land parcels which were purchased by the companies (Purkis, 2014). Consequently, the 1980s witnessed not only increasing volume of housing productions by the large-scale producers but also the conversion of the giant constructors to holding companies by owning (or purchasing assets from) banks (Gültekin-Karakaş, 2009).

Contrasting to the 1980s' strong authoritarian governments, the successive weak coalition governments had to deal with the political and economic turmoil during the 1990s. As discussed in chapter 4, the process of the liberalisation of the financial system and banking sector was completed by the full liberalisation of capital account and the activation of the Istanbul stock exchange market in 1989 (Ergüneş, 2009). Although high inflation was a continuous problem in Turkey since the 1970s, coupled with the devaluation of TL, it became a chronic problem since the 1990s. Specifically, the fiscal situation of the public sector continuously deteriorated and the public funds used to support the private sector gradually decreased. Hence, TOKI loans were indexed to the semi-annual salary increases in the public sector in 1989 which led to a serious decrease in the implicit interest rate subsidy for TOKI-provided loans since the mortgage credits increasingly lost value against high inflation (Erol, 2019a). Also, with a new budget law in 1988 and 1989, 30% of the MHF revenues were transferred to the government's national budget and then this rate rose to 50% in 1990 and finally all revenues of TOKI were allocated to the state budget in 1993 (Türel, 2015). Henceforth, TOKI developed new methods to solve its financial bottleneck, which became the first financialisation experience in housing. Right after the capital account liberalisation and capital market regulations in 1989, TOKI developed housing certificates to raise funds from capital markets. The housing certificates were debt securities corresponding to one square meter of a dwelling in mass housing projects; in this model, TOKI would sell these certificates whose prices would be determined monthly by TOKI according to construction costs and market conditions. However, this model remained limited with one project, Halkalı-Istanbul Mass Housings built by TOKI in 1989 and the capital gains through the issuance of the securities were transferred to MHF (Coşkun, 2015). With these housing certificates, TOKI aimed at mobilising the household savings through capital markets and make these "small-savers" homeowners in the long run; but the macro-economic atmosphere of the 1990s which not only suppressed demand but also led the capital gains from the certificates to fall below inflation rates (ibid., 216).

Similarly, the land certificates put into practice in 1989 were sold to 6,436 people (18,930 certificates in total) initially by the Land Office and later by TOKI, until 2007. However, this program failed due to pressure from land speculators and a lack of interest of the public whose savings declined in the 1990s (Pakdemirli, 2006, as cited in Coşkun, 2015). Consequently, the prices of sold certificates were paid back to the beneficiaries. Following the failure of the housing and land certificates, another attempt was made through the development of real estate certificates by the state-owned Emlak Bank which were issued within the bond market as part of the Istanbul Stock Exchange in 1996. However, the initiative was limited to one project, namely the 380 dwellings in Ataköy-Istanbul built by Emlak Bank in 1995. Hence, following the unsuccessful attempts of TOKI for raising housing funds from the capital markets under the successive crises of the second half of the 1990s, TOKI turned to an almost idle institution, contrary to the 1980s' monopoly housing financier and, in 2001 with the abolishment of the MHF, TOKI was transferred to the national budget again, which was already impacted by the 2000–2001 crisis.

Although during the 1990s commercial banks were allowed to give mortgages for the first time, they only gave housing loans for highest-income groups, in a very small percentage within their asset portfolios (Coşkun, 2016). The most active ones became the state-owned banks (Emlak Bank and Vakıf Bank) that gave fully amortised mortgages with maximum 5 years maturities and 50 to 80% loan-to-value ratios, in contrast to TOKI mortgages which had 15-year maturity (ibid., 404). However, since Emlak Bank's housing loans were Deutsche Mark-denominated, with the devaluation of TL against foreign currencies and soaring mortgage defaults, Emlak Bank stopped its mortgage lending activities in 1995 and later in 1998 the bank began to give wage-indexed payment mortgages, "specifically designed for the high inflationary environment" (Erol and Patel, 2004: 275). Finally, within the context of the successive economic crises in 1994, 1999 and 2001 in Turkey, a significant part of the banks went bankrupt.

Regarding the construction companies, the 1990s witnessed significant transformations in the capital accumulation strategies of large construction capital in that a fierce competition started for owning banks directly or via foreign partners (Gültekin-Karakaş, 2009; Tanyılmaz, 2015). Therefore, during the 1990s, construction companies substantially decreased housing production and developed four new strategies to survive, namely expanding their construction activities to the international market,[17] merging with foreign construction firms, increasing their activities in other sectors of domestic markets, particularly other fields of the constructions sector apart from housing industry and in the banking sector,[18] acquiring the bankrupt construction companies (Batmaz *et al.*, 2006; Şengül, 2012; Öztürk, 2010; Purkis, 2014). Therefore, it is not coincidental that the large construction companies which achieved to stand against the subsequent crises of the 1990s became the financialised ones[19] in the 2000s.

To sum up, the stimulation of the housing sector as a newly-discovered field of capital accumulation, throughout the 1980s, thanks to the ANAP government's specific housing policies, resulted in the high growth of the housebuilding sector. Moreover, with the neoliberal turn in 1980, the big metropolitan cities, not least Istanbul, started the de-industrialisation and redesign into a hub of global trade and finance, accompanied by the replacement of the industrial areas with skyscrapers, commercial buildings and luxury residential vicinities (Türkün, 2011; Şengül, 2003). With the changing macroeconomic and political atmosphere of the 1990s, this positive environment was reversed and the large construction capitalist followed new capital accumulation strategies outside the housing production. However, the biggest blow to the sector came with the 1999 earthquake, due to which hundreds of buildings were demolished and a great number of people died, and following the 2000–2001 financial crisis. Notably, the earthquake caused people to lose their trust to the constructors since the earthquake reports put forward the fact that low-quality construction materials (such as cement and steel) had been used in the production of most of the buildings in Turkey. Consequently, although the early neoliberal era represented the first attempt to formalise housing SoP in general, housing finance in particular, it was only achieved in the 2000s under the AKP governments.

---

17   In addition to the MENA region, they also moved to new countries, primarily to Russia. According to Batmaz *et al.* (2006: 215), when they were operating in 16 countries in 1980, the number of countries rose to 63 in 2000.

18   Capital gains from the GDS trade were largely invested into construction projects in Russia following the dissolution of the USSR. Usually, Turkey-based construction companies and Western partners (e.g. Enka-Bechtel partnership) were involved in these projects. Thanks to projects in the Russian market, as of 1995, Turkish construction companies already captured 10% of the construction industry in the world market (Öztürk, 2010).

19   Some of them are Enka, Sabancı, Akkök, Çukurova, Uzanlar, Toprak, Zorlu, Calik, Ihlas (Öztürk, 2010: 139).

3   Conclusion

This chapter provided a historical background of the housing provision in Turkey regarding the periodisation of capitalism and the changing form of state capacity in housing. In this respect, two periods were defined as the co-existence of formal and informal housing and the land regime in the ISI period and the formalisation of the housing SoP in the early neoliberal era. The post-war era under the first wave of urbanisation and industrialisation in Turkey was marked by an overwhelming sheltering need of the working classes, the lack of a formal state policy to housing problem, the formation of gecekondu and the dominance of the yapsatçıs as a peculiar and early form of speculative housebuilding in Turkey. The second period between 1980 and 2001 witnessed the establishment of a formal housing market through the foundation of TOKI, the entrance of large capital groups into housing for the first time, the urban expansion through mass housing complexes, the commercialisation of gece-kondu and the concentration of the gecekondu-yapsatçı model and ultimately the decline in housing production and effective demand following the fiscal crisis of TOKI in the 1990s.

Although the early neoliberal period witnessed the establishment of a for-mal housing market thanks to TOKI and a few state-owned banks, under the high inflationary and crisis-ridden economic environment of the 1990s, com-mercial banks were not willing to direct their attention to the housing market, nor secondary mortgage markets developed in Turkey. Therefore, apart from the deregulation of the financial system including the allowance of commer-cial banks to give housing loans, and the state's efforts to increase effective demand and mobilise households' savings through MHF, the housing system was not financialised in the narrow sense during the 1990s, except for very lim-ited activity of TOKI and Emlak Bank of raising fund from the capital market through certificate-issuance. Nevertheless, this period became the foundation years of the neoliberal principles in housing in Turkey.

CHAPTER 6

State in Housing Provision

Having presented a historical overview of the housing provision in the pre-AKP period in Turkey, this chapter turns to the analysis of the housing SoP in the post-2002 period. This chapter, as the first one of the empirical chapters, explores the role of the state in housing SoP in the AKP period by focusing on TOKI. The analysis of the state's intervention into land and housing is not limited to this chapter but continues in the subsequent chapters, analysing production and consumption of the housing SoP in the post-2002 period. Although the role of the state in the provision system is not restricted to TOKI, and other state institutions such as state-owned banks, Central Bank, and different levels of local government are also important in the formation of the housing SoP in the 2000s, TOKI has been the main apparatus in land and housing markets in the AKP era and, therefore, the focus of this chapter.

1   TOKI as a Particular Articulation of Political and Economic Intervention

After coming into power in 2002, AKP rigorously implemented the IMF-devised post-crisis recovery programme (TSEP) until the GFC. In line with TSEP, Erdoğan also announced the government's one-year Emergency Action Plan (EAP) in a press conference after they came into power, which outlined the primary sectors[1] to restructure to overcome the 2001 crisis by increasing free-market competition and efficiency via tax reforms, privatisations, PPPs and other new governance mechanisms, in line with the suggestions of IMF (DPT, 2003). In the EAP, there was a special section called 'Housing Mobilisation' in which the primary target of the government was determined as rehabilitating gecekondu and solving the housing problem via a comprehensive mass housing program, a five-year goal of 250,000 housing units to be built by the end of 2007, which was implemented in 2003 (ibid.).

Although 'Housing Mobilisation' was presented as a welfare program, there were three aims behind the plan: i) restructuring of the state in the housing

---

[1]   Housing, energy, mining, tourism, health and infrastructure sectors were mentioned in the declaration.

sphere as a self-financing agency, as part of the ambitious fiscal discipline measures of the structural reform package; ii) facilitating the capital accumulation by opening up housing as a new attractive space for private capital; and iii) legitimating the commodification of land and housing for popular masses by employing a debt-based affordable housing program. Hence, during the years following the announced housing mobilisation, the institutional, organisational and financial structure of TOKI was radically restructured. Its authorisation was strikingly enlarged via tens of laws and statutory decrees and, consequently, it became a unique institution with the full power in land and housing markets. Although TOKI had been empowered before for a short period during the second half of the 1980s under ANAP governments, the power, the authority and the political and economic role of TOKI in the 2000s are different from that of the 1980s. Its economic and political tasks were restructured in accord with both the changing balance of class forces and the new mode of the social and economic reproduction.

TOKI, as the main state institution in the urban and housing sphere, was restructured in line with the consolidation of neoliberalism, in which not only economic reproduction but also social reproduction has been financialised. Also, as shown below, TOKI not only became a facilitator of the financialisation of land and housing in the post-2002 era but also became a subject of financialisation itself. Moreover, although TOKI became the key institution in the privileged representation of the second-generation bourgeoisie in the power bloc thanks to the government's use of the housing sector as a favourable terrain for the political manoeuvre, TOKI's role in land and housing cannot be reduced to the preferential treatment of the newly-empowered fraction of the bourgeoisie. As discussed in this chapter and more broadly in Chapter 8, TOKI was crucial in expanding the capitalist relations in the housing sector, creating lucrative spaces for the flow of private capital for all fractions to the built environment and aiding the organisation of the production and consumption of housing around the appropriation of monopoly rents thanks to its massive authorisation in planning, land development, slum renewal and urban transformation. Apart from promoting economic reproduction in housing by leading the private sector to enter to the previously-unattractive spaces, being a pioneer in the financial innovations in the sector, and extending private property rights, it had a crucial role in legitimising the unprecedented commodification and privatisation of public commons by partially ensuring the social reproduction of labour-power, either via subsidised credits for owner-occupied affordable houses or creating a huge employment opportunity in the construction sector (see below).

Moreover, TOKI's concentrated and renewed economic role equipped the Administration with private enterprise qualifications through which it becomes both "a catalyst for the private sector" and an accumulator of fiscal revenue thanks to its operational mode in the form of PPPs (Atasoy, 2016: 671). Also, the increasing intra-class struggles in the power bloc, particularly between the early participants and late participants to the accumulation process, and the growing contradictions between the accumulation and legitimising functions of the state in the housing SoP made TOKI to organise in a new mode of authoritarian administration (Chapter 8). Hence, TOKI became a sign of the contemporary form of the authoritarian statism, thanks to its restructuring as the main representative of the strong executive power in land and housing markets.

At a closer look, the process of the reorganisation of TOKI encompassed the rearrangement of TOKI's place in the administrative hierarchy. Although it was temporarily affiliated to the Ministry of Public Works and Settlement in 2003, in 2004 TOKI was directly tied to the Prime Ministry Office[2] with a presidential decree (No. 25348). This made it "a political institution" in the words of TOKI's director (interview III) since its targets have been directly determined by Erdoğan and it became a strategic field for political manoeuvre of the government. According to the top-level bureaucrat in TOKI, the Administration's direct attachment to the Prime Ministry enabled Erdoğan to "transform a rather idle institution [of the 1990s] to a machine thanks to the fact that TOKI and the construction sector have been the main project in Erdoğan's mind ever since he was the mayor of Istanbul" (interview III). Moreover, with the same presidential decree in 2004, TOKI was exempted from the control of the Exchequer and the Audit Department and became an unaccountable state agency reporting directly and only to the PM. The top-down administrative restructuring of TOKI, as part of the executive centralisation, "enabled the projects to proceed very rapidly without the intervention of bureaucrats, ministers etc. with a direct approval of the PM" (interview III).

However, such relative autonomy placed the institution at the centre of clientelism and corruption allegations (Gürek, 2008; Çavuşoğlu, 2013; Sönmez, 2012). Indeed, the non-transparency of TOKI contradicted with the IMF

2 Later on, due to the transition from the parliamentary system to the presidential government system and the election of Erdoğan as the President of Turkey in 2018, TOKI was attached to the Ministry of Environment and Urban Planning (Decree No. 703, 2018). The Ministry has been already working like TOKI's subsidiary before this change in 2018 as it was also mentioned by the interviewee from TOKI "we are the institutions of the same party; so we are together actually" (interview IV).

conditionality regarding the public sector restructuring of TSEP in the early 2000s. Nevertheless, TOKI strongly adhered to the neoliberal principles and become the main mechanism of deepening capitalist relations in the housing SoP in Turkey. Moreover, this book considers clientelism between the state and certain fractions of bourgeois as inherent to the modern capitalist state, although grounded historically, but not being an abnormality, since "the state is a system of political domination rather than a neutral instrument, and state power is a complex social relation that reflects the changing balance of social forces in a determinate conjuncture" (Jessop, 1978: 11). Based on this, TOKI represents a specific modality of changing state-capital relations in the 2000s and the particular institutional form these relations give rise to, as the representative of the contemporary form of the authoritarian state in housing SoP in Turkey.

The rest of the chapter investigates TOKI by examining its role and authorisations regarding land, planning, housing provision, finance and urban transformation, respectively.

2   Land

The legal changes making TOKI the principal land developer on a vast amount of public land in Turkey include the abolishment of the General Directorate of Land Office and all the duties and land bank of the Office which include empty plots in the outskirts of the cities, agricultural land and brownfield of the former SOEs transferred to TOKI in 2004 (Law No. 5273). This added 64.5 million m^2 new land stock to its portfolio, which is 302 million m^2 (TOKI, 2019). Secondly, by taking over the authorisations of the Land Office, TOKI was charged with developing land not only for residential investment but also for other infrastructure and superstructure fields such as education, tourism and health (Law No. 5273, 2004). For these investments, TOKI could either sell public land to private companies or develop public-private projects on it (TOKI, 2011). Fourthly, the administration had the right to buy required land from private owners for developing residential and non-residential projects (ibid.). Lastly, TOKI was authorised to obtain public land belonging to the Treasury, Military and different ministries at no cost, but with approval of the PM and the related ministries (Law No. 4966). Particularly, the allowance of the appropriation of any land owned by the Treasury for any purpose became a crucial privilege given to TOKI. Consequently, TOKI became the biggest landowner, having the rights to manage, use, develop and sell 54% of the total land stock of Turkey (TOKI, 2016).

3   Planning

Within the scope of the EAP, regeneration of gecekondu areas was announced as one of the primary targets of the government. Following this, TOKI was empowered with making plans for urban regeneration projects in gecekondu settlements alongside implementing these projects (Law No. 5162, 2004). With follow-up laws, this new urban planning power of TOKI was extended to the planning of the historical areas and dilapidated inner-city zones (Law No. 5366, 2005) and the planning of all state-owned lands (Law No. 5018, 2009). Furthermore, thanks to the transfer of all the planning duties of the Ministry of Public Works and Settlement (Law No. 5069, 2007), TOKI became the highest authority in the planning of the public land by overriding the power of local governments.

Such authorisation was part of a broader transformation in the strategic centralisation of the planning system of Turkey. Specifically, together with TOKI, more than twenty institutions, including the Ministry of Culture and Tourism, which approves the tourism investments in coastal areas, the Privatisation Administration, which privatises public properties and facilities on state-owned land, and the Iller Bank, which is a state-owned investment bank specialised on traditional municipal services such as sewage collection and disposal and drinking water supplies were granted urban planning powers in the AKP period (Şengül, 2012).

On the one hand, the concentration of planning powers in the central government's institutions associated with the certain strategic sectors lifted the extra bureaucratic steps for easing and speeding up investments and bending the legal rules for liberalising the capital investments in the sectors in question (Balaban, 2017: 24). Especially large-scale construction companies and REITS were strongly in support of the centralisation of planning power since they "demand reduction in the planning bureaucracy and for more power to be given to the [TOKI] as the central planning authority equipped with guarantor role to reduce the risks of the investors" (Çelik et al., 2016: 45).

On the other hand, such unprecedented centralisation of planning enabled direct and unmediated control of the national government on the strategic sectors — as a reflection of the neoliberal authoritarian state organisation in which the administrative units directly attached to the Executive can take decisions by bypassing the parliamentary decisions and even sometimes by overriding local governments' decisions (Purkis, 2014). Therefore, the empowerment of TOKI and the Ministry of Environment and Urbanisation together with TOKI after 2011 with such an urban planning authority in addition to its landownership role, gave TOKI enormous power to create and manipulate the effective demand for housing. Planning regulations allocated and redistributed ground rent in certain locations. As put by Berry (2014: 397), "the conditions for the existence and appropriation of monopoly rents depend on the continuing creative acts of capital, residents and state actors, [particularly] political action focused on planning [...] and renewal projects."

In Turkey, the authoritarian planning system which unprecedently centralised the land-use planning and zoning decisions in the hands of TOKI and the Ministry created a top-down mechanism to determine residential differentiation of cities and to create differentiated monopoly rents on different localities. Hence, the centralisation of the planning system in Turkey signifies a centralised intervention of the state over monopoly rents through the top-down determination of the land use decisions, the degree of intensive investment, the creation of artificial scarcities in urban land, i.e. a supply of shortage of landed property in desirable locations, and reproducing different qualities of residential land. In addition to TOKI's and the Ministry of Environment and Urbanisation massive empowerment in land planning at all scales, the centralisation of planning power, i.e., "upward scaling of planning powers", also happened in the city-scale planning institutions during the AKP governments (Çelik *et al.*, 2016: 41). For instance, metropolitan municipalities in the biggest cities of Turkey had "strategic planning powers that override the district municipalities [that] weakened the role of the local state and reduced the ability of dwellers to participate in the planning process" (ibid.). Despite the widespread objections against the enactment of these laws, especially from the professional chambers, academics and political parties and organisations, none of the legal or political struggles resulted in the cancellation of these laws, which radically altered the institutional structure of the city planning system in Turkey (Şengül, 2012; Penpecioğlu, 2017).

4   Housing Provision: Is TOKI a Robin Hood[3] or an Unrivalled Monopoly?

Following the housing mobilisation announcement, the AKP government changed the state's role in the housing SoP by way of transforming TOKI from a mortgage institution to direct housing provider thanks to a new law (No. 4966, 2003), which allowed TOKI to establish its own companies and to develop a partnership with domestic or foreign private companies for building residential

---

3   As a heroic figure who takes from the rich and gives to the poor.

units, infrastructure and other social facilities including hospitals, schools, military quarters, police stations, roads, commercial centres, mosques, dormitories, sport centres and water dams both in Turkey and abroad. Although after the abandonment of the MHF in 2001, TOKI gave housing loans in gradually decreasing amounts, it stopped[4] in 2005. This radical change and the following mortgage law (No. 5582, 2007), which enabled banks and other financial institutions to give long-term mortgage loans and securitise them, resulted in a transition from the state housing finance system to private financial capital.

As a social welfare institution, the main responsibility of TOKI was to solve the housing problem by providing affordable houses to low and middle-income households. For this, TOKI "finds the land parcel on which the mass housing project will be developed [either from its own land bank or from the Treasury and other public institutions]; makes the construction plan and submit the project to the approval of the Ministry of Environment and Urban Planning"[5] (interview III). The specific emphasis of the top-level bureaucrats of TOKI was "if the land parcel is so valuable, we do not use this parcel for affordable housing project but for luxury housing" (interview III, interview IV). Therefore, the selection of the peripheral urban land for the development of affordable houses is a deliberate strategy. Secondly, a tender process is initiated for choosing the private builders, who will implement the project prepared by TOKI which does not undertake the building work but works with contractor companies. A TOKI manager said: "the contractor firm makes the work cheaper than us since they already have their own subcontracted workers, technical equipment and team and; in the case of Anatolian cities, they already have geographical expertise in their own regions and we also want to boost the private building sector" (interview III).

Thirdly, when the winning company of the tender is announced, the building process starts on the land parcel determined by TOKI that "takes generally 14–24 months for completion" (Palancıoğlu and Çete, 2014: 130). The mass housing designs are identical for all the projects as they have the same-designed multi-storey apartments with three-sized dwellings according to income criteria determined by the Ministry of Family and Social Policy, which are 45–65

---

4 Excluding exceptional cases including providing credit for war victims and the restoration of historic buildings.

5 Before the establishment of the Ministry in 2011, there was not any approval process thanks to the PPL, which enabled TOKI to develop its projects without submitting the construction plan, zoning and land use plans to any other authority. Nonetheless, the new regulation and subsequent approval requirement coming with the establishment of the Ministry became just a procedural work.

m² for the poor group, 65–87 m² for the low-income group and 87–146 m² for the middle-income group. Also, the exemption of TOKI from construction and land development fees, taxes and other project expenses and the lack of land cost "substantially decreases the projects' production expenses" (interview IV). Based on this, the sale prices of affordable housing units, below the market prices, are determined by TOKI according to land value and total construction costs including infrastructure, social facilities, consultancy and other technical expenditures (interview IV).

Furthermore, while the production process continues, the housing units are put up for sale to the households according to income categories. Beneficiaries make down-payments and then monthly instalments are calculated. These monthly instalments are based on a single-index repayment plan and their increases are adjusted to the changes in PPI, CPI and the increases in public employees' salaries. Following the determinations of payment schemes according to eligibility criteria (see Table 3), the beneficiaries take mortgage loans from public banks by signing a contract with banks on behalf of TOKI, which becomes the guarantor for repayment since the property rights of houses belongs to TOKI until households fully pay their mortgage debts. The bank receives monthly payments, "gets commission from down payments [and] collects real estate taxes and insurance premiums on behalf of TOKI" (ibid., 131). As seen in Table 2, except for the poor group, the other beneficiaries must make down-payments. The head of Finance Department of TOKI explains:

> according to the Turkish customs and traditions, the first thing is buying a house as soon as having a little income. Turkish people are not like Europeans or American. For instance, we received TL1.5 billion from social housing projects. Half of this was paid out of peoples' pockets, the rest by mortgage loans. Everybody in Turkey has under-the-mattress money or gold. So, we invigorate the banking sector through social housing. Neither this level of savings nor such population increase can be seen in Europe. After you buy a house for yourself, you should buy for your children, then for your grandchildren.
>
> interview IV

Lastly, TOKI makes the progress payments of contracting firms during two years from their start to production.[6] This progress payment method has become the biggest criticism of the contractor firms as they need to spend

---

6   Chapter 8 explains the details of this process.

TABLE 2   Payment schemes for affordable houses

Beneficiaries	Down-payments	Monthly instalments	Maturities (years)	Sizes (m²)
Poor group	—	Starting from TL150 (US$25)	25	45–65
Low-income group	10–15 % of the housing price	Starting from TL300 (US$50)	15–25	65–87
Middle-income group	10–25 % of the housing price	varies	8–10	87–146

SOURCE: TOKI, ACCESSED FROM HTTPS://WWW.TOKI.GOV.TR/EN/HOUSING-PROGRAMS .HTML

from their equities (or borrow) until they get their payments from TOKI (interviews; IMO, 2008).

Therefore, not only a wide scope of business space has been created for private house-builders, especially for local capitalist classes in Anatolia (Chapter 8) but also thousands of households, who have never had a chance to get credits from financial institutions, have been involved into the financial system as new debtors who can be considered as "low and middle-income subprime borrowers" of Turkey (Atasoy, 2016: 15). Although financialisation of household debt cannot be treated in the narrow sense since there is no securitisation or trade of issued mortgages in capital markets, the explicit commodity form in this housing SoP indicates financialisation of affordable housing system in a broader sense thanks to TOKI-issued mortgages. Moreover, the prevalence of homeownership over all other tenure forms[7] has led many people from lower classes to accord their lives according to monetary criteria and discipline themselves to pay their mortgage debt (Karaçimen, 2014; Ergüder, 2015). This, broadly argued as a part of the financialisation of daily life within the literature (Martin, 2002;

---

7   The affordable houses are advertised in the official website of TOKI as such: "Your dreams will come true. Buying a house will be like paying rent monthly" (www.toki.gov.tr).

Langley 2008), is also considered an indirect impact of financialisation of social reproduction in the form of commodity calculation in the book.

TOKI developed a second mode of housing provision, which is the revenue-sharing model, based on the utilisation of its massive land stock through the production of luxury housing for upper-income groups as well as shopping malls and private schools on high-value land by large-scale construction companies and the appropriation of the resultant monopoly rents by TOKI in return of its land contribution. Since TOKI became a financially autonomous institution and did not receive any funding from the state budget, it could generate own financial resources. In this sense, the revenue-sharing scheme, as the biggest component of TOKI's 'fund-raising' businesses, is a special housing SoP in that TOKI does not take place in the production process but becomes a landowner (TOKI, 2016). However, unlike the usual landowner, TOKI does not sell land directly but becomes the shareholder of the private construction company and appropriates a part of the development gain of this private builder, after the project is completed and residential units are sold.

The process entails a high-quality urban land[8] on which the project is carried out and construction companies are called for the tender. Here, the head of the Finance Department of TOKI emphasises that "in our revenue-sharing model, we only go out to the tender of land plot, we are not get involved the project, neither in land development nor in construction process; but the winning contractor prepares it" (interview IV). Therefore, during the tender process, bidding companies do not present their projects to TOKI; instead, they make an offer for the respective land plot based on their anticipated development gain. Bidding contractors calculate their anticipated development gains by taking into consideration TOKI's share which is around 35–45% of the total sales revenue and all the investment costs, excluding development fees and tax premiums. Although this exemption was initially applied to TOKI's affordable housing projects, in 2011 it was extended to its all activities (Law No. 6111). This became one of the reasons for the public discontent and biggest criticisms made to TOKI.

Furthermore, TOKI chooses the winning contractor company based on the highest payment offered to the Administration. However, offering the highest revenue does not guarantee selection as the head of the Finance department explains:

---

8   The land for the revenue-sharing projects is chosen from the biggest cities, with priority on Istanbul.

for instance, a company makes an offer by saying there is, let's say, 100,000 m² parcel here; I can sell 1 m² with x lira and my expected profit from the project is y lira so I will give 37% of my total sale revenue to you. On the other hand, another company says that I can sell 1 m² with z lira based on my project and customer portfolio so I will give 35% to you. I mean this is lower than the former, but we can choose the second one if we think it is risk-free.

interview IV

This arbitrariness is the reason for substantial discontent among different fractions of construction capital in Turkey since TOKI favours the business groups with organic ties to the government in its tenders,[9] as discussed in Chapter 8. Moreover, according to tender agreements, winning contractors must make payments to TOKI according to agreed payment schedules even if they cannot sell the residential units or get their expected development gains. While this agreed amount of payment determined in the contract is considered as the sub-limit, if the residential units are sold at higher prices than expected, the obtained development gain is shared between TOKI and the contractor company, according to the agreed percentage. Although TOKI "does not deal with the sales of the residential units of the revenue-sharing projects", which are luxury houses with social facilities such as parks, swimming pools, gardens etc, "the contractor company should receive approval for the sale prices before they start to sell the units to customers on the market" (interview IV).

Lastly, TOKI takes its share as follows:

TOKI and [the] contractor firm have a common bank account, the sale revenues deposit in this joint pool. TOKI can use this money as soon as it is deposited but the contractor cannot that is a precaution against the danger of their fleeing by ripping-off. Instead, we have a progress payment method. As long as they build houses, we transfer its share and in this way the company makes payments to us for the land plot from the sale revenues by instalments. In every six months, we determine the instalment amounts. We pay attention not to bother the contractor company.

interview IV

---

9 Because TOKI's revenue-sharing projects are not liable to the PPL, the tendering process is exempt from any control mechanism. This is justified by TOKI's autonomous financial structure, although its massive land bank is public property.

Therefore, in this model of PPP, large-scale contractor firms enjoy several unique advantages being a partner with TOKI, such as the exemption of fees and taxes in each stage of the investment, the rapid provision of infrastructural services regarding the projects in question by municipalities, completing the required bureaucratic steps and permissions within the shortest time thanks to TOKI's prerogatives, and "having the advantage of high marketing and sales capabilities" as from the construction stage of the project (Erol, 2019a: 255).

TOKI tries to legitimise its revenue-sharing activities based on cross-subsidisation of their affordable housing projects and closing the gap between their short-term investment expenses and long-term receivables in their saying (TOKI, 2016). In the interview (IV), the head of Finance department of TOKI says that "we are actually capitalising idle land of the public institutions". This supports De Soto's idea around the necessity of unlocking under-utilised land as dead capital for stimulating economic growth (De Soto, 2001). The other top-level bureaucrat was clearer: "when we open our parcels for development, we actually create rent, then we turn this rent into social housing" (interview III). There is a caveat, though, since during the 2000s, 'rent creation' became a buzzword in Turkey. For almost fifteen years, it is possible to see this discourse in newspaper headlines to academic analyses, to reports of political parties and professional organisations in Turkey. It is either used for criticising the AKP government, TOKI and hegemonic bourgeois fraction, or praising them for their contribution to the economy and needy people. TOKI has, therefore, been either considered a Robin Hood, as stated by a top-manager: "they [we] are transferring rent created in metropolises to the Anatolia" (interview III) or an unrivalled monopoly (IMO, 2008; Çavuşoğlu 2017; Erol 2019a; Ergüder 2015).

The revenue-sharing model can be examined based on the theoretical analysis in Chapter 2. Based on this, MR is the main form of the ground rent in the context of the residential use of land that is appropriated out of the circulation of revenues of the housing consumers and the amount of MR is determined by human-made scarcities vis-a-vis effective demand arising from the desirability of residential land, i.e., location advantages to services and facilities (and the brand image of neighbourhoods) and payment capacity of people. Since MR is the main source of profit for the speculative house-builders and speculative landowners, state land bank is privatised for capturing a part of the MR. In the revenue-sharing scheme, the state via TOKI appropriates MR as the shareholder of the capitalist house-builder. Nevertheless, in this case, there is not an individual landowner who can be unaware of the market potential of her land against the speculative house-builder who always chases for capturing higher amount of MR by manipulating land values between the purchase of land and sale of houses. Instead, TOKI not only gets assistance from its own Real Estate

Valuation Corporation (GEDAS)[10] but leads the land market thanks to its massive land portfolio. Therefore, similar to the analysis of Ram and Needham (2016: 101) on India, in Turkey "state mirror the practices of speculative developers (in terms of having a land bank, aggressive marketing campaigns, and competitive building practices)" and as Aalbers (2019: 154) argues, the "state is no longer merely the enabler of property speculation but has become a speculator itself". Nevertheless, it is important to consider such restructuring of the state, its increasing economic role and self-financing, within the context of periodisation of capitalism. Namely, MR appropriated by TOKI should also be considered as fiscal revenue[11] in the face of fiscal austerity measures in the aftermath of the 2001 crisis in Turkey, in that state institutions were restructured based on raising their capital instead of getting a share from the government budget.

Going back to the main explanation of TOKI behind this revenue-sharing model, which is cross-subsidisation, the luxury-housing production of TOKI consists only of 14–17% of its total production. However, while all the luxury-housing projects via this model take place on the rarely-available central locations of Istanbul and Ankara or around limited forested spaces of Istanbul, the number of affordable houses built in these metropolises with the highest housing shortage is far lower compared to the smaller Anatolian cities as shown in Table 3. Moreover, although revenue-sharing projects are proportionately lower within TOKI's total housing provision, they are much higher in exchange value-terms, generating enormous capital gains to both TOKI and its private partners (see Figure 10). Therefore, unlike its justification, this model is based on the MR-generation and boosting private construction business rather than providing housing for lower classes.

Table 3 shows the distribution of the affordable and luxury housing projects in the three biggest metropolises, namely Istanbul, Ankara and Izmir, and the poorest cities of Turkey, including Mardin, Batman and Şırnak, according to the TurkStat 2018 data on equivalised household disposable median income. Because there is no available data for the distribution of the residential units provided by TOKI according to the cities, we used TOKI's housing projects between 2003 and 2014. As can be seen from Table 3, while Istanbul leads the

---

10   GEDAS Real Estate Valuation Corporation, established in 1994 and listed in the Capital Market Boards of Turkey as the first property valuation company in 1995, is a subsidiary of TOKI, which has 49% of the total shares of the corporation.

11   Haila (2016) defines this rent appropriated by the state (regarding neoliberal fiscal discipline measures) as "the fiscalisation of rent", meaning rent as the source of public revenue.

luxury-housing production for the upper-income groups and Ankara follows it in the revenue-sharing model, the housing projects for the poor group, which has the largest housing shortage, are almost negligible in these three metropolises. Similarly, the poorest three cities have very low or no affordable housing production by TOKI and there is no acknowledgement of the provision of housing for the squatters as a result of their relocation through slum transformation projects. Through the slum-transformation projects, the new business spaces have been created for the revenue-sharing projects. If the housing production for slum transformation projects is included in the scope of poor group projects, these affordable housing numbers are still well behind the housing need for Istanbul, Izmir and Ankara, which constitute nearly one-third of the total population and the biggest share of the labour force of Turkey.

As seen in Table 4, as of 2018, 837,572 residential units were built by TOKI via PPP, of which 655,194 were sold. Apart from luxury and affordable houses, including new dwellings for relocated squatters, peasants and people living in the areas affected by natural disasters, TOKI has built many social facilities again via PPP. Regarding residential units, approximately 85% of it takes place in the affordable housing category, against 14% luxury housing. Firstly, as shown in Table 4, the biggest slice of 44% belongs to the narrow and middle-income group. However, middle-income housing projects are not within the scope of the poor and low-income projects mainly because there is no condition of

TABLE 3   TOKI's housing projects between 2003–2014 — selected cities

Cities	Population (million)	Poor group projects	Low-income group projects	Middle-income group projects	Revenue-sharing projects (%)	Slum-transformation projects
Istanbul	15.520	0	27	45	80	39
Ankara	5.504	3	19	66	13	45
Izmir	4.368	2	8	12	n/a	5
Mardin	0.839	1	1	8	0	1
Batman	0.609	0	1	9	0	0
Sirnak	0.530	0	0	11	0	0
Turkey	82	76	351	872	100	199

SOURCE: CALCULATED BASED ON THE INDICATORS FROM TOKI (2014) AND TOKI WEBSITE (HTTPS://WWW.TOKI.GOV.TR/PROJE-TIPINE-GORE-UYGULAMALAR#9)

purchasing houses to shelter in the contracts of the middle-income projects. As confirmed by the TOKI manager, "there are some people purchasing these dwellings with the aim of investment" (interview III), although there is no data regarding the percentages of the purchases for sheltering and investing.

Moreover, TOKI stopped providing data for poor groups and low-income groups separately but cumulated the total produced units for these groups, which was 151,301 between 2003 and 2018. This makes it unclear to what extent TOKI-produced houses meet sheltering needs of different income groups, especially when taking into consideration that defined income level of the low-income group is two-times more than the one of the poor groups. Moreover, while the maximum monthly net household income was determined as 5,500 TL (6000 TL for Istanbul), to the limit for applying to the TOKI's low-income houses in 2019 is 2,020 TL. Therefore, when considering that nearly 32% of the employed labour force gained minimum income or less than minimum income in 2017 (Aslan, 2019) and the unemployment rate is 14% in Turkey, meeting the financial application requirement for the TOKI's low-income houses is not achievable for a substantial part of the population.

Also, in the low-income houses, there is a legal gap allowing investments. The TOKI manager explains:

> For the low-income projects there are two kinds of sales. The first is the sales by lot in that beneficiaries cannot have any other house. The second is the open sales for the unsold low-income houses in that everybody can apply to these dwellings, which are not on valuable land parcels, since TOKI does not want them to remain unsold but rather want to make everyone homeowner.
>
> interview III

Although TOKI's affordable houses cannot be sold to third parties because the property rights of houses belong to TOKI until the payment of all instalments is made, Atasoy (2016: 17) shows that "a few who cannot afford the monthly payments are informally selling their shares to others through highly personalised 'trust' relations". The formal beneficiary as the real debtor to TOKI pays her instalments after receiving the payments, including the down-payment, from the informal purchaser (ibid.). Moreover, the motivation behind this informal transfer of houses from the insolvent households to the financially better ones has been "the future financial worth of the units" (ibid., 18). This is already common for revenue-sharing projects. As mentioned by the TOKI manager, "most of the houses we built through revenue-sharing have been purchased with the aim of investment by people. There are dozens of examples buying for instance

TABLE 4   Total housing units provided by TOKI (2003–2018)

	Poor and low-income group	Narrow and middle-income group	Slum-transfor mation	Disaster houses	Agricultural village	Revenue-sharing	Total housing units*	Sold housing units	Other social facilities
Residential units	151,301	374,042	143,021	37,734	6,415	112,265	837,572	655,194	14,351
Ratio (%)	18	44	17	5	1	14	100	76	—

Note: Within total housing units, 12,794 units (nearly 1.5% in total) are not shown in any category in TOKI sources.
SOURCE: TOKI (2018); THE ANATOLIAN AGENCY HTTPS://WWW.AA.COM.TR/TR/INFO/INFOGRAFIK/10292

15–20 residential units in one go" (interview IV). The president of the Istanbul branch of the Chamber of Architects confirms that: "you can't imagine how people buy these branded-luxury residencies; it is like buying one kg tomatoes from market" (interview VIII). In the context of continuously increasing house prices during the 2000s and 2010s, many people from Turkey and abroad considered the housing investment as a safe haven (Chapter 7). In conjunction, Atasoy's study (2016) shows a similar trend even for the low-income houses. Therefore, the commodity form in the TOKI-provided affordable houses that have already risen via the privatisation of social housing (through PPP-based production with the aim of TOKI to support private house-builders) and the articulation of the beneficiaries to the financial system as new mortgage debtors also takes the form of commodity calculation, due to the increasing importance of exchange value of houses regarding their use-value among the lower classes.

At this point, I must analyse whether TOKI is not a Robin Hood but an unrivalled monopoly. The answer of this question for me is both yes and no. Although TOKI has monopolistic qualifications thanks to its massive land-bank, institutional privileges and financial exemptions, the underlying mechanism of the housing SoP of TOKI suggests the contrary. When calculating the proportion of TOKI-provided units (837,572) in total residential units produced between 2003–2018 (11,414,202), which is 7.4%, one can notice that more housing units were produced by the private house-builders directly, except for TOKI's PPP model, during this period. Also, as emphasised by TOKI managers in our interviews (III; IV), one of the main purposes of its housing production model is boosting the private housebuilding sector, "pulling the private sector as locomotive force". Via TOKI, the state socialises not only the costs of private construction companies by exempting them from public taxes and fees but also their investment risks by allocating the highest quality of urban land for their residential projects in the case of revenue-sharing and by taking merchant activities of the housing provision, finding customers, selling units and collecting payments, from the private builders in the case of affordable housing. Only between 2003 and 2011, TOKI (2011: 15) employed 600 contractor firms in different scales operating in the construction industry via its tenders. As a landowner and developer, TOKI triggers a huge mobilisation in the construction industry, although not all fractions of construction capital enjoy the same conditions. So far, TOKI is a monopoly as a landowner but not as a housing developer. Its biggest subsidiary, Emlak Konut REIT, needs to be investigated for a complete picture.

5   Emlak Konut REIT

TOKI has seven subsidiaries[12] operating in real estate marketing, contracting, trading, management, consultancy and property valuation fields. Emlak Konut REIT, formerly a state-owned commercial bank (Emlak Bank), was later transformed into a state-owned REIT and affiliated to TOKI in 2002. TOKI had 100% share of Emlak Konut REIT until 2010. However, when it had its first public offering in 2010, TOKI's share fell to 74.99%. With the second IPO, TOKI's share became 49.34%. These IPOs were significant not only in terms of being the 5th biggest public offering in the history of the country but also making Emlak Konut the largest investment trust of Turkey, 6th in Europe and MENA region and 26th at the global level[13] in terms of market value, real estate portfolio and land stock (Emlak Konut Activity Report, 2013). As seen in Figure 9, the total assets of Emlak Konut REIT substantially increased in 2010 and 2013, the years of IPO issuances.

Table 5 shows the structure of the current partnerships of Emlak Konut. TOKI is the main shareholder with 49.34% share of A-type mutual fund, an equity fund with opportunity for higher capital gains, albeit with more volatility, and B-type mutual fund, also known as fixed-income fund or bond fund and safer compared to stocks, albeit with comparatively lower capital gains. 80% of the remaining bearer stocks were purchased by international investors and 20% by domestic investors. TOKI gets substantial amounts of capital gains from dividend pay-outs of Emlak Konut REIT each year, despite its decreasing share, as shown in Table 6.

As discussed in Chapter 8, the number of REITs skyrocketed during the 2000s and the REITs became the main indicator of the financialisation of housing in Turkey through real estate-securitisation and land-trading on capital markets. However, Emlak Konut has some differences compared to other REITs due to its unique place in both public and private sectors, like both a private financial institution and a state institution. Unlike other REITs, Emlak Konut was involved in the PPL and hence its projects must have been responsive to the requirements of the law due to its affiliation with TOKI.[14] Nevertheless, unlike TOKI, Emlak Konut REIT does not have a social welfare role as its "primary

---

12   These are Emlak Konut REIT; GEDAS Real Estate Valuation Corp.; TOKI-Metropolitan Municipality Construction Property Corp.; Vakıf REIT; Boğaziçi Housing Service Management and Commerce Corp. and Vakıf Construction Restoration Corp.

13   As of 2019, it is 2nd in MENA and 79th in the world (Emlak Konut, 2019).

14   As TOKI's share decreased to 49.34% after the second IPO in 2013, Emlak Konut was excluded from the PPL after 2013.

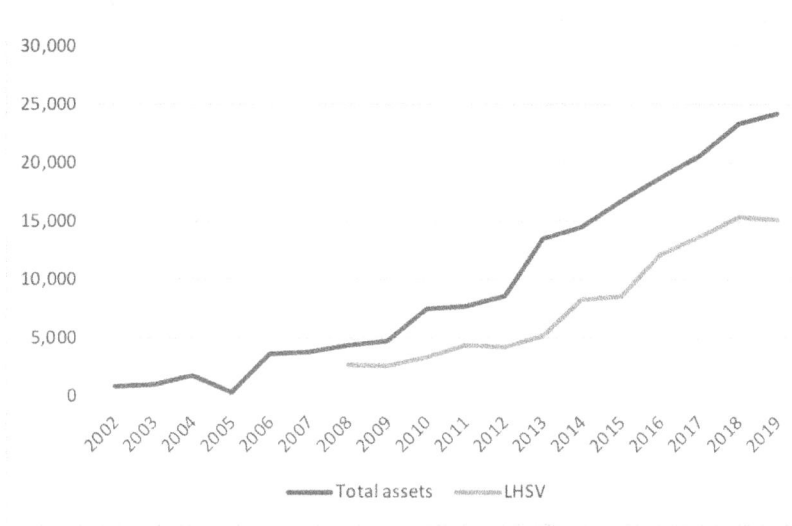

FIGURE 9   Total assets and the land and housing stock value (LHSV) of Emlak Konut
REIT — in million TL (2003–2019)
SOURCE: PREPARED BASED ON THE ANNUAL ACTIVITY REPORTS OF EMLAK
KONUT REIT HTTP://WWW.EMLAKKONUT.COM.TR/EN-US/ACTIVITY-REPORTS

goal is to increase the number of (tangible and intangible) values its shareholders and other stakeholders" by developing real estate projects for upper
classes and undertaking marketing and sales activities (Emlak Konut, 2017: 6).
However, as the subsidiary of TOKI, it has some prerogatives including access
to TOKI's land stock and carrying out revenue-sharing projects by purchasing
land from TOKI (interview XXII). Emlak Konut REIT also has a priority of buying land from TOKI's stock without any tendering procedure which has generated controversies around TOKI. However, the main point of the criticisms was
not the sale of public land for profit-making projects or trade-in capital markets as an asset but their land transaction below market values[15] and the use of
these lands for the projects undertaken by the certain fractions of construction
capital through the revenue-sharing activities of Emlak Konut (CHP, n.d.).

The revenue-sharing projects of Emlak Konut are the same with those of
TOKI, except that Emlak Konut REIT purchases land from TOKI[16] without

---

15   The Chamber of Account's report (2015) documented that TOKI have sold public land to
Emlak Konut REIT below their market values.
16   Or other third parties although they mostly purchase land from TOKI (interview XXII).

TABLE 5   The current shareholder structure of Emlak Konut REIT

Trade tittle	Type of mutual fund	Type of share	Share amount (TL)	Number of shares	Percentage of share (%)
TOKI	A	Registered share	253,369,919	25,336,991,900	6.67
TOKI	B	Bearer share	1,621,460,838	162,146,083,835	42.67
Open to Public	B	Bearer share	1,925,120,331	192,512,033,148	50.6
Others	B	Bearer share	48,911	4,891,117	< 1
Total			3,800,000,000	380,000,000,000	100

SOURCE: HTTP://WWW.EMLAKKONUT.COM.TR/EN-US/PARTNERSHIP-STRUCTURE

being subject to any tendering requirements, unlike other REITs. Similar to TOKI's revenue-sharing projects, Emlak Konut does not undertake any building process itself but via contractor companies. However, a new protocol was signed between TOKI and the Emlak Konut REIT at the end of 2019 which enabled Emlak Konut REIT to carry out the revenue-sharing projects on behalf of TOKI, instead of purchasing land, in return of 15% of the resultant development gain and by paying 85% of it to TOKI.

Hence, Emlak Konut is the industry leader by having the highest market value (34% of the total market value of other REITs) which is why Emlak Konut REIT is also considered a monopoly in the sector (Erol, 2019a; Çelik and Karaçimen, 2017). Despite the advantages it enjoyed due to its affiliation to TOKI, the continuously increasing numbers (35 REITs currently) and market share of REITs after 2002, indicate that Emlak Konut REIT's high capital gains from the land uplift encouraged several other capital groups to establish their REITs. Hence, as discussed in Chapter 8, TOKI's and Emlak Konut REIT's unique positions in the real estate and housing sectors created broad discontent among different fractions of construction capital with the complaints of unfair competition, while their operations in the market boost the housing and land markets by attracting foreign and domestic capital (interview XVIII; interview XXV).

TABLE 6   TOKI's capital gains from Emlak Konut's annual profits (2003–2019)

Years	Total (undistributed) profit for the financial year (million TL)	TOKI's share ratio (%)	TOKI's capital gains (million IL)
2019	1,385	49,34%	683
2018	1,621	49,34%	800
2017	2,216	49,34%	1093
2016	1,915	49,34%	945
2015	907	49,34%	448
2014	751	49,34%	370
2013	1,006	49,34%	494
2012	530	74,99%	397
2011	256	74,99%	171
2010	554	74,99%	415
2009	344	99,99%	344
2008	563	99,99%	563
2007	947	99,99%	947
2006	168	99,99%	168
2005	143	99,99%	143
2004	151	99,99%	151
2003	99	99,99%	99
2002	52	99,99%	52

SOURCE: PREPARED BASED ON THE ANNUAL ACTIVITY REPORTS OF EMLAK KONUT REIT
HTTP://WWW.EMLAKKONUT.COM.TR/EN-US/ACTIVITY-REPORTS

Also, Emlak Konut REIT, as the main subsidiary of TOKI, linked it indirectly to the derivative markets by capitalising and trading TOKI's massive public land bank in capital markets. Therefore, the unique relationship between TOKI and Emlak Konut REIT signified a particular example of commodification and, therefore, financialisation of public land in Turkey.

6   Finance of TOKI

With the new mass housing law (No. 4966) in 2003, TOKI was given the authority to create its own financial resources. The main income resources of TOKI included the sale of real assets (land and houses) and the revenue-sharing projects, according to the annual reports of Chamber of Accounts. The main issue in evaluating the balance sheet of TOKI is the inconsistency of data since the same indicators are not reported every year. Therefore, the only available data source (for figures below) is the Undersecretariat of Treasury's annual reports (2005–2011) and the Chamber of Account's annual reports (2012–2018). As shown in Figure 10, more than 80% of the net sales revenue of TOKI comes from the sales revenues of land, houses and commercial units. Although the revenue-sharing projects constitute the second biggest income source, it is still far below the revenues from the sale of real assets for the available years. Therefore, the biggest landowner of Turkey on behalf of the Turkish state has been the main agent of the privatisation of public land in the post-2002 period.

Moreover, based on these reports, TOKI has been by far the most profitable public institution of Turkey during the 2000s and 2010s. The profit-loss statement of TOKI is positive since annual profits increased from TL0.7 billion in 2005 to TL4 billion in 2017, while net sales revenue rose from TL4.5 billion to TL7 billion between 2011 and 2016, as shown in Figure 11. Figure 12 shows the substantial increase in the total assets of TOKI in that the market value of land and real estate stock more than doubled between 2011 and 2016.

Despite being the most profitable public institution in Turkey, the main financial problem of TOKI is its liquidity unbalance resulting from running many construction activities and managing partnerships with several private firms at the same time. As the head of the Finance Department of TOKI says, when the volume and pace of projects are high, they have liquidity shortage and, for closing these short-term liquidity shortages, TOKI "borrows loans from banks frequently" (interview IV).

TOKI initiated two other fund-raising activities recently. Firstly, TOKI started to issue real estate certificates on BIST. As discussed above, the first real estate certificates, which are capital market instruments representing the paper claims for independent units of real estate assets, had already been developed and sold by TOKI in 1989 to Halkalı-Istanbul Mass Housing projects to raise funds, although it failed due to the lack of a well-developed financial infrastructure and the 1990s' volatility. In 2017, TOKI issued real estate certificates for a revenue-sharing project in Istanbul, Park Mavera III, on BIST encompassing 3,370,410 certificates, each of which with TL42.50 market value and sold to domestic individual investors (52.7%), and institutional investors (47.3%). Although the performance of these certificates was below expectations and they lost value within 6-months following their issuance by TOKI, they are considered a pilot project for the newly developing real-estate certificates system in Turkey, designed as a long-term financial project by the AKP government to

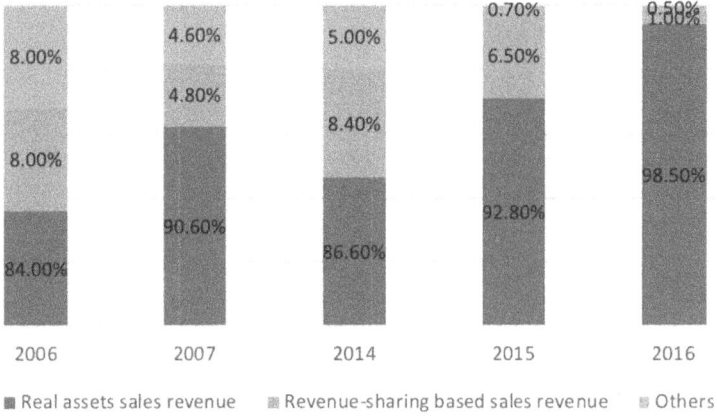

FIGURE 10   Distribution of TOKI's net sales revenue — selected years (%)

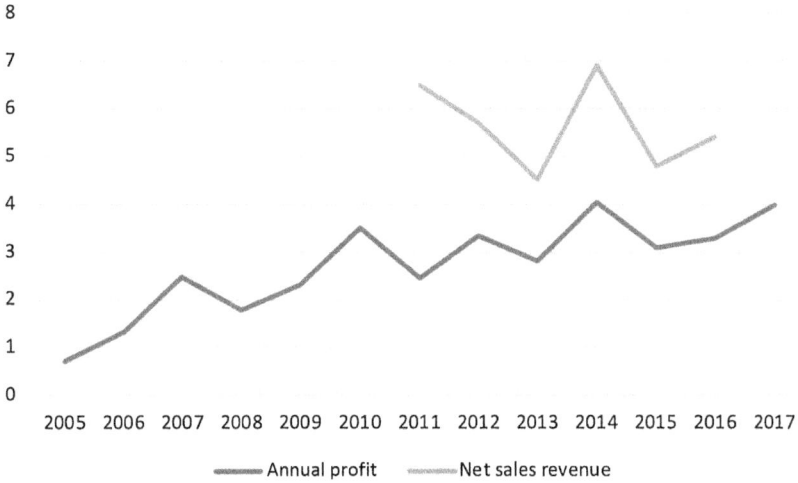

FIGURE 11   Annual profit of TOKI — in billion TL (2005–2017)

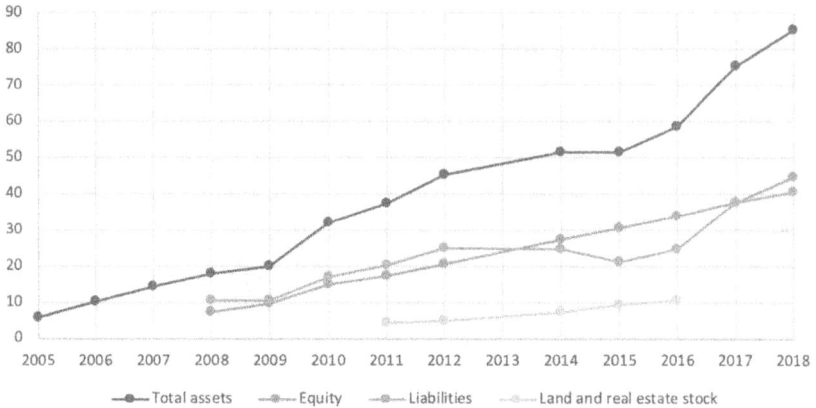

FIGURE 12   The financial position of TOKI — in billion TL (2005–2018)

increase the demand by channelling small savings of lower-class people to the sector.

Moreover, TOKI was empowered to issue both domestic and international bonds and stocks in 2007 (Law No. 5582). This would be based on the collateralisation of its land and real estate stocks and their sale on the securities market. However, it was not before 2019 that TOKI issued its first asset-guaranteed security of TL2 billion. Therefore, TOKI took on a task not only as the catalyser of private housebuilding in Turkey but also as the leader of financial deepening in the sector, "being a model for other developers" (interview III). Therefore, this book considers TOKI as a relevant example of financialisation in Turkey.

7   Urban Transformation: from Slum Upgrading to Mass Regeneration

After the announcement of the EAP, TOKI started implementing urban renewal and gecekondu transformation projects alongside zoning and making development plans for them. Although TOKI is not the only actor in these projects but cooperates with local municipalities, it is equipped with greater power than local governments. Urban regeneration projects were critical for transforming inner cities into new financial and commercial hubs and creating high-value land for private capital investments, especially in Istanbul. The most important role of TOKI in this process became "solving the legal and bureaucratic obstacles for investors, giving financial and technical support to the municipalities, and organising resident relocations resulting from regeneration projects, and weakening possible civil resistance by both subtle and brutal methods" (Çelik *et al.*, 2016: 42–3).

Gecekondu transformation or slum upgrading projects have become significant for their political, demographic and economic implications since a substantial part of these gecekondu areas are located in or around highly precious inner-city zones. Gecekondu transformation process mainly includes the demolishment of shanty settlements, rehabilitation of these areas and provision of new housing units for squatters in-situ transformation or transformation through relocation. For both models, municipalities determine the gecekondu areas which need to be transformed and apply to TOKI. If the area is considered appropriate to carry out a regeneration project, a protocol is signed between TOKI and the relevant municipality. Then, the legally entitled right-holders are identified by a commission of officials from TOKI and municipalities, where TOKI establishes the details of the project by evaluating the land, population, property rights on that land, the expected cost of the project and the future real estate values. After the project is established by TOKI, the municipality contacts the right-holders and informs them about the transformation. The next step changes according to the method of the project. In the in-situ transformation model, right-holders are moved to the TOKI-built houses in the same neighbourhood following the clearance of gecekondu areas by municipalities. When right-holders accept the transformation project, they also accept the transfer of their property rights to TOKI. Then TOKI calculates the cost of the production (excluding land cost) of new housing unit that would take place in the same neighbourhood and offers two alternatives to squatters, either accepting cash payments equivalent to the land[17] price or paying their debt which is the difference between the market value and the cost of the new housing unit, by monthly instalments. With the second method of displacement and relocation of squatters in different parts of cities, squatters are offered new houses, that were already built by TOKI in another part of the city, in exchange for the transfer of the property rights of their land. This offer is initially forwarded by the relevant municipality but if the right-holder-squatters are not persuaded by the municipality, the negotiations for getting their consent are run by TOKI. Following this, if squatters are still not convinced for transferring their property rights to TOKI, either in return of a new housing unit in another neighbourhood or cash payments as the compensation of

---

17   If squatter is a landowner, the compensation (and the price difference for the new house) is calculated based on the land price. However, if squatter does not have the legal ownership of land but just the gecekondu on it, TOKI calculates the compensation based on the market value of that gecekondu.

their land, TOKI has a legal right to forcefully evict squatters and expropriate these lands, which are in historical or central locations and generally used for revenue-sharing projects. In short, squatters are obliged to accept TOKI's offer. Similar to the first model, if right-holders accept to move to the new housing units of TOKI, which are often on outskirts of cities, they also accept paying the remaining cost of the new homes by 180-month instalments.

Consequently, since 2004, TOKI, in collaboration with local governments, started many gecekondu transformation projects, a great majority of which have been located in Istanbul (see Table 3), and completed 143,021 housing units for squatters as of 2019 (see Table 4). However, there have been several problems for squatters. Firstly, the distant peripheral and isolated locations of new dwellings were far from squatters' workplaces which made them lose their connections with city centres, which are better in terms of the social reproduction facilities such as hospitals, schools, and transportation and deteriorated their living conditions instead of improving them. For instance, the transformation of the Sulukule neighbourhood in Istanbul, which was a historical home to the Anatolian Romani people since Byzantian times, was one of the first examples of the transformation of historical and dilapidated neighbourhoods. Some of the Sulukule-squatters, who accepted the resettlement option instead of compensation, were moved to TOKI blocs 40 km away and lost their community links (Gough and Gündoğdu, 2009: 21). Although the mortgage rates for these new houses were low and maturities were long, the debt amounts were still high for many, who are either unemployed or employed in informal, flexible and precarious jobs (interview XV).

Moreover, while some squatters in the urban renewal areas prefer directly selling their lands to TOKI instead of resettlement, a substantial part of the resettled squatters have difficulties in paying the monthly instalments and end up selling their new houses (Türkün, 2014; Karaman, 2014). For instance, 320 out of 327 resettled families from Sulukule could not afford their mortgage payments as they did not have any regular job or income (Özdemir, 2010: 110) and, consequently, sold their title to third parties and built new gecekondu elsewhere (interview XV).

Also, as discussed before, many gecekondu had been granted with property rights via amnesty laws enacted by different governments in different times of the Turkish political history. These periodical and unsystematic amnesties generated ambiguities and differences in the legal title deeds of squatters, who became landowners or tenants. Therefore, gecekondu transformation projects have brought forth these legal differences and created further inequalities and segregation among squatters. While the landowner-squatters have a chance to bargain the amount of ground rent that they can appropriate from TOKI and municipalities, the tenant-squatters, who cannot legally verify their tenancy status, "are typically not offered any form of compensations and therefore face direct eviction" (Karaman, 2014: 297). In other words, gecekondu transformation projects caused the partial repossession of some squatters, while leading the dispossession of some others. Moreover, consent and coercion coexisted as the modalities of state intervention against squatters. For instance, several resistance movements were organised by squatters against these transformation projects with the support of social and political organisations, professional chambers, NGOs and, some of them stopping the upgrading projects (Kuyucu, 2018; Ahunbay et al,, 2016). However, in some other cases, TOKI and municipalities managed to break the resistance by either offering compensation payments or evicting the inhabitants by using police or judicial force (Kuyucu and Ünsal, 2010; Türkün, 2011).

However, neither of these interventions has been hassle-free for TOKI. The gentrification of historical neighbourhoods and the eviction of resisting squatters received reactions from national and international media, political organisations, human rights organisation and campaigns (Özdemir, 2010). Also, the landowner-squatters have increasingly been aware of the value of the land on which their gecekondu are located and asked for higher amounts of compensation payments. The latter was especially troublesome for TOKI and municipalities. The top-level bureaucrat of TOKI said: "We make the ones living in dump home-owner. Instead of being grateful, they are seeking for rent. This is why urban transformation is very hard." (interview III). The zoning and urban transformation manager of Istanbul Metropolitan Municipality argued that

> maybe municipalities impose transformation projects on inhabitants but actually this is not bad for them. However, citizens are not contented as they always ask for more. Instead of blessing us for the payment we made them for these illegally occupied places, they accuse the state as being the rent-seeker. The real rent-seekers are gecekondu owners!.
> interview XXIV

The same idea was expressed by two other interviewees, an activist scholar from the Assembly of Socialist Engineers and Architects (interview XV) and the president of the Istanbul branch of the Chamber of Architects (interview VIII), based on their experiences of some resistance movements, although urban activists were expecting the inhabitants to continue their struggles and transform it to anti-gentrification and anti-commercialisation struggle.

Such prevalence of financial motives and rationales in the decision-making processes of the urban poor sets an important example of financialisation of

social reproduction concerning housing, in the form of commodity calculation. Although increasing financial awareness of squatters contradicts the
interests of TOKI and its private partners, it can be argued that the ideological orientation of lower classes towards individualised responsibility for their
social reproduction and increasing ideological segregation between possessed
and dispossessed urban poor have successfully hampered the organisation of
decommodified and collective forms of housing provision.

Furthermore, this book does not consider the coercive relocation of masses
incompatible or contradictory with the consent-building mechanisms since
both have been employable in "class-cleansing"[18] of valuable metropolitan
areas; the re-organisation of these rare central and historical areas as new hubs
for tourism and commerce and, therefore, the creation of effective demand for
luxury residential units in and around these neighbourhoods. TOKI, which is
the embodiment of the authoritarian management in the urban scale, orches-
trates this process, while the role of local governments is reduced to dealing
with technical issues of the renewal process such as communicating with
squatters for informing them about renewal projects without any consultation
with inhabitants, clearing the emptied areas and providing infrastructural services if required. Moreover, apart from coordinating the general process, TOKI
also takes place in these projects as the planner of historical areas and inner-
city zones, landowner and developer.

As discussed in Chapter 8, these expropriated land parcels, which have
rarely-found qualities due to their locations, were directly used as a mechanism to create and distribute significantly high amounts of monopoly rents to
the second-generation bourgeoisie via revenue-sharing projects. Nevertheless,
the construction capitalists who have ideological and political unity with the
AKP governments were not the only beneficiaries of the urban transformation
process, although privileged in this TOKI-driven rent distribution mechanism.
Specifically, the enactment of 2/B law (No. 6292), which allowed privatising[19]
forested lands to development for urban generation projects and the Law on
the Transformation of Areas under Disaster Risk (LTADR) (No. 6306) in 2012
provide a great example of the state's encouragement for revitalising the

---

18   The term, which refers to the clearance of lower classes from high-value inner-city land
      to expand the private housing market for upper classes, is borrowed from Gough and
      Gündoğdu (2009).

19   Following the completion of the cadastral work in 2013, almost 50% (1,573 km²) of the
      (state-owned) forested land, which covers 3,450 km², was sold to private capital at the
      expense of forest villagers and peasants, who have used the land in question for years
      (Atasoy, 2016: 662).

housebuilding and real estate sectors as a whole, by expanding the geographical scope of the urban transformation projects.

In this sense, LTADR authorised TOKI and the Ministry of Environment and Urbanisation to determine[20] and declare the disaster-prone zones on which regeneration projects will be implemented. LTADR, as the last statutory decree and law made since 2002, can be considered the latest step in the extraordinary centralisation of urban governance and the enormous empowerment of TOKI and the Ministry. Because most the regions in Turkey are in the 1st and 2nd-degree earthquake zone, LTADR enables TOKI and the Ministry to declare all areas in all levels and scales regeneration areas without any juridical obstacle.

Besides, after an area is declared regeneration area by TOKI or the Ministry, the urban transformation may happen either in the full area or only in a single building. Particularly, the allowance of the regeneration of single buildings is the main novelty that LTADR brought to the urban transformation system. For this, the age and robustness of buildings are controlled by licensed institutions and if the expert report shows that building is susceptible to possible disaster,[21] an urban regeneration project has to start on this land plot. According to the LTADR, the building must be demolished by the homeowners within 60 days following the expert report which declared it as a risky construction. If this is not done, water, natural gas and electricity supplies are cut off and, if homeowners still do not comply, the building is demolished by the Ministry, TOKI or municipalities. The cost of the demolishment, in any case, belongs to homeowners. After the demolishment, homeowners become joint landowners and their share over the land changes according to the market values of their former dwelling units calculated by the Directorate of Land Registry under the Ministry. Within 30 days following the notification, the decision regarding how the empty land will be used must be taken by the shareholders through a majority system. If a minimum 2/3 of shareholders cannot be constituted, TOKI and the Ministry have a right of enforcing 'an urgent expropriation for the common good' (Law No: 5162). The joint landowners can decide the construction of a new building, combine their land with nearby parcels,[22] sell the

---

20   The approval of the decision of the risky areas belonged to the cabinet but later with the transition to the Presidential system, the article changed and currently the President is the only authority to approve (or not) this decision.

21   Most of the buildings built before the 1999 earthquake are considered risky by the licensed institutions since the quality of construction materials was not controlled by the authorities before.

22   For instance, if two buildings next to each other are both declared transformation parcels, the owners of both lands can decide to combine their land parcels and then agree with a developer to reconstruct a new bigger building for them. This is preferred especially for

land or hold it as an asset. Although the LTADR permits several options, the most widespread practice is the reconstruction of a new apartment since most of the shareholders are residents and they need sheltering. If shareholders decide the renewal of the building, they suffer the cost of the reconstruction. This meant compulsory mortgage indebtedness for a great number of people. For supporting this process and getting the consent of people, the Ministry signed a protocol with banks in which the state provides interest support at the rate of 3 to 4% with 7 to 10 year-maturity. If a shareholder does not consent to the renewal decision taken by the majority (2/3), her share is offered to other shareholders via an auction that is managed by the property valuation corporations registered in the capital markets board. In case the other shareholders do not want to buy this share, it is purchased by the Ministry on behalf of the Treasury and transferred to TOKI.

For the construction of their new houses, shareholders can agree either with TOKI and municipalities or private developers. However, TOKI and municipalities do not aim to develop social housing but to generate profit through these transformation projects, similarly to private developers, except for their responsibilities for "directing the sector" (interview III) and "serving as a model for the private developers" (interview XXIV). The production method takes the form of PPPs. Municipalities work with their construction firms while TOKI collaborates with municipalities and private construction firms. The head of the urban transformation department of the Metropolitan Municipality of Istanbul provides an example:

> if it is a big project, a few institutions work together. For instance, we made a protocol with TOKI and Şişli Municipality for the transformation of Kuştepe neighbourhood. We, as the Metropolitan Municipality, took the task of the coordination of the project, Şişli Municipality cleared the area and TOKI undertook the development work. Because politically we are the institutions of the same party [AKP], the project was very successful. But in some cases, if the district municipality is from the opposition party [CHP], they do not want to work with us.
>
> interview XXIV

The manager from TOKI came up with a similar explanation: "in these projects, TOKI takes place if they make an agreement with municipalities but some

---

the developers as the planning authorities give higher floor permissions for bigger land parcels.

municipalities, for instance Yenimahalle Municipality from Ankara [from CHP] did not want to sign a protocol with us instead they finished the project by themselves" (interview III). Because LTADR authorises different branches of government, such tensions are common even though in a significant conflict requiring an urgent solution TOKI is the last resort. Also, not only TOKI and its private allies but also municipalities and their own construction companies chase capital gain similar to private developers (interview XV; interview VIII; interview XXVIII). Although the opposition parties have always been critical to TOKI's extraordinary empowerment, when they were authorised with the LTADR, the local government from opposition parties also started to chase profit.

Nonetheless, the principal actor of the urban transformation under LTADR has been private developers rather than TOKI and municipalities which "prefer to step in larger projects and full area transformations" (interview III). Especially considering the number of risky buildings that required an urgent renewal, announced at 7.5 million housing units (Hürriyet, 2018), TOKI, municipalities and their private partners can only undertake a very small part of the transformation projects. Yet, what I conclude about the LTADR is that even though the devastating earthquake in 1999 showed that several buildings had been constructed with low-quality construction materials and there is a need for the renewal of several buildings in Turkey, the AKP governments have used the earthquake risk as an excuse for declaring several neighbourhoods as transformation areas, "reshaping of urban landscapes in response to the needs of capital", controlling the effective demand in neighbourhood and city levels, legitimising the demolishment and reconstruction of millions of houses, generating a huge investment area for construction capitalists and reinvigorating the housebuilding sector (Fine *et al.*, 2015: 32). As shown by several scholars (Ünver and Suri, 2020; Gündeş *et al.*, 2017; Kuyucu, 2014), the urban transformation of certain neighbourhoods has been prioritised by the Ministry not according to the degree of damage of buildings but based on the quality of their land, the desirability of its location. Therefore, after the enactment of the law, "a very fast and unrestrained transformation started in the most desired districts and neighbourhoods of the big metropolis" (Kuyucu, 2017: 377) and with a popular expression within the society, the whole country rapidly turned to a 'construction site'.

As Rolnik (2019: 181) rightly identified and compared with floods in Indonesia, "the Turkish case casts light on how risks associated with natural disasters — in this case, earthquakes — [can be selectively used] what should be demolished and what should remain; who should be displaced and who should not". Because the law empowering TOKI for zoning, planning and the

transformation of historical and dilapidated neighbourhoods was largely criticised, and several projects met with resistance of residents and social movements, the political power formulated a more rational and scientific basis for
urban transformation by the LTADR. Moreover, the reduction of the scale of
projects by enabling the renewal of single buildings served for individualising
urban transformation and weakening social opposition against projects (interview XV; Kuyucu, 2017).

Moreover, the timing of the LTADR indicates the purpose of reinvigorating
the housebuilding sector by creating a consistent demand for the construction capital (see Chapter 7 and 8). The head of the Association of Real Estate
and Real Estate Investment Companies (GYODER) declared at the international real estate fair (Cityscape Global): "The post-GFC period provides a safe
and rich investment area in Turkey thanks to political and economic stability.
Apart from the already available opportunities, the residential units which will
be renewed as a part of the disaster law will create a 400-billion-dollar financial mobility in the sector" (NTV, 2012). Most importantly, the LTADR exempts
private developers which undertake the transformation of risky buildings from
all fees and taxes.

While the main beneficiaries of the LTADR became private developers,
there have been two sides of the coin for the demand side. On the one hand,
the landlords, who are not residents in the transformation areas but rather use
their properties as an investment tool or lease out, are highly likely to obtain
capital gains at the end of the urban transformation since values of properties increase in renewed buildings or areas. Moreover, some landlords buy old
apartment units in certain neighbourhoods with the expectation of a future
declaration of them as transformation areas (interview XV; interview VIII). On
the other hand, resident homeowners, who do not have financial savings to
cover the expenses of the renewal, are obliged to either get involved into the
financial system by receiving mortgages or lose their homes by selling their
shares. Yet, tenants have become voiceless and neglected; while they have
been excluded from their neighbourhoods even after the transformation is
completed as they do not become financially capable of meeting increasing
rents in general (interview VIII; Purkis, 2014), the state's main offer to evicted
tenants have been mortgage subsidies in the form of interest rate (4% with
10 year-maturity) to encourage home ownership.

8 Conclusion

This chapter focused on the role of the state in housing SoP in the post-2002 period by examining the restructuring of TOKI, which is the main state institutions in land and housing markets in Turkey. The restructuring of TOKI under AKP rule has been considered as a new moment of the articulation of the economic and political in the housing sphere. Specifically, TOKI is a historical and institutional outcome of both financialised neoliberalism and the contemporary form of authoritarian statism. For the former, the reorganisation of the Administration as a public enterprise with private firm qualifications, its transformation from a mortgage institution into a kind of Privatisation Institution under the shadow of the state's welfare apparatus, its turn to a self-financing entity against the fiscal austerity measures of the 2000s and its gradual move towards capital markets for financing itself have been a crucial example of the financialisation of social housing and financialisation of the state in Turkey. For the latter, as a consequence of the changing of the balance of class forces in Turkey under AKP rule and the increasing contradictions between accumulations and legitimating functions of the state in housing, TOKI has been restructured in a new authoritarian institutional form as the main representative of the strong executive power in the urban sphere. This authoritarian restructuring of the Administration was presented in this chapter with its new qualification in six spheres that are land, planning, housing provision, real estate investment, finance and urban transformation, respectively. The enhanced state capacity in production and consumption of housing and TOKI's relationship with different fractions of construction capital were examined in more detail in the subsequent chapters.

CHAPTER 7

Consumption of Housing

The consumption of housing occurs through two formal tenure forms in Turkey, namely owner-occupation and private rented. This chapter focuses on the owner-occupation as the ideologically dominant tenure form in the Turkish housing SoP during the 2000s and 2010s. Alongside being the dominant mode of consumption of the financialised housing provision in Turkey, the other reason of focusing on owner-occupation in this chapter is the absence of official data for private rented sector. The post-2002 era witnessed the state's systematic and continuous intervention to ensure the precedence of owner-occupation. TOKI's direct housing provision for low and middle-income people, who become indebted via the state-sponsored mortgage credits, indicates that the Turkish state's main demand-side policy is creating a leveraged homeownership society. However, the peculiarity of the 2000s does not only stem from TOKI's unique role, but also the participation of new actors to the housing SoP of Turkey, notably the heavy involvement of commercial banks into the mortgage market for the first time in the Turkish history. This chapter will start an examination of the housing purchase finance and mortgage boom in the post-2002 period. The subsequent sections analyse financial inclusion and exclusion dynamics, the rise of a shadow banking system, the general determinants of housing effective demand, the residential land and house price inflation and housing inequality.

1   Housing Purchase Finance and Mortgage Boom?

Due to the diminishing financial returns from the purchase of the GDS and the remarkable fall in inflation rates in the 2000s, the commercial banks increasingly switched their investment activities towards consumer lending, making housing loans the most important component of their overall consumer loan portfolio with its nearly 50% share since 2004, when TOKI was eliminated from the housing finance system of Turkey. Therefore, the most important source of the housing purchase finance in Turkey became the mortgages provided by the commercial banks in the post-2001 crisis period.

However, the milestone for housing purchase finance in Turkey is the year 2007, when a new mortgage system was established. Following the significant drop in inflation and interest rates and the restructuring of the banking sector, the AKP government started to work on the formation of a legal mortgage market in the country and the collaborative work of the government with the Capital Markets Board (CMB) resulted in the enactment of the Housing Finance Law (No. 5582) in 2007. The law established the institutional and legal infrastructure of both primary and secondary mortgage markets. The novelties brought by the law include: i) mortgage finance corporations, financial leasing companies, REITs and investment funds are allowed to provide mortgage loans to house buyers on condition that they must get approval and licencing from the BRSA, ii) banks and mortgage financing institutions are allowed to give both long-term fixed and floating-rate (CPI-pegged) mortgages and therefore the fixed-rate mortgages became available for the first time in Turkey, iii) banks and mortgage financing institutions are permitted to pool mortgages and securitise them, iv) mortgage-covered bonds (MCB) and mortgage-backed securities (MBS) are introduced as the new capital market instruments, v) the CMB was authorised to regulate and supervise Turkey's secondary market institutions and issue the required capital market legislations and vi) several laws (Financial Leasing Law, Consumer Protection Law, Mass Housing Law, Capital Markets Law, Execution and Bankruptcy Law, Civil Law, and Tax Law) were modified and amended within the framework of the Housing Finance Law (Erol, 2016). Therefore, the institutional and legal bases for the transformation of monopoly rent into fictitious capital and its trade in capital markets were created for the first time in the Turkish history.

Although during the 2000s and early 2010s, there was no development regarding the secondary mortgage market and the boom happened through the primary market, the second half of the 2010s witnessed some attempts to vitalise the secondary mortgage market due to the reversal of favorable conditions for the expansion of consumer credit market in accord with the fluctuations in the global financial markets, the heavy external indebtedness of the banks, the resultant urge for increasing their liquidity to fund housing loans and increasing pressure of the hegemonic capital fractions of the construction sector on the government to speed up the turnover times of their unsold housing stock (Sabah, 2012; IMF 2017; 2018).

In 2014, the CMB released "the Communiqué on Covered Bonds, which introduced a single piece of legislation to govern both mortgage- and asset-covered bonds" and the Communiqué on Asset-Backed and Mortgage-Backed Securities, which determined the principals and details of the issuance of MBS (Erol, 2019b: 735). Following this, in 2016, Vakıfbank, one of the largest

TABLE 7 Mortgage-backed covered bonds in Turkey

Years	2015	2016	2017	2018
Total mortgage-backed covered bonds outstanding (EUR million)	128	628	1,923	2,334
Total mortgage-backed covered bonds issuance (EUR million)	128	500	1,334	766

SOURCE: EUROPEAN COVERED BOND COUNCIL, HYPO.ORG/ECBC/

state-owned banks of Turkey, issued the first residential mortgage-backed covered bond, worth €500 million (Table 7), and the European Bank for Reconstruction and Development (BERD) invested €50 million in this MCB. This first attempt to raise capital for mortgage loans via the bond market was followed by another large private bank (Garanti Bank) which issued €130 million worth residential MCB. Since then, other public and private banks rapidly started to apply to the Capital Market Board to get a licence for issuing residential MCBs. Although the size and volume of the MCB are still low and underdeveloped comparative to the European MCB market (EMF Hypostat, 2019), its slowly increasing growth and desire of the commercial banks to find new financial sources to fund mortgages in the recent years signals that soon the CMB issuance will be highly likely one of the main financing methods of the house purchase finance.

Secondly, for the first time in Turkey, the state-owned Turkey Development and Investment Bank completed the issuance of the mortgage-backed securities, worth TL3,15 billion in December of 2018 and TL1 billion in 2019, to raise funds for mortgage loans and to "free up bank balance sheets and improve lenders'[1] access to liquidity" (Karakaya and Kandemir, 2018). Moreover, in March of 2020, the Central Bank also announced the inclusion of MBSs in its collateral pool, accept these mortgage securities as collateral to enhance banks' liquidity

---

[1] For this, in 2018, the risk weight of the banks for the MBSs was reduced to zero from 1.25% by the BDDK to enable banks to use their portfolio mortgages to issue in the secondary market.

and use these mortgage securities in its swap operations. Although this is a very recent development and, therefore, underdeveloped to show an indicator of the precedence of IBC in the house-purchase finance in Turkey, this step shows that the AKP government searches for new financial sources for funding housing demand, aims to develop a subprime market and uses the state-owned banks and the Central Bank to drive this process.

Finally, as shown in the former chapter, following the release of the Communiqué on Real Estate Certificates in 2013 and the legislation of supporting regulations in the years 2016 and 2017 by the CMB, TOKI issued nearly 3.4 million real estate certificates on BIST for its revenue-sharing project in Istanbul and sold these derivative products to domestic individual and international investors in 2017. This project is considered a pilot project by TOKI to fund its future housing projects, to set an example for other actors of the construction sector and to initiate a new funding method for the construction and real estate sectors in Turkey. The trade of these certificates in the secondary market is expected to raise funding for both housing production and consumption. Regarding the consumption side, each certificate was sold at a very small price (TL 42.50) to include people from the lowest income groups who can mobilise their savings for a future purchase. The following message was given by the President of Borsa Istanbul in a panel to introduce the certificates to the public: "the investment you made to the securities via these certificates may turn to the ownership of a house if you accumulate enough certificates. You can also sell them whenever you want and make it liquid again. [...] With these certificates, we will reach to the bottom end of the population if we can solve the financial literacy problem of Turkish population" (Milliyet, 2017). The use of this new derivative product is expected to feed the land and house price inflation in the country by expanding effective demand and the amount of MR and to make households as the new financial investors and risk-takers. This novel instrument applied by TOKI has been a significant step in the financialisation of housing in the form of both commodification, meaning increased deployment of IBC via the trade of revenue streams in the capital market, and commodity calculation. Although the performance of the certificates sold within the scope of the pilot project of TOKI was below the expectations discussed before, this was considered due to the financial illiteracy of the households as mentioned by President of the Borsa Istanbul.

Therefore, it is not coincidental that in the same period, an official financial inclusion and education campaign was launched by the AKP government and a state strategy document, namely the Strategy for Financial Access, Financial Education, the Protection of Financial Consumers and Action, was published by the PM office. This campaign aimed at expanding the formal financial tools to all segments of the society as 'finance for all' to educate citizens for using the existing and future financial instruments and services and facilitate their active participation, to equip them with financial literacy to deal with risk elements in financial markets (i.e. households as risk-absorbers) and to help the poor to make rational decisions around their savings (i.e. households as financial investors and calculators). Therefore, for guaranteeing the future success of the securitisation of mortgages and the use of derivative products by society, the state has proactively developed entrepreneurship programmes and seminars since 2014 (Güngen, 2017).

To summarise, the development of a secondary mortgage market started with the enactment of the mortgage law in 2007, became idle for nearly seven years but accelerated in the second half of the 2010s with the development and use of new mortgage-backed capital market instruments. At this point, the effort for developing secondary a mortgage market in the 2010s is a policy response of the AKP government (in the form of further financial deepening) against the negative impacts of the crisis-ridden economic environment of the post-2013 era on the construction sector and banking sector. Although financing house purchase via MBSs and MCBs are relatively new practices in Turkey and, therefore, the secondary mortgage market is still less developed compared to the ACCs and some LCCs, such as Malaysia and Chile (EMF Hypostat, 2013; Micco *et al.*, 2012), this process will likely gain speed and result in the creation of a sub-prime market in Turkey, due to the current narrowing in the housing effective demand (see below) and the unaffordability of the political and economic risks arising from the crisis in the construction sector.

On the other hand, the primary mortgage market showed an unprecedented development in Turkey since 2004 and its spectacular growth resulted in a mortgage boom in the country. Firstly, this boom was driven by commercial banks. Although mortgage finance institutions, REITs, REIFs and investment banks are also allowed to provide housing loans through the Housing Finance law in 2007, they did not get involved in financing housing demand, but the main mortgage lenders became the commercial banks. As shown in Figure 13, from 2003 to 2015, private domestic banks became the dominant lenders with their 55.7% and 47.13% shares respectively, while the state-owned banks were also gradually increasing their weight in mortgage lending, whose shares in overall lending rose from 10.1% in 2003 to 36.7% in 2015. However, since 2016, there has been a significant increase in the share of the state-owned banks in overall mortgage lending and, currently, they dominate the mortgage market because of the use of the state-owned banks by the AKP in stimulating domestic credit expansion and household consumption (indebtedness) against the

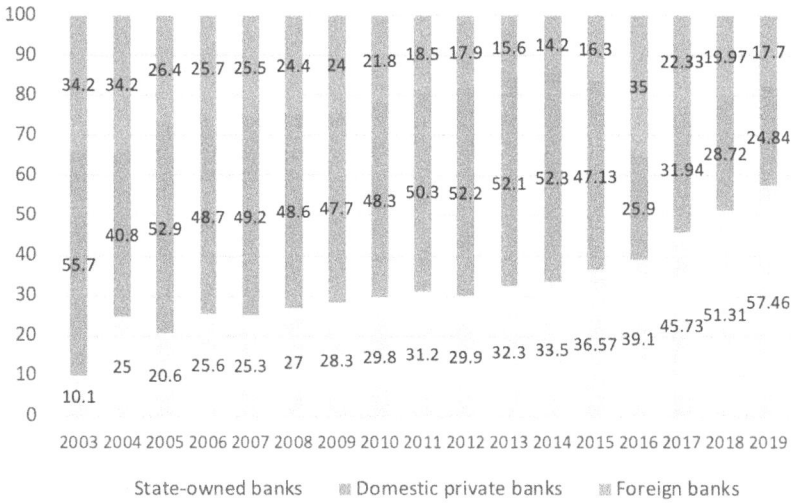

FIGURE 13   Share of the state-owned, private and foreign banks in overall mortgage lending
             (2003–2019)
             SOURCE: BRSA (BDDK.ORG.TR); BAT (TBB.ORG.TR)

decreasing growth rates following the coup attempt in 2016 and the debt and
currency crash of the private sector in 2018.

Furthermore, because of the underdeveloped secondary mortgage market,
Turkish banks fund housing loans mostly through their deposit base (EMF
Hypostat, 2013). However, because the Turkish banks tried to improve their
balance sheets and deposit basis by borrowing from international financial
markets and therefore financed TL-dominated housing loans through foreign exchange funds, an indirect expansion of IBC in Turkey's primary mortgage market and an indirect impact of "global factors [on the house purchase
finance] given the banking sector's heavy reliance on external funding" took
place (IMF, 2017: 56). One of the most direct indicators of the volatility in the
global financial markets on mortgage loans through the banking system has
been the monthly interest rates on mortgages. Although the fall in the mortgage rates since the beginning of the 2000s is spectacular, this has been very
volatile during the 2000s and 2010s (Figure 14).

Also, housing loans with relatively long maturities became available after
2004 for the first time in Turkey and since then the banks gradually extended the
maturities of housing loans to enable more people to access the formal mortgage market. Although in the early 2000s, the maturities officially extended
to 20 years, such a long repayment period was not welcomed by the banks in

Mortgage loan rates (the end of each month - %)

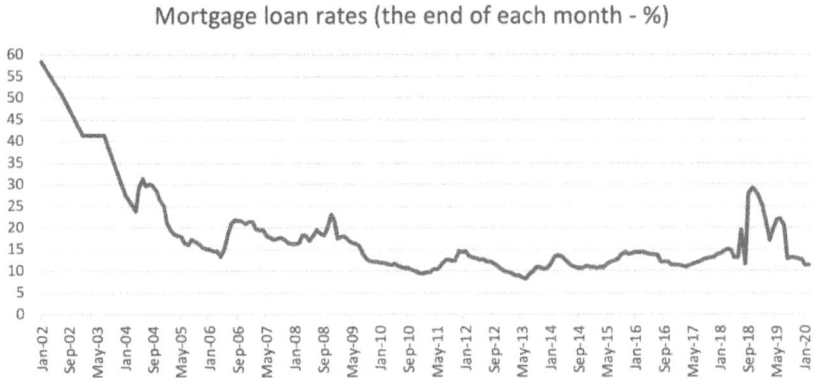

FIGURE 14   The change in the ratio of mortgage loan rates (the end of each month — %)
              (2002–2019)
              SOURCE: CBRT HTTPS://EVDS2.TCMB.GOV.TR/

practice and "nearly half of households prefer[ed] a maturity of 5 to 10 years, while the share of loans with maturities of longer than 10 years [was] 19 per-cent, which [was] quite low when compared to international figures" (Turhan, 2008: 4). Similarly, between 2006 and 2010, the average maturities of the loans were 7.2 years and in the early 2010s, the preferred mortgage loan maturity varied around 7 to 10 years (TBB, 2013; 2019). The main reason why households did not prefer to use mortgages with longer periods is the application of much higher interest rates for the loans with longer maturities. However, because the AKP government initiated a mortgage campaign by using the state-owned banks, as a part of its anti-crisis strategy based on stimulating the domestic credit-market expansion and debt-based household consumption, the public banks and some private banks offer mortgages with 20-year maturity by reduc-ing the interest rates applied for this term on an unprecedented scale (Hürriyet, 2020). Nonetheless, because most of the housing loans of the banks have been funded by their 3-months deposits, there has been a maturity mismatch risk for the Turkish banks due to the increasing gap between the maturities of their liabilities and mortgage loan maturities. This can also be considered one of the reasons why the commercial banks in Turkey accelerated their search for alternative funding methods for house purchase finance through the securities and bond markets since 2014.

Three important regulations were made by the BRSA to prevent the poten-tial risks of the rapidly developing mortgage market on the banking system and borrowers. The first one is the allowance of banks to disburse both floating-rate and fixed-rate loans with the Housing Finance Law in 2007, which saw nearly all loans given at a fixed rate (Gökçeimam, 2019). This measure aimed to protect both banks and house purchasers against the risk of volatile interest rates (Vural, 2019). Secondly, while the Turkish banks offered US Dollar and Euro-denominated mortgages alongside the TL-dominated mortgages until 2011 (Erol and Çetinkaya, 2009), the BRSA set a maximum limit for FX-dominated mortgage loans at 25% in 2011 and, therefore, legally prohibited external indebtedness of households against a potential FX risk, which happened in some Central and Eastern European countries (CEECs), such as Hungary and Poland (CBRT, 2011; IMF, 2014; dos Santos, 2013; Lis, 2015). Therefore, almost all mortgage loans in Turkey have been TL-dominated since then and only a very small amount of FX-dominated loans have been given to the foreign citizens with residences in Turkey (Gökçeimam, 2019: 522). Thirdly, in 2011, the BRSA also brought a maximum LTV (loan-to-value) limit for residential mortgages at 75% in that the number of extended mortgage loans cannot exceed 75% of the appraised market value of the housing unit and house purchasers must have 25% down-payment. However, within the scope of the counter-cyclical policies of the AKP, which aimed to expand the domestic credit market and household consumption, the government increased the LTV rate to 80% in 2016, temporarily decreased the VAT on luxury houses from 18% to 8%, and reduced the risk weight of the mortgage loans from 50% to 35% to stimulate housing demand and encourage people to invest in housing. Another important government regulation is the mortgage interest rate subsidy for people purchasing houses to rent but not for the ones who buy housing for their own use (Türel and Koç, 2015). Therefore, for the property investors, the law allowed "the interest paid on the mortgage credit [to be] deducted from the part of the rent that is subject to income tax" (ibid., 57). In other words, the state directly encourages the use of housing as an investment tool (see below).

Consequently, the significant fall in the mortgage rates and increase in maturities, particularly from 2004, caused unprecedentedly and exponentially increasing numbers of households to be involved in the mortgage market (see Figure 15) and to purchase housing via formal financial mechanisms for the first time in Turkish history. On the one hand, such large participation of people to the formal financial system led to a substantial surge in effective demand and general monopoly rent in the country, which had been constrained by the lack of a formal and institutional mortgage finance system for decades. Specifically, the financialisation of housing in the commodity form, which is the formation and growth of the housing credit market enhancing the housing purchase capacity of people, emancipates monopoly rent from the decades-long limitations of effective demand. Nonetheless, the mortgage rates are still too high comparative to not only the ACCs in the Euro zone but some other CEECs too,

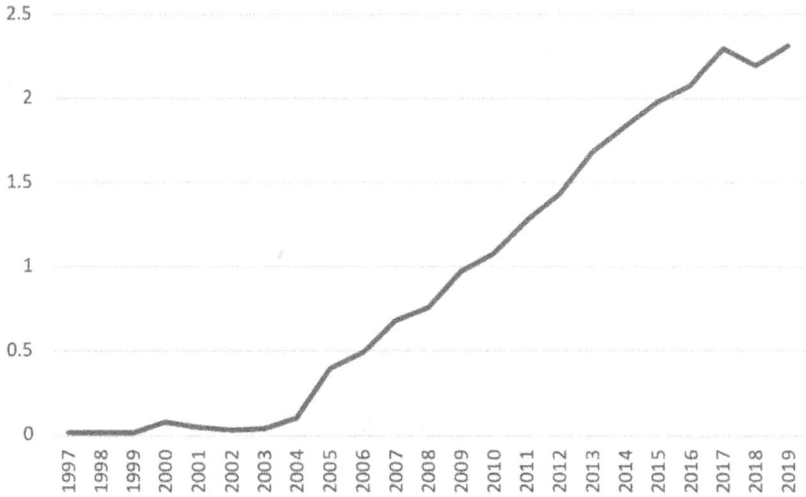

FIGURE 15   The total number of people using mortgage loans (million people) (1997–2019)
SOURCE: BAT ANNUAL REPORTS HTTPS://WWW.TBB.ORG.TR/EN/BANKS
-AND-BANKING-SECTOR-INFORMATION/STATISTICAL-REPORTS/20; * THIS
NUMBER IS FOR OUTSTANDING MORTGAGE LOANS

such as Bulgaria, Czech Republic, Hungary and Lithuania (EMF Hypostat, 2013; 2018; 2019). This contributed to the exclusion of the poor from the mortgage market and the development of a shadow banking system in financing housing purchase especially from the second half of the 2010s (see below).

Thanks to the establishment of a formal mortgage system and the commercial banks' increasing attention to the mortgage market, the demand for mortgage loans expanded nearly from the scratch and the volume of outstanding mortgage loans, which was TL2 billion in 2004, rose to TL200 billion in 2019 by growing 10,000%, as can be seen from Figure 16, that created a mortgage boom in the county lasting more than a decade. In line with this, the ratio of mortgage loans in GDP increased from 0 to 8% in 2017 — that is a substantial rise within Turkey's history but very low compared to the ones in ACCs varying between 25% (Austria in 2008, but 29% in 2018) to 80% (the USA in 2008, but 53% in 2018) (EMF Hypostat, 2018: 116). Although the share of the mortgage loans in GDP had a general upward trend until 2017, it started to swiftly fall since 2017, as displayed in Figure 16.

Moreover, as seen in Figure 17, the mortgage loans accounted to almost half of the total consumer loans (excluding credit cards) given by the commercial banks in the country, increasing from 10% in 2002 to 49% in 2016, thanks to the rapid decline in the mortgage rates and extension of maturities. Similarly,

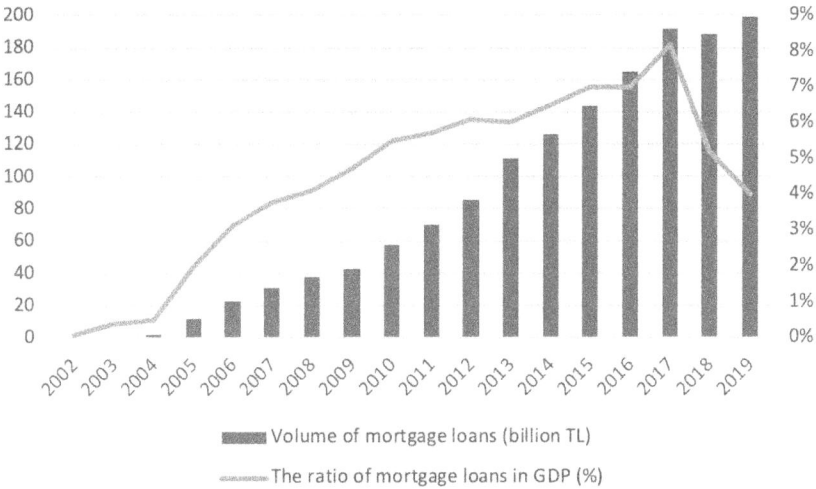

FIGURE 16   The volume of the outstanding mortgage loans (billion TL) and the ratio of
mortgage loans in GDP (2002–2019)
SOURCE: CBRT AND BRSA

when looking at the ratio of mortgage indebtedness within total household liabilities, including credit card debts, health, education and other expenses, it is possible to observe that more than one-third of the total indebtedness of households has been composed by the mortgage indebtedness since 2006 as a nearly flat line. Therefore, households have been under the heavy burden of financial indebtedness to sustain their housing needs since the early 2000s.

Despite this striking growth, the share of the mortgage loans in total assets of banks reached 7% in 2012 and varied between 4% and 7% during the late 2000s and the 2010s, due to the underdeveloped secondary mortgage market and the financing of mortgage loans through the deposit base of the commercial banks in Turkey, although Turkish banks expanded their mortgage portfolios by borrowing from international financial markets (Erol, 2019a).

Finally, the fluctuations in the primary mortgage market can be examined through the number of mortgage loans extended, as displayed in Figure 18. This shows periodically extended loans, unlike the outstanding loans in Figure 16, and helps track the impact of the institutional regulations and macroeconomic volatility on the mortgage market. As it can be noticed, the flow of mortgage loans swiftly increased from 2004, particularly after the enactment of the mortgage law in 2007. However, the growth of mortgage loans extended temporarily halted in 2010 and 2011 because the BRSA "attempted to monitor the skyrocketing loans by tightening the regulations concerning capital adequacy and credit

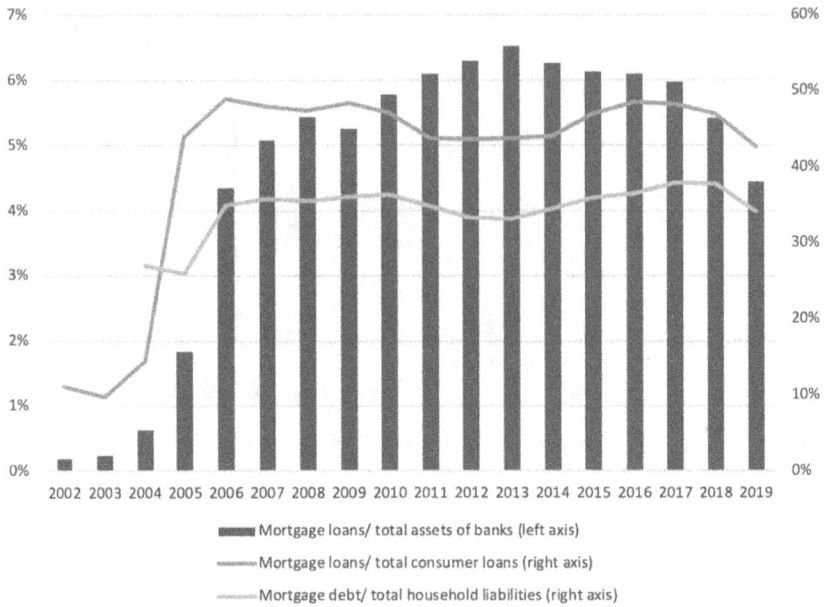

FIGURE 17   The ratios of mortgage loans in total consumer loans and total assets of banks
             and the ratio of mortgage debt in total household liabilities
             SOURCE: BRSA, BDDK.ORG.TR; CBRT, ANNUAL FINANCIAL STABILITY
             REPORTS, HTTPS://TCMB.GOV.TR/WPS/WCM/CONNECT/EN/TCMB+EN/MAIN+
             MENU/PUBLICATIONS/REPORTS/ANNUAL+REPORTS/ *EXCLUDES NON-
             PERFORMING MORTGAGE LOANS

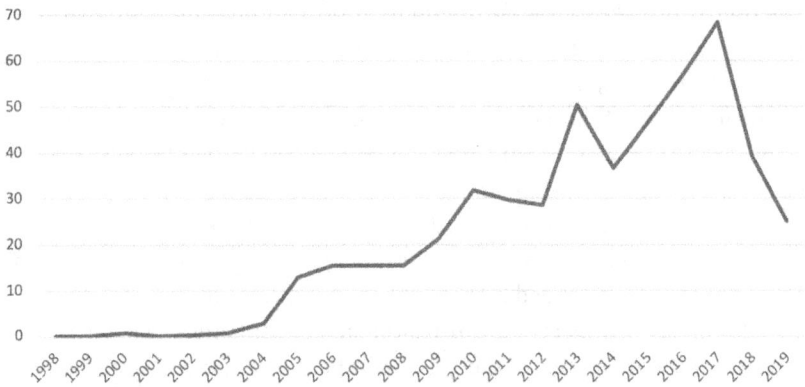

FIGURE 18   The number of mortgage loans extended, billion TL (1998–2019)
             SOURCE: BAT (TBB.ORG.TR); *EXTENDED TERM LOANS

risks, which forced the banks to be more prudent concerning consumer loans particularly in housing loans" as part of the measurements taken against the GFC (Topal *et al.*, 2015: 41). After the sharp growth in the amounts of mortgage debt in 2012, the Central Bank and the BRSA unwillingly[2] put some macro-prudential measurements into practice in 2013, such as further increasing mortgage credit risk weightings and borrowers' income and credit score requirements to restrict the expansion of domestic consumer credit market in the face of depreciating domestic currency, increasing risks of currency mismatch due to the heavy FX-indebtedness of the NFCs and commercial banks and the potential balance sheets problems of the banks.[3] Therefore, the year 2013 witnessed a relative slowdown in mortgage demand that reflected the decline in the amounts of the housing credits, which decreased from TL50 billion in 2013 to TL36 billion in 2014. However, since the end of 2015 and especially after the failed coup attempt in 2016,[4] the regulatory risk weights on consumer loans were lowered, LTV ratio of mortgages increased from 75% to 80%, minimum wages increased by 30%, the purchase of luxury houses were exempted from taxes and AKP announced a new national housing mobilisation promising "to contribute 15% to 20% of household savings for first single-home purchases to improve debt affordability for low-income households" (Erol, 2019b: 730). The amount of the extended housing credits massively expanded from TL36 billion in 2014 to TL68 billion in 2017. Despite this effort of the government to sustain the mortgage boom in the country, from 2017 on, the accumulated fragilities in the economy, not only in the form of potential currency and debt crisis of the private sector but also the explosion in inflation and unemployment rates

2 The restriction on the expansion of domestic credit markets meant the decrease in the growth rates of the economy because the AKP governments used the households' debt-based private consumption, the expansion of idle loanable money capital and the resultant asset price inflation to stimulate economic growth since the early 2000s (Orhangazi and Özgür, 2015; Bahçe *et al.*, 2015; Güngen, 2017).

3 However, at the end of 2011, the Central Bank introduced the Reserve Options Mechanism "which allows banks to keep a certain ratio of their Turkish lira reserve requirements in foreign exchange and/or gold" to smooth "exchange rate and balance sheet effects of [short-term] capital flow volatility" (Alper *et al.*, 2013: 211).

4 Right after the coup attempt in 2016, President Erdoğan urged the banks to cut the mortgage rates by giving them the target rate of 9%. Interestingly, Erdoğan said that "interest rates on consumer loans put by penny-pincher banks are cruel to people. Banks must pile it high and sell it cheap or renounce their gains to support the economy and the country against the treason" (Milliyet, 2016). Even the PM Binali Yıldırım "joined the push, telling lenders: You either do this on your own or we make you do it" (Courcoulas and Ercan, 2016). The Turkish banks responded to Erdoğan by collectively decreasing the interest rates on mortgage loans from 13.8% compounded in June to 11.5% in November.

caused the decrease in the housing effective demand. Consequently, the ratio of mortgage loans in GDP fell from 8% to 4%, the amount of the extended housing credits decreased from almost TL70 billion in 2017 to TL25 billion in 2019, and the mortgage rates spiked in 2018 and 2019.

This shows that the boom-bust cycles of the mortgage market followed the general trends of the macroeconomic expansion and contraction phases in Turkey through the banking system. However, what makes Turkey different is the state's massive intervention to delay the bust phase of the housing and mortgage markets. While this intervention stems from the vital role of the expansion of loanable money-capital and the circulation of revenues in the AKP government's consumption and credit-driven economic growth strategy, the political and economic importance of the construction sector in the hegemonic project of the AKP fuelled the endless struggle for keeping the housing effective demand alive and enabling the turnover of the accumulated housing stock of construction capitalists (Chapter 8). Therefore, against the recent economic turmoil in 2018, the AKP government's response became the expansionary fiscal and monetary policies to boost housing purchases via the mortgage market. For this, minimum wages were increased, the benchmark interest rates were successively reduced by the CBRT during the second half of 2019; lower TL reserve requirements were introduced for banks to stimulate their fund-raising activities from international financial markets and therefore to enhance their (mortgage) lending portfolios; the VAT exemption on luxury housing purchases were prolonged, the title deed fees paid when purchasing dwellings were reduced from 4% to 3%, a mortgage campaign was initiated by the state-owned banks in that below-market-rate mortgages with long maturities, and inflation-indexed mortgage loans and those with the option of one-year payment delay have been offered and continuously advertised by the large media outlets as 'homeownership like paying a monthly rent' (Sabah, 2019; Takvim, 2020; Sözcü, 2020). According to the IMF (2019: 9) report on Turkey,

> [This] rapid credit growth by state-owned banks has weakened their balance sheets, hampered needed deleveraging, and fueled dollarization. New lending and restructuring deals have eroded capital, and TL28 billion (0.7 percent of GDP) was injected into state-owned banks in April 2019 to strengthen their capital base. To support net interest margins while providing credit below the cost of CBRT funding, state-owned banks kept lira deposit rates low, and borrowed heavily in FX, contributing to a sharp increase in deposit dollarization.

Therefore, the cost of the debt-led growth is socialised by the state-owned banks and the fragilities of Turkey's financialised accumulation model is transferred into the public sector. During 2020, it seems that this mortgage campaign driven by the state-owned banks starts to revitalise housing purchase demand again although it is early to interpret this very recent rise as a new mortgage boom in Turkey, unless recent capital market instruments like MBSs and MCBs develop further, which would liberate the banks' balance sheets from mortgage liabilities, dispose their risks to other investors and expand the lending capacities, and the ongoing high inflation and high unemployment rates are reversed.

2   Two Sides of the Same Coin: Financial Inclusion and Exclusion

So far, it has been argued that the AKP era witnessed the remarkable development of primary mortgage market and a slow but obvious expansion of the secondary mortgage market thanks to the invention of new mortgage-backed capital market instruments, a mortgage boom between 2005 and 2017, a historical growth in the volume of outstanding mortgages (reaching to TL200 billion as of 2019) and a heavy mortgage indebtedness for an increasing part of the population that reached to nearly 4.5 million people as of 2019. However, because a subprime market could not be developed in Turkey, this new formal and institutionalised housing finance market only served the middle and high-income households. Conversely, the low-income people were excluded. Since the LTV ratio at 75% (80% after 2016) requires people to accumulate a substantial amount of money, only a fraction of the society with accumulated wealth, a good credit score, and a (sufficient) regular income to pay monthly instalments has a chance to access the mortgages.[5] This is the main reason why mortgage loans have very low non-performance ratio in Turkey. This is particularly the case for housing loans which reached a maximum 2.14% in 2009, when the unemployment rate temporarily soared as a reflection of the GFC, but reduced to 0.84% in 2012, as can be seen in Table 8. Even during the economic turmoil of 2013, 2016 and 2018, the share of the NP mortgage loans within total mortgage loans declined at 0.69%, 0.47% and 0.44% respectively. Another reason for these very low default rates in mortgage payments is the social and cultural significance of homeownership in Turkey. In my interviews, almost all participants mentioned that the debtors sell their cars, gold and

---

5   There is no data showing the distribution of the housing loans according to income groups.

TABLE 8   The ratios of non-performing (NP) mortgage loans in total mortgage loans and
           total non-performing (NP) consumer loans

Years	The ratio of NP mortgage loans in total mortgage loans (%)	The ratio of NP mortgage loans in total NP consumer loans (%)
2005	0.23%	1.25%
2006	0.17%	1.62%
2007	0.52%	5.28%
2008	0.99%	3.00%
2009	2.14%	11.63%
2010	1.82%	11.45%
2011	1.08%	10.51%
2012	0.84%	8.72%
2013	0.69%	7.55%
2014	0.54%	4.32%
2015	0.00%	4.32%
2016	0.47%	4.11%
2017	0.44%	4.59%
2018	0.44%	4.31%
2019	0.65%	6.16%

SOURCE: CALCULATED BASED ON THE ANNUAL REPORTS OF THE BRSA

jewellery, borrow from the extended family members and even work in multiple jobs to keep their homes.

Therefore, as stated by Yalman *et al.* (2019: 13), "rising household debt and the growing reliance on consumer credits have not been class-neutral phenomena, entailing the transfer of resources from non-capital-owning classes to those who are in a position to benefit". Hence, financial inclusion and the mortgage indebtedness are not class-neutral. Although the mortgage market became accessible for the middle-classes for the first time in the Turkish history, the lower-classes and the poor continued to be excluded from the mortgage markets. Instead, for the urban poor, there are four options to meet their sheltering needs, namely, to wait on a line for TOKI's affordable houses and be by lottery, to be a private tenant, to live in a family-financed housing, to be either a tenant or owner of a gecekondu, which has been much harder in the AKP era since there is no tolerance[6] to gecekondu dwellings anymore.

Regarding the informal housing, no official published statistics shows the current ratio of gecekondu dwellings. According to the study of Turk and Altes (2010: 30), "29% of the urban population, a total of 12.5 million people, live in 2.5 million squatter houses in Turkey". Similarly, according to the media research of the Ajans Press (2019), the ratio of the population living in the gecekondu dwellings within the total population is 12%. Based on these estimations, a substantial part of the population continues to meet their sheltering needs through gecekondu dwellings, despite the AKP governments' unremitting fight against the squatters, TOKI's power to clear squatter areas on the high-value lands and resultant gentrification projects since the early 2000s.

As the only available data, the TurkStat's Population and Housing Survey report (2011) shows that households living in the dwellings owned by their relatives or friends without paying any rent composes 7.3% of the total population. Although the TurkStat does not release any specific indicator for the private tenancy rates divided by income groups, according to the Institute's Annual Income and Living Conditions reports, the share of the people meeting their sheltering needs as private tenants within total population rose from 21% in 2011 to 25% in 2018.[7] Because the spread of owner-occupation was largely driven by the middle and upper-class, it is highly likely that most of the lease-holders are from the low and low-middle classes, especially in the big cities.

Lastly, the poor and low-income group, which is the segment with the largest housing deficit, was largely underserved with its 18% share within total housing units produced by TOKI. Nevertheless, these inclusion-exclusion dynamics in Turkey occurred based on the state-driven partial possession of some lower classes and the dispossession of some others since the materialisation of the homeownership dream for at least a part of the society was crucial for the state to get the political support from the poor and to legitimise the privatisation of public land and distribution of massive-scale ground rent to the hegemonic construction capitalists.

---

6   The approach of the AKP government to gecekondu dwellings can be understood from the speech of the former head of TOKI in a panel in 2007: "Squatting is a terror problem in Turkey. Gecekondu host drug trafficking and terrorists. In our struggle against this, everybody must support us" (Sabah, 2007).

7   According to the same report, nearly 95% of the non-institutional population with the income range below 60% of the median income suffer from a heavy burden of housing costs between 2006 and 2018 (see figure in Appendix 2).

Alongside the exclusion of the lower-classes from the mortgage market (except TOKI-provided houses), the high and volatile mortgage interest rates and the average 7 to 10-year maturities also created a burden for the middle classes and discouraged some potential house purchasers to take mortgage loans from banks. Therefore, despite being marginal, a part of the population continued to apply to the traditional method for house purchasing, that is borrowing from the extended family members.

3   Alternative Searches for Further Financial Inclusion: a Shadow
        Banking-System in Turkey

The volatile interest rates on mortgage loans and the narrowing effective demand, especially after 2013, prompted the private housing developers and REITs to develop a shadow banking system as an alternative financial method in the housing purchase. This refers to the provision of house purchase finance by the private housing developers and REITs based on their equity capital or borrowing from financial institutions, by collateralising their assets including landbanks and properties. In this system, the private developers, like unofficial mortgage finance institutions, issue a bill to house purchasers to be paid in monthly instalments that offer below-market mortgage rates and longer maturities.

Moreover, as the most widespread financing of this type, the developer takes out a business loan from private domestic banks for a certain housing project and then makes a special agreement with a shadow bank where the developer puts up its assets as collateral to the bank and in return, the bank provides mortgage loan to the developer's customers for this specific housing project according to the terms and conditions of the bill issued by the developer (see Figure 19). Although in practice the house purchaser gets the mortgage loan from the agreed bank, this mortgage debt is financed by the construction company. This way, the developer company, instead of the bank, undertakes the default risk of the house purchasers.

Through this shadow banking activities, the private housing developers started to provide "subsidized mortgage loans at more favorable lending terms compared to the terms of banks' mortgage loans" and with higher LTV ratios and uncontrolled eligibility criteria, which is highly likely significantly below the criteria of the banks (IMF, 2017: 57). Looking at the ratio of the housing sales via mortgage loans within total housing sales in Figure 20, the share of the mortgage-backed sales within total housing sales rose from 4% to 41% in 2009 but significantly dropped after 2013, when the first financial shock in the

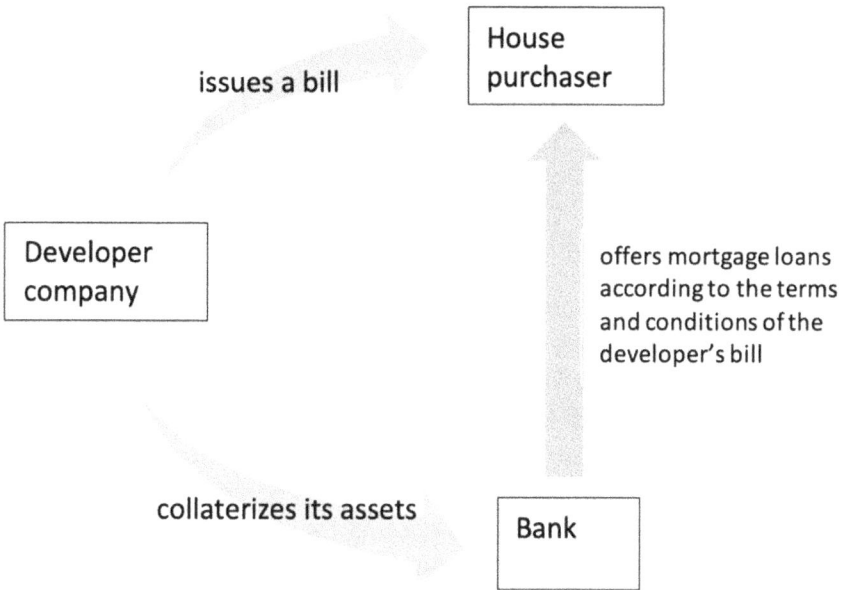

FIGURE 19   Shadow banking system in housing purchase finance

Turkish economy occurred and the resultant spike in interest rates and follow-ing macroprudential measures restricted the mortgage demand, and then in 2018, when the biggest currency and debt crash of the post-2001 era happened in the private sector.

Figure 21 also shows the number of housing sales according to the financ-ing methods. The financial methods other than mortgage loans dominate the house purchasing since 2009. The TurkStat does not give any details about the other financing methods, which include cash payments, shadow banking sys-tem and the FDI to the residential market (foreigner's residential purchases). Although there is no indicator about which percentage of this 'other housing sales' is financed through the shadow banking system, it is high likely that a substantial part of the 'other sales'[8] is financed through the developers' asset collateralisation.

Because there is no institutional tracking or control on these housing cred-its, which are raised out of the formal mortgage market, and the housing supply side directly undertakes the default risks of the house purchasers to speed up

---

8   According to another interpretation, some people launder unrecorded money by purchasing residential units in Turkey (Aşıcı, 2016; Purkis, 2016). This is probably true but we think that it constitutes only a marginal part of the total housing sales.

Mortgage sales to total house sales (%)

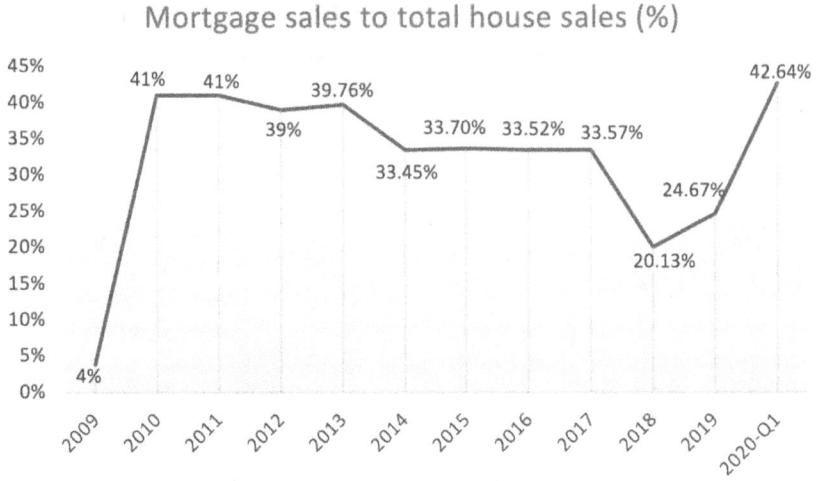

FIGURE 20   The ratio of mortgage-backed sales in total house sales (2009 and 2019)
SOURCE: TURKSTAT HTTPS://CIP.TUIK.GOV.TR/#

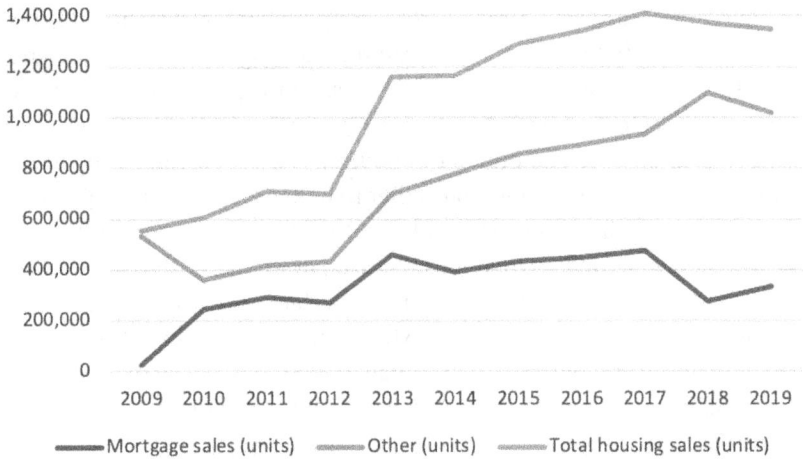

FIGURE 21   The financial methods in the house sales in Turkey (2009 and 2019)
SOURCE: TURKSTAT

their turnover time and deplete their unsold accumulated stock, this shadow banking system creates significant uncertainty and increases bankruptcy risk for housing developers, especially when considering the heavy FX indebtedness of the construction companies (see Chapter 8).

Moreover, this non-institutional house purchase finance has been offered not only by the medium-scale constructors of the individual housing projects but also the largest housing developers and REITs of Turkey, including the Emlak Konut REIT. While for the medium-scale builders, this method provides lump-sum money, to finance a portion of their on-going housing production in the case of the pre-sale agreements, for the large-scale developers and REITs, the shadow financing method helps to deplete their unsold luxury housing units, which have been accumulated during the 2010s. As displayed in Figure 22, there is not a consistent trend around the financing methods in the purchasing of luxury houses. Coupled with Figure 23, the figures show that in the months with higher mortgage rates, the housing purchasers turn towards shadow financing while in the months with lower mortgage rates, the purchasing via the mortgage market directly expands. In any case, the weight of the shadow financing in the case of sales of the luxury houses is quite high, varying from 14.8% to 66% within total sales, during the entire period. The boom phases of shadow financing overlap with the periodisation made to show the crisis in the accumulation model of the AKP governments, meaning the years 2013, 2016 and 2018.

Moreover, although this shadow financing system becomes a black hole in the housing finance of Turkey, the indirect support of the state can be observed. For instance, in the economic turmoil of 2016 and the post-2018, the mortgage campaign and housing sale campaigns via shadow financing were carried out. While the dominant fractions of the construction capital joined President Erdoğan's mortgage campaign in the name of National Housing Mobilization, the private developers and REITs supported their housing sale campaigns[9] with 90–95% LTVs, 2-year deferred repayment, longer-term housing credits with below-market mortgage rates (Milliyet, 2017; Sözcü, 2018). However, all these campaigns and housing mobilisation which is driven by the collaboration of the central government and the shadow financing system of the private developers address to the middle and upper classes and aim to make them invest in housing. However, the sheltering needs of the lower classes and urban poor continue to be ignored and the prevention of informal housing, as the

---

9   The names of the housing sale campaigns are interesting to mention which were the 'Union of Forces in the Real Estate' in 2016 and 'Time to Win in the Real Estate' in the post-2018 period. Moreover, it is important to say that these campaigns had very broad media coverage.

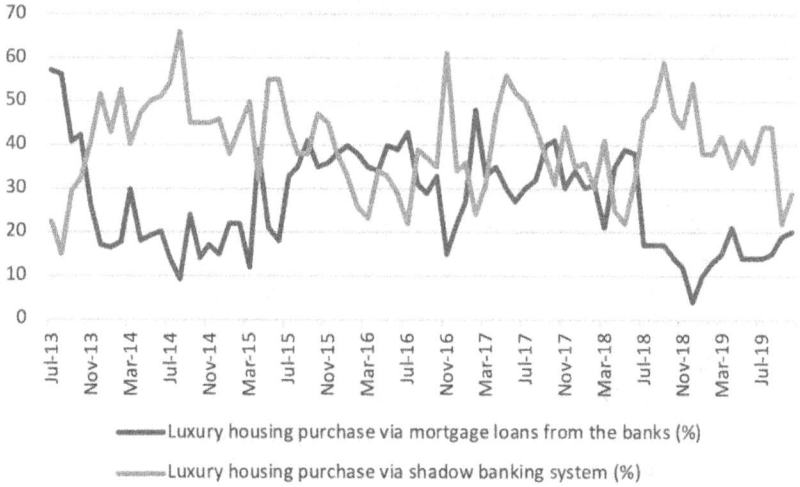

FIGURE 22   The financial methods in the luxury (branded) housing purchases —
             selected months
             SOURCE: GYODER REAL ESTATE SECTOR INDICATORS HTTPS://WWW.GYO
             DER.ORG.TR/EN/PUBLICATIONS/GYODER-INDICATOR

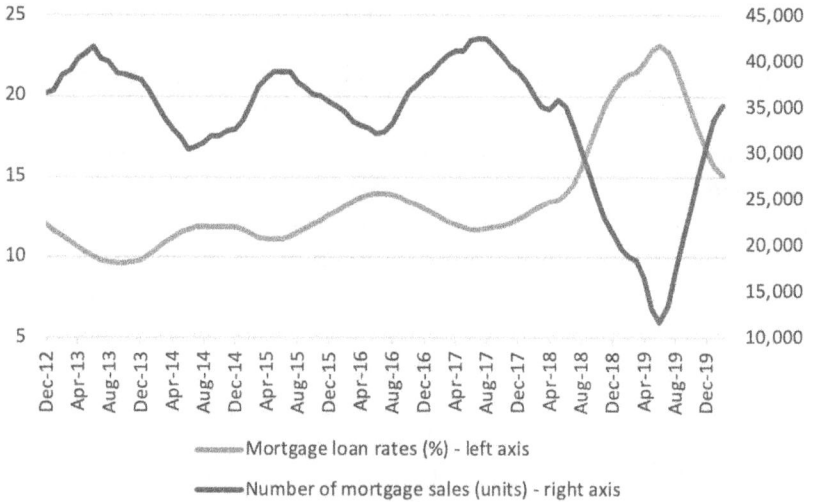

FIGURE 23   The relationship between the number of mortgage-backed sales and interest
             rates on mortgage loans
             SOURCE: CBRT

only decommodified sheltering, obliged them to meet their sheltering needs in market conditions that create a much heavier burden on them, by spending increasing proportions of disposable income on housing, due to the continuously inflating house and rent prices (see below).

4   Effective Demand in Housing

The formal mortgage market and the shadow financing system became the main factors behind the unprecedentedly heightened housing effective demand in Turkey that fuelled the size of the ground rent. However, apart from the housing purchase finance, six other dynamics need to be considered within the scope of housing demand in the post-2001 period. While the population in Turkey was 64.7 million in 2000, it reached nearly 83 million in 2019. Moreover, household formation dramatically changed in Turkey in the recent period. While households traditionally consisted of "large and multigenerational cohabitation", the 2000s witnessed the formation of "the Western model of small households" (The report: Turkey, 2012: 140). Therefore, the average household size decreased from 5.7 in 1970 to 4.12 in 2002 and then to 3.3 in 2019.[10] Decreasing household size together with the increasing young population generated a structural demand for housing in Turkey. Secondly, while only 31% of the total population was living in cities in 1960, 92% of the population lives in urban areas as of 2019.[11] Hence, the continuing migration from rural to urban areas created heavy demand for urban land and housing, especially in large cities. Thirdly, Turkey hosts more than 3.5 million registered Syrian refugees since 2011. This unexpected demographic shock generated an important housing demand especially in the cities near the Syrian border and in Istanbul.

Moreover, there has been an increasing amount of foreign demand on the residential property market in Turkey thanks to the allowance of the foreign investment on real estate by foreigners for the first time in 2003. This has been accelerated with the enactment of a new Reciprocity law (No. 2644) in 2012 that facilitated the FDI on real estate by significantly easing the conditions of foreign purchasing of the properties in Turkey. This recent law in 2012 not only further lifted the former restrictions on FDI to the real estate but offered the Turkish citizenship to the ones who buy real estate worth of at least

---

10   https://data.tuik.gov.tr/Bulten/Index?p=Statistics-on-Family-2020-37251&dil=2 [Accessed 19 February 2023].

11   https://data.tuik.gov.tr/Kategori/GetKategori?p=Nufus-ve-Demografi-109 [Accessed 19 February 2023].

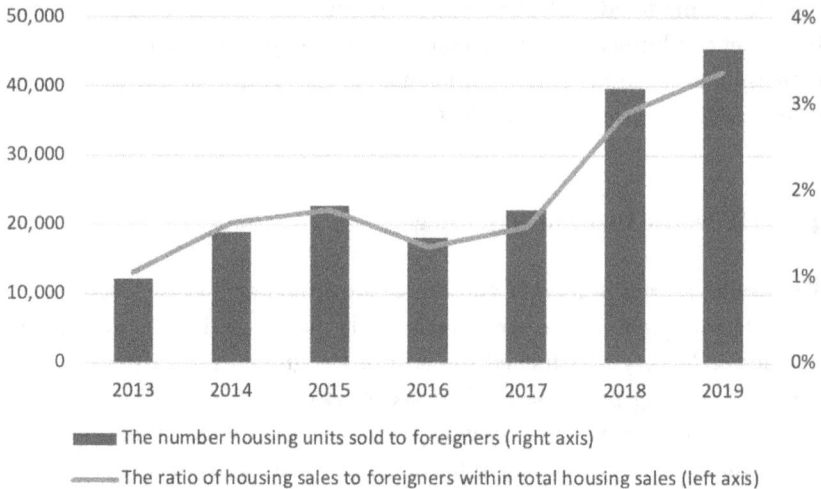

FIGURE 24   Foreign demand for housing in Turkey (2013–2018)
SOURCE: TURKSTAT

$1 million and later reduced to $250,000 in 2018. With this law, the property investors notably from the MENA region and European countries substantially increased their investment in residential real estate in Turkey.[12] Alongside the investment-linked property purchases by foreigners, for some house purchasers, especially from the countries with heavy political turmoil such Iraq, Iran and Afghanistan, the right to citizenship became the main motivation of buying a house in Turkey (Bloomberg, 2016). However, on the one hand, the foreign demand in the housing market is not compelling in terms of the number of housing units. As displayed in Figure 24, the percentage of housing sales to foreigners within the total housing sales rose from 1% in 2013[13] to 3.4% in 2019.

Unlike the number of residential units sold to foreigners, the amount of foreign investment to housing has been very high. This is why foreign demand became very significant for the turnover of the stock of the branded houses. As shown in Figure 25, the share of the sales to foreigners, within total housing sales in the case of the branded houses, which are developed by the largest construction companies and REITs, increased from 2.3% in July of 2013 to 54% in April of 2015 but recently varied between 8 to 20%.

---

12   https://data.tuik.gov.tr/Bulten/Index?p=House-Sales-Statistics-December-2020-37464&
      dil=2 [Accessed 19 February 2023].

13   The year of 2013 is the earliest date which TurkStat start to publish housing sale statistics.

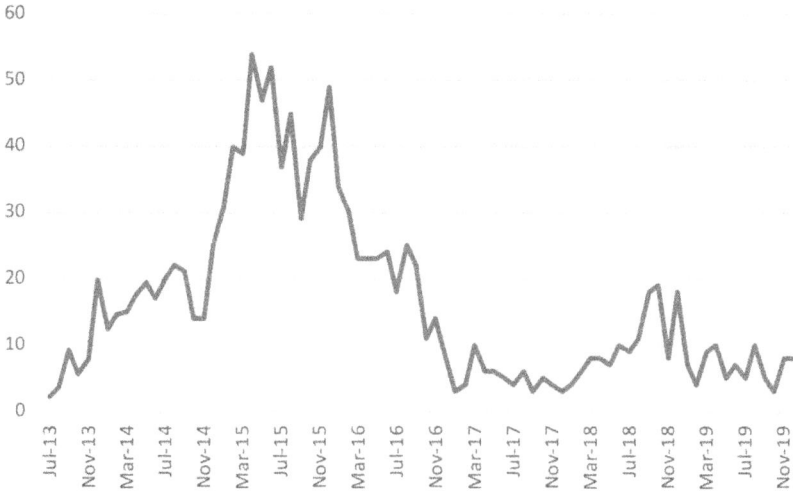

FIGURE 25   The ratio of the branded-housing sales to foreigners within total branded-
housing sales
SOURCE: GYODER REAL ESTATE SECTOR INDICATORS

Therefore, the reciprocity law not only facilitated the expansion of FDI to
the Turkish housing market but linked the monopoly rent from the residential
real estate to the globally circulating IBC, "by allowing rents to be drawn from
the global pool of surplus-value rather than determined by [merely] local factors" (Robertson, 2016: 34).

Also, the 1999 Marmara earthquake became a turning point for housing
SoP in Turkey in the 2000s. The collapse of more than 134,000 buildings in
the Marmara region brought the vitality of the renewal of all risky buildings in
Turkey which became another root of the solid demand for housing. Another
dynamic which needs to be considered regarding the housing effective demand
in Turkey is TOKI's intervention into land and housing markets. Since housing
effective demand is not only a social need for sheltering but also artificially
expansion of housing need and manipulation of demand, the capitalist state
having land planning and zoning powers can generate effective demand by
creating artificial scarcities in urban land and reproducing different qualities of
residential land. While this pace and rhythm of the social and economic reproduction have been extremely rapid in the current phase of capitalism, both
the quality of land parcel and the quality of built environment surrounding
that parcel have been subject to very dynamic and rapid alterations. This rapid
differentiation in the qualities of residential land is accompanied with the creation of new housing sub-markets, not only according to the social class of

people but also their lifestyles, consumption habits and ideological positions.[14] Therefore, the size and amount of localised monopoly rents become different in different housing sub-markets that reflects different conditions of housing effective demand arising from the income and wealth levels, tastes, lifestyles, ideological segregations alongside the closeness of the residential land to the employment opportunities, urban services and amenities such as transportation, school, hospital. Moreover, state, media and capital collectively manipulate the consumption behaviours of people by making housing an object of desire or an investment tool by overshadowing its use-value. This way, the size and amount of residential monopoly rents extracted by developers, investors and financial institutions are swollen. Here, the particularity of the Turkish case stems from the extraordinarily encompassing empowerment of TOKI, its authoritarian intervention into the urban land market and its manipulative and over-politicised planning practices. Because TOKI had the authority to develop shopping malls, commercial buildings, business areas, hospitals, mosques, universities and other social facilities through PPPs, as well as gentrifying urban space by displacing gecekondu residents in high-quality lands, the creation of state-made artificial scarcities happened at an astronomically rapid pace and rhythm in the AKP era.

Consequently, the combination of the structural factors of urban housing demand (including high population rise, new household formation, internal and external migration to urban areas and compulsory demand for earthquake resistant houses) and the main determinants of the housing effective demand (including the mortgage boom during the 2000s and 2010s, the further expansion of housing credit via the shadow financing system during the 2010s, the international capital flows to the residential real estate and the urban planning power of TOKI continously reproducing artificial scarcities in urban land and differentiation in the quality of residential land) lie behind the dramatically inflating land and house prices in Turkey.

---

14 For instance, in Turkey, especially in Istanbul, the conservative middle-class neighbourhoods differ from the residential vicinities of the secular middle-class (interviews; Öncü and Balkan, 2016; Batuman, 2019). Nevertheless, there are several other different determinants of the housing sub-markets such as being a member of religious minorities, different ethnical backgrounds and migrant communities, which are beyond the scope of this book.

5   Residential Land and House Price Inflation

To examine the residential land and house price inflation, the house price index (HPI) is used. However, the most important limitation here is the lack of a long-term official HPI in Turkey, which would allow tracking the historical changes in land and housing prices. The Central Bank (CBRT) started to prepare its HPI in 2010 for the first time. On the other hand, Reidin, a private real estate information company, has released its index since 2007 based on the seven large cities of Turkey by also including the retrospective data since 2003. However, they have significant differences in terms of the methodology and coverage and therefore their results are different from each other (IMF, 2017: 50), and there is no consensus about which one is more reliable for tracking the trends in house price changes in Turkey. Therefore, I will initially employ HPI for Turkey and three biggest cities (Ankara, Istanbul and Izmir) by using the CBRT data set from 2010 to 2019 (Figure 26) and then compare the HPI in Istanbul and the rest of the country by using the Reidin's data set which provides the longest period available (from 2003 to 2019) (Figure 27).

   Figure 26 shows monthly nominal and real housing sales prices for Turkey, Istanbul, Ankara, and Izmir from January 2010 to January 2019. The volume of the house price inflation, boom-bust phases of the housing market and real returns from the residential property investments can be more accurately followed by a real HPI, given high inflation rates in Turkey. The reason for also considering the nominal price changes is because this has been the main determinant for the housing purchase and investment motivations of Turkish households. As seen in Figure 26, while the nominal prices show a continuously upward trend until the end of 2018 at the national level in the three biggest cities, the inflation-adjusted values show different trends; the housing sale prices in Istanbul and Ankara started decreasing at the end of 2016, although Ankara never had a significant increase in housing prices and its price appreciation was always below the general trend of Turkey. Besides, in Izmir, this contraction was not until the end of 2018, whereas the housing prices in Turkey had the first reduction in 2016, then temporarily recovered in 2017 but continuously decreased in real terms after the end of 2017. Comparing the house price increases in the boom phase of Turkey's housing market, roughly from January 2010 to September 2016, we can see that the HPI of Turkey, Istanbul, Ankara and Izmir respectively rose by 128%, 190%, 88% and 122% in nominal terms and 40%, 79%, 16% and 37% in real terms. These values show that Istanbul's housing prices significantly deviates from both Turkey and the other two biggest cities. This excessive-inflation in housing prices in Istanbul stems from several factors including continuously increasing migration to the city from

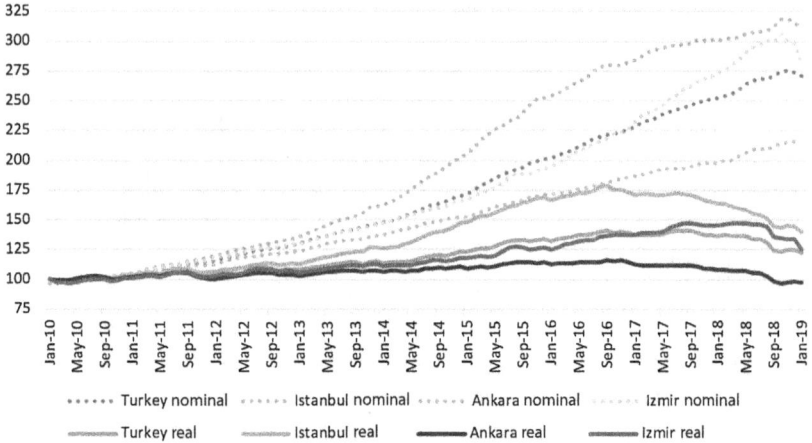

FIGURE 26   Nominal and Real House Price Index in Turkey, Istanbul, Ankara and Izmir
(2010=100)
Note: Real values were calculated through the division of nominal values by CPI
SOURCE: CBRT

the Anatolian cities due to the availability of job opportunities, the role of the
city as the financial and commercial hub of the country, its attractiveness for
the international property investors and a serious scarcity in the availability of
urban land. The above country-wide house price appreciation in Izmir after
2016 results from the increasing internal migration to Izmir, particularly from
Istanbul (Gazete Duvar, 2018).

Figure 27 gives a better idea about the weight of Istanbul in the housing
market of Turkey. To grasp the domination of Istanbul's housing market and
the differentiation between Istanbul and Turkey, the figure includes three
variables, namely real HPI for Istanbul, Turkey and 'Turkey without Istanbul'.
Between 2003 to 2008, the inflation-adjusted prices in both Turkey and
Istanbul are nearly stagnant and similar between Istanbul and the rest of the
country. Between 2008 and 2010, the housing market shows a very strong negative shock due to the GFC in that mortgage rates had a cumulative 78% rise,
the housing effective demand had a first significant contraction and housing
prices dropped by 29% from mid-2007 to mid-2008. Until the end of 2011, the
stagnant trend in real prices continues. Between 2012 to 2016,[15] an excessive

15   When compared with the international trends, Turkey was on the 6th place having high-
      est real house price increases in the world between 2010 and 2015 (IMF 2017; data.oecd.
      org) and on the 1st place in Europe from 2010 to 2017 (EMF, 2018).

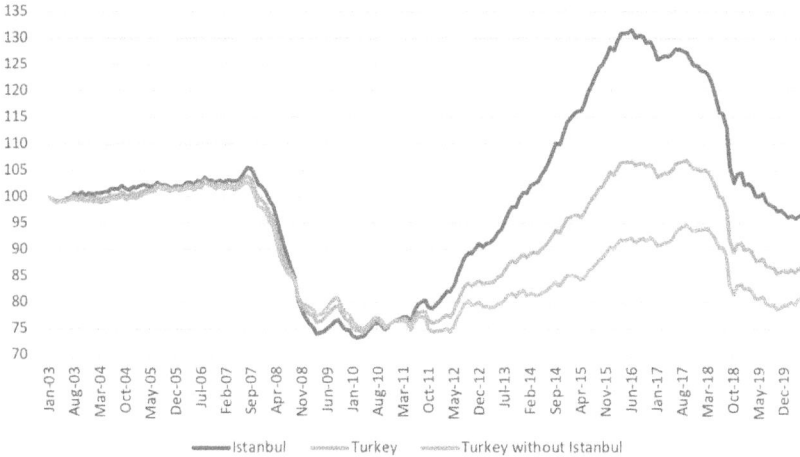

FIGURE 27   Real House Price Index (2007=100)
SOURCE: AUTHOR'S CALCULATION BASED ON THE REIDIN DATA SET (REAL
VALUES WERE CALCULATED THROUGH THE DIVISION OF NOMINAL VALUES
BY CPI)

boom in housing prices witnesses a very sharp house price inflation in Istanbul
and Turkey. The remarkable deviation of prices between Istanbul and 'Turkey
excluding Istanbul' shows that while prices in Istanbul rise by 75.5% in real
terms, the real price appreciation becomes 22% in 'Turkey excluding Istanbul'
and 42% in Turkey. Hence, the bubble-like formation between 2012 and 2016 is
more obvious in the housing market in Istanbul compared to 'Turkey excluding
Istanbul'.[16] Nevertheless, due to the weight of Istanbul in the country's housing
demand, the housing price trends in Istanbul determines the general housing trends of Turkey. Lastly, after the coup attempt in 2016, the house prices
decrease in real terms until 2017, have a short recovery period during 2017 and
then sharply deflate after the end of 2017. From June 2016 to December 2019,
during the bust phase, real prices dropped by a cumulative 35.5% in Istanbul,
24% in Turkey and 15.6% in 'Turkey without Istanbul'.

   Unlike the approaches of the neo-classical idea of market equilibrium
and rational agents, this book suggests "a theoretical understanding of house
price behaviour in terms of ground rent" (Robertson, 2014a: 94). As argued in

---

16   In some other cities, especially in the ones hosting large Syrian migrants, such as
      Gaziantep, Hatay, Adana, and Sanliurfa and in the touristic coastal cities such as Antalya
      and Mugla, where there is a very high demand for summer houses, there might be similar
      bubble-like formations but I do not separately examine them in the book.

the theoretical chapters, differently from other asset price inflations, in the case of housing, price inflations are largely underpinned by the expansion of monopoly rent. However, MR is determined by both country-level and localised factors. While the general MR for housing arises "from the differences in the relative speeds of the circuit of production and the circuit of revenue" in an economy, localised MR "reflects the excess demand relative to the supply of housing on a particular city" (or area)[17] although they are also interrelated and impact each other (ibid., 125). Therefore, the level and volume of revenues circulating in the economy is the main determinant for both of country-level MR and localised MR. This is why the remarkable expansion of the loanable money-capital (either in the form of interest-bearing capital or money-dealing capital) in the housing market expanded the housing effective demand and MR at an unprecedented scale and, therefore, heavily inflated land and housing prices in Turkey, to a lesser extent, and in Istanbul. Although MR is volatile by nature due to its dependence on the circuit of revenue, financialisation of housing not only linked the cycles of the housing market to the financial cycles in general but also further increased the level and volume of the volatility of MR. In other words, MR is always bubble-prone by its nature, but its excessive inflation (above the historical trends) arising from the intensive and extensive expansion of finance creates larger speculative bubbles of MR, followed by larger burst. Alongside the unprecedented intervention of finance into housing in the post-2001 period of Turkey, because land and housing increasingly started to be treated like a financial asset by the agents in the housing SoP who speculate on land and pursue appropriating larger amounts of capital gains from inflating house prices, house prices took an increasingly fictitious (bubble) form that burst in 2016/7.

On the other hand, because the mortgage boom in Turkey was accompanied by a construction boom, the house price inflation in Turkey was to some extent limited by high levels of supply. Hence, expanded effective demand not only fuelled the house prices but also encouraged high levels of housing production. However, as discussed in the next chapter, because housing supply in Turkey was sustained without taking into consideration the demand factors and the volatility of the rent-based accumulation, the unsold housing stock accumulated regarding the gradual contraction of effective demand from 2016 on and became one of the factors in the recent depreciation of housing prices. Although the demand factors became the main determinant of the house price

---

17   Hence differentiated MR arises from the disequilibrium between demand and supply in certain locations.

inflation thanks to the speed of the circulation of revenues regarding the circulation of production and the rapid moving capacity of revenues (unlike the production) according to changes in macroeconomic conditions, the examination of the supply-side is also necessary for a better understanding of land and housing price behaviours, hence the next chapter analyses the supply side factors of housing SoP in Turkey.

6 Housing as a Speculative Investment Tool: Consumption of Housing for the Appropriation of Monopoly Rents

There is consensus in the literature that one of the most important dynamics behind the house price inflation in Turkey was the widespread use of housing as an important investment instrument by Turkish households (WB, 2018; IMF, 2017; TSKB, 2015; Erol, 2015; Coskun, 2016; Yeşilbağ, 2018). Although culturally housing is considered the most secure and preferred asset in Turkey, the novelty of the 2000s arises from middle-class individuals investing in housing. According to the WB Turkey Economic Monitor report (2018: 17), the ratio of the real estate within total household investment instruments preferences is nearly 23%, while the ratios of other traditional investment tool preferences such as gold, bank deposits and FX, become respectively 36%, 19% and 12%. The underdevelopment of the capital market instruments and its complexity for individual investors is one factor behind the motivation of households towards housing investment (Coşkun and Ümit, 2016). Also, the low-interest rate-cheap FX monetary policy of the AKP's economy administration discouraged people to invest in deposit accounts. Therefore, the increase in housing prices above interest rates and inflation until 2016/7 made housing investment attractive for wealthy households in the post-2001 period. However, the leveraged homeownership with the expectation of high capital gains from the price appreciation made housing an increasingly risky and speculative asset. According to the report of the Turkish Contractors Association (2014), 60% of the total housing purchases in Turkey is made with the intent of a speculative investment, in pursuit of augmented capital gains in the form of monopoly rent, either through leasing out or buying to sell later with higher prices.[18]

Highly unequal distribution of income regarding the increasing GDP in Turkey in the post-2001 era created "a 'new' middle-income class—the urban

---

18   The most important regulation to buy-to-sell market by the state became the legislation
      allowing "untaxed capital gains on real estate when sold 5 years after acquisition" (Türel
      and Koç, 2015).

rich, who take risks, demand and consume a lot" who became the main driver and beneficiary of the inflated land and house prices (Erol, 2019a: 243; Ergüder, 2015; Onaran, 2006; Öncü and Balkan, 2016). Because the middle and the upper-classes had optimistic beliefs and expectations on future price increases in housing, that were largely created by the state and media collaboration in the AKP era,[19] they increasingly utilised their savings by investing in housing. While the treatment of housing as an object of speculation was driving up land and housing prices, the inflated house prices, in turn, encouraged more people to invest in housing. However, the absence of a reliable measurement of housing investment prevents us not only to accurately track housing inequality but to understand the housing wealth effect (Hepşen *et al.*, 2017). The decreased rate of homeownership in Turkey, which dropped from 61% in 2006 to 59% in 2018,[20] is a sign of the increasing level of housing investment. Besides, the number of secondary home sales can be considered another sign of the prevalence of investment-linked housing purchase among households. As seen in Figure 28, since 2013,[21] the ratio of transactions in the secondary home market is higher than the primary home market; after the debt and currency crisis of 2018 this ratio had the highest increase. This high percentage of the second-hand sales may be linked to the growing importance of the buy-to-sell property market in Turkey, while the recent spike in the second-hand housing sales[22] may be related to significant decreases in housing production by the developers since 2017.

To understand the extent and volume of the capital gains from housing investment and the relative cost of owning versus renting, the price-to-rent ratio (PRR) index in Turkey[23] and the annual gross yield rate of housing

---

19   Some of the headlines of the newspapers include "House purchaser will be coining money" (Gazete Vatan, 2012); "Now knock the door of the bank, do not miss these mortgages" (Habertürk, 2013); "Do not miss the best time for housing investment" (Milliyet, 2016); "The future Istanbul will boom these neighbourhoods" (HaberTürk, 2013); "Investment in true projects in the real estate always yields" (Hürriyet 2016).

20   According to the calculations of Kahveci (2018), based on population growth, new household formation and new building ratios, the homeownership ratio should have been 65.4% if the housing purchases had happened according to the housing need.

21   2013 is the earliest year of the data available.

22   Very recently, for vitalising the first-hand house sales, the state-owned banks started to offer lower (monthly 0.64%) interest rates on mortgages for new houses compared to second-hand houses (monthly 0.74%).

23   According to the IMF Country Report on Turkey (2017: 52), the cumulative changes in the housing price-to-rent ratio is the highest among other 'emerging market economies' such as Chile, Brazil, Malaysia, Mexico, Poland between 2010 and 2015 and this increase shows a significant overheated housing market in Turkey according to both IMF (2017) and WB (2018).

FIGURE 28   The first-hand and second-hand housing sales (2013–2020)
SOURCE: TURKSTAT HTTPS://BIRUNI.TUIK.GOV.TR/MEDAS/?KN=73&LOC
ALE=EN

investments have been calculated. Figure 29 shows both PRR index and residential investment gross yield rate for Turkey and Istanbul. The PRR significantly decreases from 2003 to 2007; it becomes relatively stable from 2007 to 2009 and steadily grows until 2018, followed by a decrease. Therefore, the increase in rent prices is dramatically higher than house prices between 2003[24] and 2007, while the constant trend during the GFC shows that there was a parallel decrease in both house and rent prices in 2008 and 2009. However, the 2010–2018 period indicates that house price inflation surpasses rent price increases but never reaches the level of the beginning year of the index, 2003. Moreover, the housing market in Istanbul is not substantially different from Turkey. In terms of the returns on housing investment, while the annual gross yield rate of buy-to-let investment is 4% of the market value of houses in both Istanbul and Turkey in 2003, it increases to 7% in 2008. After the highest level in 2009 of 9%, the gross rental returns from housing investment continuously drop and the annual gross yield rate became 5% of the market value of houses in both Istanbul and Turkey in 2018. Since 2018, rental incomes start to increase with the house price depreciation in nominal terms. Specifically, the faster

24   Because the data between 2003 and 2007 was prepared retrospectively by Reidin and there is not any available data for earlier years, whether the high level of the beginning of the index in 2003 is exceptional compared to the historical trend or not becomes a question for us.

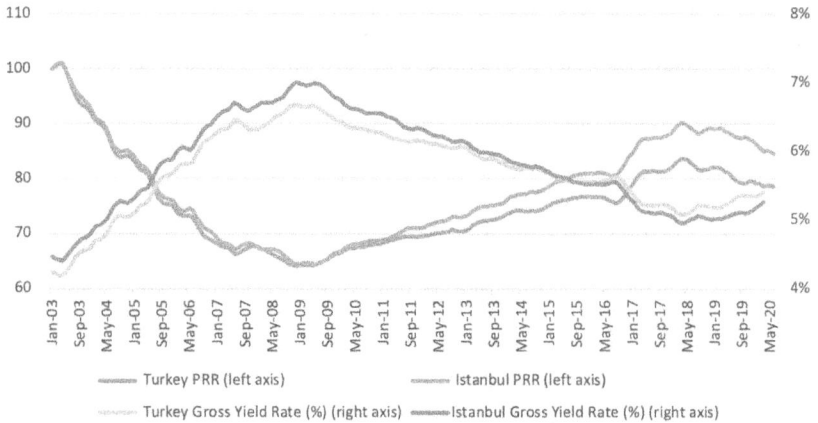

FIGURE 29   Housing price to rent ratio (2003=100) and residential investment gross yield
rate (%)
SOURCE: REIDIN

increase in house prices compared to rental prices in both Istanbul and Turkey
between 2010 and 2018 lowers the capital gains of the buy-to-let residential
investment, although the capital gains from the buy-to-sell market for housing
investors becomes higher.

7   Housing Inequality: Wealth Effect and Crisis of Social Reproduction

The investment on housing by households and the potential capital gains
through house price volatilities impact the wealth of those who use most of
their accumulated wealth on residential investment. The report of the Turkish
Contractors Association (2014) argues that only 40% of the total home purchasers in Turkey buy dwellings to live while 60% is for investment. As shown
above, the increase in housing sale prices above the rent prices lowered the
rental returns of the housing investors while significantly increased the capital gains arising from the secondary housing sales. However, because home
equity loans and mortgage equity withdrawal in Turkey are not as widespread
as in the ACCs (Erol, 2019b), the bust phase of housing does not create a high
negative equity risk for households in Turkey as it happened in the US, Spain
and Ireland in the last decade. Nevertheless, since the rent-based accumulation, similar to interest-bearing capital, arises from a redistribution of the total
surplus-value produced in the entire economy towards a fraction of the society,

the wealth effect of that fraction of the society means the further impoverishment of the rest. Therefore, as the other side of the coin, the dramatic house price inflation in Turkey in the last decade created a crisis of social reproduction for the non-homeowners whose housing costs and the VLP attached to housing increased.

To analyse the housing affordability, international housing research generally uses an index based on 'price-to-income ratio' which is not available in Turkey. However, an affordability (housing purchase power) index prepared by Reidin (Figure 30) shows the ratio of the median equated household disposable income to the required income to buy a median-priced home by using housing credit for 10-year maturity. The index values of 100 and above indicate an individual having median income that can purchase a home by using housing credit in the interest rate environment of the relevant period, while values below 100 show that individuals encounter difficulties in making monthly instalment payments for mortgage-backed housing purchases. According to Figure 30, the index values in both Turkey and Istanbul are below 100 between 2003 and mid-2019, except for 2013 when the mortgages had the lowest interest rate, indicating that median-income household cannot afford a median-priced home, neither in Turkey nor in Istanbul. Because the index is strongly sensitive to the changes in the mortgage rates, the fluctuations in the affordability rates coincide with the fluctuations in mortgage rates. In any case, the index shows that house price increases are very high compared to household income increase. For instance, in the boom period of housing (2010–2016), the cumulative increase in equivalised household disposable income was 87% while house prices increase at the rates of 190% in Istanbul and 128% in Turkey. Although the recent value in the index of 120 points shows that the housing purchasing power of households increased, these results ignore not only the spike in unemployment rates[25] but also the labour market conditions, such as the increasing precarity and flexibility of labour. Although an accurate housing inequality can only be tracked by separate affordability indices for each income group, Figure 30 helps to determine that the purchase of a median house was not possible for a family gaining median income without some inheritance money or other sources of accumulated wealth during the 2000s and 2010s.

Hence, the owner-occupation and house price inflation in Turkey was largely driven by the high-middle and upper-classes (Sarı and Khurami, 2018). However, the increasingly speculative treatment of housing made the housing

---

25   As of December 2019, 4.4 million people were unemployed, and from mid 2018 to mid 2019, 840,000 jobs were lost, corresponding to 3% of total employment. (www.tuik.gov.tr).

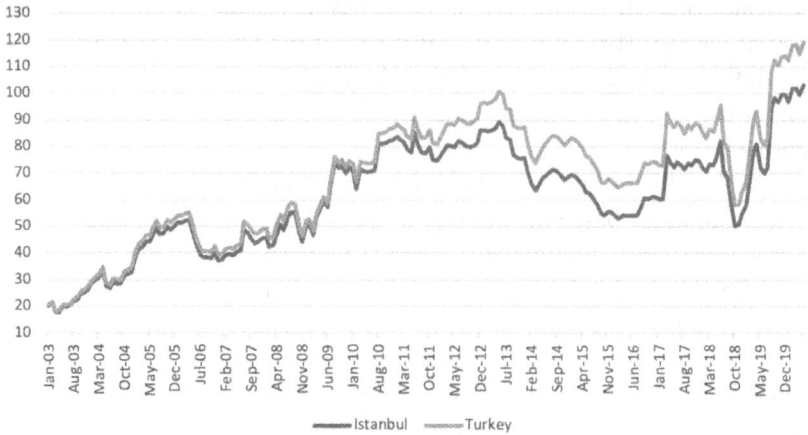

FIGURE 30   Housing Affordability Index [for 10-year maturity]
             SOURCE: REIDIN

need of the working classes and urban poor a chronic problem in Turkey, which is impossible to solve in the market conditions. While the poor and low-income group became the most vulnerable in the housing ladder, the middle-income households became highly indebted to meet their sheltering needs, especially in the face of inflated housing and rent prices. Consequently, finan-cialisation of housing SoP of the post-2001 Turkey manifested in the form of a highly leveraged homeownership society, escalated housing inequality and the unprecedented victory of the exchange value of housing over its use-value.

8   Conclusion

This chapter started with an investigation of the house purchase finance. The most important novelty of the post-2002 era is the establishment of a com-prehensive mortgage system in Turkey for the first time. Despite being under-developed, the secondary mortgage market slowly grew from the second half of the 2010s, as a response to the reverting conditions for the expansion of con-sumer credit market in accordance with the fluctuations in the global financial markets, the heavy external indebtedness of the banks, the resultant urge for increasing their liquidity to fund housing loans and increasing pressure of the hegemonic capital fractions of the construction sector on the government to speed up the turnover times of their housing stock. As this chapter showed, the AKP era witnessed the remarkable development of primary mortgage market thanks to heavy involvement of the commercial banks into the mortgage market for the first time in Turkey, resulting in an unprecedented mortgage boom in the country. Since the banking system heavily relied on external funding and linked the domestic mortgage system to the global circulation IBC, financialisation indirectly but strongly impacted the housing purchase finance in Turkey.

The boom-bust cycles of the mortgage market followed the general trends of the macroeconomic expansion and contraction phases in Turkey through the banking system. However, the Turkish state's massive intervention into housing SoP through state-owned banks, TOKI and Central Bank's manipulative monetary policy delayed the bust phase of the housing and mortgage markets. Particularly, the state-owned banks' substantial role in expanding housing loans indicates that the cost of the debt-led growth in Turkey is socialised by the state-owned banks.

Moreover, this chapter argued that the exponential increase of households involved in the mortgage market in Turkey is a historical record which led to a substantial surge in effective demand and, therefore, general monopoly rent in the country, which had been constrained by the lack of a formal and institutional mortgage finance system for decades. Therefore, the financialisation of housing in the commodity form, which is the formation and growth of the housing credit market enhancing the housing purchase capacity of people, emancipates monopoly rent from the decades-long limitations put by effective demand in Turkey. While the mortgage market became accessible for the middle-classes for the first time in Turkish history, the low-class and the poor continued to be excluded from the mortgage markets. Hence, financial inclusion and the mortgage indebtedness as one of the most concrete outcomes of the financialisation is not considered as a class-neutral phenomenon in this book. Therefore, this chapter discussed that financial exclusion composes the other side of financialisation, where the wealth effect is paired with impoverishment of a large segment of the society trapped between unequal access to owner-occupied sector, the burden of high rent prices and underserved affordable housing.

The chapter also examined the general determinants of the effective demand in the post-2002 Turkey, including the mortgage boom during the 2000s and 2010s, the further expansion of housing credit via shadow financing system during the 2010s, the international capital flows to the residential real estate and, the urban planning power of TOKI continuously reproducing artificial scarcities in urban land and differentiation in the quality of residential land, the high population rise, new household formation, migration to urban areas and compulsory demand for earthquake-resistant houses. Therefore, the land

and house price inflation in Turkey were examined by HPI which shows that Istanbul housing prices deviate from both Turkey and the other two biggest cities, Ankara and Izmir. The index also shows that the period from June 2016 to December 2019 signifies the bust phase of the housing market in Turkey and Istanbul as the real prices started to drop, despite the long-standing effort of the state to sustain land and house price appreciation in the country.

Moreover, the unprecedented intervention of finance into housing in the post-2001 period, the organisation of consumption of housing over appropriating monopoly rent, and the increased household indebtedness became the main indicators of the financialisation of housing SoP in Turkey. The treatment of housing as a speculative investment tool manifested through multiple homeownership by wealthy households, with the expectation of high capital gains. Nevertheless, because the rent-based accumulation arises from a redistribution of the total surplus-value produced in the entire economy towards a fraction of the society, the dramatic house price inflation in Turkey in the last decade created a crisis of social reproduction for the non-homeowners whose housing costs increase simultaneously. The Housing Purchase Power Index showed that purchasing a median house is not possible for a family gaining median income, without inheritance money or other sources of accumulated wealth during the 2000s and 2010s. However, because the index does not take the labour market conditions and unemployment into consideration, there is a need for a more detailed examination of the housing inequality that requires the release of official statistics.

CHAPTER 8

Production of Housing

Three producers in the Turkish housing SoP are construction cooperatives, private or public developers. As discussed before, the traditional housing producers in Turkey are yapsatçıs that appeared with the first industrialisation-urbanisation wave in the 1960s but the 1980–2001 period witnessed the emergence of medium and large scale housing developers and the establishment of several housing cooperatives which are regarded as non-profit producers and whose members were generally middle-class professionals (Türel and Koç, 2015). The public sector also developed social housing projects in the pre-2002 era (see Figure 31), however, the main role of the state in this period was funding both house-building and purchase since there was not a comprehensive housing finance system for housing purchase or development. Hence, TOKI was more of a mortgage institution than a housing provider and the main receivers of TOKI-credits between 1980 and 2000 were housing cooperatives, which had significant state support not only in the form of credit but also in the form of land provision at below-market rates and VAT exemptions.

As seen in Figure 31, private developers have already dominated the housing supply since the 1980s, however, after 2004, the cooperatives' share of 20–30% in the housing production shifted to the private sector and the public sector.

Alongside the increasing weight of the private sector in the housing production, the 2000s witnessed a significant differentiation of private developers not only based on their size but also business models, production techniques, financing methods, their financialisation levels and their engagement with other actors in the housing SoP, such as the state, landowners and financial institutions. Before a detailed investigation, it is important to present the main factors triggering the fractioning among housing producers and the peculiar dynamics shaping the housing production in Turkey. Therefore, this chapter examines the general dynamics behind the housing supply-side in the post-2002 era and then continue with the analysis of housing production process, housing development finance, volume of housing production and housing stock respectively.

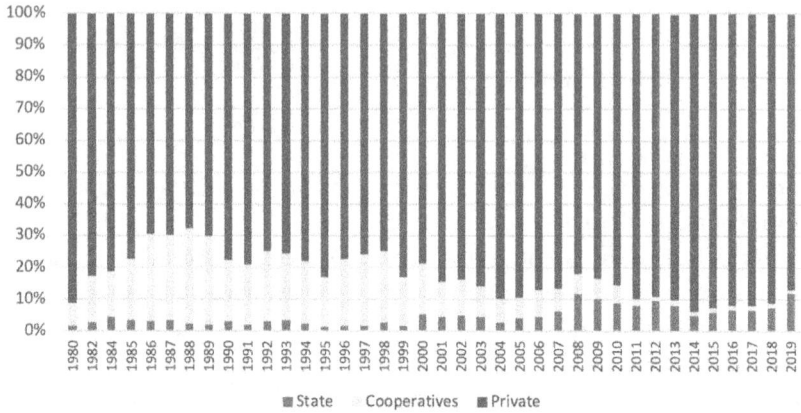

FIGURE 31   Share of housing producer groups in annual housing starts (number of dwellings)
SOURCE: TURKSTAT

1   A Bird's Eye Shot to the Housing Supply-Side Dynamics in the Post-
         2002 Era

Firstly, the mortgage boom in Turkey was accompanied by a construction
boom at the record level (see below). After the election of the AKP government
in 2002, the party started to employ a country-wise 'Construction Move' that
has been widely defined as 'construction-oriented economic growth strategy'[1]
by researchers, media organisations, business groups, political organisations,
public debates and even by the party bureaucrats (BSB, 2015; Sönmez, 2015;
Orhangazi, 2019; Ergüder, 2015; Bülten, 2018). The first and most important
manifestation of this strategy was the re-creation of TOKI to lead the construction move in the country. Hence, TOKI was designed as a giant state enterprise
that has several roles of property developer, landowner, land developer, zoning
and planning power, and the largest shareholder of the biggest REIT of Turkey,
as the embodiment of new neoliberal authoritarian state in housing, signifying
the administrative centralisation and enhanced state capacity in commodification and privatisation of housing SoP, as the main arm of the strong executive power in the urban sphere and as an intermediary agent between political
power and economic power. As one of the top bureaucrats of TOKI argues,

---

1   The book focuses on the housebuilding sector and the evaluation of the construction sector
     in general is out of scope for this book. However, because housing is the most important
     component of the construction and real estate sectors in Turkey, I will shortly discuss the use
     of the housebuilding sector as a macroeconomic tool in the end of this chapter.

> We, as TOKI, were empowered with a special purpose, with the instruction of dear Erdoğan that is encouraging business groups to invest in construction sector. Of course, this primarily stems from the shortage of earthquake-resistant houses in Turkey. Except this, after 2001 crisis, the textile sector, as the favourable sector of the 1990s, collapsed. The other segments of the manufacturing sector received a significant blow. The information sector and heavy industry have been already underdeveloped in Turkey; therefore, the construction sector was chosen for weathering the storm of 2001 as an engine of growth.
>
> interview III

The interviewee was open in expressing the use of the construction boom as a macroeconomic tool by the government, but this is only half of the picture. Therefore, what I argue is that the construction move under AKP was not only a capital accumulation strategy but also a political project to create and strengthen the hegemonic bourgeoisie.

The empowerment of TOKI was the most vital step in the realisation of this project. Also, a great number of legislative changes, namely 198 laws and by-laws in zoning, urban planning, land use and development were adopted under the party rule to enable the use of land for the most profitable investments (Penpecioğlu, 2017). Such changes are not a result of the uninterrupted election of AKP since 2002 but its success in neoliberal authoritarian state-building that shows its increasing strength within the state apparatus by overshadowing the parliamentary and judiciary branches and even transforming these branches, as it happened with the transition from the parliamentary regime to the presidential regime in 2018.

Therefore, the primary dynamic behind the construction boom of Turkey was the excessively-centralised and personalised authoritarian mode of governance admitting the required legal and institutional alterations. Consequently, the flow of capital onto construction and real estate sectors in Turkey is not a simple replica of the worldwide importance of built environment production (thanks to its role in absorbing over-accumulated capital) in the age of financialisation but strongly related with the restructuring of the state, internal class struggles and power relations attached to the construction and housing sectors. This is not to say that financialisation did not have an impact in housing production in the country but rather that financialisation had a peculiar character in the housing SoP of Turkey, as shown below.

Hence, the distinctiveness of the construction boom in Turkey comes from its strong class character, namely the inter-bourgeoisie struggle on the appropriation of ground rent. As discussed before, what makes TOKI a monopoly is its land stock after being authorised to use, develop, and privatise all public land that is half of the total land stock of Turkey. For the other half of the country, the land ownership is highly fragmented with a great number of private individuals and enterprises possessing small pieces of land. Therefore, commodification of land in Turkey included the enactment of several legislations that opened up the nature reserve areas and conservation areas to development. Specifically, enterprises having land banks in forested, agricultural, industrial or historical areas had a chance to develop residential buildings on these previously restricted parcels. The commodification of land also happened by direct privatisation of public land and through revenue-sharing projects of TOKI. While the construction capitalists equally benefitted from the former, the latter mostly favoured the capital fractions having a close relationship with the government. In other words, PPP projects of TOKI or different ministries in infrastructure and energy sectors rewarded the second-generation bourgeoisie by allocating and redistributing ground rent (Sönmez, 2015; Karatepe, 2016). This hegemonic capital fraction became dependent on state licences to get high development gains, while the first-generation bourgeoisie was largely excluded from public procurements although they also benefitted from the construction move of the party and accompanied legislative changes allowing the commodification of land (see below).

Despite of the party effort to encourage investment in the construction and real estate sectors, without financialisation of the Turkish economy this would not be possible since mortgage and construction booms became possible through the internal and external expansion of finance to both housing consumption and housing production. The anti-inflationary monetary policy and low interest rate environment of the 2000s bolstered by global liquidity and foreign capital inflows not only decreased the mortgage rates and expanded housing effective demand but created favourable conditions for housing development finance. Hence, the flow of cheap loans to housing and increasing interest of individual and institutional investors to Turkish real estate market drastically inflated housing prices particularly after 2010 and created booms of monopoly rent and led housing developers and landowners to get high capital gains that encouraged developers to further invest in residential production.

Although the construction boom in Turkey was primarily housing-centred,[2] the significant level of production in commercial buildings and infrastructural facilities also contributed to this boom. While TOKI was a facilitator of the

---

2 Housing investments composes nearly 80% of all construction investments (www.tuik .gov.tr).

high-level investments in non-housing components of the construction sector, infrastructural mega-projects such as highways, railways, tunnels, third bridge in the Bosporus, third airport and Canal Istanbul were developed by domestic and foreign construction companies through public procurements (Çarıkçı, 2017).

A significant challenge for the examination of the housing supply side is the absence of a specialised industry, given that nearly all medium and large scale developers which produce houses also produce commercial centres, offices, shopping centres and other superstructure facilities, fewer of them were also active in the infrastructure installations. The decreasing specialisation and the resultant diversification of the investment around different branches of the construction sector in the Turkish case stem from the over-politicisation of the sector. Within the interviews with 19 private construction and real estate companies, including 2 holding groups, 2 REITs, 9 SMEs and 6 large-scale developers, 6 of 9 SMEs are specialised house-builders, 2 holdings, 2 large-scale developers and 1 REIT invest in residential, non-residential buildings and infrastructural facilities, and one REIT, 4 large-scale developers and 3 SMEs invested in residential and non-residential buildings. The firms developing infrastructural projects have higher technological expertise, machine, equipment and skilled labour force while the production of non-residential buildings and high-rise residential buildings do not require a differentiated production method and technological development level. Nevertheless, as it stems from the interviews, one technological threshold for the superstructure of 12 or more floored building requires deeper excavation, more sophisticated bored piling equipment, different expertise certificates and elevators. Therefore, some of the small-scale housing developers which cannot produce more than 12 floored buildings also cannot produce shopping malls, commercial centres, etc. Also, the interviewees that invest in infrastructural projects say that they do not prefer to develop residential buildings if the project is not profitable since the competition in housebuilding sector is higher than infrastructure; hence, they prefer to differentiate themselves from other construction companies through a high-level of expertise and technological development. Moreover, according to them, the infrastructural construction is less politicised[3] compared to the residential construction due to this technological threshold eliminating a significant part of the enterprises.

---

3   The caveat is that several works in infrastructure such as dam, barrage, road, tunnel, metro and road building require different technological and engineering expertise (Interviews). These works in Turkey are also carried out by PPPs and the contractor companies are chosen by the public tenders. It has been largely shown by several reports and articles that the main

Moreover, the post-2002 era witnessed an unprecedented flow of capital from other sectors into the construction and housebuilding sectors. The number of enterprises in the construction sector rose 95.2% only between 2008 and 2011 (Kurtuluş *et al.*, 2012) and, as of 2018, the total number of private building companies reached 233,388, the vast majority of which are small-scale firms.[4] This number is nearly ten times the construction companies in the whole Europe (Cumhuriyet, 2020), mainly due to the absence of a board structure regulating the access to the market and a licensing that checks the institutional and technological expertise. However, the flow of capital into construction and real estate activities did not mean the withdrawal of the relevant capital groups' investments in other sectors but a more diversified investment portfolio of the Turkish business groups that operate in tourism, media, logistics, commerce and energy sectors alongside the construction and real estate sectors (Uzunkaya, 2013; interviews). For instance, among the interviewed firms, the major shareholder of one REIT also has companies in energy and jewellery sectors, the founder of the other REIT also has a company in the tourism sector, the owner of one large-scale construction company is also the owner of a private university, the owner of another large-scale construction company also has furniture firms, and two holding companies are also active in education, automotive, software and energy sectors. For some of the traditional industrialists of Turkey (the first-generation bourgeoisie), the reason for entering the housebuilding industry by establishing new subsidary firms is their desire of utilising their land which was hosting their factories before. For instance,

> two biggest pharmaceutical producers of Turkey, Eczacibasi Holding and Deva Holding, turned their factories in Istanbul to building complexes including residential and commercial buildings. Similarly, Tekfen Holding closed down their bulb factory (established in 1964); carried the bulb factory to China and developed a satellite city project (includes luxury houses and offices) on this brownfield land. These are prevalent practices in the 2000s. Most old industrial buildings were turned to places of real estate production by core industrialists.
>
> interview VII

---

contracting firms of these projects are the construction companies which have close ties to the government such as Limak, Cengiz, Albayrak, Kolin, Kalyon and Çeçen (Sönmez, 2015; Çarıkçı, 2017; Buğra and Savaşkan, 2014).

4   https://data.tuik.gov.tr/Bulten/Index?p=Kucuk-ve-Orta-Buyuklukteki-Girisim-Istatistikl eri-2021-45685 [Accessed 19 Feb 2023].

For a better understanding of the prevalence of this practice among the business groups in Turkey, while 25 holding companies were already in the construction sector before 2002, 52 other holding companies, most of which have been active in manufacturing and trade since the early decades of the Republic, also established new subsidiary companies operating in housebuilding and real estate sectors since 2002.

On the other hand, there are also cases where the entrance into the sector caused existing firms to exit other sectors of the economy. For instance, most of my interviewees mentioned that many new SMEs in the housebuilding, which was established in the 2000s, were active in the textile industry in the 1990s but went bankrupt in the 2000–2001 crisis. The owner of a small-scale firm explains:

> My brothers and I run a textile mill in Ümraniye, Istanbul in the 1990s. In the first years, it was a lucrative business but after the 1998 crisis, the worst years started. Not to speak of exporting, even Laleli market[5] went through a crisis. We went bankrupt. After that, firstly, in 2004, we started to build up laminated flooring. For 11 years we have been in this business, now my brother leads this firm. And three years ago [in 2012] we established a new firm to build houses in this region [Beylikdüzü, Istanbul]. Five years ago, Beylikdüzü was a restricted area, but it was rezoned for construction. During the first two years after Beylikdüzü being rezoned as residential area, we firstly did laminated flooring, fire-check indoors and steel outdoors of newly-built apartments; in return, instead of receiving cash payment, we accepted the barter payment; that is owning one residential unit in return of doing laminated flooring, doors and PVS windows of whole building. After selling these units, we accumulated enough capital to establish a new firm in construction. So, none of the new enterprises entered the housebuilding sector with hefty sums. This business was a plan B for us. But Beylikdüzü became a new favourite place for residential buildings so this business became more lucrative than we expected.
>
> interview XVII

Similarly, three other SMEs and one large-scale firm in my interviews entered the housebuilding sector after being bankrupt in the 2001 crisis before which they were running a rubber factory, a textile mill, a bread factory and a furniture factory, respectively.

---

5   Laleli market is a well-known textile hub of Istanbul.

Therefore, the rise in the construction and real estate activities in the economy (see Figure 32 and 33) under the AKP generated heated public debates. While the party officials insistently advocated that the growth in construction and real estate activities is at normal levels, the ex-minister of Economy, Ali Babacan, called out the imbalance on resource allocation between real estate activities and industry sectors:

> Fixed capital formation by private sector is not hopeful. Share of private sector's fixed capital expenditure is not at the levels we desire. This phenomenon restrains our recent growth and worries us about the growth in future. There are imbalances among sectors. Especially the demand in real estate is so high. An economy, without production and undeserving the luxury residential property and luxury consumption which are funded by external debt, might direct Turkey into a dead-end. ... The easy gains from housing reduce the interest in industrial sector that is not a thing we desire.[6]
>
> HÜRRIYET, 2014

Based on this, Demiralp *et al.* (2016) tested whether there is a transfer from industrial sectors to the construction sector and found that the decline in the share of industry in the economy, particularly before 2006, partially results from excessive rents generated in the construction sector. Yeldan (2018), Pamuk (2014), Aşıcı (2016) and Hepşen *et al.* (2017)[7] also analysed the fixed capital formation in the economy and discussed that the ex-minister Babacan was right about the imbalances in allocation of fund and resources among sectors and this imbalance favouring the real estate sector expose the country to currency risk, due to the heavy FX indebtedness of the sector, despite producing for the domestic market, as shown below.

As discussed in the theoretical chapters, in the case of housebuilding, the main profits of speculative builders come from the appropriation of monopoly rents, i.e. the circulation of revenues. However, this is not to say that the

---

6   The response of Erdoğan to the ex-Minister of Economy is: "During my prime ministry period, we never said stop to investments while experiencing a world crisis. ... This was what made us especially in those troubled times: We never stopped the construction industry. We said, go to the construction industry. TOKI was the head. If you say stop to the construction industry and advance to the [manufacturing] industry, the collapse begins. This sector with Turkey's urban transformation must uphold." (Fortune, 2014).

7   Hepşen *et al.* (2017: 5) argue that the actual housing investments are not reflected in the GDP accurately and, therefore, "the official statistics do not capture the real conditions of the economy".

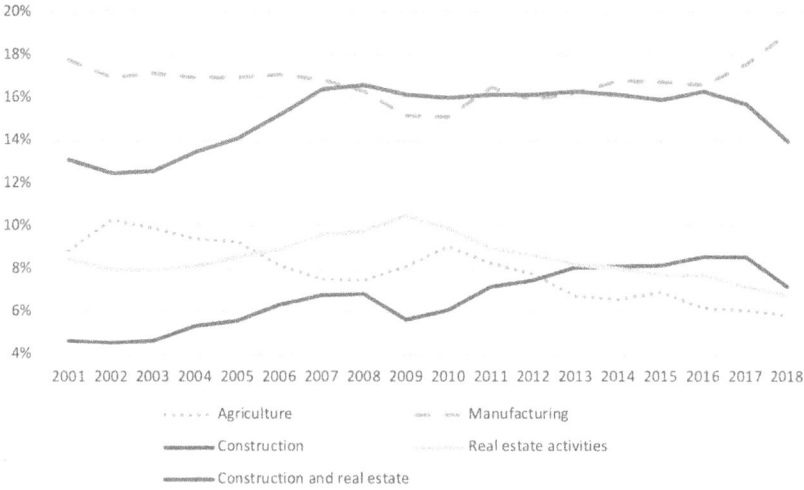

FIGURE 32   Distribution of GDP (by production approach) across construction and real
estate activities (2000–2018)
SOURCE: TURKSTAT HTTP://WWW.TURKSTAT.GOV.TR/

building capitalist does not get a part of profit out of circulation of capital but
that a substantial part of the development gain of speculative house-builders
comes from the revenues of the consumers, including wages, inheritances and
future revenues (mortgage debt). However, it is impossible to know empirically (quantitatively) how much of the development gain of developers comes
from the monopoly rent and how much of it comes from the surplus-value.
Yet, analytically, the best part of the development gain of speculative builders
or capital gain of speculative landowners and financial institutions are determined by the level, volume and speed of circulation of revenues but this level
ultimately depends on the circulation of the surplus value produced across the
economy and is, therefore, limited by the level of the productive activities, i.e.
the social pool of surplus-value. Consequently, the imbalance on resource allocation among sectors by the ex-minister of the Economy means capturing an
increasing part of the total value produced in the economy as monopoly rent
by the developers, landowners, housing investors and financiers. In a broader
framework, this refers to an increasing capital move from productive sectors to
rentier sectors.

   Although the main fractioning of construction capitalists is between public and private contractors, the increasing number of enterprises in the sector,
particularly small-scale yapsatçıs, is a common problem for both fractions.
Therefore, they both put pressure on the government to implement a law to

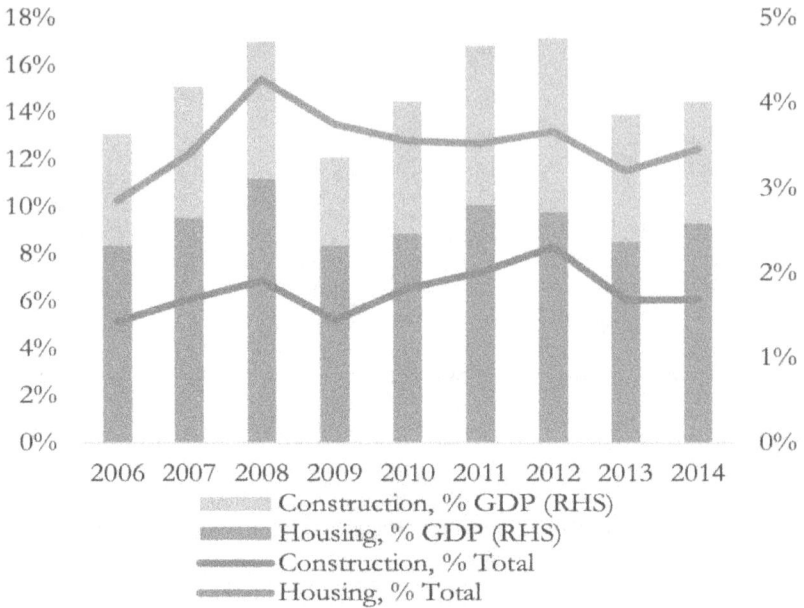

FIGURE 33   Housing and construction (non-residential), percentage of total investment and
             GDP (2006–2014)
             SOURCE: WB TURKEY COUNTRY ECONOMIC MEMORANDUM, 2016 P.8 HTTP://
             DOCUMENTS1.WORLDBANK.ORG/CURATED/EN/533991494216391559/PDF/111
             701-REVISED-PUBLIC-FINALTURKEYINVESTMENTCEMAPRIL.PDF

eliminate small-scale non-institutionalised builders with informal practices
in the building process. For instance, INTES (Turkish Employers Association
of Construction Industries), the union of the first-generation large-scale
internationalised businesses, wants the introduction of a legal condition
based on engineering and architecture certificates to establish a building firm
(Gülöksüz, 2009). TMB (Turkish Constructors Association), which represents
the first-generation medium to large-scale companies, asks for the legal regulations which will bring consolidation into the sector:

> the easy entry to the sector created an excessive competition and low-
> ered profits. Now, all of us operate with far less profits. If the market con-
> tinues to be dispersed, we can never achieve a consolidation in the sector.
> ... This creates an unfair competition between the institutionalized and
> non-institutionalized firms as they pay far less tax than us but produce
> houses for our segment [middle and high-income group].
>
> TMB, 2015: 50

While INTES and TMB are the representatives of the first-generation bourgeoisie as the early participants in the accumulation process in the construction sector,[8] the representative business associations of the construction capital in the second-generation bourgeoisie have also been lobbying for a control mechanism for market access. Specifically, the head of the KONUTDER (Association of Housing Developers and Investors), which is the representative of the large-scale housing developers having close relationships with the party and frequently working with TOKI, notes that "60% of the Istanbul housing market comprises of thousands of small-scale firms. In Anatolia, this ratio is much higher. If the entrance to the sector cannot be stopped, we cannot make the sector institutionalized" (TMB, 2015). One of the firms in KONUTDER explains the problem as such: "We need urgent regulations. There is not a technical or capital criterion for entering to the sector. Especially if we work like banks [raise shadow financing], the regulation becomes a more urgent need" (Çelik, 2018). Therefore, the prevalence of the shadow financing in the sector carries the problem beyond the bankruptcies of construction firms but the spread of the risk to the banking sector. Consequently, as a result of loud-voiced objections from the representative association of both fractions, in 2014, the Ministry of Environment and Urbanisation declared that they are working on a new law to regulate entrance to the sector based on financial and technical qualification (SBB, 2018), although this law was still not enacted. The main reason for the unwillingness of the government to eliminate the small-scale builders is the political importance of the SMEs in the support of the power bloc. For instance, the owners of 6 SMEs in housebuilding in my interviews said that although they do not have any ideological and political ties with the party, they vote for them since the strength of the party and "the political and economic stability" are important for the continuity of their businesses.

8　TMB was founded in 1952 and INTES in 1964. TMB and INTES have respectively 120 and 130 member firms. However, currently, 51% of TMB members are also INTES members and 65% of INTES members are also TMB members. The close relations between TMB and INTES were not limited to a large overlap between members and managers, and in the years following the establishment of INTES, the two organizations used the same place and the same administrative staff. While moving towards institutional maturation between 1980–2001, first its managers and administrative staff and then its venues have differentiated, although their activities have become increasingly similar (INTES, 2014).

2 Housing Developers and Housing Production Process

After discussing the general dynamics behind the fractioning among construction capitalists in general and house-builders in particular, this section investigates the business models of production and financing methods of the building capitalists in the housing SoP in the post-2002 Turkey. Most housing developers in Turkey, varying from one-man to multinational firms, are also part of mercantile capital, which means that they get main part of their profit by playing on land market. Therefore, speculative housebuilding is the dominant pattern of the housing SoP. Nonetheless, the scale of the building firms is crucial for the business strategies, production and financing methods of housing development. To examine housing developers, they are divided into two groups: small, medium and large-scale developers. Although there are not official statistics showing the weight of these two groups in overall housing production in Turkey, it has been estimated that nearly 80% of the total private-sector production belongs to the first group (IMO, 2008; TMB, 2015).

A significant part of the first group comprises yapsatçıs who became the only housing producers, during the decades when there was no institutionalised source of development finance, thanks to their unique financing model. This was based on an equity-sharing agreement between a builder and a landowner in that the builder does not pay in advance but delivers the agreed number of flats to the landowner and the rest remains in the builder's hands. After this stage, yapsatçıs realised their development gain after selling their share in the market and then by using this development gain as initial capital to purchase means of production excluding land, they chase another landowner who wishes to use the land for residential purposes. Because these small builders depend on returns to start to a new production cycle, they do not work on the multiple sites simultaneously unlike large developers. While in the first urbanisation-apartmentisation period, these small-scale players enjoyed the availability of land in the central location of cities by making deals with gecekondu owners and, therefore, replaced the single-storey gecekondu with maximum four-floor apartment buildings, in the post-2002 era, the gentrification of shantytowns were carried out by large construction firms through their partnership with TOKI. Therefore, in today's cities, yapsatçıs can only make the equity-sharing agreement with landowners of the old buildings having typically 3–4 floors. Therefore, in new equity-sharing agreements, they have to demolish old buildings and build new apartment blocks with higher floors to be able to pay the share of the landowner and get higher development gains. Although increasing the number of floors of a residential building ultimately depends on getting building permits from the relevant municipalities, local governments generally accept floor increases due to the requirement of replacing old buildings with earthquake-resistant ones.[9]

Moreover, unlike old buildings, which need to be demolished and rebuilt, the new ones have several property owners sharing the ownership of the relevant land plot. Therefore, until 2012, when the enacted earthquake law (LTADR) qualified the consent of the two-third majority[10] of shareholders to take the demolishment-rebuilding decision, yapsatçıs had to persuade all flat-owners sharing the ownership of the relevant land and bargain with all land-owners regarding their equity shares. However, after 2012, when tax and fee exemptions were brought for promoting urban regeneration, landowners were obliged to accept the replacement of old buildings. Considering that a significant urban land scarcity showed up in the big cities particularly in Istanbul in the 2010s (interviews), this law aimed at reinvigorating the housebuilding sector by legitimising the demolishment and reconstruction of millions of houses and generating a huge investment area for construction capitalists. Therefore, after 2012, large construction companies increasingly moved to this demolishment-reconstruction business and the traditional equity-sharing model of yapsatçıs became widespread for all housing developers in all scales. While yapsatçıs succeeded to survive in the 2000s thanks to the absence of competitivity from large capital groups in the equity-sharing based housing production, the situation reversed after 2012 with the increasing interest of large construction companies in parcel-based urban regeneration projects. Hence, this became the primary reason why large construction companies started to lobby for the elimination of yapsatçıs from housebuilding market. Nearly all small-scale firms interviewed in our survey mentioned that the pressure has been increasing:

> we cannot take building permits as easy as before. Municipalities now direct people to housing estates. They do not want single plot-based apartment buildings but building complexes on larger land parcels. For example, municipalities ask for car parking lot for each project. This is impossible for single-parcel production. This is for sending off us and opening space for large companies. They want to kill small-scale builders

---

9   At this point, yapsatçıs in my interviews noted the discretionary treatment of building firms by the local governments in obtaining building permits for higher floor increases.

10 As discussed before, all buildings constructed before the 1999 Marmara earthquake are considered risky and expected to be renewed with this law. However, if the expertise report classifies the relevant building as high-risk, then no majority is needed for the replacement of the building.

for the sake of monopolies. The municipality in this region [Bağcılar] hold a meeting with us [small builders] and told us to merge with others.

interview xx

Hence, M&A took place among yapsatçıs although there is no data to understand how widespread it is. For instance, two medium-size companies interviewed in my survey were established through the merging of three yapsatçıs. This merging enabled them to purchase land and develop their housing projects and access finance. One of these firms explains:

> Flat-for-land method is preferable for a developer because you don't have to worry for land cost when starting a project. However, in this region [Beylikdüzü], there are nearly 100 yapsatçıs. It is very competitive; you should decrease your share to persuade landowners to choose you instead of others. ... When we made the decision of coming together in 2005, peasants were living in this region. So we put our capital together; purchased land from them and developed our first housing project.
>
> interview xi

Besides, the most common practice among small and medium-scale developers is working as sub-contractors of large construction companies alongside their speculative housebuilding activities. Subcontracting is widespread in the Turkish construction sector, especially among the business groups which entered the building sector from other sectors for the first time. Therefore, in the post-2002 period, a significant part of small-scale builders became the subcontractors of large-scale construction firms in that they undertook different parts of the production of the large residential estates having several on-site amenities such as fitness centres, car parks, and community gardens. Nevertheless, the prevalence of subcontracting in the construction sector created a hierarchical, multi-layered and complex production chain. One medium-scale firm, which recently shifted their activities from the speculative building towards subcontracting works, explains the process:

> In our business, again, there is a landowner and developer firm which agrees on a very big project, that is not a project with 10–20 flats but 1000–2000 flats. We do not take part in any agreement/bargaining process between them. This is not our business. Instead, the developer firm comes to us and say that you will undertake whole construction process according to my agreed project, engineering and designing. So we start from rough construction, do plastering, coating, flooring, windows,

internal doors, everything until giving keys of flats to the developer firm. In return, the developer firm makes progress payment to us each month. We have 220 permanent employees but apart from this, we also have several subcontractors for different parts of the construction. Our profit margin is maximum 15% of the total project. For instance, if the project value is 10 million, we are paid a cumulative 1.5 million during the building process, roughly 1,5 years. All in all, they are developer firms; they do not lay a finger on anything. All expenses belong to us, labour cost, building materials, payments to other subcontracting firms. They only deal with the sale of the dwelling units.

interview XXI

As it can be seen, the contracting-subcontracting works became a complex process since the developer firm has a core subcontracting firm, but the subcontracting firm also has several other sub-contractor firms. Thanks to this hierarchical production chain, newly established and inexperienced construction firms leave all industrial production to smaller capital groups and become only traders, which speculate on land purchase at the beginning and then sell the completed dwelling units for realising their development gain. A part of the future gain of the developer firm, whose size changes according to how much their bet on land (monopoly rent) is realised, goes to the industrialist-builder and landowner and the rest becomes their share.

Consequently, large construction companies dominate the housing provision in metropolises and the touristic cities having high domestic and foreign demand, while the small and medium-scale house-builders compete for the production of single-plot apartment buildings and undertake to subcontract large construction companies. However, some of the local medium-scale firms become monopolies in their cities and regions (WB, 2015: 49). According to Dursun (2015), the local monopolies have power on the entry-exit conditions of local housing markets by lobbying with relevant local government, although they cannot intervene in PPP projects of TOKI. Yet, because PPP projects of TOKI in small cities are only for the production of affordable houses, they do not see TOKI as a competitor. Moreover, according to the survey by Dursun (2015), small building firms in these relatively small cities also work as subcontractors of these regional monopoly firms.

On the other hand, when investigating the large-scale housing developers, three groups stand out, as mentioned above. The first and oldest initially grew by undertaking infrastructural works through public procurements in the 1950s and 1960s. Then, they were internationalised in the 1970s by expanding their activities to MENA but later intensified their activities in the domestic housebuilding market in the 1980s for accessing public funds. The second group, the TOKI developers, grew through the revenue-sharing projects of TOKI and Emlak Konut REIT and the third one appeared as a result of the entrance of already big business groups in other sectors of the economy into the construction and real estate sectors to benefit from lucrative returns from continuously inflating land and house prices in the 2000s. For now, ignoring these differences, I examine the housing production process of large-scale developing firms.

Unlike the single-plot apartment building production of small builders, large construction firms develop big-scaled, high-rise, luxurious residences on large tracts of land with several on-site amenities (Erol, 2019a). Also, unlike SMES, forming and extending land bank is an important part of their activities. While in some instances, they purchase land from landowners and directly start production, in others, they buy land from the agricultural edges of the cities or reserve areas which are not zoned for development and hoard these lands as assets to use them as collateral to raise capital from financial institutions. Plus, while small-scale house-builders generally require the realisation of development gains from the previous project to start a new production cycle, large construction firms operate housing production on several sites at the same time. One of my interviewees explained:

> The shift of construction business from the small groups to big groups brought a factory-style production. This is not a classical small-scale housing production such as finding land, completing the construction, selling of these dwelling units and waiting for a new work. In big construction companies, there are staffed architects, engineers, technical personnel, task masters, skilled workers. They have giant machineries and marketing companies. They have complementary companies in horizontal and vertical levels. They should be always active; there must always be a product on the production line, whatever it is, a house, hotel, office, stadium, shopping malls, schools, hospitals, bridges. If their production stops, the factory knocks off.
>
> interview VII

Although the interviewee was well enough in explaining the alteration in the volume, size and level of the production of real properties in general and housing in particular in the post-2002 Turkey, I need to make correction at one point. The factory does not knock off when the developers stop production, on the contrary, it only works until effective demand is shaken somehow. When the boom period of property market cycle ends, if developers cannot realise the gains from the built structures, if they cannot exit the production line before the bust phase and if they do not have strong balance sheets to resist against the market downturn, they remain with overaccumulated capital (unsold dwelling and substantial amounts of capital locked up in land), being highly leveraged or bankrupt. This is what happened in the housing supply side after 2017, as detailed below.

Compared to the small-scale house-builders, large-scale ones experience a harder exit due to their higher level of fixed capital tied up production (resulting from simultaneous production in multiple plants), although their high-risk profile means higher-level development gains. Moreover, while some of the large-scale housing developers undertook all or some part of the industrial production themselves, others only dealt with mercantile activities by hiring hundreds of subcontracting firms for industrial production (interviews). The subcontracting not only eliminated the technological know-how disadvantage of new players but also enabled them to lower labour costs due to the prevalence of the employment of informal precarious workers by small subcontractors in Turkey (Çoban, 2018; Çınar, 2018; Gürcanlı and Müngen, 2013). Although the casual nature of building employment and the cost-reduction through employing subcontracted workers is a well-known practice in the housebuilding sector in the Global South and Global North countries such as France and Germany (Ball, 2012), in Turkey, the employment of migrant Syrian workforce in the lowest segment of of very hierarchical structure of the building labour led construction capitalists to take advantage of further cost-cutting (Çoban, 2018; Çınar, 2018). Moreover, the mobility of the construction workers, the ethnical antagonism between the construction workers, and the temporary employment contracts for each project significantly destroy the collective bargaining power and class solidarity among the construction labouring class and even prevents the establishment of a trade union for construction workers in Turkey, except for the Construction Workers Association established in 2012 (Çınar, 2014). Therefore, the prevalence of the multi-layered and hierarchical production chain in the housing SoP led big companies to take advantage of cheap labour through subcontracting firms, which cut down labour costs not only by wages but also by under-provision of health and safety equipment (Toksöz, 2008; Çınar, 2015). The neglect of health and safety conditions by these private companies contributed to work accidents among all construction sectors in Turkey. Only between 2008 and 2012, 754 construction workers died, and 940 workers became permanently disabled (DISK, 2014).

A new business model became very common among the large-scale housing developers in the 2010s. The sell-and-build or pre-selling system completely reversed the order of speculative building activity. Whilst for a classical speculative builder, the industrial activity (building residential blocs) follows the mercantile activity (selling them to house purchasers), in the sell-and-build model, housing developers sell the dwelling units on mock-up models before (and during) the construction process. This business model gained terrain especially after 2013 due to the depreciation of TL which directly affected construction companies having high FX debts. Therefore, "financing housing projects by advances from house buyers" became a coping strategy of large and medium-scale companies to sustain their production in an environment where they left behind the golden era of borrowing cheap FX loans (IMF, 2017: 63). Moreover, as a common practice, for facilitating and speeding up the 'pre-sales' agreements with home-buyers, these firms run advertising campaigns aggressively and "launch subsidized sales campaigns offering mortgage loans at below-market rates [i.e., through shadow financing]" (IMF, 2017: 63). Therefore, when referring to the factory example of the interviewee above, a significant part of the large-scale developers did not stop running their factory but increased the volume of production to compensate for the increasing FX debts. While the sell-and-build model was a solution for developers thanks to financing their on-going housing projects with advances from homebuyers, these homebuyers took on the risk of developers' potential failure in completing their projects. Looking to the activity reports of GYODER, showing the sales of branded houses developed by large-scale companies, indicates the size of this activity. While the share of the incomplete houses within total housing sales made in January 2014 was 63.6%, its ratio became 82% in December 2017 and 74% in January 2018. Therefore, 'sell-to-build' model and financing the ongoing projects by advances from home-purchasers became the most widespread business and financing model for large-scale housing developers particularly since 2013 when the TL started to depreciate. Nevertheless, 'building completion insurance' was introduced in 2014 (Consumer Protection Law, No. 6502) for regulating the sell-to-build housing market. A developing firm had to conduct building completion insurance from an insurance company or a bank letter of guarantee to be able to make pre-paid sales on models. However, there have been only a few firms conducting a building completion insurance since the enactment of the law, because neither insurance companies are willing to make building completion insurance nor the developers want to take out insurance (Sigorta Dünyasi, 2020).

As mentioned above, after the enactment of LTADR in 2012 exempting the developer firms, which undertake urban transformation projects, from several taxes and fees, the equity-sharing business model also became an attractive model for large-scale housing developers. Moreover, when considering that land prices dramatically inflated and urban land scarcity showed up in the big cities in the 2010s (interviews), this law also became a saviour for the large-scale developers since it created a compulsory housing demand and made the already occupied urban land available for new house-building activities. Although M&A is available for the large-scale housing developers, it is not widespread in the sector. Instead, joint-venture agreements became popular with particular projects (Uzunkaya, 2013). When national large-scale developer firms enter local markets for developing housing projects for the upper-segment of these cities, they partner with smaller, local firms on certain projects. An interviewee from a large-scale construction company explains:

> We do not prefer merging with others because it is meaningless if two firms have the same power. Coming together only matters if you have something which I do not have, for instance knowing the local market. ... We sometimes make joint venture agreements with firms having the control of local markets. We put our capital onto project; they solve all the potential problems such as getting building permits, land purchasing, etc.
>
> interview XXVII

Moreover, although the post-2002 era witnessed the multiplication of large-scale construction companies, not all of them can be classified as institutionalised firms in the sense that a substantial part have family-run business structures without a professional management team; hence, company owners also work as managers (Uzunkaya, 2013; SBB, 2018). The finance manager of a large-scale company explained the struggle with the company owner:

> I started to work for this company after retiring from a bank in 2005. When I started to work here, firstly they made me the manager of both finance and accounting departments. It took me several months to be able to explain that accounting and financing are different things. This is a big company. But the mentality is same with the small-scale ones. I do not say all the firms are like that but I think 90% of these large construction companies are unprofessional, whatever the boss says it happens. The boss steps in everything, in technical issues, in financing. Then they go bankrupt. For instance, I tell the owner of the company that there is a crisis in Turkey, an unnamed crisis since 2014. Moreover, for our segment [the high-end houses], there is a housing oversupply. They still continue to build. The profit margins decreased compared to previous years but they make more construction as a response.
>
> interview II

Although all large-scale housing developers produce houses for medium and high-income groups, they try to differentiate themselves from others by their branded houses, which is key for understanding the consumption behaviours of the home-purchasers in the 2000s. The business development manager of a large-size company and the major shareholder of a REIT said:

> Our customer profile is young secular white-collar people. They use their homes as home offices. They want to say that they live in this branded house because we do not sell houses but we sell a lifestyle. As Churchill[11] said, 'we shape our buildings and afterwards our buildings shape us'. Indeed, people adopt themselves to the living aura and system you built. For instance, we put unalterable welcoming mats; they cannot change their doormats in all of our housing projects since we do not want people to have different doormats. This is a metropolitan life; there must be some rules. This is the brand we sell.
>
> interview IX

Apart from their scale, the business strategies of construction capitalists also differ according to their relationship with the state. As discussed in Chapter 6, there are two groups of companies in the PPP projects of TOKI,[12] including the local small and medium-scale developing firms in Anatolian cities which undertake the production of affordable houses, and some large-scale companies undertaking comparatively more profitable[13] affordable housing projects of TOKI, which are produced for the medium-income group in big cities. In this model, TOKI provides land and sells the completed dwellings to the beneficiaries chosen by lot but do not intervene in the actual production. The contractor companies cover all the expenses during the construction period and

---

11   Winston Churchill's (1943) statement about the rebuilding of the House of the Commons in the UK.

12   There are more than 600 private construction companies working in TOKI's housing projects. A significant part of them are small and medium-scale local construction firms undertaking the production of affordable houses in their own regions. However, in the case of revenue-sharing projects, which are conducted by large-scale national construction firms, there is much more concentration.

13   According to the calculations of Sönmez (2011), while the average value of these projects is between TL100–200 million, 45 construction companies undertake most of the affordable housing projects for middle-income groups. The Chamber of Civil Engineers (IMO, 2011) also lists up 21 construction companies which frequently win tenders for affordable housing production. These companies are members of the representative business associations of the small-scale Islamic capital fractions MUSIAD and TUSKON.

receive the progress payments from TOKI during two years as from their start to production. Although the contractor companies are exempt from construction and land development fees, taxes and other project expenses thanks to TOKI's prerogatives, they become highly leveraged for covering the expenses of the building process (interviews). Because affordable housing projects of TOKI are in the form of large mass housing estates, small and medium companies generally do not have sufficient equity capital to sustain such a large volume of production and they have serious financing problems. The owner of a medium-size company explains the process like that:

> We are currently constructing TOKI's social houses for medium-income group with 1312 flats. The value of this work is TL105 million. However, financing this project is very hard for us. Until we finish 30% of the total work we already spent 20 million TL but the first-instalment of the progress payment, which we received from TOKI, is only TL11–12 million. TOKI starts to pay the principal amount after we finish 70% of the total work. So you should have a power to resist until this point. However, the completion of this work takes at least 1.5 year. This means that we have to finance all the expenses during 1.5 year. This includes the payments to many subcontracting firms we work together. Hence, we always have TL10–12 million budget deficits for this project. Our internal financing is not sufficient to cover this so we borrow from banks but the cost of commercial credits is nearly 15% nowadays [in 2015]. I mean there is always a risk of failure to complete the project. This risk is not only for us. All the companies working with TOKI is in the same situation; company statements are horrible; nearly all of us have budget deficit with high liabilities. Then what we do is salvaging the day. How do we do this? If we took one work from TOKI, then we take another, then another ... With the gain from the first work, we pay a part of our debts and then use this capital for the second project. This goes on like this. Actually the smallest shock in the economy damages cash-flows.
>
> interview XXVI

Therefore, although with affordable housing projects of TOKI, a wide scope of business space has been created for particularly local capitalist classes in Anatolian cities and these projects were lucrative for them until 2013, the increasing cost of debt financing in the face of depreciating TL from 2013 harmed the balance sheets of these contractor firms. According to the activity reports of TMB (2019; 2020), particularly after the debt and currency crisis in 2018, several contractor companies had problems in receiving their progress payments from TOKI. Also, with increasing costs of building materials, some of which are imported[14] and their costs are sensitive to exchange rate fluctuations, contractor companies' expenses mounted their tendered amounts and several of them failed in completing the projects (TMB, 2020). For saving these companies from bankruptcy, a new Enforcement and Bankruptcy Code was enacted in January 2019 in that the contractor companies failing to complete the TOKI projects had a right to apply for liquidation or project transfer.

The second group of companies undertaking the revenue-sharing projects of TOKI and its subsidiary Emlak Konut REIT are large-scale construction companies, which grew significantly in the post-2002 era by undertaking luxurious housing production on the highest-value urban land in big cities, particularly in Istanbul. In this model, unlike the affordable housing projects, TOKI (and Emlak Konut REIT) is not responsible for any part of the land development, construction, finding homebuyers or selling the completed dwelling units; instead, it is only a landowner, which provides a high quality of urban land, namely high MR-generating land, on which the project will be carried out. This model is based on the privatisation of public land controlled by TOKI, however, unlike the usual landowner-capitalist house-builder bargaining at the beginning of the sale of land, TOKI does not sell land directly but rather becomes the shareholder of the successful tender company and so appropriates its share, such as a part of the development gain of this private builder, after the project is completed and residential units are sold.[15] TOKI's capital gains from the sale of land are around 35–45% of the total sale revenue (interview III, interview IV). Moreover, thanks to the prerogatives of TOKI, the construction company becomes exempt from all kinds of development fees and tax premiums in each stage of investment, which are normally compulsory payments for private

---

14   Although building materials such as cement and iron have been produced in Turkey, the required energy for their production has been imported. 59% of the cost of cement production comes from imported electricity and fuel and 86% of the cost of iron production consists of imported scrap, ore or energy (Güngör, 2018). However, according to the IMF report on Turkey (2017: 60), "on the supply side of the housing market, real changes in the construction cost seem to have a negative but statistically insignificant relationship with the real house price growth". While the increase in construction costs were constantly below the house price inflation until November 2016, with the substantial deflation of the house prices since then, construction costs overwhelmingly outpaced the house prices in that "the annual change difference between cost of construction and house prices is more than 29% as of September 2018, reflecting housing developers' inability to pass on costs to buyers given the slowdown in demand" (WB, 2018: 19). See figure in Appendix 3.

15   Because TOKI gets its share as cash payment, it is different from the flat-for-land model.

developers, and takes the required "legal permissions in the shortest term under TOKI's public guarantee" (Çelik *et al.*, 2016: 24). Moreover, the construction companies enjoy national and international-level marketing campaigns by using the network of TOKI since the beginning of the project.

Therefore, one can easily say that TOKI is a profit-oriented public institution utilising its public land stock for the benefit of private capital. However, here, the source of the biggest discontent among the construction capitalists in Turkey is the tendering process for the mass housing projects conducted by TOKI which favours a particular group of developers. In the tendering process, after determining the land on which the project will be carried out, TOKI calls private developers for tender. The bidding companies make offers for the land plot in question based on their anticipated development gains. In such tenders, the winning company is expected to be chosen according to the highest payment offered for land; however, TOKI applies ambiguous criteria, such as "the most risk-free offer" (interview III, interview IV). Because TOKI's revenue-sharing projects are not liable to the PPL, its tenders are exempt from all kinds of formal control and public auditing mechanism. Therefore, numerous reports, news and articles reveal that the firms enjoying these housing projects on the most valuable and largest land parcels of big cities have direct or indirect political affiliations with the government, either through "ideological kinship (e.g. board members of politically connected media channels, Islamic Charities, and Foundations)" or the familial and personal ties with the party executives (Gürakar, 2016: 10; Sönmez, 2011; IMO, 2008; 2011; BSB, 2015; Gürek, 2008; Çavuşoğlu, 2017; Demiralp *et al.*, 2016; Buğra and Savaşkan, 2012; 2014; Karatepe, 2016). For instance, according to the report of IMO (2011), while construction companies having close connections with the party won 68% of the total tenders conducted by TOKI, this ratio became 90% when the successful tenderers' membership into Islamic business organisations is taken into consideration. According to Gürek's calculations (2008) the Islamic fraction of construction capitalists won the tenders at the value of 10 quadrillion within the total TOKI tenders until 2008, the value of which was 16 quadrillion in total. Moreover, it is also possible to understand the degree of concentration of tendering activities among these 'privileged companies' by analysing the tender list of TOKI. When looking at the revenue-sharing projects of TOKI and Emlak Konut REIT, including urban renewal projects, it is possible to see that they were carried out by nearly 60 firms including Varyap, Metal Yapı, Kuzu, Mesa, İçtaş, Gap, Torunlar, Ağaoğlu, Aşçıoğlu, İhlas, Egeyapı. Examining the representative business associations of these firms, the overwhelming majority of

them are members of KONUTDER and GYODER,[16] which are the business associations of the large-scale pro-government housing developers and real estate
investors, as part of the second-generation bourgeoisie. According to the head
of KONUTDER, 17 firms in their association have 1.6% market share in housing
production, apart from the revenue-sharing works that they carried out with
the partnership of TOKI and Emlak Konut REIT (Milliyet, 2013). This confirms
that an overwhelming part of their total development gain comes from the projects of TOKI and Emlak Konut REIT. While more than half of these firms were
established during the AKP rule (IMO, 2011; Perouse, 2015), some of them were
already active in the construction sector during the 1980s and 1990s, despite
being only mid-level developers in the sector. Therefore, what made them the
biggest players in the domestic housing market in Turkey is their privilege in
winning the public tenders and undertaking the largest housing production in
the post-2002 period.

Moreover, because TOKI developers undertaking these projects work with
dozens of subcontractors and they generally work with the same subcontractors regularly (Dursun, 2015), these projects also indirectly create a second-
layer of beneficiaries of public tenders, although their profit margins are much
lower than the main contractors. Therefore, I argue that this 'rent coalition'
surrounding the TOKI tenders created a hegemonic capital group as the receivers of the lion share of the monopoly rents arisen from housing projects on the
most valuable land parcels of the country and hundreds of small-and medium-
level capital groups as the small beneficiaries within the process of the rent-
distribution. Moreover, the legitimation and political support of this TOKI-led
rent coalition became possible thanks to the affordable housing projects by
materializing homeownership dream of a segment of low and low-middle-
classes' through subsidized credits (Marschall *et al.*, 2016; Özdemir, 2010).

From this point forth, it can be argued that the biggest discontent from
the existence of TOKI in Turkish housing SoP comes from the long-standing
actors of the constructions sector, i.e., first-generation bourgeoisie, which were
already large-scale developers before the 2000s. My interviewee from one of
the oldest and largest construction-origin conglomerate groups in Turkey,
which has been active in the domestic and international construction sector
since the 1950s evaluates the impacts of changing conditions in the sector as
following: "These newly emerging companies were previously working as our
subcontractors. We have been in the construction industry for over 50 years.

---

16   While the GYODER was founded in 1999, KONUTDER was established in 2011. They collab-
      orate in the lobbing activities.

These companies normally cannot compete with us in free market conditions, but we cannot compete with them in tenders. Finally, we closed our tendering department. Instead our projects are mostly abroad." (interview XXIX). Similarly, the technical manager of a first-generation construction-centred holding company described the changing strategy of the company in the 2000s as follows:

> The founder of our company entered the construction sector by building railways in the 1960s. In the 1980s-90s, the company also took over the construction of several mass housing projects. We are currently focused on infrastructural works. For instance, recently we completed a tunnel construction in Turkey by winning the public tender for it. The founders of our company are not close at all to the government. They won this tender because there were only two companies bidding for the project. There are not many companies that can compete with us in the works requiring high technological expertise. ... 90% of our works is in overseas now, in North Africa, Saudi Arabia, Qatar, generally railway construction works. ... Although we were not active in residential building until recently, after the enactment of urban transformation law in 2012, we established a new real estate company as part of the group companies. This new firm make land development, house and office building works. We also carry out large-scale urban transformation works in Istanbul but independently, not with TOKI. We did not even try to enter TOKI tenders. We know the result why should we?
>
> interview I

While these two holding companies responded to the rise of new (privileged) big players in the domestic housing market by intensifying their works on infrastructural construction and decreased the volume of housing production (for the latter) or completely quit residential production (for the former); the existence of TOKI in luxury housing production becomes a much more burning issue for the large-scale construction companies specialising in the super-structure construction and housing. They think that TOKI is a competitive firm for them and advocate a complete withdrawal of TOKI from the luxury housing production. The owner of one large-scale construction firm explains this as follow:

> Governments cannot change laws based on the benefits of the people around them. When Özal founded TOKI, he wanted to revive the construction industry for all of us. He completely privatised the construction

sector. Today, TOKI is the biggest trouble for us. They take place in the construction of everything, housing, schools, and hospitals. The rest of us compete with the rest of the market. Now [in 2015], we already used all of our land stock. Land prices are very high now and competition in the domestic market is very tiring for us. Finally, we decided to change our strategy. Our new projects are now in Turkmenistan, Algeria and Kazakhstan, on the construction of public buildings and schools.

interview XVI

Based on the interviews, the first-generation large construction capitalists tend to expand their operations to the international market by abandoning the domestic residential production. The reports of TMB and INTES, which are the representative business associations of the first-generation large construction firms, confirm these findings that 90% of the total international construction works of Turkish construction firms[17] were undertaken by the member firms of INTES/TMB, while these firms also undertake 70% of all construction works in the domestic market. Moreover, when examining the projects of INTES/TMB member firms active in international markets, some of these companies also undertake housing production in Oman, Russia, Libya, Algeria, Saudi Arabia and Iraq, although housebuilding in overseas is not dominant compared to other construction services.

Furthermore, considering the strong clientelism in the housebuilding sector and the AKP era witnessed the new privileged firms commonly named as TOKI riches, construction barons of AKP or partisan companies, the unprecedented flow of capital onto construction and real estate sectors during the 2000s and 2010s is difficult to explain. The number of firms in the construction sector is more than 200,000 as of 2018. Although a significant part of them are small and medium-level developers, the biggest conglomerates composing the traditional industrial and commercial bourgeoisie of Turkey since the early decades of the Republic, also established new construction companies for housing production and real estate investments. Therefore, the question is whether it is sufficient to describe the intervention of Turkish state into housing SoP referring to clientelism, cronyism, corruption, patronage. At this point, this book advocates the necessity of moving beyond such shortcut definitions and understanding the construction capitalists' relation with the state and TOKI, based on our Poulantzas-inspired analysis. The growing

---

17   Turkey is the second country after China in the Top 250 Global Contractors List and also in the second place in the world in the export of construction services (ENR, 2018).

political and economic role of the state in authoritarian statism when combined with the intensification of antagonistic inter-class relations may deepen the selective aid to particular capital fractions at the expense of others. Hence, clientelism and corruption are the modes of asymmetrical representation of particular short-term interests of certain fractions of capital in certain apparatuses of the state, such as TOKI. In this mode of representation, "political support is exchanged for particular benefits [...] which is mostly related with the allocative, distributive or redistributive role of the state" (Jessop, 1996: 163). Although TOKI's PPP projects primarily allocated and redistributed ground rent towards the second-generation construction capitalists, the urban planning, land development and zoning power of TOKI, Ministry of Environment and Urbanisation, metropolitan municipalities and many other institutions created the conditions for the generation and appropriation of ground rent for all fractions of the construction capital. Hence, the relations between the state and different fractions of construction capitalists do not refer to a simple coalition (monolithic power bloc) but a complex contradictory reconciliation among its constituents.

As a result, TOKI, as a specific institutional form, is generated through the balance of social class forces in the 2000s. Also, TOKI represents a particular example of the state-driven financialisation of housing SoP in Turkey, not only through privatisation and commercialisation of public land and social housing but also as an economic agent providing new opportunity structures for all fractions of private developers through pioneering the introduction of new financial tools, such as real estate certificates, bonds and stocks issuing in domestic and international markets and REITs. Thirdly, the systematic fight of the state against informal land and housing market by way of TOKI's expropriation rights not only formalised tradable property rights in the country but also facilitated the creation of new attraction centres in cities. The extra-economic intervention of the state to housing and land markets by radically altering the conditions of urban planning enabled all fractions of business groups to utilise their land banks for housing production. Moreover, the authoritarian neoliberal restructuring of the state systematically repressed the democratic channels for the expression of popular dissents and eliminated the popular opposition for the sake of deepening expansion of capitalist relations in housing provision.

The Turkish state not only completely withdrew from the financial sphere but also established a formal and institutional housing finance system that motivated the flow of capital onto housing and real estate sectors. Lastly, in the critical moments of the narrowing of the housing effective demand or when the urban land scarcity showed up, the intervention of the state into housing helped to delay the bust phase of housing as it happened via the enactment of the reciprocity law accelerating FDI to housing, the earthquake law paving the way for the reconstruction of approximately 7 million dwellings and bringing tax and cost exemption for the developers, and the 2/B law permitting to open up forested lands to development, the reduction of VAT charge from the housing developers from 18% to 1% in 2013, the announcement of housing sale campaigns and the introduction of mortgages with lower interest rates by the state-owned banks. Therefore, although the short-term economic-corporate interests of the politically hegemonic second-generation bourgeoisie were largely favoured in the PPP projects, the long-term interests of different fractions of capital were represented in the Turkish state's intervention into housing SoP, not least by enabling the neoliberalisation and financialisation of housing that expanded the volume and scale of capital accumulation in housebuilding for all fractions in the power bloc.

Hence, it is not coincidental that all the housing developers in my interviews, which define themselves as opposed to the government, also mentioned how they benefitted from the neoliberal economic policies under the AKP and from the significant steps taken by the government in crisis-ridden times. For instance, the owner of a medium-sized construction company, which develops its housing projects as a speculative developer, explains this as follow:

> The political and economic stability helped the sector grow, despite bureaucratic obstacles. We definitely advocate the retreat of TOKI from the metropolises, as we also develop houses for middle-income groups in Istanbul as TOKI does [by its affordable housing projects]. ... TOKI's first projects were also good for us. When it developed a housing project in a region, infrastructure was provided by municipalities there, so we had a chance to enter these [sub-] markets. They also saved us from gecekondu trouble. However, they already cleared the way for us. Now they should stop.
>
> interview XXI

Moreover, the owner of a first-generation large-scale firm also mentioned the advantages of the changing conditions in the 2000s as follows:

> In the 2000s, the creditworthiness of Turkey increased, a significant amount of foreign capital flew into our sector, from foreign banks, foreign funds and especially from Arab countries. This became possible by political and economic stability. When banks started to give credits to everyone, demand for housing increased this much for the first time, although

> people are indebted more than they gain. So the most important thing
> the government did for us was the banking law.
>
> interview XVI

The business development manager of a large-size company, which define
themselves as the housing developers of young secular white-collar people,
also evaluates the state's intervention into housing in a similar manner:

> All in all, we cannot say that AKP did everything wrong. Above all, they
> were backed by the IMF wind for the first 6–7 years. They stimulated the
> economy thanks to foreign capital inflows, and they created new rich
> who invest in housing. Also, they knew how to play into the Turkish peo-
> ple's admiration for real estate. Erdoğan created an adoration in the Arab
> world, that in turn created foreign demand for housing. And indeed the
> truest thing AKP government did was the strategy of expanding the bor-
> ders of cities.
>
> interview IX

Lastly, one of the most worrying aspects for all the developers in my interviews
was going back to the political and economic turmoil years of the 1990s. When
I interviewed the firms right after the June 2015 general elections, the AKP had
lost the parliamentary majority for the first time since 2002. Hence, the firms
explained that they were waiting for "the re-establishment of political and economic stability" "in alarm" (interview XXVI). The reason behind the desper-
ate need for 'political and economic stability' of all fractions of construction
capitalists in Turkey was their FX-dependent financing structure. Therefore,
I return to the examination of the housing development finance.

3   Housing Development Finance

As discussed before, the process from land purchase to the sale of the completed dwelling units, which realises the developers' development gain in the
form of MR, takes a long time (1.5–3 years only for production process) and
imposes large costs on producers, hence housing developers frequently need
credit to finance the production process. Regarding the housing development
finance in the post-2002 era, three funding sources can be mentioned including commercial credits from banks, REITs and real estate investment funds
(REIFs), and stock and bond issuance. While the last two signify the financialisation of housing developers in the narrow sense, meaning that is the extensive

expansion of IBC, the first one is part of the broader impact of financialisation, due to the exposure of developers to the volatilities in domestic and global financial markets through their high FX liability.

Regarding capital markets, stock and bond markets in Turkey are less-well established compared to the ACCs and some LCCs, such as South Korea and South Africa (Demiröz and Erdem, 2019). Corporate bond issuance of US$200 million was only tried by Yüksel İnşaat in 2010 that has operated not only in luxury residential building but also in several sectors including infrastructure, energy, and defence industry. Regarding the stock market, nine large-scale construction companies have been traded on BIST and raised capital for their projects through stock market, although the market capitalisation rates of their stock shares have been very volatile, given the total market capitalisation of nine construction companies on BIST is TL38.463 billion as of July 2020.[18] Therefore, there has been a slow and gradual increase in raising capital through stock market among some large-scale construction companies since 2010, although this did not become a common phenomenon among developer firms in Turkey.

On the other hand, REITs became both the most expeditiously growing source of development finance and one of the most important actors of the Turkish housing SoP. Although the legal framework for the establishment of REITs was formed in 1996, the number of REITs sprouted in the 2000s thanks to the allocation of certain legal privileges, including the exemption from paying any corporate tax and income tax or dividends (Erol and Tırtıroğlu, 2011). Therefore, REITs in Turkey "enjoy complete freedom in their dividend policy choices" that enable their "dividend withholding tax rate to be zero percent" (Erol, 2019a: 261). Also, according to the legal code regulating the conditions of the establishment of REITs, one of the shareholders must own at least 25% share and all REITs must offer at least 25% of their share to the public (IPOs). However, as a general trend in Turkey, the major shareholders hold more than 50% of the equities of REITs that gave some big construction companies (from both first-generation and second-generation bourgeoise) concentrated control on some REITs, such as Torunlar, Doğuş, Kiler, Nurol, Sinpaş and Yeşil REITs. Moreover, according to the CMB, Turkish REITs must invest at least 50% of their portfolio values to real estate activities and real estate-backed securities. While this ratio was 75% before, its reduction to 50% enabled Turkish REITs to enjoy "considerably more diversified asset portfolios than their counterparts

---

18   https://www.borsaistanbul.com/en/sayfa/3269/public-offering-and-listing-in-borsa
      -istanbul [Accessed 19 Feb 2023].

in other countries" such as purchasing, selling and leasing houses and land, trading capital market tools and in this way getting rental income and capital gains from these activities (ibid., 262).

Hence, as expressed by Erol (2019a: 267), compared to counterparts in other countries, Turkish REITs have a more hybrid structure. Although REITs cannot undertake the construction work themselves, they can purchase land for housing projects and finance construction companies to develop these projects. Therefore, as publicly listed real estate companies, Turkish REITs collect funds from domestic and international institutional investors and use them for financing particular large-scale housing projects. This way, while land and buildings are securitised and become paper claims to the property for the institutional investors, the money pooled from third-parties are used to finance owner-occupied housing in Turkey.

However, since there is no consolidated data regarding the share of REITs investments allocated to housing investments, the share of the REITs in total housing development finance cannot be examined. Nevertheless, REITs' financing of housing development is limited to the top-end luxury projects. Figure 34 shows the number of REITs and their overall portfolio values. As can be seen, the number of REITs listed on BIST continuously increased during the 2000s and 2010, particularly after the GFC thanks to a strong new wave of hot money flows from the ACCs as a consequence of QE, although their market capitalisation rates have been fluctuant, in line with the volatility in capital inflows and interest rates on mortgages. As of the end of 2019, there are 33 REITs with a total portfolio of $5.497 billion.

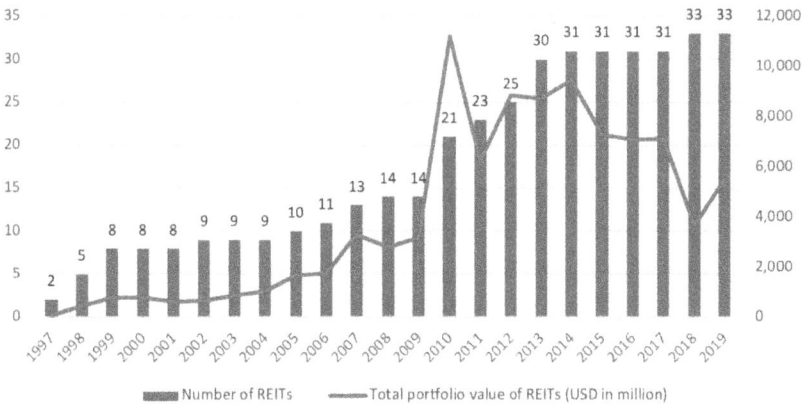

FIGURE 34   Number of REITs and total portfolio values — in US$ million (1998–2019)
SOURCE: CMB HTTP://WWW.CMB.GOV.TR/

Hence, REITs became the main capital market instruments linking the housing into global financial circuits. Moreover, they became the main drivers of financialisation of housing in Turkey but also the primary beneficiaries of financialisation after 2002. Due to the majority control of the parental construction companies on REITs, they also represent the financialised segments of first and second-generation construction capital. Although the Turkish REIT market is less developed compared to, for instance, REIT market in the US, it "predates those in developed economies such as Japan, France and the UK" as a strongly growing source of housing development finance (Erol, 2019a: 261). Thus, unlike the underdeveloped secondary mortgage market of Turkey, REITs are moderately strong financial tools.

Apart from REITs, REIFs, whose necessary legal regulations were implemented in 2014, were designed as new capital market instruments to finance real estate projects including housing. Unlike REITs, REIFs are hedge funds. Specifically, if institutional investors invest in REITs, they become shareholders of companies; while in the case of REIFs, they invest in a certain project and become the shareholder of this certain project (Çelik and Karaçimen, 2017). The first REIF was established in 2015 and, as of the end of 2019, their number rose to 42 with a total of TL6.6 billion net asset values.[19] Although REIFs are gradually increasing their share in development finance, they are less developed compared to REITs.

Lastly, the corporate loans given by the commercial banks have been the most important source of development finance of residential builders. As in the case of mortgage loans, the relatively low interest rates accompanied by increased international capital inflows in the post-2001 era created a favourable environment for corporate loans for private house-builders. Especially in the case of small and medium-sizes house-builders, domestic loans became the primary way of funding their housing production. However, for applying to corporate loans for a specific project, developer firms must show a certain level of credibility to banks. Therefore, the common application for developer firms considers their land and other properties as collateral as well as showing their credibility via the already completed projects and previously-taken letter of guarantee from other banks and financial institutions (interviews). As mentioned before, developer firms can take corporate loans both in domestic currency and foreign currency. Hence, Figure 35 shows the total domestic debt of construction companies, characterised by a continuous increase

---

19   https://www.spk.gov.tr/kurumlar/fonlar/yatirim-fonlari/gayrimenkul-yatirim-fonlari [Accessed 19 Feb 2023].

in construction sector's domestic debt that rose from TL4.6 billion in 2004 to TL245.5 billion in 2019, which composes nearly 9% of total corporate loans given by banks. Therefore, this figure confirms that construction companies have been rapidly and increasingly leveraged during the 2000s and 2010s. However, the share of NPLs within total loans significantly increased after 2016 and especially after the 2018 crisis; while the ratio of NPLs was 4.1% in 2013, it increased to 9.8% in 2019 (BRSA, 2020). It is important to mention that following the coup attempt in 2016, the AKP government started to give Credit Guarantee Funds (CGF) for SMEs that needed financing for their ongoing projects. Hence, a part of the domestic loans after 2017 was given as the Treasury-sponsored commercial credit as part of CGF.

Apart from the increase in their domestic debt at an unprecedented scale, a more burning problem for construction companies was their external debt. Although developer firms get their FX loans from both foreign creditors and local lenders, the general trend was taking these loans from commercial banks. As already discussed, the combination of the monetary policy of the AKP government in the post-2001 recovery period and extremely favourable global conditions made the foreign borrowing attractive for NFCs. Especially after the GFC, monetary expansion and decrease in interest rates in the ACCs led this favourable global economic picture to continue for LCCs including Turkey through a new wave of hot money inflow. Hence, this process, underpinned by

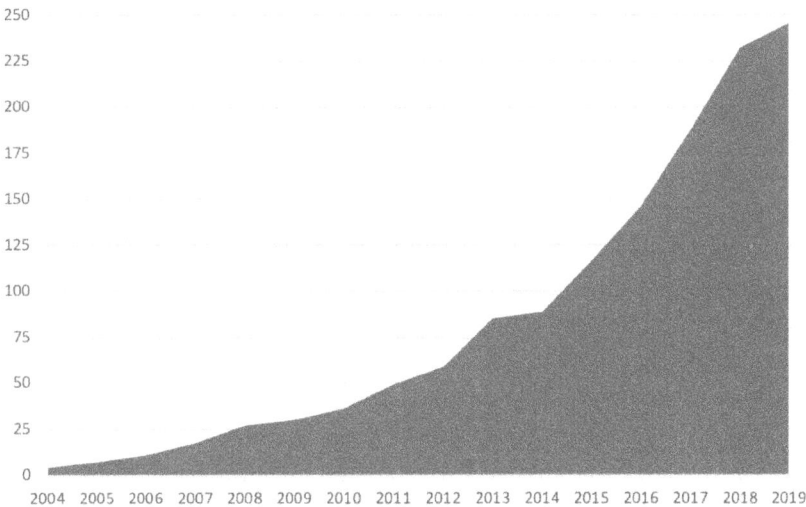

FIGURE 35   Outstanding domestic debt of construction companies (billion TL)
SOURCE: CBRT AND BRSA

increasing capital inflows facilitated the appreciation of the national currency and resulted in increasing FX-dominated indebtedness of the NFCs by making foreign borrowing a cheaper alternative. Nevertheless, as discussed before, the process starting with the announcement of FED's tapering QE policies in 2013 and continuing with the political and economic turmoil in 2016 ended up with a significant currency and debt crisis of the private sector in 2018, whose impacts have continued. Consequently, especially huge currency depreciation after 2015 resulted in highly leveraged private sector in that the construction and real estate sectors take the lead because of the predominance of external borrowing in these sectors. As shown in Table 9, the ratio of external debt to internal debt was 76.6% in 2007 and rose to 86% in 2016, while this was 24% in 2007 and 72% in 2016 for the real estate sector. Moreover, while the volume of external debt of construction sector was US$1290 million in 2004; it rose to US$17,938 million in 2019. Whereas the ratio of external debt of construction and real estate sectors within totals NFCs' external debt was 6.39% in 2004, their share rose to 22.34% in 2019.

Consequently, high FX indebtedness of construction and real estate companies made them vulnerable to currency shocks such as the depreciation of TL that has been an ongoing process in Turkey. Taking into consideration the development gains of house-builders in the national currency, due to the prevalence of domestic housing demand, the currency mismatch becomes a survival issue for them. Therefore, the recent years witnessed the news about bad loans of construction firms and an increasing number of bankruptcies (see below). Although the official figures show that the construction industry's total bad loans rose from TL15 billion (US$2.63 billion) in May 2019 to TL23.8 billion (US$3.71 billion) in February of 2020 (BRSA 2020), there is no exact figure showing the weight of the foreign-currency-denominated NPLs within the total bad debt. Adding the risk of shadow financing, which exists in the sector as a black hole to the construction sector's own highly leveraged structure, a great number of developer firms are under the threat of debt defaults.

Initially, for averting the bankruptcies of construction companies, the AKP government brought a new bankruptcy regulation, namely the Decree Law No. 669, 2016, that enabled firms to declare concordat (bankruptcy postponement). Highly leveraged construction companies had a chance to apply for debt restructuring with banks without attachment proceeding.[20] While the number of construction companies declaring concordat was 45 in 2016, it rose

---

20   The approval to concordat is given by court decisions. However, courts only approved the
      firms which are believed to repay their debts.

TABLE 9   The external debt of the construction and real estate sectors and their percentage within the external debt of the NFCs (2004–2019)

Years	Construction sector external debt (USD in million)	Real estate sector external debt (USD in million)	The ratio of the external debt of the construction and real estate sectors within total NFCs' external debt	The ratio of the external liabilities to total liabilities in the building construction sector	The ratio of the external liabilities to total liabilities in the real estate sector
2004	1,290	219	6.39%	n/a	n/a
2005	2,026	222	7.32%	n/a	n/a
2006	3,274	650	8.62%	n/a	n/a
2007	5,810	2,887	12.35%	76.6%	24%
2008	6,884	4,301	12.57%	77.6%	27%
2009	6,161	4,664	13%	75%	28%
2010	5,320	5,158	13.43%	74.6%	45%
2011	4,874	5,254	13%	78.5%	48%
2012	4,984	5,135	12%	77%	47.4%
2013	5,377	5,439	12.58%	76%	40.4%
2014	6,849	5,237	14%	81%	65%
2015	8,968	4,850	15%	84%	71%
2016	10,779	5,381	16.50%	86%	72%
2017	12,150	5,345	16%	n/a	n/a
2018	16,170	5,767	20%	n/a	n/a
2019	17,938	5,520	22.34%	n/a	n/a

SOURCE: CALCULATED BASED ON THE DATA SET OF THE CBRT, HTTPS://EVDS2.TCMB.GOV.TR/

to 172 in 2018 (Emlakkulisi, 2018). In September of 2018, a temporary supplementary article (no: 30536) also entered into force for preventing bankruptcies for companies with TL value of the foreign exchange debt exceeding the registered capital due to the currency crisis. With this provisional article, *de facto* bankrupt companies were allowed to not reflect their foreign exchange losses on their balance sheets until 2023 and, therefore, they had a chance to get new loans for continuing their operations. The technical bankruptcy postponement arrangement can be considered an effort of the government for keeping several zombie firms alive, which is important for the continuity of their support to the power bloc. Moreover, in 2018, sovereign Turkey Wealth Fund borrowed a treasury-guaranteed loan of €1 billion from international financial markets to rescue (by purchasing debts of) the three large construction companies, that have been with close relations with the government since the early 2000s. Regarding small and medium-scale construction companies, state-owned banks also continue to give corporate loans "at rates below the cost of funding from the CBRT", by borrowing from international financial institutions (IMF, 2019). In December 2019, the Bank Association of Turkey announced a new financial restructuring framework agreement to decrease the concordat declarations, so that SMEs and large companies having trouble to repay their debts have a chance to restructure their debts, with longer maturities and interest rate cut, without stopping their investment and employment activities. However, it is important to note that, as of 2019, the Turkish banks already seized 14,750 unsold dwellings of construction companies, who failed to repay their debts, and try to sell these houses as part of their claims (Cumhuriyet, 2019).

Apart from these, the government has tried to find other alternatives for save construction companies. For instance, it established a new real estate fund to buy the troubled assets of developers and, with the money they receive from the fund, they will cover their debts to banks and other financial institutions (Daily Sabah, 2019). Similarly, another plan is the 'depletion of housing stocks' program in that Emlak Konut REIT, with the support of the Ministry of Treasury and Finance, will buy the unsold dwellings of the construction companies at the price valued by their expertise and, with 70% of the purchased price, the bank debt of the companies will be paid by the Emlak Konut, while 30% will be given to the companies to be used in their own business. With these rescue plans announced, the government aims to rescue insolvent construction companies, prevent the insolvent construction firms to bring down the banking system, and deepen the symbiotic relationship between the saved capital groups and the government (Swyngedouw, 2017). Another bailout scheme on the government's agenda is the establishment of "centralized asset management companies for NPLS in the energy and construction sectors" (IMF, 2019) since energy sector is as critical as construction sector for the hegemonic class fractions in the power bloc. However, so far, these alternatives are only in the government's agenda and ongoing currency devaluation seems to create an impediment.

Despite these efforts to bailout construction companies, according to the data published by TOBB, from the mid-2018 to mid-2019, 4,579 construction companies, which undertake the construction of residential and non-residential buildings, went bankrupt, while the number of bankruptcies in the construction sector was 1,185 in 2016 and 2,510 in 2017 (Yeşilbağ, 2018). Among these firms, there are also companies which worked in PPP projects of TOKI and are active in the sector for 50 years. On the other hand, the construction capitalists from both first and second-generation bourgeoisie, which still try to survive, lobby for new methods to reinvigorate the sector, such as 'Second Urban Transformation Period' with new rules and regulations (GYODER, 2019) and deepening the capital market instruments, which will channel international institutional investors' funds to Turkey, to vitalise both housing demand and development finance by moving beyond the ongoing interest rate-exchange rate trap of the economy administration (TMB, 2020). Moreover, TMB and INTES, as the representatives of the first-generation large construction capitalists, insistently invite the government to focus on economic issues and continue to put market-friendly policies into application, instead of ongoing political struggles with the CHP, following AKP's losing the biggest metropolitan municipalities in the local elections of 2019 (TMB, 2019; 2020).

4   The Volume of Housing Production and Housing Stock

Alongside the ongoing financial problems of construction companies in Turkey, another problem has been the unsold housing stock of large developers that accumulated since 2013. As discussed in the former chapter, the narrowing housing effective demand in accordance with increasing unemployment rates, deteriorating financial conditions and saving rates of households, not only burst highly inflated house prices but also led the housing developers to remain with unrealised dwelling units in their hands. As discussed before, capital accumulation through land and house price inflation (in the form of bubbles of monopoly rent in the era of financialisation) is inherently unsustainable in the long-term and always prone to burst. The prevalence of monopoly rent appropriation in the housebuilding industry is the main reason for the cyclical nature of the housebuilding industry. While developers may have high development gains by increasing their production capacity in the cyclical upswings on condition that they can complete the turnover of capital before the cyclical downturn in the housing cycle, being stuck in the sector without liquidating land values (MR) make developers liable to fail (Wellings, 2006: 261, 265). The crucial point is a true calculation of strategic moves of building capitalists of when to purchase land, when to start production and when to liquidate. Nevertheless, since the combination of industrial and mercantile activities of housebuilding capitalists makes them act based on the anticipations and expectations in the last instance, the industry itself is very risky as much as being lucrative (Ball, 2012). Moreover, uncertainties about the bust time may lead to the over-borrowing of both house-purchasers and developers.[21] In the case of Turkey, over-borrowing with the expectation of the continuity in the upswing phase of housing was also accompanied with over-production for some construction capitalists, especially the ones producing for the top-segment of the market. In the era of financialisation, the housing effective demand and cyclicality of housing itself is strongly attached to the financial expansion and contraction phases that depend on several factors such as global liquidity conditions, capital inflows and sudden reversals, monetary policies and so on. In the case of Turkey, in addition to these factors, the strong state intervention into housing and land markets, the Central Bank and banking sector made construction capitalists continue their over-ambitious production until 2017, when the housing effective demand strongly shrank and the house price inflation severely decelerated. While one reason behind the construction companies' continuance to housing production, despite being highly leveraged is excess trust to the government, the second reason is related to the increasing number of new actors in the sector. The second point emphasized by the first-generation firms in the interviews was the necessity of controlled growth, meaning slowing production and focusing on realisation before the downturn of the housing cycle.

The volume of housing production can be seen in Figure 36. In Turkey, there are two indicators for evaluating housing production according to years, which are building permits and occupancy permits. These certificates are given by the relevant municipalities on the locations where dwellings are built. While building permits are taken right before the construction starts, occupancy permits are granted after the construction completed and dwelling units become available for selling or residing. To show the level and scale of the housing boom, the analysis starts in 1980.[22] As seen in Figure 36, annual housing production starts to vitalise in 2003, reaching 600,000 units in 2006 but slightly decrease during the GFC. The reason why annual housing starts first increased

---

21   As put by Ball (2003: 902), "housing market cycles can be the opportunity for spectacular profit-making, but equally spectacular loss-making during downswings".

22   The difference between building and occupation permits before the 2000s stem from the illegal buildings' granting with construction permits under amnesty laws without occupation permits (Türk and Altes, 2010).

in 2010 and then significantly decreased in 2011 is because "geographical coverage of building regulations [was enlarged] up from 19 to cover all 81 provinces"
and because "new regulations involved additional costs, many house-builders
aimed to avoid those costs by obtaining construction permits prior to the regulations taking force in their provinces" (Erol, 2019a: 247). Consequently, construction permits peaked at 1.375 million in 2017, which refers to the bust phase
of the housing cycle in Turkey. Although occupation permits followed a similar
trend, the difference between building and occupation permits can be considered to stem from the urban transformation projects since when the buildings
were demolished and rebuilt construction permits require to be regranted but
occupation permits for the residents are not necessary. Therefore, the figure
confirms that there is an unprecedented growth in housing production in
Turkey during 2003–2017.

The annual unsold housing stock from 2013 can be calculated since the housing sales according to both first-hand and second-hand sales were published by
TurkStat from this date forward. If we remove the second-hand housing sales
from the total housing sales, it is possible to reach the number of new dwelling
units which could not be realised by developers. According to Table 10, annually, 27–29% of newly-built houses could not be sold between 2013 and 2018
and added to unsold housing stock of the country. There is a consensus in the
literature that this unsold housing stock concentrates on luxury houses produced by the large-scale construction companies (IMF, 2017; 2018; WB, 2015;

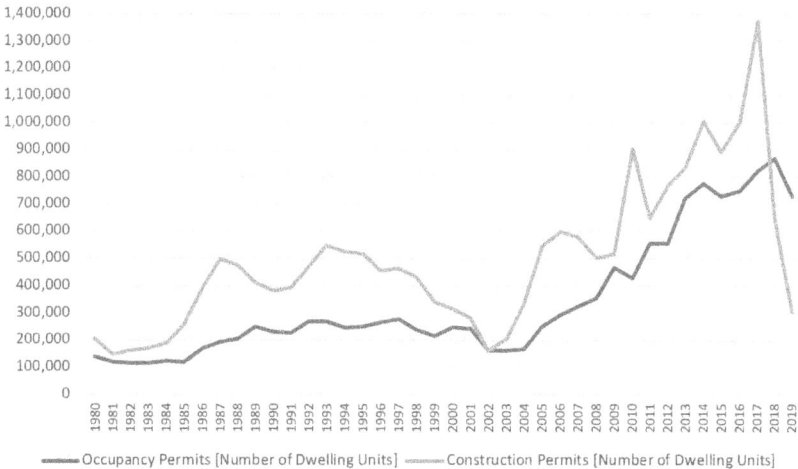

FIGURE 36   Annual building permits and occupancy permits (number of dwelling units)
            SOURCE: TURKSTAT

TABLE 10   Housing stock, number of dwelling units (NDU)

Years	Construction permits [NDU]	Occupancy permits [NDU]	First-hand housing sales [NDU]	Annual additions to unsold housing stock [NDU]
2013	836,138	723,540	529,129	194,411
2014	1,004,938	775,007	541,554	233,453
2015	893,427	730,012	598,667	131,345
2016	1,002,725	750,743	631,686	119,057
2017	1,375,676	821,439	659,698	161,741
2018	651,038	869,506	651,572	217,934
2019	304,544	730,585	511,682	218,903

SOURCE: TURKSTAT

TSKB, 2015; Purkis, 2016; Türel, 2015). By playing on the trend of upper-middle and upper-income groups' investments on housing, large construction companies focused their production on this segment, while the housing deficit and real housing need concentrate in the low and middle-income groups (Purkis, 2014; 2016; Türel, 2015).

5   Construction Move: a Political Project and a Macroeconomic Tool

This chapter also highlights the main motivation of the AKP governments to support housing centred-construction boom in the post-2002 era. Namely, the 'construction move' has been used both as a political project and a macroeconomic tool. As a political project, AKP governments ensured the contradictory unity of the different fractions of construction capital under the hegemony of the second-generation privileged developers as the party's organic bourgeoisie. In this process, a specialised intermediary agent between political power and economic power (TOKI) was designed to represent the interests of the hegemonic construction capitalists by dominating other state institutions, thanks to the organisation of the state in a neoliberal authoritarian form. As the success of hegemony depends on the reconciliation of different interests within the power bloc, the first-generation and second-generation construction capitalists, financial capital, and small and medium construction capital groups were integrated into the power bloc and their economic-corporate interests were also favoured, albeit asymmetrically. Moreover, the use of the construction sector as "an instrument to accommodate the growing labouring classes" (Saraçoğlu and Demirtaş-Milz, 2014: 192), materialisation of the homeownership dream for part of the lower classes through affordable housing projects, presentation of the housing ladder as the most favourable way of prosperity and the use of the financialised regime of social reproduction for disuniting and passivising popular masses became crucial for the success of this political project.

Nevertheless, strong economic and extra-economic state intervention into housing and land markets backed by an intensive and extensive expansion of finance paved the way for a large real estate and housing economy in Turkey that has been discussed as the 'construction-sector based economic growth' by a large number of scholars (Boratav *et. al.*, 2018; Orhangazi, 2019; Orhangazi and Yeldan, 2020; Hepşen *et al.*, 2017; Sönmez, 2015; Erol, 2019b; Akçay, 2018; IMF, 2019).

Because the main focus of this book is housing, an analysis of construction sector in general is beyond the limits of this book. However, since the biggest component of the booming construction and real estate sectors has been housing economy, its role in economic stimuli needs to be mentioned. The extant literature emphasizes four points in the evaluation of the construction sector's weight in total economic growth that I also agree with. The first point is that its impact to the economic growth is not limited to the value-added of the sector within total GDP since manufacturing sector is still the primary sector in value-added, despite its decreasing share. Here, the stimulating impact on other sectors makes the construction sector's share substantial in the distribution of GDP across sectors. Hence, together with real estate activities, construction sector's share rises to 16–18% within total GDP between 2007 and 2016. The second point is that the positive impact of the construction sector on the economy is linked to its backward and forward linkages with other sectors. Specifically, only for residential construction, the sector "receives input from a total of 24 fundamental sectors, namely from 3 main productions, 15 manufacturing and 6 service sectors" (Özkan *et al.*, 2012: 362). The third point is that due to its labour-intensive nature, the construction sector became the second sector in employment creation; its share in total employment rose from 5.5% in 2005 to 7.5% in 2017.[23] Nonetheless, it is also the most vulnerable segment of the debt-currency crisis of 2018 since two-thirds of total job losses happened in the construction sector. Lastly, the construction-oriented system

---

23   https://data.tuik.gov.tr/Bulten/Index?p=Labour-Force-Statistics-August-2020
     -33792&dil=2 [Accessed 19 Feb 2023].

of accumulation is strongly linked with the AKP government's credit-fuelled domestic-consumption based growth strategy, due to the direct reliance of the housing sector to domestic housing demand.

Hence, based on these four points, the construction sector was used by the economy administration as an important macroeconomic policy instrument for stabilising economy and stimulating economic growth. In addition, the accumulation via the asset price appreciation attached to land and housing must be mentioned. Namely, construction and real estate-focused economic growth mean an increase in asset values rather than an increase in value-added, meaning accumulation through the redistribution of revenues rather than surplus-value production. Hence, the house and land price inflation led the actors in the housing SoP to get their profits from the distribution of revenues and wealth, in the form of monopoly rent and interest-bearing capital, that depends on the total amount of real value produced or yet to be produced in the economy.

6   Conclusion

This chapter focused on the production of housing in Turkey in the post-2002 period. By starting with an analysis of the general political and economic dynamics that pave the way for the contemporary mode of housing production, the chapter shows that the housebuilding sector, a part of the larger construction and real estate economy, had a significant macroeconomic and political role within the financialised system of accumulation in Turkey. This role was shaped by the deepened and broadened expansion of finance into housing SoP that attracted the housing developers to focus on maximising their development gains by appropriating larger amounts of ground rents and by sacrificing housing needs of the large segment of the society. However, this chapter argued that the fractioning among construction capital is a consequence of the historically-specific class formation process and the changing balance of class forces in Turkey. The overwhelming presence of TOKI as a quasi-public agency in housing and the land market is the result of this contradictory power relationships attached to the construction and housing sectors. Therefore, both deepened and broadened presence of loanable money capital in the housebuilding sector and the neoliberal authoritarian interventions of the state to housing system led the housing producers, traders, investors and landowners to pursuit the generation and appropriation of monopoly rents on residential landed property.

CHAPTER 9

Conclusion

This book has discussed the political economy of housing in general and in Turkey in particular, from an MPE perspective. In line with the SHP/SoP approach, the book argued that housing provision must be examined as a whole, by considering the spheres of production, exchange and consumption as parts of a unity. To analyse the concrete and complex social relations of housing provision, after 2002 in Turkey, the road map followed started from higher to lower levels of abstraction in an analytical order. For this, Chapter 1 included an analytical and historical examination of the production of housing as a commodity, which is inextricably linked to the capture of ground rent, and the intervention of the landed property into capital accumulation in the housebuilding industry.

Chapter 2 argued that the determination of land and housing prices are inseparably linked to ground rent. Moreover, housing investment activities generate conditions for the creation and appropriation of values as rent, determined by the location of the land and the built environment surrounding the land. Having evaluated the historically-circumscribed social relations of housing production attached to the soil, the book argued that the vast majority of housing rents does not derive from the circulation of surplus-value produced on a particular land. Instead, it derives from monopoly pricing, or the circulation of revenues in the form of MR as part of surplus-value of other commodities produced elsewhere. The identification of the main source of rent in housing has been crucial to understanding why:

i) Housing is exceptionally expensive compared to other wage-goods necessary for social reproduction;

ii) Residential production does not develop a uniform market price for dwellings unlike industrial production;

iii) The prices of housing can rise above the social values produced in the housebuilding industry in excess of the value and production price of houses;

iv) Many landed interests can potentially appropriate revenue gains during the provision of housing;

v) There are different profit rates in housing submarkets named differentiated MR deriving from different monopoly prices generated via different qualities of land for residential production and different levels of effective demand for housing;

vi) The main motivation of housebuilders is to increase their development gains by playing on land uplift and exploiting the opportunities of human-made scarcities on the landed property;

vii) The level, volume and speed of circulation of revenues in the economy determine the level and amount of development gains of builders, landowners and investors;

viii) Production rates are unsteady in the housebuilding industry and output and profits change according to boom-bust phases.

The first contribution of the book is, therefore, the theorisation of the ground rent in the context of the urban residential land and the analysis of the intervention of landed property into capital accumulation in the housebuilding industry. Since housing provision must be examined through different phases of capital accumulation, the book analysed the structural transformation of capitalism and housing provision in recent decades through the concept of financialisation. To provide an understanding of the broad impacts and outcomes, tendencies and counter-tendencies of financialisation as a historically-specific phenomenon, this book approached the concept of financialisation within Marx's theory of money and finance. Having examined IBC and other monetary forms at Marx, I argued that in an advanced credit system, the temporarily unoccupied money of all social classes (as social funds) are collected and centralised in the financial institutions to be loaned out and function as IBC. Within the context of the borrowing and lending relations of money as IBC, money capital is a commodity itself, whose use-value to the borrower is its ability to be transformed into productive capital, and whose exchange value for the money's owner is surplus-value in the form of interest ($1/X$ M). Therefore, IBC uses credit relations to expand accumulation (and therefore itself) with the ultimate aim of appropriating a certain quantity of unpaid labour produced within the overall economy ($M - M'$). While the functional and coordinative roles of IBC are crucial in the development of capitalist (re-)production, IBC has also a parasitical character due to its unique capacity of self-expansion. Within financialised capitalism, this contradiction condenses and the tendency of finance to breed itself takes precedence over its functional role, like the monopolistic role of IBC in all spheres of the economy. Since IBC tends to capitalise and trade every stream of revenue, the capacity of IBC to overcome the limits of surplus-value production and its domination over all other capitals expanses comprehensively in the financialised capitalism. This also becomes the main reason of the instabilities and crises of contemporary capitalism.

Based on these analytical foundations, the book defined financialisation as the intensive and extensive accumulation of IBC, following Fine (2009a).

Having defined financialisation narrowly as IBC, I argued that financialisation rises within and through neoliberalism because neoliberalism as the current stage of capitalism has materialised the conditions in which financialisation occurred, by enabling the internationalisation of production and finance, opening new ways for the commodification of social reproduction and, therefore, facilitating the expansion of IBC. Nevertheless, the book discussed that the incidences, forms and effects of financialisation are uneven in different social formations, taking country-specific forms determined by historical, institutional and social factors, as well as sector-specific dynamics and outcomes due to different ways in which finance is involved in the sectors of commodity production. However, since the activities of IBC have expanded to a great extent in the current capitalism, due to the commodification and privatisation of social reproduction, the boundaries between IBC and other forms of capital have increasingly become blurry and since there are broader, diverse and complex impacts of financialisation on social reproduction apart from the quantitative expansion of IBC, the book examined variegated and uneven impacts and outcomes of financialisation of housing based on the trilogy, CCFCC, developed by Fine (2017).

The book examined the intensive and extensive expansion of finance in housing focusing on general tendencies of financialisation of housing by partially ignoring the country-specific factors and the unevenness[1] (Ollman, 2003). Based on this, I argued that the intensive expansion of IBC through the use of complex financial methods and innovations in the HDF accelerates the size, rhythm and volume of MR appropriation by house-builders, financialised house-builders tend to expand the scale and scope of financial activities to attract financial agents and maximise the MR appropriation by speculating on land prices. Also, when the ground rent is capitalised through trading land on capital markets or when real estate is securitised, the relationship between MR and IBC becomes blurred.

Moreover, financial institutions, either through direct ownership or as a shareholder of building firms, maximise their capital gains in the short-term or reinforce the MR appropriation. Since capital gains of financial institutions partly derive from MR attached to the land and housing, financialisation makes the relationship between rent and interest much more intimate and interwoven. Also, financialisation creates the favourable conditions not only for the localised MR which can be captured through individual productive activities

---

1   This investigation was made based on a survey on different countries housing SoPs.

but also the general monopoly rent by increasing the speed and scale of the circuit of revenue regarding the circuit of production.

The book also shows that financialisation accelerates the pace and volume of boom-bust cycles and volatility in the housebuilding industry. Increasing amount of IBC flowing to mortgage finance, land and residential markets heavily inflates land and house prices. The demand stimulated by the expansion of finance does not necessarily cause an increased supply, it may merely inflate prices or; the increase in effective demand may lead to both construction boom and inflating house prices, that also apply to Turkey.

While financialisation accelerates the size and volume of both localised and general MR and brings lucrative opportunities for huge capital gains, it also makes all the agents in the housing SoP vulnerable to economic shocks and huge losses. Plus, financialisation leads the transformation of the consumption standards of housing by increasingly attaching the VLP to IBC.

The revolutionary expansion of mortgage markets and accompanying changes in the VLP attached to housing transform the monetary payments on housing into a commodity form because streams of revenues flowing into financial companies and banks create the scope for financialisation. Even if there is no securitisation, growing mortgage loans feed house prices and, in turn, increasing capital gains make further lending an attractive operation for financial institutions.

Increasing the amount of MR circulated in the economy that comes from the inflated land and house prices is partly and potentially accrued to capital gains of banks and other lenders out of arranging those mortgages in the form of interest. Financialisation creates a tendency for the domination of mortgage-funded owner-occupation over all other tenure forms. Commodification of housing provision creates a tendency of the consumption of housing in pursuit of capital gains. In the financialised welfare systems, homeownership can be used as collateral for social reproduction or wealthier households can appropriate capital gains by investing in housing that is only sustainable during which house prices continue to soar. Commodification of housing provision and accompanying house price inflation lead much more people to be excluded from this form of wealth accumulation and to become indebted to access to houses. Therefore, house price inflation not only conceals the unequal and uneven distribution of wealth among households but also reproduces class inequality by causing the already-disadvantaged groups to have the heaviest burden against increasing MR.

Financialisation creates an ideology of homeownership as part of the neoliberal consumption culture. The adaption of speculative accumulation strategies by the housing associations or by the state institutions not only brings a

new commodified criteria and ideology but also contributes to the financialisation of social housing. Financialisation of social housing provision transforms
public housing programmes into an industrial policy which aims to improve
construction sector's performance and transforms the social dimension of
public housing policy into an affordability concern.

Another key contribution of this book is that it analysed the general tendencies and counter-tendencies in the structural transformation of housing
provision in recent decades. The book argued that housing provision needs to
be examined according to different forms of the state because the production
and consumption of housing is primarily a national relation and the dominant
capitalist relations are managed, reproduced and realised through different
historically and socially-specific class features and institutional forms. Both
the transition to neoliberalism and financialisation and the consolidation and
institutionalisation of neoliberalism and financialisation in the post-2001 era
were realised through an authoritarian state form in Turkey; therefore, the
book contributes to the financialisation literature by adopting a state perspective. Also, during the consolidation and institutionalisation of neoliberalism
and financialisation in the post-2001 era, the institutional, organisational and
financial structure of TOKI was radically restructured, its authorisation was
strikingly enlarged and consequently, it became a unique institution with the
full power in land and housing markets. Under the AKP governments,

i)   TOKI's economic and political tasks were re-articulated based on the
       changing balance of class forces and the new mode of social and eco-
       nomic reproduction;

ii)   It became a sign of the contemporary form of the authoritarian statism
       in Turkey, thanks to its restructuring as the main representative of the
       strong executive power in the housing market;

iii)   It became a catalyst for the private sector, a pioneer for financial inno-
       vations in the sector and, aimed to legitimise the unprecedented com-
       modification and privatisation of public commons by partially ensuring
       the social reproduction of labour-power;

iv)   TOKI became not only a facilitator of the financialisation of land and
       housing in the post-2002 era but also a peculiar example of the finan-
       cialisation of state in Turkey;

v)   TOKI became a key institution for the privileged representation of the
       second-generation bourgeoisie in the power bloc;

vi)   TOKI was also crucial in creating lucrative spaces for the flow of private
       capital to the built environment, and aiding the organisation of the pro-
       duction and consumption of housing around the appropriation of MR;

vii)   TOKI has strongly adhered to the neoliberal principles and became the main mechanism of the deepening capitalist relations in the housing SoP in Turkey;

viii)   It had an enormous power in the creation and manipulation of effective demand for housing and in determining residential differentiation of cities and creating differentiated MR on different localities thanks to its extremely centralised planning power and landownership role;

ix)   By employing a new mode of financialised social housing provision, TOKI became the main agent enabling the involvements of thousands of households into the financial system as new debtors. Alongside this explicit commodity form in the social housing SoP of Turkey, many people from lower classes accord their lives according to monetary criteria and discipline themselves for being able to pay their mortgage debt;

x)   Emlak Konut REIT, as the main subsidiary of TOKI, worked as a financial arm of the institution and linked it indirectly to the derivative markets by capitalising and trading TOKI's massive land bank in capital markets. Therefore, the unique relationship between TOKI and Emlak Konut REIT signified a particular example of financialisation of public land in Turkey;

xi)   Through gecekondu projects, TOKI transformed inner-cities into new financial and commercial hubs and created scarcely-found valuable land stock for private capital investments;

xii)   Gecekondu transformation projects caused the partial repossession and dispossession of squatters and created further inequalities and segregation among the urban poor.

The book argued that the post-2002 era witnessed the state's systematic and continuous intervention to ensure the precedence of owner-occupation primarily via TOKI. Nevertheless, the particularity of the 2000s consists of the heavy involvement of commercial banks into the mortgage market and the establishment of the institutional and legal basis for the financialisation of housing for the first time in the Turkish history. Although the institutional basis for the secondary mortgage market was formed in the 2000s, only the second half of the 2010s witnessed some attempts to revitalise the secondary mortgage market in Turkey due to the reverting conditions for the expansion of the consumer credit market in accordance with the fluctuations in the global financial markets, the heavy external indebtedness of the banks and the resultant urge for increasing their liquidity to fund housing loans and increasing pressure of the hegemonic capital fractions of the construction sector on the government to speed up the turnover times of their unsold housing stock. Contrary to the underdeveloped secondary mortgage market, the primary mortgage market showed an unprecedented development in Turkey and its spectacular growth resulted in a mortgage boom in the country. Chapter 4 argued that because the banking system heavily relied on external funding and, hence, linked the domestic mortgage system to the global circulation of IBC, there is an indirect but strong impact of the financialisation on housing purchase finance in Turkey. While the boom-bust cycles of the mortgage market followed the general trends of the macroeconomic cycle in Turkey through the banking system, the state's massive intervention into housing SoP through state-owned banks, TOKI and Central Bank's manipulative monetary policy had a significant impact on delaying the bust phase of the housing and mortgage markets.

Regarding housing consumption, this book highlighted that the involvement of an increasing number of households in the mortgage market in Turkey led to a surge in effective demand and, therefore, in general monopoly rent. Also, financialisation of housing in the commodity form emancipated monopoly rent from the decades-long limitations put by effective demand in Turkey. Although the mortgage market became accessible for the middle-classes for the first time in the country's history, the lower classes and the poor were excluded from the mortgage markets. Financial inclusion and heavy mortgage indebtedness became a direct outcome of financialisation, however, financial exclusion composed the other side of financialisation in Turkey.

While financialisation led the consumption of housing for the pursuit of capital gains for wealthier households and this became the most important reason of heavily inflated house prices in Turkey, particularly between 2010 and 2017, the inflating land and house prices and the state's intolerance against informal housing paved the way for the impoverishment of a large segment of the society trapped between unequal access to the owner-occupied sector, the burden of high rent prices and underserved affordable housing.

Furthermore, the combination of the structural factors of urban housing demand and the main determinants of the housing effective demand in Turkey lie behind the dramatically inflating land and house prices in Istanbul and in Turkey, to a lesser extent, since the early 2000s.

Arising from the unprecedented expansion of finance in the housing SOP and the treatment of land and housing like a financial asset by the state, landowners, developers, REITS and households, who speculate on land prices and appropriate large amounts of capital gains from inflating house prices and MR, this book noticed that house prices, especially in Istanbul, took an increasingly bubble-like form that burst in 2016–2017. However, because the mortgage boom in Turkey was accompanied by a construction boom, the house price inflation in Turkey was, to some extent, limited by high levels of supply.

Although MR is volatile by nature due to its dependence on the circuit of revenue, financialisation of housing in Turkey not only linked the cycles of the housing market to the financial cycles in general, i.e. monetary expansion-tightening phases of Turkey that are directly linked to the global liquidity conditions and foreign capital inflows, but further increased the level and volume of the volatility of MR. Consequently, financialisation of housing SoP in the post-2001 Turkey manifested itself in the form of highly leveraged homeownership society, escalated housing inequality and the unprecedented victory of the exchange value of housing over its use-value.

Regarding the sphere of production of the Turkish housing SoP, the book argued that, alongside the increasing weight of the private sector in the housing production at the expense of cooperatives, the post-2002 period witnessed a significant fractioning among housing producers. The three main factors triggering the fractionalisation within the construction capital include the inter-bourgeoisie struggle on the appropriation of ground rent between the early participants and late participants to the accumulation process that manifested itself within the institutional existence of TOKI, the scale of developers and their location within the hierarchical, multi-layered and complex production chain and their relationship with HDF. Consequently, TOKI's PPP projects created a rent coalition, which created a hegemonic capital group as the receivers of the lion share of the monopoly rents arisen from housing projects on the most valuable land parcels of the country and hundreds of small-and medium-level capital groups as the small beneficiaries within the process of the rent-distribution. The legitimation and political support of the TOKI-led rent coalition became possible thanks to the affordable housing projects by materialising the homeownership dream of a segment of the low and middle-classes through subsidised credits. Although the short-term economic-corporate interests of the politically hegemonic second-generation bourgeoisie were largely favoured in the TOKI's PPP projects, the long-term interests of different fractions of capital were also represented in the Turkish state's intervention into housing SoP, not least by enabling the neoliberalisation and financialisation of housing that expanded the volume and scale of capital accumulation in housebuilding for all fractions in the power bloc.

The book also argued that while the primary dynamic behind the housing-centred construction boom of Turkey was the excessive-centralised and per-sonalised authoritarian mode of governance admitting whatever the required legal and institutional alterations are, this would not be possible without financialisation of the Turkish economy. This manifested itself broadly through the internal and external expansion of loanable money-capital to both housing consumption and housing production, the anti-inflationary monetary policy and low interest rate environment of the 2000s bolstered by global liquidity and foreign capital inflows, the flow of cheap loans to housing and increasing interest of individual and institutional investors to Turkish real estate market, notably via REITS. Lastly, I argued that the 'Construction Move' in Turkey was used by the AKP rule both as a macroeconomic policy instrument, and as a political project to strengthen the second-generation bourgeoisie.

The theoretical and empirical contributions of the book presented here also suggest fruitful avenues for future research. First, the labour regime and employment conditions of construction workers in Turkish housing SoP are an under-researched area. This book identified limited secondary sources in analysing the construction workforce in Turkey; therefore, future research needs to fill the vital gap in this area. Second, the lack of official data prevented an accurate track of housing inequality and poverty, for quantitative analysis. Moreover, because the field research of the book focused on the state institutions and the construction companies, further research also needs to carry the fieldwork on households for a better understanding of the housing consumption in the Turkish housing SoP. Third, the methodological and theoretical framework formulated in this book provides a comprehensive approach for comparative housing research from an MPE perspective.

Interview Schedule and Codes

Interview number	Occupation of interviewee	Location	Date
I	The Technical Manager of a holding company	Istanbul	16.06.2015
II	The Finance Manager of a large-scale construction company	Ankara	20.06.2015
III	A top-level bureaucrat in TOKI and later a mayor from the AKP	Istanbul	30.06.2015
IV	The Head of Finance Department of TOKI	Istanbul	30.06.2015
V	The Technical Manager in one of TOKI's affordable housing projects	Istanbul	30.06.2015
VI	The owner of a small-scale construction company	Istanbul	03.07.2015
VII	Mustafa Sönmez (Journalist/ Economist)	Istanbul	03.07.2015
VIII	Mücella Yapıcı (Activist/ President of the Istanbul Chamber of Architects)	Istanbul	04.07.2015
IX	The Business Development Manager of a large-scale company	Istanbul	07.07.2015
X	The Technical Manager of a large-scale company	Istanbul	11.07.2015
XI	The owner of a medium scale construction company	Istanbul	11.07.2015
XII	The Finance Manager of a medium scale construction company	Ankara	14.07.2015

Interview number	Occupation of interviewee	Location	Date
XIII	An expert academician	Ankara	15.07.2015
XIV	An expert academician	Ankara	15. 07.2015
XV	Gürkan Emre Gürcanlı (an activist scholar from the Assembly of Socialist Engineers and Architects)	Istanbul	18.07.2015
XVI	The owner of a large-scale construction firm	Istanbul	24.07.2015
XVII	The owner of a small-scale construction firm	Istanbul	24.07.2015
XVIII	The Business Development Manager of the parental company of a REIT	Istanbul	02.08.2015
XIX	The owner of a small-scale construction company	Istanbul	04.08.2015
XX	The owner of a small-scale construction company	Istanbul	04.08.2015
XXI	The Finance Manager of a medium-scale company	Istanbul	05.08.2015
XXII	Tender and Rights Manager in EmlakYapı	Istanbul	12.08.2015
XXIII	An expert academician	Istanbul	13.08.2015
XXIV	The Head of the Zoning and Urban Transformation Department of the Metropolitan Municipality of Istanbul	Istanbul	16.08.2015
XXV	The Assistant Chairman in a REIT	Istanbul	27.08.2015
XXVI	The owner of a medium-scale construction company	Ankara	29.08.2015
XXVII	The owner of a large-scale construction company	Ankara	20.12.2015

Interview number	Occupation of interviewee	Location	Date
XXVIII	The owner of a small-scale construction company	Istanbul	15.01.2016
XXIX	The Quality Control Manager of a holding company	Istanbul	15.01.2016
XXX	The General Manager of a large-scale company	Istanbul	23.01.2016

Distribution of Non-institutional Population by Equivalised Household Disposable Median Income Groups and Housing Living Conditions Indicators (2006–2018)

Non-institutional population and housing living conditions indicators	Income group			
	Total	Below 60% of the median income	Between 60%-120% of the median income	Above 120% of the median income
2006				
Non-institutional population (thousand person)	67,631	17,165	3,229	27,237
Housing costs				
A heavy burden (%)	28.2	45.6	32.1	13.8
A slight burden (%)	58.8	48.8	59.0	64.7
Not burden at all (%)	13.0	5.7	8.9	21.5
2007				
Non-institutional population (thousand person)	68,484	16,054	25,685	26,744
Housing costs				
A heavy burden (%)	29.8	49.7	33.7	14.1
A slight burden (%)	57.4	45.5	58.0	64.0
Not burden at all (%)	12.8	4.8	8.2	21.9
2008				
Non-institutional population (thousand person)	69,231	16,714	25,306	27,212
Housing costs				
A heavy burden (%)	25.4	42.5	28.1	12.3
A slight burden (%)	60.6	49.8	61.9	66.1
Not burden at all (%)	14.0	7.6	10.0	21.7

Non-institutional population and housing living conditions indicators	Income group			
	Total	Below 60% of the median income	Between 60%-120% of the median income	Above 120% of the median income
2009				
Non-institutional population (thousand person)	70,542	17 123	25 785	27 633
Housing costs				
A heavy burden (%)	29.6	47.8	31.5	16.4
A slight burden (%)	58.9	47.3	59.8	65.4
Not burden at all (%)	11.5	4.9	8.8	18.2
2010				
Non-institutional population (thousand person)	71 343	16 963	26 713	27 667
Housing costs				
A heavy burden (%)	28.2	45.6	32.1	13.8
A slight burden (%)	58.8	48.8	59.0	64.7
Not burden at all (%)	13.0	5.7	8.9	21.5
2011				
Non-institutional population (thousand person)	72,377	16,569	27,301	28,506
Housing costs				
A heavy burden (%)	23.2	41.2	25.4	10.7
A slight burden (%)	61.1	50.1	62.8	65.7
Not burden at all (%)	15.7	8.7	11.7	23.6
2012				
Non-institutional population (thousand person)	73,604	16,741	28,124	28,738
Housing costs				
A heavy burden (%)	22.2	40.4	24.5	9.2
A slight burden (%)	62.6	52.3	63.9	67.2
Not burden at all (%)	15.3	7.2	11.6	23.5

Non-institutional population and housing living conditions indicators	Income group			
	Total	Below 60% of the median income	Between 60%-120% of the median income	Above 120% of the median income
2013				
Non-institutional population (thousand person)	74,457	16,706	28,724	29,027
Housing costs				
A heavy burden (%)	21.0	39.1	23.4	8.2
A slight burden (%)	63.4	54.1	65.0	67.3
Not burden at all (%)	15.6	6.7	11.6	24.6
2014				
Non-institutional population (thousand person)	75,693	16,501	29,676	29,516
Housing costs				
A heavy burden (%)	19.4	32.4	21.5	10.2
A slight burden (%)	59.9	58.4	64.4	56.1
Not burden at all (%)	20.7	9.3	14.1	33.7
2015				
Non-institutional population (thousand person)	76,369	16,706	30,169	29,494
Housing costs				
A heavy burden (%)	23.2	35.9	25.8	13.4
A slight burden (%)	57.2	53.8	62.0	54.2
Not burden at all (%)	19.6	10.3	12.2	32.4
2016				
Non-institutional population (thousand person)	77,110	16,328	30,775	30,006
Housing costs				
A heavy burden (%)	17.4	31.4	18.3	8.8
A slight burden (%)	59.2	58.6	65.5	53.0
Not burden at all (%)	23.4	10.0	16.2	38.1

Non-institutional population and housing living conditions indicators	Income group			
	Total	Below 60% of the median income	Between 60%-120% of the median income	Above 120% of the median income
2017				
Non-institutional population (thousand person)	78,862	15,864	32,582	30,416
Housing costs				
A heavy burden (%)	13.4	22.7	14.7	7.1
A slight burden (%)	55.9	61.1	61.2	47.5
Not burden at all (%)	30.7	16.2	24.2	45.3
2018				
Non-institutional population (thousand person)	79,762	16,889	31,931	30,942
Housing costs				
A heavy burden (%)	11.5	23.6	11.6	4.9
A slight burden (%)	55.0	57.8	63.1	45.2
Not burden at all (%)	33.4	18.6	25.3	49.9

SOURCE: TURKSTAT HTTPS://TUIKWEB.TUIK.GOV.TR/PREHABERBULTENLERI.DO?ID=33820

Divergence between Construction Costs and House Prices in Turkey (June 2016–September 2018)

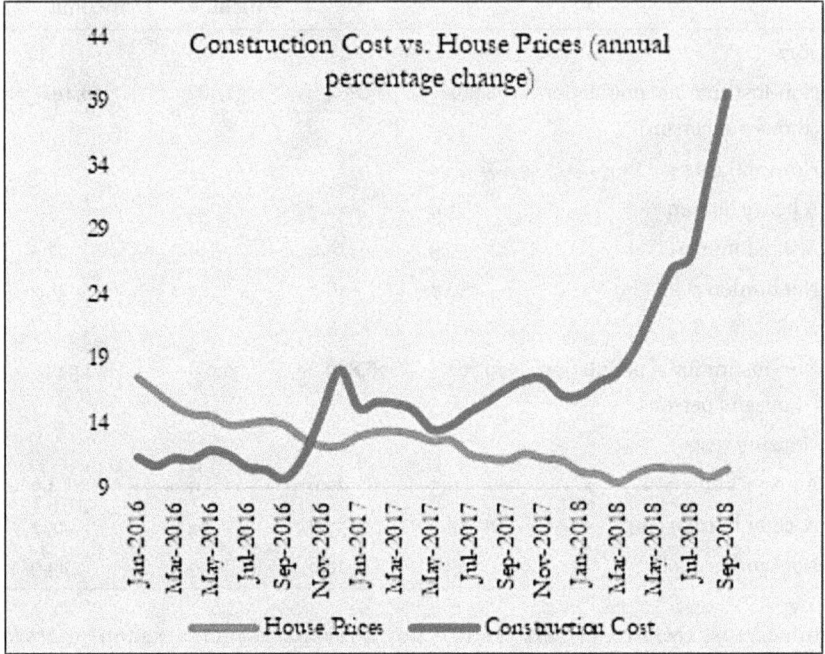

Construction Cost vs. House Prices (annual percentage change)

SOURCE: THE WORLD BANK, *TURKEY ECONOMIC MONITOR*, DECEMBER 2018: *STEADYING THE SHIP*, P. 19. HTTPS://ELIBRARY.WORLDBANK.ORG/DOI/ABS/10 .1596/31129

Bibliography

Aalbers, M.B. (2008). 'The financialization of home and the mortgage market crisis'. *Competition & Change*, 12(2), pp. 148–66.

Aalbers, M.B. (2011). *Place, Exclusion, and Mortgage Markets*. Oxford: Wiley-Blackwell.

Aalbers, M.B. (2016). *The Financialization of Housing: A Political Economy Approach*. London: Routledge.

Aalbers, M.B. (2017). 'The variegated financialization of housing'. *International Journal of Urban and Regional Research*, 41(4), pp. 542–554.

Aalbers, M.B. (2019). 'Financial geographies of real estate and the city: A literature review'. *Financial Geography Working Paper No. 21*. Available at: http://www.fin geo.net/fingeo-working-paper-series/. [Accessed 1 Dec 2020].

Aalbers, M.B., Loon, J.V. & Fernandez, R. (2017). 'The financialization of a social housing provider'. *International Journal of Urban and Regional Research*, 41(4), pp. 572–587.

Aalbers, M.B. & Haila, A. (2018). 'A conversation about land rent, financialisation and housing'. *Urban Studies*, 55(8), pp. 1821–1835.

Adaş, E.B. (2009). 'Production of trust and distrust: Transnational networks, Islamic holding companies and the state in Turkey', *Middle Eastern Studies*, 45(4), pp.625–636.

Agartan, K. (2017). 'Beyond politics of privatization: a reinterpretation of Turkish exceptionalism', *Journal of Balkan and Near Eastern Studies*, 19(2), pp.136–152.

Aglietta, M. (1998). 'Capitalism at the turn of the century: Regulation theory and the challenge of social change'. *New Left Review I*, 232, pp.41–90.

Agnello, L. & Schuknecht, L. (2011). 'Booms and busts in housing markets: Determinants and implications'. *Journal of Housing Economics*, 20(3). pp.171–190.

Ahunbay, Z; Dinçer, İ. & Şahin, Ç. (eds.) (2016). *Neoliberal kent politikaları ve Fener-Balat-Ayvansaray: Bir koruma mücadelesinin öyküsü*. İstanbul: İş Bankası Kültür Yayınları.

Akça, İ. (2014). 'Hegemonic Projects in Post-1980 Turkey and the Changing Forms of Authoritarianism'. In: Akça, İ., Bekmen, A. & Özden, B.A. (eds.), *Turkey Reframed: Constituting Neoliberal Hegemony*, pp. 13–46. London: Pluto Press.

Akçay, Ü. (2013). 'Sermayenin Uluslararasılaşması ve Devletin Dönüşümü: Teknokratik Otoriterizmin Yükselişi'. *Praksis*, 30/31, pp. 13–42.

Akçay, Ü. (2018). 'Müteahhit Düzeni Battı. Alternatifler Neler?'. *Gazete Duvar*, November 08. Available at: https://www.gazeteduvar.com.tr/yazarlar/2018/11/08/muteah hit-duzeni-batti-alternatifler-neler. [Accessed 19 February 2023].

Akçay, Ü. & Güngen, A.R. (2016). *Finansallaşma, Borç Krizi ve Çöküş: Küresel Kapitalizmin Geleceği*, 2nd ed. Ankara: Nota Bene.

Akın, C. (2008). 'Housing market characteristics and estimation of housing wealth in Turkey'. *SSRN Electronic Journal.* Available at: https://papers.ssrn.com/sol3/pap ers.cfm?abstract_id=1331324. [Accessed 1 Dec 2020].

Akyüz, Y. (2014). 'Internationalization of Finance and Changing Vulnerabilities in Emerging and Developing Economies'. In: *United Nations Conference on Trade and Development.* Available at: https://unctad.org/system/files/official-docum ent/osgdp20143_en.pdf. [Accessed 1 Dec 2020].

Akyüz, Y. (2015). 'Internationalization of finance and changing vulnerabilities in emerging and developing economies', *South Center Research Paper No. 60.*

Akyüz, Y. (2018). 'External balance sheets of emerging economies: Low-yielding assets, high-yielding liabilities'. *PERI Working Paper Series No. 476.* Amherst, MA: Political Economy Research Institute.

Akyüz, Y. & Boratav, K. (2003). 'The making of the Turkish financial crisis', *World Development,* 31(9), pp. 1549–66.

Albo, G. & Fanelli, C. (2014). *Austerity against Democracy: An Authoritarian Phase of Neoliberalism?* Canada: Socialist Project. Available at: https://socialistproject.ca /pamphlets/austerity-democracy-authoritarian-phase-neoliberalism/. [Accessed 1 Dec 2020].

Albo, G., Gindin, S. & Panitch, L. (2010). *In and Out of Crisis: The Global Financial Crisis and Left Alternatives.* Oakland, CA: PM Press.

Albritton, R. (2012). 'Commodification and Commodity Fetishism'. In: B. Fine & A. Saad-Filho (eds.), *The Elgar Companion to Marxist Economics,* pp. 66–71. Cheltenham: Edward Elgar.

Alcaly, R.E. (1976). 'Transportation and urban land values: a review of the theoretical literature'. *Land Economics,* 52, pp. 42–53.

Alonso, W. (1964). *Location and Land Use: Toward Theory Land Rent.* Cambridge, Mass: Harvard Univ. Press.

Alper, K., Kara, H. & Yorukoglu, M. (2013). 'Reserve option mechanism'. *Central Bank Review,* 13, January 2013, pp. 1–14. bourgeoisie.

Althusser, L. (2010). *For Marx.* London: Verso.

Arrighi, G. (2004). 'Spatial and other 'fixes' of historical capitalism'. *Journal of World Systems Research,* 10(2), pp. 527–539.

Ashman, S. & Fine, B. (2013). 'Neo-liberalism, varieties of capitalism, and the shifting contours of South Africa's financial system'. *Transformation,* 81–82, pp. 145–178.

Aslan, S. (2004). *1 Mayıs Mahallesi.* İstanbul: İletişim.

Aslan, A.S. (2019). 'Barınma Problemine Çözüm Olarak Sunulan İpotekli Konut Kredilerine Erişilebilirliğin Değerlendirilmesi'. *Megaron,* 14(1), pp.177–191.

Aşıcı, M. (2016). *Sermayenin Verimli Kullanımında İnşaat — Sanayi Çelişkisi*[online]. Available at: https://ssrn.com/abstract=2733329. [Accessed 1 Dec 2020].

Atacan, F. (2005). 'Explaining religious politics at the crossroad: AKP-SP'. *Turkish Studies*, 6(2), pp. 187–199.

Atasoy, Y. (2016). 'Repossession, re-informalization and dispossession: The 'muddy terrain' of land commodification in Turkey'. *Journal of Agrarian Change*, 17(4), pp. 657–679.

Atikcan, E.Ö. & Öge, K. (2012). 'Referendum campaigns in polarized societies: The case of Turkey'. *Turkish Studies*, 13(3), pp. 449–470.

Baharoğlu, D. (1996). 'Housing supply under different economic development strategies and the forms of state interventions'. *Habitat International*, 20(1), pp. 43–60.

Baharoğlu, D. & Leitmann, J. (1998). 'Coping strategies for infrastructure: How Turkey's spontaneous settlements operate in the absence of formal rules'. *Habitat International*, 22(2), pp. 115–135.

Bahçe, S. *et al.* (2015). 'Financialisation and the financial and economic crises: The case of Turkey'. *FESSUD Studies in Financial Systems No. 21*, July 2015. bourgeoisie.

Bajunid, A.F.I. & Ghazali, M. (2012). 'Affordable mosaic housing: Rethinking low-cost housing'. *Procedia — Social and Behavioral Sciences*, 49, pp. 245–256.

Bakır, C. & Öniş, Z. (2010). 'The regulatory state and Turkish banking reforms in the age of post-Washington consensus', *Development and Change*, 47(1), pp. 77–160.

Balaban, O. (2008). *Capital Accumulation, the State and the Production of Built Environment: The Case of Turkey*. PhD. Thesis, Ankara: Middle East Technical University.

Balaban, O. (2017). 'İnşaat Sektörü Neyin Lokomotifi?' In Bora, T. (ed.), *İnşaat Ya Resulallah*, pp. 19–26. İstanbul: İletişim.

Balkan, E. & Yeldan E. (2002). 'Peripheral Development under Financial Liberalisation: The Turkish Experience'. In: Balkan, N. & Savran, S. (eds.). *The Ravages of Neoliberalism: Economy, Society and Gender in Turkey*, pp. 39–54. New York: Nova Science Publishers.

Ball, M. (1978). 'British housing policy and the house-building industry'. *Capital and Class*, 2(1), pp. 78–99.

Ball, M. (1983). *Housing Policy and Economic Power: The Political Economy of Owner Occupation*. London; New York: Methuen.

Ball, M. (1985a). 'Land Rent and the Construction Industry'. In: M. Ball, V. Bentivegna, M. Edwards, & M. Folin (eds.) *Land Rent: Housing and Urban Planning*, pp. 71–86. London: Croom Helm.

Ball, M. (1985b). 'The urban rent question'. *Environment and Planning A*, 17, pp: 503–525. bourgeoisie.

Ball, M. (1986). 'Housing analysis: Time for a theoretical refocus?' *Housing Studies*, 1(3), pp.147–166.

Ball, M. (1988). *Rebuilding Construction: Economic Change and the British Construction Industry*. London: Routledge.

Ball, M. (2003). 'Markets and the structure of the housebuilding industry: An international perspective'. *Urban Studies*, 40(5–6), pp. 1229–1271.

Ball, M. (2010). *The Housebuilding Industry: Promoting Recovery in Housing Supply*. London: DCLG.

Ball, M. (2013). 'Spatial regulation and international differences in the housebuilding industries'. *Journal of Property Research*, 30(3), pp.189–204.

Ball, M. (2012). 'Housebuilding and Housing Supply'. In: Clapham, D.F., Clark W.A.V. & Gibb, K. (eds.), *The SAGE Handbook of Housing Studies*, pp. 27–46. SAGE Publications.

Ball, M. (2016). *Housing Policy and Economic Power: The Political Economy of Owner Occupation*. London: Routledge.

Ball, M. & Harloe, M. (1993). 'Rhetorical barriers to understanding housing provision: What the 'provision thesis' is and is not'. *Housing Studies*, 7(1), pp.3–15.

Baran, P.A. & Sweezy, P.M. (1966). *Monopoly Capital*. New York: Monthly Review Press.

Barker, K. (2004). *Review of Housing Supply*. London: HM Treasury.

Barlow, J. & King, A. (1992). 'The state, the market, and competitive strategy: The housebuilding industry in the United Kingdom, France, and Sweden'. *Environment and Planning A: Economy and Space*, 24(3), pp. 381–400.

Barnes, T.J. (1988). 'Scarcity and agricultural land rent in the light of the capital controversy: three views'. *Antipode* 20, pp. 207–238.

Barras, R. (1994). 'Property and the economic cycle: building cycles revisited'. *Journal of Property Research*, 11(3), pp. 183–197.

Barroso, J.B.R.B., da Silva, L.A.P. & Sales, A.S. (2016). 'Quantitative easing and related capital flows into Brazil: Measuring its effects and transmission channels through a rigorous counterfactual evaluation'. *Journal of International Money and Finance*, 67, pp. 102–122.

Basu, D. (2018). Marx's analysis of ground-rent: Theory, examples and applications. *UMASS Amherst Economics Working Papers*, 241. Available at: https://scholarwo rks.umass.edu/econ_workingpaper/241. [Accessed 1 Dec 2020].

Batmaz, E.S., Emiroğlu, K. & Ünsal, S. (2006). *İnşaatçıların Tarihi*. Ankara: Türkiye Müteahhitler Birliği Yayını.

Batuman, B. (2019). *Milletin Mimarisi: Yeni İslamcı Ulus İnşasının Kent ve Mekân Siyaseti*. İstanbul: Metis Yayınları.

Bayliss, K., Fine, B. & Robertson, M. (n.d.). 'From financialisation to consumption: The systems of provision approach applied to housing and water'. *FESSUD Working Paper No. 02*.

Bayliss, K., Fine, B. & Robertson, M. (2016). 'The role of the state in financialised systems of provision: Social compacting, social policy, and privatisation'. *FESSUD Working Paper No. 154*.

Bayliss, K., Fine, B. & Robertson, M. (2017). 'Introduction to special issue on the material cultures of financialisation'. *New Political Economy*, 22(4), pp. 355–370.

Bayramoğlu, S. (2005). *Yönetişim Zihniyeti: Türkiye'de Üst Kurullar ve Siyasal İktidarın Dönüşümü*, İstanbul: İletişim.

Baysan, T. & Blitzer, C. (1991). 'Turkey's Trade Liberalization in the 1980s and Prospects for Its Sustainability'. In: Arıcanlı, T. & Rodrik, D. (eds.), *The Political Economy of Turkey: Debt, Adjustment and Sustainability*. New York: St. Martin's Press.

Bedirhanoğlu, P. (2009). 'Türkiye'de Neoliberal Otoriter Devletin AKP'li Yüzü'. In: Uzgel, İ. & B. Duru (eds.), *AKP Kitabı: Bir Dönüşümün Bilançosu*, pp. 40–65. Ankara: Phoneix.

Bedirhanoğlu, P. & Yalman, G. (2010). 'State, Class and the Discourse: Reflections on the Neoliberal Transformation in Turkey'. In: Saad-Filho, A. &Yalman, G. (eds.), *Economic Transitions to Neoliberalism in Middle-Income Countries*, pp. 107–127. New York: Routledge.

Bedirhanoğlu, P., Comert, H., Eren, I., Erol, I., Demiroz, D., Erdem, N., Gungen, A.R., Marois, T., Topal, A., Turel, O., Yalman, G., Yeldan, E., and Voyvoda, E. (2013). 'Comparative perspective on financial system in the EU: Country report on Turkey'. *FESSUD Working Paper No. 11*.

Bedirhanoğlu, P. (2020). 'Social Constitution of the AKP's Strong State through Financialization: State in Crisis, or Crisis State?' In: Bedirhanoğlu, B., Dölek, Ç., Hülagü, F. and Kaygusuz, Ö. (eds.), *Turkey's New State in the Making: Transformations in Legality, Economy and Coercion*. London: Zed Books.

Bekmen, A. (2014). 'State and Capital in Turkey during the Neoliberal Era'. In: Akça, İ., Bekmen A. & Özden, B.A. (eds.), *Turkey Reframed: Constituting Neoliberal Hegemony*, pp.47–74. London: Pluto.

Ben-Shahar, D., Gabriel, S. & Golan, R. (2019). 'Housing affordability and inequality: A consumption-adjusted approach'. *Journal of Housing Economics*, 45, pp. 1051–1377.

Bernt, M., Colini, L. and Förste, D. (2017). 'Privatization, financialization and state restructuring in Eastern Germany: The case of Am südpark'. *International Journal of Urban and Regional Research*, 41(4), pp. 555–571.

Berry, M. (1981). 'Posing the housing question in Australia: Elements of a theoretical framework for a Marxist analysis of housing'. *Antipode*, 13(1), pp. 3–14.

Berry, M. (1986). 'Housing provision and class relations under capitalism: Some implications of recent Marxist class analysis'. *Housing Studies*, 1(2), pp.109–21.

Berry, M. (2010). 'Housing Wealth and Mortgage Debt in Australia'. In: Smith, A. & Searle, B. (eds.), *The Blackwell Companion to the Economics of Housing: The Housing Wealth of Nations*, pp. 126–146. Chichester: Wiley-Blackwell.

Berry, M. (2014). 'Housing provision and class relations under capitalism'. *Housing, Theory and Society*, 31(4), pp. 395–403.

Bieler, A., Bruff, I. & Morton, A.D. (2010). 'Acorns and fruit: From totalization to periodization in the critique of capitalism'. *Capital and Class*, 34(1), pp. 25–37.

Bina, C. (2006). 'The globalisation of oil: A prelude to a critical political economy'. *International Journal of Political Economy*, 35(2), pp. 4–34.

Blackwell, T., & Kohl, S. (2018). 'The origins of national housing finance systems: A comparative investigation into historical variations in mortgage finance regimes'. *Review of International Political Economy*, 25(1), pp. 49–74.

Boddy, M. (1976). 'Political economy of housing: Mortgage-financed owner occupation in Britain'. *Antipode*, 8, pp. 15–23.

Bonefeld, W. (1992). 'Social Form and Constitution of Capitalist State'. In: Bonefeld, W., Gunn, R. & Psychopedis, K. (eds.), *Open Marxism Vol. 1: Dialectics and history*, London: Pluto.

Bonizzi, B. (2017). 'International financialisation, developing countries and the contradictions of privatised Keynesianism'. *Economic and Political Studies*, 5(1), pp. 21–40.

Boratav, K. (1994). 'Contradictions of 'Structural Adjustment': Capital and the State in Post-1980 Turkey'. In: Keyder, Ç. & Öncü, A. (eds.), *Developmentalism and Beyond: Society and Politics in Egypt and Turkey*. Cairo: American University in Cairo Press.

Boratav, K. (2003). *Türkiye İktisat Tarihi: 1908–2002*. Ankara: İmge.

Boratav, K. (2014). 'AKP Ekonomisi: Artan Bağımlılık'. *soL Haber Portalı*, April 22. Available at: http://haber.sol.org.tr/yazarlar/korkut-boratav/akp-ekonomisi-artan -bagimlilik- 91313. [Accessed 1 Dec 2020].

Boratav, K. (2018). *Türkiye İktisat Tarihi: 1908–2015*. Ankara: İmge.

Boratav, K. (2019). 'Krugman'ın Senaryosu ve Türkiye Krizi', *Mülkiye Dergisi*, 43(1), pp. 285–292.

Boratav, K.,Yeldan, A.E. & Köse, A.H. (2000). 'Globalization, distribution and social policy: Turkey 1980–1998'. *CEPA Working Paper series No.1*. New York: New School University.

Boratav, K. & Yeldan, K. (2006). 'Turkey, 1980–2000: Financial Liberalization, Macroeconomic (In)-stability, and Patterns of Distribution'. In: Taylor, L. (ed.), *External Liberalization in Asia, Post-socialist Europe and Brazil*, pp. 417–455. Oxford and New York: Oxford University Press.

Boratav, K., Bulutay, T., Ege, Y., Türel, O., Türeli, R.A. & Uygur, E. (2018). 'Yeni Ulusal Gelir Serileri Üzerine Gözlem ve Değerlendirmeler', *Ekonomi-tek*, 7(2), pp. 61–70.

Boratav, K. & Orhangazi, Ö. (2022). 'Neoliberal Framework and External Dependency versus Political Priorities, 2009–2020'. In: Özçelik, E and Özdemir, Y. (eds.), *Political Economy of Development in Turkey: 1838 — Present*. Singapore: Springer Nature Singapore.

Bortz, P.G. & Kaltenbrunner, A. (2017). 'The international dimension of financialization in developing and emerging economies'. *Development and Change*, 49(2), pp. 375–393.

Boyer, R. (2000). 'Is a finance-led growth regime a viable alternative to Fordism'. *Economy and Society*, 29(1), pp. 111–145.

Boyer, R. (2001). The financialization of capital: an interpretation along "regulation" theory. *Paper presented at the workshop on 'Regulation in East Asia's Mode of Development'*, Taichung, Taiwan.

Bozkurt, U. (2013). 'Neoliberalism with a human face: Making sense of the justice and development party's neoliberal populism in Turkey'. *Science & Society*, 77(3), pp. 372–396.

Bozkurt-Güngen, S. (2018). 'Labour and authoritarian neoliberalism: changes and continuities under the AKP government in Turkey'. *South European Society and Politics*, 23(2), pp.219–238.

Brenner, R. (2006). *The Economics of Global Turbulence*. London: Verso.

Broome, A. (2009). 'The Politics of Capital Gains: Building an Asset-Based Society in New Zealand'. In: Schwartz, H.M. & Seabrooke, L. (eds.), *The Politics of Housing Booms and Busts*, pp. 76–96. London: Palgrave Macmillan.

Bruegel, I. (1975). 'The Marxist Theory of Rent and the Contemporary City: A Critique of Harvey', In: *Political Economy and the Housing Question Workshop*, pp. 34–46. London: CSE Books.

Brunhoff, S. de. (1976). *Marx on Money*. New York: Urizen Books.

Brunhoff, S. de. (1998). 'Money, Interest and Finance in Marx's *Capital*'. In: Bellofiore, R. (ed.) *Marxian Economics: A Reappraisal, Vol.1*. London: Macmillan.

Brunhoff, S. de & Foley, D.K. (2006). 'Karl Marx's Theory of Money and Credit'. In: Arestis, P. & Sawyer, M. (eds.) *A Handbook of Alternative Monetary Economics*. Cheltenham: Edward Elgar.

Bryan, D. & Rafferty, M. (2014). 'Political economy and housing in the twenty-first century — From mobile homes to liquid housing?' *Housing, Theory and Society*, 31(4), pp. 404–412.

BSB (Bağımsız Sosyal Bilimciler) (2015). *AKP'li Yıllarda Emeğin Durumu*. İstanbul: Yordam.

Buchanan, B.G. (2017). *Securitization and the Global Economy: History and Prospects for the Future*. Basingstoke: Palgrave Macmillan.

Buğra, A. (1994). *State and Business in Modern Turkey: A Comparative Study*. Albany, N.Y.: State University of New York Press.

Buğra, A. (1998). 'The immoral economy of housing in Turkey'. *International Journal of Urban and Regional Research*, 22(2), pp. 303–307.

Buğra, A. (2007). 'Poverty and citizenship: An overview of the social-policy environment in republican Turkey'. *International Journal of Middle East Studies*, 39(1), pp.33–52.

Buğra, A. & Savaşkan, O. (2012). 'Politics and class: The Turkish business environment in the neoliberal age'. *New Perspectives on Turkey*, 46, pp. 27–63.

Buğra, A. & Savaşkan, O. (2014). *New Capitalism in Turkey: The Relationship between Politics, Religion, and Business*. UK: Edward Elgar.

Butcher, S. (2020). 'Appropriating rent from greenfield affordable housing: developer practices in Johannesburg'. *Environment and Planning A: Economy and Space*, pp.1–25.

Byrne, M. (2019). 'The financialization of housing and the growth of the private rental sector in Ireland, the UK and Spain'. *Geary Institute Working Paper*. Available at: https://www.ucd.ie/geary/static/publications/workingpapers/gearywp201 902.pdf. [Accessed 1 Dec 2020].

Byrne, M. (2020). 'Generation rent and the financialization of housing: a comparative exploration of the growth of the private rental sector in Ireland, the UK and Spain', *Housing Studies*, 35(4), pp.743–765.

Byrne, M. & Norris, M. (2019). 'Housing market financialization, neoliberalism and everyday retrenchment of social housing'. *Environment and Planning A: Economy and Space*, o(o), pp. 1–17.

Čada, K. (2018). 'They seemed like super businessmen': Financial instruments in social housing policy. *Critical Housing Analysis*, 5(2), pp. 56–67.

Campling, L. & Havice, E. (2014). 'The problem of property in industrial fisheries'. *The Journal of Peasant Studies*, 41(5), pp. 707–727.

Cardoso, A.L. & Aragão, T.A. (2012). 'Reestruturação do setor imobiliário e o papel do Programa Minha Casa Minha Vida'. *Conference Paper. Belo Horizonte: Seminário Internacional da Rede Ibero-Americana de Pesquisadores sobre Globalização e Território (RII)*.

Celasun, M. (1991). 'Trade and industrialisation in Turkey: Initial conditions, policy and performance in the 1980s'. Paper presented at UNU/WIDER Conference, Paris, 31 August–3 September 1991.

Cerutti, E., Dagher, J. and Dell'Ariccia, G. (2017). 'Housing finance and real-estate booms: A cross-country perspective'. *Journal of Housing Economics*, 38, pp.1–13.

Chang, D. (2008). 'Global construction and Asian workers: Expansion of TNCs in Asia and implications for labour'. *Building and Wood Workers' International and Asia Monitor Resource Centre*. Available at: https://eprints.soas.ac.uk/7860/. [Accessed 1 Dec 2020].

Charles, S. (1977). *Housing Economics*. London: Macmillan.

Charney, I. (2001). 'Three dimensions of capital switching within the real estate sector: A Canadian case study'. *International Journal of Urban and Regional Research*, 25(4), pp.740–758.

Chesnais, F. (2001). *La théorie du régime d'accumulation financiarisé: contenu, portée et interrogations*. Presented at the Forum de la régulation, Paris: Université de Paris-Nord. Available at: https://rechercheregulation.files.wordpress.com/2012/12/03_c hesnais.pdf. [Accessed 19 February 2023].

Chesnais, F. (2002). 'A teoria do regime de acumulação financeirizado: conteúdo, alcance e interrogações'. *Economia e Sociedade*, 11, pp. 1–44.

Cho, J.W. (2004). *Korean Construction Workers' Job Centre, Seoul, South Korea*. Paper for In-focus Programme on Socio-economic Security, ILO, Geneva.

Choi, C. (2018). 'Subordinate financialization and financial subsumption in South Korea'. *Regional Studies*, 54(2), pp. 209–218.

CHP. (n.d). *Yolsuzluğun Kitabı-2 TOKI*. Available at: https://content.chp.org.tr/file/tok iraporu.pdf. [Accessed 1 Dec 2020].

Christophers, B. (2010). 'On voodoo economics: theorising relations of property, value and contemporary capitalism'. *Transactions of the Institute of British Geographers*, 35(1), pp.94–108.

Christophers, B. (2015). 'From financialization to finance'. *Dialogues in Human Geography*, 5(2), pp. 229–232.

Christophers, B. (2017). 'The state and financialization of public land in the United Kingdom'. *Antipode*, 49(1), pp. 62–85.

Churchill, W. (1943). Quote from http://www.winstonchurchill.org/learn/speec hes/quotations.

Cizre, Ü. & Yeldan, E. (2005). 'The Turkish encounter with neo-liberalism: Economics and politics in the 2000/2001 crises', *Review of International Political Economy*, 12(3), pp. 387–408.

Clarke, S. & Ginsburg, N. (1976). 'The Political Economy of Housing'. In: Political Economy of Housing Workshop (ed.) *Political Economy and the Housing Question*, pp. 3–33. London: CSE Books.

Clarke, S. (1992). 'The Global Accumulation of Capital and the Form of the Capitalist State'. In: Bonefeld, W., Gunn, R. & Psychopedis, K. (eds.), *Open Marxism Vol. 1: Dialectics and History*, London: Pluto.

Coiacetto, E. (2006). 'Real estate development industry structure: Consequences for urban planning and development'. *Planning Practice & Research*, 21, pp. 423–441.

Coiacetto, E. (2009). 'Industry structure in real estate development: Is city building competitive?' *Urban Policy and Research*, 27(2), pp. 117–135.

Cook, N., Smith, S. and Searle, B. (2009). 'Mortgage markets and cultures of consumption'. *Consumption, Markets and Culture*, 12 (2), pp. 133–54.

Copello, M.M.M. (2007). 'The Nuevo USME and Pereira Projects: Mobilization of Land Value Increment for Provision of Serviced Land for Social Housing'. In: Freire, M., Lima, R., Cira, D., Ferguson, B., Kessides, C., Mota, J.A. and Motta, D. (eds.), *Land and urban policies for poverty reduction*. World Bank and Brazilian Institute of Economic and Administrative Studies (IPEA). Washington, DC.

Coq-Huelva, D. (2013). 'Urbanisation and financialisation in the context of a rescaling state: The case of Spain'. *Antipode*, 45(5), pp. 1213–1231.

Coşkun, Y. (2015). Türkiye'de Konut Finansmanı: Sorunlar ve Çözüm Önerileri. Publication No. 310. The Banks Association of Turkey. April. Istanbul. Available at: https://papers.ssrn.com/sol3/papers.cfm?abstract_id=2602713. [Accessed 1 Dec 2020].

Coşkun, Y. (2016). 'Housing Finance in Turkey over the Last 25 Years'. In: Lunde, J & Whitehead, C. (eds.), *Milestones in European Housing Finance*, pp. 393–411. John Wiley & Sons.

Coşkun, Y. and Ümit, O. (2016). 'Cointegration analysis between stock exchange and TL/FX saving deposits, gold, housing markets in Turkey'. *Business and Economics Research Journal*. 7(1), pp. 47–69.

Costa-Font, J., Gil, J. & Mascarilla, O. (2010). 'Housing Market, Wealth, and "Self-Insurance" in Spain'. In: Smith, S. & Searle, B.A. (eds.), *The Blackwell Companion to the Economics of Housing*, pp. 279–294. Chichester: Wiley-Blackwell.

Courcoulas, C. & Ersoy, E. (2016). 'Nothing like a threat of treason to make Turkish banks cut rates'. *BloombergQuint*, November 2016. Available at: https://www.blo ombergquint.com/business/erdogan-leans-on-turkey-s-banks-and-slowly-rates -come-down. [Accessed 1 Dec 2020].

Crouch, C. (2009). 'Privatised Keynesianism: An unacknowledged policy regime'. *The British Journal of Politics & International Relations*, 11(3), pp. 382–399.

Çarıkçı, Ç. (2017). 'The Place of Contingent Liabilities in Public Investments and Their Importance in Public Finance Management'. In: *Current Debates in Public Finance, Public Administration and Environmental Studies*, Volume 13, London: Ijopec Publication.

Çavuşoğlu, E. (2013). 'Kadim İdeoloji Korporatizme AKP Makyajı: İnşaat Dayalı Büyüme Modelinin Yeni Osmanlıcılıkla Bütünleşerek Ulusal Popüler Proje Haline Gelişi'. *Birikim*, 296, pp. 70–81.

Çavuşoğlu, E. (2017). 'İslâmcı Neo-Liberalizmde İnşaat Fetişi ve Mülkiyet Üzerindeki Simgesel Hâle'. In Bora, T. (ed.), *İnşaat Ya Resulallah*, pp. 40–51. İstanbul: İletişim.

Çelik, Ö. (2018). 'Ziya Yılmaz: Banka gibiysek bize düzenleme lazım'. *Emlak Rotası*, April 17. [online]. Available at: https://www.emlakrotasi.com.tr/banka-gibiysek-bize -duzenleme-lazim/. [Accessed 1 Dec 2020].

Çelik, Ö., Topal, A., & Yalman, G. (2016). 'Finance and system of provision of housing. The case of Istanbul, Turkey'. *FESSUD Working paper No. 152*.

Çelik, Ö. & Karaçimen, E. (2017). 'Türkiye'de Gayrimenkul ve Finansın Derinleşen ve Yeniden Yapılanan İlişkisi'. In: Bedirhanoğlu, P., Çelik Ö. & Mıhçı, H. (eds.), *Finansallaşma Kıskacında Türkiye'de Devlet, Sermaye Birikimi ve Emek*. Ankara: Nota Bene.

Çınar, S. (2014). 'Taşeron Çalışma İlişkilerinde İnşaat İşçileri'. *Journal of Sociological Research*, 17(2). [online]. Available at: https://dergipark.org.tr/en/download/arti cle-file/404862. [Accessed 1 Dec 2020].

Çınar, S. (2015). 'Taşeronlaşmanın İnşaat İşçileri Üzerindeki Etkileri'. *TÜBITAK*, Program Code: 3001, Project No: 114K629, Ankara.

Çınar, S. (2018). 'İnşaat İşgücü Piyasasında Yeni Aktörler ve Yeni Çatışmalar: Türkiyeli İşçilerin Gözünden Suriyeli İnşaat İşçileri'. *Çalışma ve Toplum*, 1(56), pp. 121–137.

Çoban, B. (2018). 'Türkiye'de İşsizlik Profili Bağlamında Suriyeli Gençlerin İstanbul İşgücü Piyasasına Katılım Sorunları'. *Çalışma ve Toplum*, 56, pp. 193–216.

David, L. (2012). 'The social construction of real estate market risk. The case of a financial investments cluster in Mexico City'. *Articulo — Journal of Urban Research*, 9. Available at: https://journals.openedition.org/articulo/2163. [Accessed 1 Dec 2020].

David, L. & Halbert, L. (2010). 'Constructing "world-class cities": Hubs of globalization and high finance'. *Dialogues in Urban and Regional Planning*, 5, pp. 99–114.

De Soto, H. (2001). *The Mystery of Capital. Why Capitalism Triumphs in the West and Fails Everywhere Else*. London: Black Swan Books.

Demir, F. (2008). 'Financial liberalization, private investment and portfolio choice: Financialization of real sectors in emerging markets'. *Journal of Development Economics*, 88(2), pp. 314–324.

Demir, O., Acar, M. & Toprak, M. (2004). 'Anatolian tigers or Islamic capital: Prospects and challenges'. *Middle Eastern Studies*, 40(6).

Demiralp, S., Demiralp, S., & Gümüş, İ. (2016). 'The state of property development in Turkey: Facts and comparisons'. *New Perspectives on Turkey*, 55, pp. 85–106.

Demiröz D. & Erdem, N. (2019).'The Turkish Corporate Sector in the Era of Financialization: Profitability and M&As'. In: Yalman, G.L., Marois, T. & Güngen, A.R. (eds.), *The Political Economy of Financial Transformation in Turkey*. London, New York: Routledge.

Dinç, C. (2018). *Debating Islamism, Modernity and the West in Turkey: The Role of Welfare Party*. Ankara: Savaş Yayınevi.

D'Lima, W. & Schultz, P.H. (2019). 'How Wall Street investors rescued the market for single family homes' (SSRN Scholarly Paper ID 3457303). *Social Science Research Network*. Available at SSRN: https://ssrn.com/abstract=3457303.

Doğan, A.E. (2006). 'İslamcı Sermayenin Gelişim Dinamikleri ve 28 Şubat Süreci'. *Mülkiye*, 252, pp. 47–68.

Doling, J. & Ronald, R. (2010). 'Home ownership and asset-based welfare'. *Journal of Housing and the Built Environment*, 25(2), pp. 165–173.

Doling, J., & Ronald, R. (2014). *Housing East Asia: Socioeconomic and Demographic Challenges*. Basingstoke: Palgrave Macmillan.

Dorling, D., Ford, J., Holmans, A., Sharp, C., Thomas, B. & Wilcox, S. (eds) (2005). *The Great Divide: An Analysis of Housing Inequality*, London: Shelter.

dos Santos, P.L. (2009). 'On the content of banking in contemporary capitalism'. *Historical Materialism*,27(3), pp. 316–338.

dos Santos, P.L. (2013). 'A cause for policy concern: the expansion of household credit in middle-income economies'. *International Review of Applied Economics*, 27(3), pp. 316–338.

DPT. (2003). 58. *Hükümet Acil Eylem Planı*. Ankara: Devlet Planlama Teşkilatı.

Duménil, G. & Lévy, D. (2001a). 'Periodizing Capitalism: Technology, Institutions and Relations of Production'. In: Albritton, R., Itoh, M., Westra, R. & Zuege, A. (eds.), *Phases of Capitalist Development: Booms, Crises, and Globalization*. Basingstoke: Palgrave, pp. 141–162.

Duménil, G. & Lévy, D. (2001b). 'Costs and benefits of neoliberalism: A class analysis'. *Review of International Political Economy*, 8(4), pp. 578–607.

Duménil, G. & Lévy, D. (2004). *Capital Resurgent. Roots of the Neoliberal Revolution*. Cambridge, MA: Harvard University Press.

Duménil, G. & Lévy, D. (2011). *The Crisis of Neoliberalism*. Cambridge, MA: Harvard University Press.

Duncan, S.S. (1986). 'House building, profits and social efficiency in Sweden and Britain', *Housing Studies*, 1(1), pp. 11–33.

Durand-Lasserve, A. (2007). 'Market-driven eviction processes in developing country cities: The cases of Kigali in Rwanda and Phnom Penh in Cambodia'. *Global Urban Development Magazine*, 3(1), pp. 1–14.

Durand-Lasserve, A. & Selod, H. (2009). 'The Formalisation of Urban Land Tenure in Developing Countries'. In: Lall, S.V., Freire, M., Yuen, B., Rajack, R. and Helluin, J-J. (eds.), *Urban Land Markets: Improving land Management for Successful Urbanization*, pp. 101–132. Dordrecht: Springer Netherlands.

Dursun, D. (2015). *The Effects of Restructuring in the Property Development Sector on Urban Processes: A Case Study on Erzurum and Kayseri*. PhD. Thesis, Middle East Technical University.

Dymski, G.A. (2009). 'Racial exclusion and the political economy of the subprime crisis'. *Historical Materialism*, 17(2), pp. 149–179.

Ebenau, M. (2014). 'Comparative capitalisms and Latin American neodevelopmentalism: A critical political economy view'. *Capital & Class*, 38(1), pp.102–114.

Economakis, G.E. (2003). 'On absolute rent: Theoretical remarks on Marx's analysis'. *Science & Society*, 67(3), pp. 339–348.

Edel, M. (1976). 'Marx's theory of rent: Urban applications'. *Kapitalistate*, 4(5), pp. 100–125, and also in *Housing and Class in Britain*, Political Economy of Housing Workshop, London.

Edel, M. (1992) *Urban Regional Economics: Marxist Perspectives*. Chur: Harwood.

Eder, M. (2010). 'Retreating state? Political economy of welfare regime change in Turkey', *Middle East Law and Governance*, 2(2), pp.152–184.

Edwards, M. (2016). 'The housing crisis: Too difficult or a great opportunity?' *Soundings: A Journal of Politics and Culture*, 62, pp. 23–42.

Epstein, G.A. (2005). *Financialization and the World Economy*. Northampton, MA: Edward Elgar.

Ercan, F. (2002). 'The Contradictory Unity of the Turkish Capital Accumulation Process: A Critical Perspective of the Internationalization of the Turkish Economy'. In: Savran, S. & Balkan, N. (eds.). *The Ravages of Neo-Liberalism: Economy, Society and Gender in Turkey*, pp. 21–39. New York: Nova Science.

Ercan, F. & Oğuz, S. (2006). 'Rescaling as a class relationship and process: The case of public procurement law in Turkey'. *Political Geography*, 25(6), pp. 641–656.

Ercan, F. & Oğuz, S. (2015). 'From Gezi resistance to soma massacre: Capital accumulation and class struggle in Turkey'. *Socialist Register*, 51(1), pp. 114–35.

Ergüder, B. (2015). '2000'li Yıllarda Türkiye'de Hanehalkı Borçlanması: Konut Kredileri ve Toplumsal Refah'. *Praksis*, 38, pp. 99–129.

Ergüneş, N. (2009). 'Global integration of the Turkish economy in the era of financialisation'. *Research on Money and Finance, Discussion Paper No. 8*, February 2009.

Erman, T. (1997). 'Squatter (Gecekondu) housing versus apartment housing: Turkish rural-to-urban migrant residents' perspectives'. *Habitat International*, 28(1), pp. 91–106.

Erol, I. (2015). 'Türkiye'de Konut Balonu Var Mı? Konut Sektörü Kapitalizasyon Oranları Analizi'. In: *Türkiye Ekonomisinin Dunu, Bugünü Yarını. Yakup Kepenek'e ve Oktar Türel'e Armağan*, pp. 323–345. İstanbul: İmge Kitapevi.

Erol, I. (2016). 'Construction, Real Estate Mortgage Market Development and Economic Growth in Turkey'. In: Abdulai, R.T. *et al.* (eds.) *Real Estate, Construction and Economic Development in Emerging Market Economies*, pp. 37–63. London, New York: Routledge.

Erol, I. (2019a). 'Financial Transformation and Housing Finance in Turkey'. In: Yalman, G.L., Marois, T. & Güngen, A.R. (eds.), *The Political Economy of Financial Transformation in Turkey*. London, New York: Routledge.

Erol, I. (2019b). 'New Geographies of Residential Capitalism: Financialization of the Turkish Housing Market Since the Early 2000s'. *International Journal of Urban and Regional Research*, 43(4), pp. 724–740.

Erol, I. & Patel, K. (2004). 'Housing policy and mortgage finance in Turkey during the late 1990s inflationary period'. *International Real Estate Review*, 7(1), pp. 98–120.

Erol, I. and Çetinkaya, Ö. (2009). 'Originating long-term fixed-rate mortgages in developing economies: New evidence from Turkey'. [online] Available at: https://hdl.handle.net/11511/58377. [Accessed 1 Dec 2020].

Erol, I. & Tırtıroğlu, D. (2011). 'Concentrated ownership, no dividend payout requirement and capital structure of REITs: Evidence from Turkey'. *The Journal of Real Estate Finance and Economics*, 43, pp. 174–204.

Erturk, I., Froud, J., Johal, S., Leaver, A. & Williams, K. (2008). *Financialization at Work: Key Texts and Commentary*. New York: Routledge.

Evans, P.B. (1995). *Embedded Autonomy: States and Industrial Transformation*. Princeton, N.J.: Princeton University Press.

Evans, T. & Herr, H. (2016). 'Financialisation in currency, energy and residential property markets', *Working Paper No. 62, Berlin School of Economics and Law, Institute for International Political Economy*. Available at: https://www.ipe-berlin.org /fileadmin/institut-ipe/Dokumente/Working_Papers/IPE_WP_62.pdf. [Accessed 1 Dec 2020].

Fainstein, S. (2016). Financialisation and justice in the city. *Urban Studies*, 53(7): 1503–1508.

Fallis, G. (1985). *Housing Economics*. Toronto: Butterworth.

Feldman, M.A. (1977). 'A contribution to the critique of urban political economy: The journey to work'. *Antipode*, 9(2), pp. 30–50.

Ferguson, J. (2007). 'Formalities of poverty: Thinking about social assistance in neoliberal South Africa'. *African Studies Review*, 50, pp 71–86.

Fernandes, E. (2007). 'Constructing the "right to the city" in Brazil'. *Social and Legal Studies*, 16(2), pp. 201–219.

Fernandez, R., & Aalbers, M.B. (2016). 'Financialization and housing: Between globalization and varieties of capitalism'. *Competition & Change*, 20(2), pp. 71–88.

Fernandez, R. & Aalbers, M.B. (2017). 'Capital market union and residential capitalism in Europe: Rescaling the housing-centred model of financialization'. *Finance and Society*, 3(1), pp. 32–50.

Fields, D., Kohli, R. & Schafran, A. (2016). *The Emerging Economic Geography of Single-Family Rental Securitization*. San Francisco: Federal Reserve Bank.

Fields, D. & Uffer, S. (2016). 'The financialisation of rental housing: A comparative analysis of New York City and Berlin', *Urban Studies*, 53(7), pp. 1486–1502.

Fields, D. (2017). 'Unwilling subjects of financialization'. *International Journal of Urban and Regional Research*, 41(4), pp. 588–603.

Fields, D. (2018). 'Constructing a new asset class: Property-led financial accumulation after the crisis', *Economic Geography*, 94(2), pp. 118–140.

Fine, B. (1979). 'On Marx's theory of agricultural rent'. *Economy and Society*, 8(3), pp. 241–278.

Fine, B. (1980). 'On Marx's theory of agricultural rent: A rejoinder'. *Economy and Society*, 9(3), pp. 327–331.

Fine, B. (1983). 'The historical approach to rent and price theory reconsidered'. *Australian Economic Papers*, 22(40), pp. 132–143.

Fine, B. (1985). 'Land, Capital, and the British Coal Industry prior to World War Two'. In: M. Ball, V. Bentivegna, M. Edwards, & M. Folin (eds.) *Land Rent, Housing and Urban Planning*, pp. 107–125. London: Croom Helm.

Fine, B. (1994). 'Coal, diamonds and oil: toward a comparative theory of mining?' *Review of Political Economy*, 6(3), pp. 279–302.

Fine, B. (1996). 'Some Perspectives on the Provision of Social and Economic Infrastructure', In: *Proposed Workshop for South African Policy Makers*. [Unpublished].

Fine, B. (2002). *Labour Market Theory: A Constructive Reassessment*. Routledge.

Fine, B. (2009a). *Financialisation, the Value of Labour Power, the Degree of Separation, and Exploitation by Banking*. [Unpublished].

Fine, B. (2009b). 'Financialisation and Social Policy' Presented at the UNRISD conference on the *"Social and Political Dimensions of the Global Crisis: Implications for Developing Countries."* Available at: https://eprints.soas.ac.uk/7984/1/unrisdsoc pol.pdf. [Accessed 1 Dec 2020].

Fine, B. (2010). 'Locating financialisation'. *Historical Materialism*, (18)2, pp. 97–116.

Fine, B. (2012). 'Labour Theory of Value'. In: B. Fine & A. Saad-Filho (eds.), *The Elgar Companion to Marxist Economics*, pp. 194–199. Cheltenham: Edward Elgar.

Fine, B. (2013a). 'Consumption matters'. *Ephemera*, 13(2), pp. 217–248.

Fine, B. (2013b). 'Financialisation from a Marxist perspective'. *International Journal of Political Economy*, (42)4, pp. 47–66.

Fine, B. (2014). 'The continuing enigmas of social policy'. *Working Paper No. 10*, Geneva. Available at: https://core.ac.uk/download/pdf/208334197.pdf. [Accessed 1 Dec 2020].

Fine, B. (2017). 'A note towards an approach towards social reproduction'. *Conference Paper for International Initiative for Promoting Political Economy*. Available at: http://iippe.org/wp-content/uploads/2018/12/sroverviewben.pdf. [Accessed 1 Dec 2020].

Fine, B. (2020). 'Framing Social Reproduction in the Age of Financialisation'. In: Santos, A. & Teles, N. (eds.), *Financialisation in the European Periphery: Work and Social Reproduction in Portugal*, pp. 257–272. London: Routledge.

Fine, B. & Harris, L. (1979). *Rereading Capital*. London: Macmillan.

Fine, B. & Leopold, E. (1993). *The World of Consumption*. London; New York: Routledge.

Fine, B. & Saad-Filho, A. (2010). *Marx's 'Capital'*, fifth edition. London: Pluto Press.

Fine, B., Bayliss, K., Robertson, M. and Saad-Filho, A. (2015). 'Thirteen things you need to know about neoliberalism'. *FESSUD Working Paper No. 155*.

Fine, B., Bayliss, K. & Robertson, M. (2016). 'From financialisation to systems of provision'. *FESSUD Working Paper No.191*.

Fine, B. & Saad-Filho, A. (2018). 'Marx 200: The abiding relevance of the labour theory of value'. *Review of Political Economy*. 30(3), pp. 339–54.

Fix, M. (2011). *Financeirização e transformações recentes no circuito imobiliário no Brasil*. PhD. thesis, University of Campinas.

Florida, R.L. & Feldman, M.M.A. (1988). 'Housing in US Fordism: The class accord and post war spatial organization'. *International Journal of Urban and Regional Research*, 12(2), pp. 187–210.

Forrest, R., & Yip, N.-M. (Eds.). (2011). *Housing Markets and the Global Financial Crisis*. Cheltenham: Edward Elgar.

Foster, J.B. (2007). 'The financialization of capitalism'. *Monthly Review*, 58(11), pp. 1–14.

Freire, M., Lima, R., Cira, D., Ferguson, B., Kessides, C., Mota, J. and Motta, D. (2007). *Land and Urban Policies for Poverty Reduction.* World Bank and Brazilian Institute of Economic and Administrative Studies (IPEA). Washington, DC.

Froud, J., Johal, S. & Williams, K. (2002). 'Financialization and the coupon pool'. *Capital and Class*, 78, pp. 119–51.

Fulong, W. (2015) 'Commodification and housing market cycles in Chinese cities'. *International Journal of Housing Policy*, 15(1), pp. 6–26.

Gaffney, M. (1969). 'Land rent, taxation, and public policy'. *Papers of the Regional Science Association*, 23(1), pp. 141–153.

Gagyi, Á. & Vigvary, A. (2018). 'Informal practices in housing financialisation: The transformation of an allotment garden in Hungary'. *Critical Housing Analysis*, 5(2), pp. 46–55.

García, M. (2010). 'The breakdown of the Spanish urban growth model: Social and territorial effects of the global crisis'. *International Journal of Urban and Regional Research*, 34(4), pp. 967–980.

García-Lamarca, M. and Kaika, M. (2016). 'Mortgaged lives': The biopolitics of debt and housing financialisation. *Transactions of the Institute of British Geographers*, 41(3), pp. 313–327.

Giang, D.T.H. & Pheng, L.S. (2011). 'Role of construction in economic development: Review of key concepts in the past 40 years'. *Habitat International*, 35(1), pp. 118–125.

Gotham, K.F. (2009). 'Creating liquidity out of spatial fixity: The secondary circuit of capital and the subprime mortgage crisis'. *International Journal of Urban and Regional Research*, 33(2), pp. 355–371.

Gough, J. & Gündoğdu, I. (2009). 'Class Cleansing in Istanbul's World-City Project'. In: Porter, L. & Shaw, K. (eds.), *Whose Urban Renaissance? An International Comparison of Urban Regeneration Strategies*, pp. 16–24. New York: Routledge.

Gökçeimam, Ö. (2019). 'Turkey'. In: Kullig, S. *et al.* (eds.), *The European Covered Bond Fact Book 2019*, pp. 521–526. EMF, ECBC.

Green, R. & Wachter, S. (2010). 'The Housing Finance Revolution'. In: Smith, S. & Searle, B.A. (eds.), *The Blackwell Companion to the Economics of Housing*, pp. 414–445. Chichester: Wiley-Blackwell.

Guironnet, A. & Halbert, L. (2014). 'The financialization of urban development projects: Concepts, processes, and implications'. *LATTS Working Paper No. 4.* Available at: https://hal-enpc.archives-ouvertes.fr/hal-01097192/document. [Accessed 1 Dec 2020].

Guironnet, A., Attuyer, K. & Halbert, L. (2016). 'Building cities on financial assets: The financialisation of property markets and its implications for city governments in the Paris city-region'. *Urban Studies*, 53(7), pp. 1442–1464.

Guttmann, R. (2016). *Finance-Led Capitalism: Shadow Banking, Re-Regulation, and the Future of Global Markets*. Basingstoke: Palgrave Macmillan.

Gülalp, H. (1985). 'Patterns of capital accumulation and state-society relations in Turkey'. *Journal of Contemporary Asia*, 15(3), pp. 329–348.

Gülalp, H. (1993).*Kapitalizm Sınıflar ve Devlet*, İstanbul: Belge.

Gülalp, H. (2001). 'Globalization and political Islam: The social bases of Turkey's welfare party'. *International Journal of Middle East Studies*, 33(3), pp. 433–448.

Gülöksüz, E. (2009). 'İnşaat Sanayiinde Uluslararasılaşma ve Sermayeler Arası İlişkiler'. *Praksis*, 19, pp. 157–189.

Gültekin-Karakaş, D. (2007). 'Türkiye'nin Yapısal Dönüşüm Sürecinde Banka Reformu'. In: Ercan, F. et al (eds.), *Türkiye'de Kapitalizmin Güncel Sorunları*. Ankara: Dipnot Yayınları, pp. 269–314.

Gültekin-Karakaş, D. (2009). 'Sermayenin Uluslararasılaşması Sürecinde Türkiye Banka Reformu ve Finans Kapital-içi Yeniden Yapılanma'. *Praksis*, 19, pp. 95–131.

Gündeş, S., Atakul, N, Büyükyoran, F. & Balaban-Okten, B. (2017). 'Earthquake Preparedness: Evaluation of Urban Transformation Model in Turkey'. *Presented at the 16th World Conference on Earthquake Engineering in Chile, January 2017*. Available at: https://www.researchgate.net/publication/319955000_Earthquake _Preparedness_Evaluation_of_Urban_Transformation_Model_in_Turkey. [Accessed 1 Dec 2020].

Güngen, A.R. (2017). 'Financial inclusion and policy-making: Strategy, campaigns and microcredita la Turca'. *New Political Economy*, 23(3), pp. 331–347.

Güngen, A.R. (2019). 'The Neoliberal Emergence of Market Finance in Turkey'. In: Yalman, G.L., Marois, T. & Güngen, A.R. (eds.), *The Political Economy of Financial Transformation in Turkey*. London, New York: Routledge.

Güngen, A.R. (2019b). 'Turkey's Authoritarianism and Crisis Management It's Complicated!' Available at: https://publicseminar.org/essays/turkeys-authoritarian ism-and-crisis-management/. [Accessed 1 Dec 2020].

Güngör, T. (2018). 'İnşaat büyük ölçüde ithalata bağımlı'. *Dünya*, March 8, [online]. Available at: https://www.dunya.com/kose-yazisi/insaat-buyuk-olcude-ithalata-ba gimli/406262. [Accessed 1 Dec 2020].

Gürakar, E. (2016). *Politics of Favoritism in Public Procurement in Turkey: Reconfigurations of Dependency Networks in the AKP Era*. New York: Palgrave Macmillan.

Gürcanlı, G.E. & Müngen, U. (2013). 'Analysis of construction accidents in Turkey and responsible parties'. *National Institute of Occupational Safety and Health*, 51(6), pp. 581–595.

Gürek, H. (2008). *AKP'nin Müteahhitleri*. İstanbul: Güncel Yayıncılık.

Haila, A. (1990). 'The theory of land rent at the crossroads'. *Environment and Planning D: Society and Space*, 8, pp. 275–296.

Haila, A. (1991). 'Four types of investment in land and property'. *International Journal of Urban and Regional Research*, 15, pp.343–65.

Haila, A. (2016). *Urban Land Rent: Singapore as a Property State*. Chichester: John Wiley & Sons.

Halbert, L. & Attuyer, K. (2016). 'Introduction: The financialisation of urban production: Conditions, mediations and transformations'. *Urban Studies*, 53(7), pp. 1347–1361.

Hampton, M. (2013). 'Money as social power: The economics of scarcity and working class reproduction'. *Capital & Class*, 37(3), pp. 373–395.

Harris, L. (1976). 'On interest, credit and capital'. *Economy & Society*, 5(2), pp. 145–177.

Harvey, D. (1973). *Social Justice and the City*. London: Edward Arnold.

Harvey, D. (1974). 'Class-monopoly rent, finance capital and the urban revolution'. *Regional Studies*, 8(3–4), pp. 239–55.

Harvey, D. (1985). *The Urbanization of Capital*, Baltimore: John Hopkins University Press.

Harvey, D. (1989). *The Urban Experience*. Baltimore: Johns Hopkins University Press.

Harvey, D. (1999). *The Limits to Capital*. London: Verso.

Harvey, D. (2003). *The New Imperialism*. Oxford: Oxford University Press.

Harvey, D. (2012). *Rebel Cities: From the Right to the City to the Urban Revolution*. London: Verso.

Harvey, D. (2014). *Seventeen Contradictions and the End of Capitalism*. Oxford University Press.

Harvey, D. & Chatterjee, L. (1974). 'Absolute rent and the structuring of space by governmental and financial institutions'. *Antipode*, 6(1), pp. 22–36.

Henderson, J.V. (2009). 'The Effect of Residential Land Market Regulations on Urban Welfare'. Lall, S.V.; Freire, M.; Yuen, B.; Rajack, R. and Helluin, J-J. (eds.), *Urban land markets: improving land management for successful urbanization*. Dordrecht: Springer.

Hepşen, A., Aşıcı, M. & Olgun, A. (2017). 'Efficient use of capital: Paradox of real estate and industry in Turkey'. *International Journal of Economics and Finance*, 9(8), pp. 221–228.

Himmelweit, S. & Mohun, S. (1978). 'The anomalies of capital'. *Capital & Class*, 2(3), pp. 67–105.

Hirayama, Y. (2012). 'The Shifting Housing Opportunities of Younger People in Japan's Home-Owning Society'. In Ronald, R. & Elsinga, M. (eds.), *Beyond Home ownership: Housing, welfare and society*, pp. 173–194. Oxon: Routledge.

Hirayama, Y. (2017). 'Selling the Tokyo Sky: Urban Regeneration and Luxury Housing'. In: Forrest, R., Koh, S.Y. & Wissink, B. (eds.), *Cities and the super-rich: real estate, elite practices and urban political economies*, pp. 189–208. New York: Palgrave Macmillan.

Hirsch, J. (1978). 'The State Apparatus and Social Reproduction: Elements of a Theory of the Bourgeois State'. In Holloway J. & Picciotto, S. (eds), *State and Capital: A Marxist Debate*, pp. 57–107. London: Edward Arnold.

Holloway, J. & Picciotto, S. (1991). 'Capital, Crisis and the State'. In: Clarke, S. (ed.), *The State Debate*. New York: St. Martin's Press.

Hoşgör, E. (2011). 'Islamic capital/Anatolian tigers: Past and present'. *Middle Eastern Studies*, 47(2), pp. 343–360.

Hoşgör, E. (2015). 'Islamic Capital'. In: Balkan, N., Balkan, E. & Öncü, A. (eds),*The Neoliberal Landscape and the Rise of Islamist Capital in Turkey*, pp. 142–165. New York: Berghahn Books.

Hoşgör, E. (2016). 'New fragmentations and new alliances in the Turkish bourgeoisie'. *Journal für Entwicklungspolitik, JEP*, XXXII 1/2, pp. 114–134.

Howard, M.C. & King, J.E. (1985). *The Political Economy of Marx.* 2nd ed. Harlow: Longman.

Ilyenkov, E.V. (1982). *The Dialectics of the Abstract and the Concrete in Marx's 'Capital'.* Moscow: Progress Publishers.

Immergluck, D. & Law, J. (2014). 'Investing in crisis: The methods, strategies, and expectations of investors in single-family foreclosed homes in distressed neighbourhoods', *Housing Policy Debate*, 24(3), pp. 568–593.

Isaacs, G. (2016). 'The commodification and financialisation of low-cost housing in South Africa'. *FESSUD Working Paper No. 200.*

Işık, O. (1991). *The Penetration of Capitalism into Housing Production: Speculative House Building In Turkey: 1950-1980.* PhD Thesis, University College London.

Işık, O. & Pınarcıoğlu, .M. (2001). *Nöbetleşe Yoksulluk: Sultanbeyli Örneği.* İstanbul: İletişim Yayınları.

Itoh, M. (2001). 'Spiral Reversal of Capitalist Development: What Does It Imply for the Twenty-First Century?' In: Albritton, R., Itoh, M.,Westra, R. &Zuege, A. (eds.), *Phases of Capitalist Development: Booms, Crises, and Globalization*, pp. 110–124. Basingstoke: Palgrave.

Itoh, M. & Lapavitsas, C. (1999). *Political Economy of Money and Finance.* London: MacMillan.

Jäger, J. (2003). 'Urban land rent theory: A regulationist perspective'. *International Journal of Urban and Regional Research*, 27(2), pp. 233–249.

Jessop, B. (1978). 'Capitalism and Democracy: The Best Possible Political Shell?' In: Littlejohn, G. *et al.* (eds.), *Power and the State*, pp. 10–51. London: Croom Helm.

Jessop, B. (1985). *Nicos Poulantzas: Marxist Theory and Political Strategy.* London: Macmillan.

Jessop, B. (1996). *State Theory: Putting the Capitalist State in Its Place.* Cambridge: Polity.

Jessop, B. (2001). 'What Follows Fordism? On the Periodisation of Capitalism and Its Regulation'. In: Albritton, R., Itoh, M., Westra, R. & Zuege, A. (eds.), *Phases of Capitalist Development: Booms, Crises, and Globalization*, pp. 282–299. Basingstoke: Palgrave.

Jessop, B. (2002). 'Liberalism, neoliberalism, and urban governance: A state-theoretical perspective'. *Antipode*, 34(3), pp. 452–472.

Jessop, B. (2014). *Poulantzas's State Power Socialism as a Modern Classic*. Available at: https://bobjessop.wordpress.com/2014/03/27/poulantzass-state-power-social ism-as-a-modern-classic/. [Accessed 1 Dec 2020].

Jesus, P.M. (2016). 'The inclusion and access of social housing movements to Minha Casa Minha Vida: The emergence of the entidades modality'. *Revista Brasileira de Estudos Urbanos e Regionais*, 18(1), pp. 92–110.

Jevons, W. S. (1970) [1871]. *The Theory of Political Economy*. Edited by R. D. Collison Black. Harmondsworth: Penguin Books.

Johansson, B. (1986). 'Spatial dynamics and metropolitan change'. *Regional Science and Urban Economics*, 16, pp. 1–6.

Kahveci, İ. (2018). 'Yine 'ev sahibi' ev sahibi oldu'. *Karar*, May 27, Available at: https://www.karar.com/yine-ev-sahibi-ev-sahibi-oldu-866938. [Accessed 1 Dec 2020].

Kalaycıoğlu, E. (2002). 'The Motherland Party: The Challenge of Institutionalization in a Charismatic Leader Party', *Turkish Studies*, 3(1), pp. 41–61.

Kaltenbrunner, A. (2015). 'A post Keynesian framework of exchange rate determination: A Minskyan approach', *Journal of Post Keynesian Economics*, 38(3), pp. 426–448.

Kaltenbrunner, A. & Karacimen, E. (2016). 'The Contested Nature of Financialisation in Emerging Capitalist Economies'. In: Subasat, T. (ed.) *The Great Financial Meltdown of 2008: Systemic, Conjunctural or Policy Created?* pp. 287–307. Cheltenham: Edward Elgar.

Karaçimen, E. (2014). 'Financialization in Turkey: The case of consumer debt'. *Journal of Balkan & Near Eastern Studies*, 16(2), pp. 161–180.

Karahanoğulları, Y. (2009). *Marx'ın Değeri Ölçülebilir mi? 1988–2006 Türkiyesi İçin Ampirik Bir İnceleme*, İstanbul: Yordam.

Karahanoğulları, Y. & Türk, D. (2018). 'Otoriter Devletçilik, Neoliberalizm, Türkiye'. *Mülkiye*, 42(3), pp. 403–48.

Karakaya, K. & Kandemir, A. (2018). 'Turkey to Sell Asset-Backed Bonds to Help Ease Banks' Burden'. (2018). Bloomberg.com. [online] 28 Nov. Available at: https://www .bloomberg.com/news/articles/2018-11-28/turkey-banks-regulator-said-to-plan-to -free-up-balance-sheets?sref=pVYFKQyF. [Accessed 1 Dec 2020].

Karaman, O. (2014). 'Resisting urban renewal in Istanbul'. *Urban Geography*, 35(2), pp. 290–310.

Karatepe, I.D. (2013). 'Islamists, State and Bourgeoisie: The Construction Industry in Turkey'. *Paper presented at the World Economics Association Conference on Neoliberalism in Turkey: A Balance Sheet of Three Decades*. Available at:

http://turkeyconference2013.weaconferences.net/wp-content/uploads/sites/11
/2013/10/Karatepe_wea_application.pdf. [Accessed 1 Dec 2020].

Karatepe, I.D. (2016). 'The state, Islamists, discourses, and bourgeoisie: The construction industry in Turkey'. *Research and Policy on Turkey*, 1(1), pp. 46–62.

Karwowski, E. & Stockhammer, E. (2017). 'Financialisation in emerging economies: A
systematic overview and comparison with Anglo-Saxon economies'. *Economic and
Political Studies*, 5(1), pp. 60–86.

Kaygusuz, Ö. (2018). 'Authoritarian neoliberalism and regime security in Turkey: Moving
to an 'exceptional state' under AKP', *South European Society and Politics*, 23(2),
pp.281–302.

Kazgan, G. (1999). *Tanzimat'tan XXI. Yuzyila Turkiye Eonomisi*, Istanbul: Altin Kitaplar
Yayinevi.

Keleş, R. (1990). 'Housing Policy in Turkey'. In: Shildo, G. (ed.), *Housing Policy in
Developing Countries*, pp. 140–172. London and New York: Routledge.

Keleş, R. (2006). *Kentleşme Politikası*. Ankara: İmge Kitabevi.

Kemeny, J. (1987). 'Toward a theorised housing studies: a counter-critique of provision
thesis'. *Housing Studies* 2(4), pp. 249–260.

Kendall, R. & Tulip, P. (2018). *The Effect of Zoning on Housing Prices. Research Discussion
Paper* 2018–03. Reserve Bank of Australia.

Keyder, Ç. (1987). *State and Class in Turkey*. London: Verso.

Keyder, Ç. (2005). 'Globalization and social exclusion in Istanbul'. *International Journal
of Urban and Regional Research*, 29 (1), pp. 124–134.

Keyder, Ç. & Öncü, A. (1994). 'Globalization of a third-world metropolis: Istanbul in the
1980's'. *Review: A Journal of the Fernand Braudel Center*, 17(3), pp. 383–421.

King, R.J. (1989). 'Capital switching and the role of ground rent: Switching between circuits, switching between submarkets, and social change'. *Environment and Planning
A: Economy and Space*, 21(7), pp. 853–880.

Kitzmann, R. (2017). 'Private versus state-owned housing in Berlin: Changing provision
of low-income households'. *Cities*, 61(1), pp. 1–8.

Knoll, K., Schularick, M. & Steger, T. (2017). 'No price like home: Global house prices,
1870–2012'. *American Economic Review*, 107(2), pp. 331–353.

Kowaric, L. (1979). *A espoliação urbana*. Rio de Janeiro: Paz e Terra.

Köse, A.H. & Öncü, A. (2000), 'İşgücü Piyasaları ve Uluslararası İşbölümünde
Uzmanlaşmanın Mekansal Boyutları: 1980 Sonrası Dönemde Türkiye İmalat Sanayi',
Toplum ve Bilim, 86, pp.72–90.

Krätke, S. (1992). 'Urban land rent and real estate markets in the process of social
restructuring: The case of Germany'. *Environment and Planning D: Society and
Space*, 10(3), pp. 245–264.

Kurtuluş, H., Purkis, S. & Alada, A. (2012). 'İstanbul'da Yeni Konut Sunum Biçimleri ve Orta Sınıfların Sosyo-Mekansal Yeniden İnşası'. *TÜBITAK Araştırma Projesi Raporu No. 110K061*. Ankara.

Kuyucu, T., 2014. 'Law, property and ambiguity'. *International Journal of Urban and Regional Research*, 38(2), pp. 609–27.

Kuyucu, T. (2017). 'Two Crises, Two Trajectories: The Impact of the 2001 and 2008 Economic Crises on Urban Governance in Turkey'. In: Adaman, F., Akbulut, B. & Arsel, M. (eds.), *Neoliberal Turkey and Its Discontents: Economic Policy and the Environment under Erdogan*. London, New York: I.B. Tauris.

Kuyucu, T. (2018). 'Türkiye'de Kentsel Dönüşümün Dönüşümü: Hukuki ve Kurumsal Çatışmalar Üzerinden Bir Açıklama Denemesi', *IdealKent*, 9(24), pp. 364–386.

Kuyucu, T. and Ünsal, Ö. (2010). 'Urban transformation' as state-led property transfer: An analysis of two cases of urban renewal in Istanbul. *Urban Studies*, 47(7), pp. 1479–1499.

Kuznet, S. (1952). 'National income estimates for the United States prior to 1870'. *The Journal of Economic History*, 12(2), pp. 115–130.

Kyung-Sup, C. (2016). 'Financialization of poverty: Proletarianizing the financial crisis in post-developmental Korea'. *Research in Political Economy*, 31, pp. 109–134.

Langley, P. (2008). *The Everyday Life of Global Finance: Saving and Borrowing in Anglo-America*. Oxford; New York: Oxford University Press.

Lapavitsas, C. (2009a). 'Financialised capitalism: crisis and financial expropriation'. *Historical Materialism*, 17(2), pp. 114–48.

Lapavitsas, C. (2009b). 'Financialisation embroils developing countries'. *Papeles de Europa*, 19. pp. 108–139.

Lapavitsas, C. (2011). 'Theorizing financialization'. *Work, Employment & Society*, 25(4), pp. 611–626.

Lapavitsas, C. (2014). *Profiting Without Producing: How Finance Exploits Us All*. London; New York: Verso.

Lapavitsas, C. & Mavroudeas, S. (1999). 'Financial Systems and Capital Markets: An Alternative View'. In: Siriopoulos, C. (ed.) *Topics in Financial Economics and Risk Management Analysis*, Paratiritis.

Lapavitsas, C. & Powell, J. (2013). 'Financialisation varied: a comparative analysis of advanced economies'. *Cambridge Journal of Regions, Economy and Society*, 6(3), pp. 359–79.

Larsen, H.G. & Hansen, A.L. (2015). 'Commodifying Danish housing commons'. *Geografiska Annaler: Series B, Human Geography*, 97(3), pp. 263–274.

Lazzarato, M. (2012). *The Making of the Indebted Man: An Essay on the Neoliberal Condition*. Cambridge, MA: MIT Press.

Lee, M.J. (1993). *Consumer Culture Reborn*. London: Routledge.

Leyshon, A. & Thrift, N. (2007). 'The capitalization of almost everything: The future of finance and capitalism'. *Theory, Culture & Society*, 24(7–8), pp. 97–115.

Lim, G.-C. (1987). 'Housing policies for the urban poor in developing countries'. *Journal of the American Planning Association*, 53(2), pp.176–185.

Lima, J.R. Jr. (2012). 'Real estate: Era possível prever?' *Construção Mercado*, 65, pp. 46–49.

Lima, V. & Xerez, R. (2022). 'Social housing systems and welfare in Ireland and Portugal: A comparative analysis', *International Journal of Housing Policy*, pp.1–11.

Liodakis, G. (2016). 'An exploration of scarcity in historical perspective'. *Science & Society*, 80(2), pp. 221–247.

Lipietz, A. (1974). Le tribute foncier urbain. Circulation du capital et propriété foncière dans la production du cadre bâti. Paris: Maspero.

Lipietz, A. (1985). 'A Marxist Approach to Urban Ground Rent: The Case of France'. In: M. Ball, V. Bentivegna, M. Edwards, & M. Folin (eds.). *Land Rent: Housing and Urban Planning*, pp. 129–155. London: Croom Helm.

Lipton, M. (1989). 'Responses to rural population growth: Malthus and the moderns'. *Population and Development Review*, 15, pp. 215–242.

Lis, P. (2015). 'Financialisation of the system of provision applied to housing in Poland'. *FESSUD Working Paper No. 100*.

López, I. & Rodríguez, E. (2011). 'The Spanish model'. *New Left Review*, 69(2), pp. 5–28.

Lovering, J. & Türkmen, H. (2011). 'Bulldozer neo-liberalism in Istanbul: The state-led construction of property markets, and the displacement of the urban poor'. *International Planning Studies*, 16(1), pp. 73–96.

Mandel, E. (1975). *Late Capitalism*. London: New Left Books.

Mann, M. (1993). *The Sources of Social Power, Vol. 2*. New York: Cambridge University Press.

Markusen, A.R. & Markusen, A. (1978). 'Class, rent, and sectoral conflict: Uneven development in Western U.S. boomtowns'. *Review of Radical Political Economics*, 10(3), pp. 117–129.

Marois, T. (2011). 'Emerging market bank rescues in an era of finance-led neoliberalism: A comparison of Mexico and Turkey'. *Review of International Political Economy*, 18(2), pp. 168–196.

Marois, T. (2012). *States, Banks and Crisis: Emerging Finance Capitalism in Mexico and Turkey*. Cheltenham, Gloucestershire, UK: Edward Elgar Publishing.

Marois, T. (2014). 'Historical precedents, contemporary manifestations'. *Review of Radical Political Economics*, 46(3), pp. 308–330.

Marois, T. (2019). 'The Transformation of the State Financial Apparatus in Turkey since 2001'. In: Yalman, G.L., Marois, T. & Güngen, A.R. (eds.), *The Political Economy of Financial Transformation in Turkey*. London, New York: Routledge.

Marois, T. & Güngen, A.R. (2019). 'The Neoliberal Restructuring of Banking in Turkey Since 2001'. In: Yalman, G.L., Marois, T. & Güngen, A.R. (eds.), *The Political Economy of Financial Transformation in Turkey*. London, New York: Routledge.

Marschall, M., Aydogan, A. & Bulut, A. (2016). 'Does housing create votes? Explaining the electoral success of the AKP in Turkey'. *Electoral Studies*, 42, pp. 201–212.

Marshall, A. (1961). *Principles of Economics*, 8th ed., New York: Macmillan.

Martin, R. (2002). *Financialization of Daily Life*. Philadelphia: Temple University Press.

Martin, R. (2014). 'What difference do derivatives make? From the technical to the political conjuncture'. *Culture Unbound: Journal of Current Cultural Research*, 6(1), pp. 189–210.

Marx, K. (1968). *Theories of Surplus Value* (Vol. 2). Moscow: Progress Publishers.

Marx, K. (1990). *Capital. A Critique of Political Economy* (Vol. 1). London: Penguin Books.

Marx, K. (1991).*Capital: A Critique of Political Economy* (Vol. 3). London: Penguin Books.

Marx, K. (1992). *Capital. A Critique of Political Economy* (Vol. 2). London: Penguin Books.

Marx, K. (1997). 'On the Jewish Question'. In Pierson, C. (ed.), *The Marx Reader*. Cambridge: Polity Press.

Massey, D. & Catalano, A. (1978). *Capital and Land*. London: Edward Arnold.

Micco, A., Parrado, A., Piedrabuena, B. & Rebucci, A. (2012). 'Housing finance in Chile: Instruments, actors, and policies'. *IDB Working Paper*, No. IDB-WP-312.

Michell, J. & Toporowski, J. (2014). 'Critical observations on financialization and the financial process'. *International Journal of Political Economy*, 42(4), pp. 67–82.

Milios, J. & Sotiropoulos, D. (2009). *Rethinking Imperialism: A Study of Capitalist Rule*. New York: Palgrave Macmillan.

Mills, E.S. (1972). *Studies in the Structure of the Urban Economy*. Baltimore: Johns Hopkins University Press.

Montgomerie, J. & Büdenbender, M. (2015). 'Round the Houses: Homeownership and Failures of Asset-Based Welfare in the United Kingdom', *New Political Economy*, 20(3), pp. 386–405.

Murray, C. & Clapham, D. (2015). 'Housing policies in Latin America: overview of the four largest economies'. *International Journal of Housing Policy*, 15(3), pp. 347–364.

Muth, R. (1969). *Cities and Housing*. Chicago: University of Chicago Press.

Ngai, P. & Huilin, L. (2010). 'A culture of violence: The labor subcontracting system and collective action by construction workers in post-Socialist China'. *The China Journal*, 64, pp. 143–158.

Nielsen, M. (2022). 'Speculative cities: housing and value conversions in Maputo, Mozambique', *Housing studies*, 37(6), pp. 889–909.

Norris, M. & Byrne, M. (2015). 'Asset price Keynesianism, regional imbalances and the Irish and Spanish housing booms and busts'. *Built Environment*, 41(2): 227–243.

Oğuz, S. (2008). *Globalization and the Contradictions of State Restructuring in Turkey*. PhD. thesis, York University.

Oğuz, Ş. (2011). 'Krizi Fırsata Dönüştürmek: Türkiye'de Devletin 2008 Krizine Yönelik Tepkileri'. *Amme İdaresi Dergisi*, 44(1), pp. 1–23.

Oğuz, Ş. (2016). 'Yeni Türkiye'nin Siyasal Rejimi'. In: Tören, T. & Kutun, M. (eds.) *Yeni Türkiye'de Kapitalizm, Devlet ve Sınıflar*, pp. 81–127, İstanbul: SAV.

Ollman, B. (2003). *Dance of the Dialectic: Steps in Marx's Method*. University of Illinois Press.

Onaran, Ö. (2006). 'Speculation-led growth and fragility in Turkey: Does EU make a difference or "can it happen again"?' *Department of Economics Working Paper No. 93*, Inst. fürVolkswirtschaftstheorie und politik, WU Vienna University of Economics and Business.

Orhangazi, Ö. & Özgür, G. (2015). 'Capital flows, finance-led growth and fragility in the age of global liquidity and quantitative easing: The case of Turkey'. *Political Economy Research Institute Working Paper No. 397*.

Orhangazi, Ö. & Yeldan, E. (2020). 'Re-Making of the Turkish Crisis'. *FESSUD Working Paper No. 504*.

Orhangazi, Ö. (2019). 'Türkiye ekonomisinin yapısal sorunları, finansal kırılganlıklar ve kriz dinamikleri'. *Mülkiye*, 43(1), pp. 111–137.

Öncü, A. (1988). 'The politics of the urban land market in Turkey: 1950–1980'. *International Journal of Urban and Regional Research*, 12(1), pp. 38–64.

Öncü, A. and Balkan, E. (2016). 'Nouveaux riches of the city of minarets and skyscrapers: Neoliberalism and the reproduction of the Islamic middle class in İstanbul'. *Research and Policy on Turkey*, 1(1), pp. 29–45.

Öniş, Z. (2004). 'Turgut Özal and his economic legacy, Turkish neoliberalism in critical perspective', *Middle Eastern Studies*, 40 (4), pp. 113–34.

Öniş, Z. (2009). 'Beyond the 2001 financial crisis: The political economy of the new phase of neo-liberal restructuring in Turkey'. *Review of International Political Economy*, 16(3), pp. 409–432.

Öymen, A. (1985). 'Konut Konut Diye Diye', *Milliyet*, 1–7 September.

Özcan, G.B. & Çokgezen, M. (2003). 'Limits to alternative forms of capitalization: The case of Anatolian holding companies', *World Development*, 31(12), pp.2061–84.

Özdemir, D. (2010). 'The role of the public sector in the provision of housing supply in Turkey, 1950–2009'. *International Journal of Urban and Regional Research*, 35(6), pp. 1099–1117.

Özden, B.A., Akça, İ. & Bekmen, A. (2017). 'Antinomies of Authoritarian Neoliberalism in Turkey: The Justice and Development Party Era'. In: Tansel, C.B. (ed.), *States of Discipline: Authoritarian Neoliberalism and the Contested Reproduction of Capitalist Order*. London: Rowman and Littlefield International.

Özkan, F., Özkan, Ö. and Gündüz, M. (2012). 'Causal relationship between construction investment policy and economic growth in Turkey'. *Technological Forecasting and Social Change*, 79(2), pp. 362–370.

Özmen, E., Şahinöz, S. & Yalçın, C. (2012). 'Profitability, saving and investment of non-financial firms in Turkey'. *CRBT Working Paper No. 12/14*. Ankara: Central Bank of the Republic of Turkey.

Öztürk, Ö. (2010). *Türkiye'de Büyük Sermaye Grupları: Finans Kapitalin Oluşumu ve Gelişimi*. İstanbul: SAV.

Öztürk, Ö. (2015). 'The Islamist Bourgeoisie in Turkey'. In: Balkan, N., Balkan, E. & Öncü, A. (eds), *The Neoliberal Landscape and the Rise of Islamist Capital in Turkey*, pp. 117–142. New York: Berghahn Books.

Painceira, J.P. (2012). 'Developing Countries in the Era of Financialisation'. In Lapavitsas, C. (ed.) *Financialisation in Crisis*, Leiden: Brill.

Palancioglu, H.M. & Cete, M. (2014). 'The Turkish way of housing supply and finance for low- and middle-income people'. *Land Use Policy*, 39, pp. 127–134.

Pamuk, A. (1996). 'Convergence trends in formal and informal housing markets: The case of Turkey'. *Journal of Planning Education and Research*, 16(2), pp. 103–113.

Pamuk, Ş. (2014). *Türkiye'nin 200 yıllık iktisadi tarihi: büyüme, kurumlar ve bölüşüm*. İstanbul: Türkiye İş Bankası.

Panitch, L. (2002). 'The Impoverishment of State Theory'. In Aronowitz, S. & Gratsis, P. (eds), *Paradigm Lost: State Theory Reconsidered*, pp. 89–104. Minnesota: University of Minnesota Press.

Panitch, L. & S. Gindin, (2011). 'Capitalist Crises and the Crisis This Time'. In: Panitch, L., Albo, G., & Chibber V. (eds.) *Socialist Register 2011: The Crisis This Time*, 47. London: The Merlin Press.

Park, J. (2011). *Spatial Analysis of Housing Markets with Land Rent Theory of Political Economy: The Cases of London, Seoul and Los Angeles*. PhD. thesis, University College London.

Payne, G., Durand-Lasserve, A., & Rakodi, C. (2009). 'The limits of land titling and home ownership'. *Environment and Urbanization*, 21(2), pp. 443–462.

Pearce-Oroz, (2007). 'Limits to Large-Scale Reconstruction: Land Development for The Poor in Inadequately Functioning Land Markets'. In: Freire, M., Lima, R., Cira, D., Ferguson, B., Kessides, C., Mota, J.A. and Motta, D. (eds.), *Land and urban policies for poverty reduction*. World Bank and Brazilian Institute of Economic and Administrative Studies (IPEA). Washington, DC.

Penpecioğlu, M. (2017). 'Yapılı çevre üretimi, devlet ve büyük ölçekli kentsel projeler kapitalist kentleşme dinamiklerinin Türkiye'deki son 10 yılı'. In Bora, T. (ed.), *İnşaat Ya Resulallah*, pp. 163–180. İstanbul: İletişim.

Pereira, A.L.D.S. (2017). 'Financialization of housing in Brazil: New frontiers'. *International Journal of Urban and Regional Research*, 41(4), pp. 604–622.

Perelman, M. (1979). 'Marx, Malthus, and the concept of natural resource scarcity'. *Antipode*, 11(2), pp. 80–91.

Perelman, M. (1987). *Marx's Crises Theory: Scarcity, Labor, and Finance*. New York: Praeger.

Perelman, M. (2003). 'The History of Capitalism'. In: Saad-Filho, A. (ed.) *Anti-Capitalism: A Marxist Introduction*, pp. 119–126. London: Pluto Press.

Pérouse, J.F. (2015). 'The State without the Public: Some Conjectures about the Administration for Collective Housing (TOKI)'. In: Aymes, M., Gourisse, B & Massicard, É. (eds.), *Order and Compromise: Government Practices in Turkey from the Late Ottoman Empire to the Early 21st Century*, pp. 169–191. Boston: Brill.

Pickvance, C. (1976). *Urban Sociology: Critical Essays*. London: Methuen.

Polanyi, K. (2001). *The Great Transformation: The Political and Economic Origins of Our Time*. Boston, MA: Beacon Press.

Pollard, J. (2009). 'Political Framing in National Housing Systems: Lessons from Real Estate Developers in France and Spain'. In: Schwartz, H.M. & Seabrooke, L. (eds.), *The Politics of Housing Booms and Busts*, pp. 170–187. London: Palgrave Macmillan.

Pósfai, Z., Gál, Z. & Nagy, E. (2018). 'Financialization and Inequalities: The Uneven Development of the Housing Market on the Eastern Periphery of Europe'. In: Fadda, S. & Tridico, P. (eds.), *Inequality and Uneven Development in the Post-Crisis World*, pp. 167–190. London: Routledge.

Poulantzas, N. (1973). 'On social classes'. *New Left Review*, 78, pp. 27–54.

Poulantzas, N. (1975). *Classes in Contemporary Capitalism*. London: New Left Books.

Poulantzas, N. (1976). 'The capitalist state: A reply to Miliband and Laclau'. *New Left Review*, 95, pp. 63–83.

Poulantzas, N. (2008). 'The Political Crisis and the Crisis of the State'. In: Martin, J. (ed.), *The Poulantzas Reader: Marxism, Law and the State*, pp. 294–322. London: Verso.

Poulantzas, N. (2014). *State, Power, Socialism. London*; New York: Verso.

Powell, J. (2013). *Subordinate Financialisation: A Study of Mexico and Its Non-financial Corporations*. PhD thesis, SOAS, University of London.

Powell, J. (2018). 'Towards a Marxist Theory of Financialized Capitalism'. In: Vidal, M., Smith, T., Rotta, T. & Prew, P. (eds.) *The Oxford Handbook of Karl Marx*. New York, Oxford University Press.

Prasad, M. (2013). *The Land of Too Much: American Abundance and the Paradox of Poverty*. Cambridge, Ma: Harvard University Press.

Purkis, S. (2014). 'Hukuka Aykırı Yasalar Yoluyla Mekan Üzerinden Pervasız Birikim'. *Eğitim Bilim Toplum*, 12(46), pp. 136–163.

Purkis, S. (2016). 'İstanbul'da İnşaat Odaklı Birikimin Durdurulamayan Yükselişi: Konut Fazlasına Karşın Artan Konut Açığı'. *Mülkiye Dergisi*, 40(4), pp. 91–111.

Rafferty, M. and Toner, P. (2019). 'Thinking like capital markets — financialisation of the Australian construction industry'. *Construction Management and Economics*, 37(3), pp. 156–168.

Rajack, R. &. Lall, S.V. (2009). 'What Do We Know About Urban Land Markets?' In: Lall, S.V.; Freire, M.; Yuen, B.; Rajack, R. and Helluin, J-J. (eds.), *Urban land markets: improving land management for successful urbanization*. Dordrecht: Springer.

Ram, P. & Needham, B. (2016). 'The provision of affordable housing in India: Are commercial developers interested?' *Habitat International*, 55, pp. 100–108.

Raviv, O.C. (2021). 'Class differences in homeownership and mortgage debt burden across cohorts: the Israeli case'. *International Journal of Housing Policy*, pp.1–37.

Rethel, L. & Sinclair, T.J. (2014). 'Innovation and the entrepreneurial state in Asia: Mechanisms of bond market development'. *Asian Studies Review*, 38(4), pp. 564–581.

Ricardo, D. (2001). *On The Principles of Political Economy and Taxation*, Ontario: Batoche Books.

Robertson, M. (2014a). *The Financialization of British Housing: A Systems of Provision Approach*. PhD. thesis, SOAS, University of London.

Robertson, M. (2014b). 'Case study: Finance and housing provision in Britain'. *FESSUD Working Paper No. 51*.

Robertson, M. (2016). 'The system of provision for housing in selected case study countries'. *FESSUD Working Paper No. 193*.

Rolnik, R. (2013). 'Late neoliberalism: The financialization of homeownership and housing rights'. *International Journal of Urban and Regional Research*, 37(3), pp. 1058–1066.

Rolnik, R. (2019). *Urban Warfare: Housing under the Empire of Finance*. London: Verso.

Romainville, A. (2017). 'The financialization of housing production in Brussels'. *International Journal of Urban and Regional Research*, 41(4), pp. 623–41.

Ronald, R. & Elsinga, M. (2012). 'Beyond home ownership: An overview'. In: Ronald, R. & Elsinga, M. (eds.) *Beyond Home Ownership: Housing, Welfare and Society*, pp. 1–28. Oxon: Routledge.

Rostow, W.W. (1949). *The Stages of Economic Growth: A Non-Communist Manifesto*. London: Cambridge University Press.

Rotta, T. & Teixeira, R. (2018). 'The Commodification of Knowledge and Information'. *GPERC Working Paper No.60*, Available at: https://gala.gre.ac.uk/id/eprint/19448/13 /19448%20Rotta%20and%20Teixeira%202018%20Commodification%20of%20Kn owledge%20and%20Information%20200618%20GPERC%20wp3.pdf. [Accessed 1 Dec 2020].

Ryan-Collins, J., Toby, L. & MacFarlane, L. (2017). *Rethinking the Economics of Land and Housing*. London: Zed.

Ryan-Collins, J. (2021). 'Breaking the housing–finance cycle: Macroeconomic policy reforms for more affordable homes', *Economy and Space*, 53(3), pp. 480–502.

Rydin, Y. (1983). *Housebuilders as an Interest Group: The Issue of Residential Land Availability*, LSE: Geography Discussion Paper No. 6, pp.11.

Saad-Filho, A. (2002). *The Value of Marx: Political Economy for Contemporary Capitalism*. London: Routledge.

Saad-Filho, A. (2005). 'From Washington to Post-Washington Consensus: Neoliberal Agendas for Economic Development'. In: Saad-Filho, A. & Johnston, D. (eds.) *Neoliberalism: A Critical Reader*, pp. 113–119. London: Pluto Press.

Saad-Filho, A. (2010). 'Crisis in Neoliberalism or Crisis of Neoliberalism?' In: Albo, G., Chibber, V. & Panitch, L. (eds.), *Socialist Register*. London: Merlin Press.

Saad-Filho, A. (2015). *Money, Credit, Fictitious Capital and the Management of Accumulation in Marx's Theory of Value*. Unpublished manuscript, SOAS, University of London.

Saad-Filho, A. (2019). *Value and Crisis: Essays on Labour, Money and Contemporary Capitalism*. Leiden. Boston: Brill.

Saad-Filho, A. & Morais, L. (2018). *Brazil: Neoliberalism versus Democracy*. London: Pluto.

Saito, K. (2017). *Karl Marx's Ecosocialism: Capital, Nature, and the Unfinished Critique of Political Economy*. New York: Monthly Review Press.

Sanfelici, D. & Halbert, L. (2015). 'Financial markets, developers and the geographies of housing in Brazil: A supply-side account'. *Urban Studies*, 53(7), pp. 1465–1485.

Santoro, P. & Rolnik, R. (2017). 'Novas frentes de expansão do complexo imobiliário-financeiro em São Paulo'. *Cadernos Metrópole*, 19(39), pp. 407–431.

Saraçoğlu, C. & Demirtaş-Milz, N. (2014). 'Disasters as an ideological strategy for governing neoliberal urban transformation in Turkey: Insights from Izmir/Kadifekale', *Disasters*, 38(1), pp. 178–201.

Sarı, Ö.B.Ö. & Khurami, E.A. (2018). 'Housing affordability trends and challenges in the Turkish case'. *Journal of Housing and the Built Environment*. [online]. Available at: https://link.springer.com/article/10.1007/s10901-018-9617-2#citeas. [Accessed 1 Dec 2020].

Sarıoğlu-Erdoğdu, G.P. (2014). 'Housing development and policy change: what has changed in Turkey in the last decade in the owner-occupied and rented sectors?' *Journal of Housing and the Built Environment*, 29(1), pp. 155–175.

Savran, S. (2002). 'The Legacy of the Twentieth Century'. In: Savran, S. (ed.), *The Politics of Permanent Crisis: Class, Ideology and State in Turkey*. New York: Nova Science.

Schwartz, H.M. & Seabrooke, L. (2009). 'Varieties of Residential Capitalism in the International Political Economy: Old Welfare States and the New Politics of Housing'. In: Schwartz, H.M. & Seabrooke, L. (eds.), *The Politics of Housing Booms and Busts*, pp. 1–27. London: Palgrave Macmillan.

Scoones, I., Smalley, R., Hall, R. & Tsikata, D. (2014). 'Narratives of Scarcity: Understanding The "Global Resource Grab,"' *Future Agricultures and Institute for Poverty, Land and Agrarian Studies Working Paper 076*, Available at: https://assets.publishing.service.gov.uk/media/57a089caed915d622c0003d3/FAC_Working_Paper_076.pdf [Accessed 17 February 2023].

Scott, A.J. (1976). 'Land and land rent: An interpretative review of the French literature'. *Progress in Geography*, 9, pp. 102–45.

Scott, A J, (1980). *The Urban Land Nexus and the State*. London: Pion.

Sengupta, U. (2019). 'State-led housing development in Brazil and India: A machinery for enabling strategy?' *International Journal of Housing Policy*, pp. 1–27.

Shiller, R.J. (2012). *Finance and the Good Society*. Princeton, NJ: Princeton University Press.

Shimbo, L. (2012). *Habitação Social de Mercado: A Confluência Entre Estado, Empresas Construtoras e Capital Financeiro*. Belo Horizonte: C/Arte.

Shimbo, L. (2019). 'An unprecedented alignment: State, finance, construction and housing production in Brazil since the 2000s'. *International Journal of Housing Policy*, 19, pp. 337–353.

Skocpol, T. (1985). 'Bringing the State Back In: Strategies of Analysis in Current Research'. In: Evans, P.B., Rueschemeyer, D. and Skocpol, T. (eds.), *Bringing the State Back In*, pp. 3–35. New York: Cambridge University Press.

Smart, A. & Lee, J. (2003). 'Financialization and the role of real estate in Hong Kong's regime of accumulation'. *Economic Geography*, 79(2), pp. 153–171.

Smith, N. (1986). 'Gentrification, the Frontier, and the Restructuring of Urban Space'. In: Smith, N & Williams, P. (eds.), *Gentrification of the City*, pp. 15–34. Boston: Allen & Unwin.

Smith, S., Searle, B. & Cook, N. (2008). 'Rethinking the risks of home-ownership'. *Journal of Social Policy*, 38(1), pp. 83–102.

Smith, S. & Searle, B. (2010). *The Blackwell Companion to the Economics of Housing: The Housing Wealth of Nations*. Oxford: Wiley-Blackwell.

Smyth, H. (1985). *Property Companies and the Construction Industry in Britain*. Cambridge: Cambridge University Press.

Soederberg, S. (2005). 'The transnational debt architecture and emerging markets: The politics of paradoxes and punishment'. *Third World Quarterly*, 26(6), pp. 927–949.

Soederberg, S. (2014). 'Subprime housing goes south: Constructing securitized mortgages for the poor in Mexico'. *Antipode*, 47(2), pp. 481–499.

Soederberg, S. (2021). *Urban Displacements: Governing Surplus and Survival in Global Capitalism*. London and New York: Routledge.

Sönmez, M. (1992). *Türkiye'de Holdingler*. Ankara: Arkadaş Yayınevi.

Sönmez, M. (2010). *Teğet'in Yıkımı*. İstanbul: Yordam Yayınevi.

Sönmez, M. (2011). TOKİ'den Aslan Payı Kimlerin? *Express*, June.

Sönmez, M. (2012). AKP Rejiminin İnşaat Baronları. *Cumhuriyet*. Available at: https://www.cumhuriyet.com.tr/yazarlar/mustafa-sonmez/akp-rejiminin-insaat-baronlari-382848. [Accessed 1 Dec 2020].

Sönmez, M. (2015). *AK Faşizmin inşaat iskelesi*. Ankara: Notabene.

Sönmez, Ü. (2011). 'The political economy of market and regulatory reforms in Turkey: The logic and unintended consequences of ad-hoc strategies', *New Political Economy*, 16(1), pp.101–130.

Srivastava, R. & Jha, A. (2016) *Capital and Labour Standards in the Organised Construction Industry in India*. London: CDPR, SOAS.

Stephens, M., Lux, M. & Sunega, P. (2016). 'Post-socialist housing systems in Europe: Housing welfare regimes by default?' *Housing Studies*, 30(8), pp. 1210–1234.

Strassmann, P. (1970). 'The construction sector in economic development'. *The Scottish Journal of Political Economy*, 17, pp. 390–410.

Swyngedouw, E. (2012). 'Rent and Landed Property'. In: Fine, B. & Saad-Filho, A. (eds.), *The Elgar companion to Marxist economics*, pp. 310–315. Cheltenham: Edward Elgar.

Swyngedouw, E. (2017). 'Post-Truth and the Politics of Autocratic Neoliberalization'. In: Adaman, F., Akbulut, B. & Arsel, M. (eds.), *Neoliberal Turkey and its discontents: Economic policy and the environment under Erdogan*. London, New York: I.B. Tauris.

Şengül, H.T. (2003). 'On the trajectory of urbanisation in Turkey: An attempt at periodisation'. *International Development Planning Review*, 25(2), pp.153–168.

Şengül, H.T. (2012). 'Türkiye'nin Kentleşme Deneyiminin Dönemlenmesi'. In: Alpkaya, F. & Duru, B. (eds.), *1920'den Günümüze Türkiye'de Toplumsal Yapı ve Değişim*, pp. 405–451. Ankara: Phoneix Yayınevi.

Şenses, F. (1989). 'The nature and main characteristics of recent Turkish growth in exports of manufactures', *The Developing Economies*, 27(1), pp.19–33.

Tanyılmaz, K. (2015). 'The Deep Fracture in the Big Bourgeoisie of Turkey'. In: Balkan, N., Balkan, E. & Öncü, A. (eds), *The Neoliberal Landscape and the Rise of Islamist Capital in Turkey*, pp. 89–116. New York: Berghahn Books.

Taylor, J.B. (2007). 'Housing and monetary policy'. *Remarks for the Federal Reserve 2007 Jackson Hole Conference*. Available at: https://www.nber.org/system/files/working_papers/w13682/w13682.pdf. [Accessed 1 Dec 2020].

Taymaz, E. & Yılmaz, K. (2008). 'Integration with the global economy: The case of Turkish automobile and consumer electronics industries'. *TUSIAD-Koç University Economic Research Forum, Working Paper No. 0801*, February.

Tekeli, I. (1982). 'Türkiye'de Konut Sunumunun Davranışsal Nitelikleri ve Konut Kesiminde Bunalım'. In: Tekeli, I. & Keleş, R. (eds). *Konut 81'*, pp. 57–89. Ankara: Kent-Koop Yayınları.

Tekeli, I. (1998). 'Türkiye'de cumhuriyet döneminde kentsel gelişme ve kent planlaması'. In: *75 Yılda değişen kent ve mimarlık*. İstanbul: Türk Tarih Vakfı Yayınları.

Tibaijuka, A.K. (2009). *Building Prosperity: Housing and Economic Development*. London: Earthscan.

Toksöz, G. (2008). Türkiye'ye Yönelik Düzensiz Göçler ve Göçmenlerin İnşaat Sektöründe Enformel İstihdamı. PhD. Thesis, Ankara University.

Topal, A. (2002). 'Küreselleşme Sürecindeki Türkiye'yi Anlamaya Yarayan Bir Anahtar: Yeni Sağ'. *Praksis*, 7, pp. 63–84.

Topal, A., Özlem, C. &Yalman, G. (2015). 'Case study paper relating financialisation of the built environment to changing urban politics, social geographies, material flows and environmental improvement/degradation in Ankara'. *FESSUD Working Paper No. 116.*

Topal, A. (2019). 'The State, Crisis and Transformation of Small and Medium-sized Enterprise Finance in Turkey'. In: Yalman, G.L., Marois, T. & Güngen, A.R. (eds.), *The Political Economy of Financial Transformation in Turkey.* London, New York: Routledge.

Topalov, C. (1985). 'Prices, Profits and Rents in Residential Development: France 1960–80'. In: M. Ball, V. Bentivegna, M. Edwards, & M. Folin (eds.) *Land rent: housing and urban planning,* pp. 1–21. London: Croom Helm.

Tribe, K. (1977). 'Economic property and the theorisation of ground rent'. *Economy and Society,* 6(1) pp. 69–88.

Tsai, I.-C. & Chiang, S.-H. (2019). 'Exuberance and spillovers in housing markets: Evidence from first- and second-tier cities in China'. *Regional Science and Urban Economics,* 77, pp. 75–86.

Turhan, I. (2008). 'Housing sector in Turkey: Challenges and opportunities', *Central Bank Report.*

Türel, O. (1998). 'Türkiye'de Kamu Sektörünün Yeniden Yapılanması'. In: '*97 Sanayi Kongresi Bildiriler Kitabı,* pp. 149–156. Ankara: TMMOB.

Türel, A. (2015). 'Türkiye'de Konut Finansmanı'. In: *Konut,* pp. 61–72. Ankara: TMMOB Şehir Plancıları Odası Ankara Şubesi Yayını.

Türel, A. & Koç, H. (2015). 'Housing Production under Less-Regulated Market Conditions in Turkey'. *Journal of Housing and Built Environment,* 30, pp. 53–68.

Türk, Ş.Ş. & Altes, W.K. (2010). 'The planning system and land provision for social housing in Turkey'. *Housing Finance International,* Autumn 2010, pp. 26–32.

Türkün, A. (2011). 'Urban regeneration and hegemonic power relationships'. *International Planning Studies,* 16(1), pp. 61–72.

Türkün, A. (2014). *Mülk, Mahal, İnsan.* İstanbul: Bilgi Üniversitesi Yayınları.

Uzunkaya, M. (2013).'Uluslararası rekabet edebilirlik çerçevesinde Türk inşaat sektörünün yapısal analizi'. *The Ministry of Development of Turkey,* June 2013. Available at: https://sbb.gov.tr/wp-content/uploads/2018/11/Uluslararas%c4%b1_Rekab et_Edebilirlik_%c3%87er%c3%a7evesinde_T%c3%bcrk_%c4%b0n%c5%9faat _Sekt%c3%b6r%c3%bcn%c3%bcn_Yap%c4%b1sal_Analizi.pdf. [Accessed 1 Dec 2020].

Ünver, M. & Suri, L. (2020). 'Kentsel dönüşümün Fikirtepe'ye yansıması'. *İstanbul Ticaret Üniversitesi Teknoloji ve Uygulamalı Bilimler Dergisi,* 2(2), pp. 11–23.

Van Gunten, T. & Navot, E. (2018). 'Varieties of indebtedness: Financialization and mortgage market institutions in Europe'. *Social Science Research,* 70, pp. 90–106.

Van Loon, J., Oosterlynck, S. & Aalbers, M.B. (2018). 'Governing urban development in the low countries: From managerialism to entrepreneurialism and financialization'. *European Urban and Regional Studies*, 26(4), pp. 400–418.

Van Waeyenberge, E. & Bargawi, H. (2015). 'Moving beyond the paradox of macro-economic stability in Uganda?' *Journal of Contemporary African Studies*, 33(1), pp. 121–140.

Voyvoda, E. (2006). 'Fiscal Programming and Alternatives in Debt Management: The Turkish Experience'. In: Berglund, P.G. & Vernengo, M. (eds.), *The means to prosperity: fiscal policy reconsidered*, pp. 128–147. London: Routledge.

Vural, I.E. (2019). 'Restricted But Significant: Financialization of Households and Retail Banking Activities in Turkey'. In: Yalman, G.L., Marois, T. & Güngen, A.R. (eds.), *The Political Economy of Financial Transformation in Turkey*. London, New York: Routledge.

Waldron, R. (2018). 'Capitalizing on the state: The political economy of real estate investment trusts and the 'resolution' of the crisis'. *Geoforum*, 90, pp. 206–218.

Walker, R.A. (1974). 'Urban ground rent: Building a new conceptual framework'. *Antipode*, 6(1), pp. 51–58.

Ward, C. & Aalbers, M. (2016). 'The shitty rent business': What's the point of land rent theory? *Urban Studies*, 53(9), pp. 1760–1783.

Watson, M. (2009). 'Planning for a future of asset- based welfare? New labour, financialized economic agency and the housing market'. *Planning Practice and Research*, 24(1), pp. 41–56.

Watson, M. (2010). 'House price Keynesianism and the contradictions of the modern investor subject'. *Housing Studies*, 25(3), pp. 413–426.

Weeks, J. (1997). 'The law of value and the analysis of underdevelopment'. *Historical Materialism*, 1, pp. 91–112.

Weeks, J. (2010). *Capital, Exploitation and Economic Crisis*. London: Routledge.

Wellings, F. (2006). *British Housebuilders: History and Analysis*. Oxford: Blackwell Publishing.

Wells, J. & Jason, A. (2010). 'Employment relationships and organizing strategies in the informal construction sector'. *African Studies Quarterly*, 11(2–3), pp. 107–124.

White, P. (1986). 'Land availability, land banking and the price of land for housing: A review of recent debates', *Land Development Studies*, 3(2), pp. 101–111.

Wijburg, G. & Aalbers, M.B. (2017). 'The alternative financialization of the German housing market', *Housing Studies*, 32(7), pp. 968–989.

Wissoker, P. (2016). 'Putting the supplier in housing supply: An overview of the growth and concentration of large homebuilders in the United States (1990–2007)', *Housing Policy Debate*, (26)3, pp. 536–562.

Wood, E.M. (2002). *The Origin of Capitalism: A Longer View*. London: Verso.

Wood, E.M. (2003). *Empire of Capital*. London: Verso.

Wu, F. (2015). 'Commodification and housing market cycles in Chinese Cities', *International Journal of Housing Policy*, 15(1), pp. 6–26.

Wu, F., Chen, J., Pan, F., Gallent, N. & Zhang, F. (2020). 'Assetization: The Chinese path to housing financialization', *Annals of the American Association of Geographers*, 110(5), pp. 1483–1499.

Yalman, G.L. (2002). 'The Turkish State and the Bourgeoisie in a Historical Perspective: A Relativist Paradigm or A Panoply of Hegemonic Strategies?' In: Balkan, N. & Savran, S. (eds.), *The Politics of Permanent Crisis: Class, Ideology and the State in Turkey*, pp. 21–54. New York: Nova Science Publishers.

Yalman, G.L. (2009). *Transition to Neoliberalism: The Case of Turkey in the 1980s.* Istanbul: Bilgi University Press.

Yalman, G.L. (2019). 'The Neoliberal Transformation of State and Market'. In: Yalman, G.L., Marois, T. & Güngen, A.R. (eds.), *The Political Economy of Financial Transformation in Turkey*. London, New York: Routledge.

Yalman, G.L., Marois, T. & Güngen, A.R. (2019). 'Debating Financial Transformation in Turkey'. In: Yalman, G.L., Marois, T. & Güngen, A.R. (eds.), *The Political Economy of Financial Transformation in Turkey*. London, New York: Routledge.

Yeldan, E. (1995). 'Surplus creation and extraction under structural adjustment: Turkey, 1980–1992', *Review of Radical Political Economics*, 27(2), pp. 38–72.

Yeldan, E. (2001). *Küreselleşme Surecinde Türkiye Ekonomisi: Bölüşüm, Birikim, Büyüme.* İstanbul: İletişim Yayınları.

Yeldan, E. (2018). 'Türkiye ekonomisi nereye koşuyor?'. *T24*, July 5, [online]. Available at: https://t24.com.tr/k24/yazi/turkiye-ekonomisi,1856. [Accessed 1 Dec 2020].

Yeşilbağ, M. (2016). 'Hegemonyanın harcı: AKP döneminde inşaata dayalı birikim rejimi'. *Ankara Üniversitesi SBF Dergisi*, 71(2), pp. 599–626.

Yeşilbağ, M. (2016). 'Müteessif müteahhitler'. *soL Haber Portalı*, March 11. Available at: https://haber.sol.org.tr/yazarlar/melih-yesilbag/muteessif-muteahhitler-231161. [Accessed 1 Dec 2020].

Yeşilbağ, M. (2018). 'İnşaat sektöründe tehlike çanları'. *soL Haber Portalı*, February 18. Available at: https://haber.sol.org.tr/yazarlar/melih-yesilbag/insaat-sektoru nde-tehlike-canlari-228884. [Accessed 1 Dec 2020].

Yıldırım, D. (2009). 'AKP ve Neo-liberal Popülizm', In Uzgel, İ. and Duru, B. (eds.), *AKP Kitabı: Bir Dönüşümün Bilançosu*, Ankara: Phoenix Yayınevi, pp. 66–107.

Yılmaz, Z. (2020). 'Erdoğan's presidential regime and strategic legalism: Turkish democracy in the twilight zone'. *Southeast European and Black Sea Studies*, 20(2), pp. 265–287.

Yönder, A. (1987). 'Informal land and housing markets: The case of Istanbul, Turkey'. *Journal of the American Planning Association*, 53(2), pp. 213–219.

Zangger, C. (2021). 'The contexts of residential preferences. An experimental examination of contextual influences in housing decisions'. *Housing Studies*, pp. 1–23.

Documents

BRSA. (2002). Banking Sector Reform: Progress Report, July 2002, Ankara: BRSA.

BRSA. (2020). Key Indicators of the Turkish Banking Sector, March 2020. Available at: https://www.bddk.org.tr/Veri/EkGetir/8?ekId=44.

Bülten. (2018). Sanayinin Sorunları ve Analizleri: İnşaatla büyümede deniz bitti. Nov, 43(1), TMMOB Makine Mühendisleri Odası. Available at: https://www.emo.org.tr/genel/bizden_detay.php?kod=125719.

CBRT. (2011). Financial Stability Report. May, Volume 12, Ankara. Available at: https://www.tcmb.gov.tr/wps/wcm/connect/EN/TCMB+EN/Main+Menu/Publications/Reports/Financial+Stability+Report/2011/Sayi+12.

Chamber of Accounts. (2012). Kamu İşletmeleri Genel Raporu [Public Enterprises General Report]. Available at: https://www.sayistay.gov.tr/tr/Upload/62643830/files/raporlar/genel_raporlar/kit_genel/Kamu%20%C4%B0%C5%9Fletmeleri%202012%20Y%C4%B1l%C4%B1%20Genel%20Raporu.pdf.

Chamber of Accounts. (2013). Kamu İşletmeleri Genel Raporu [Public Enterprises General Report]. Available at:https://www.sayistay.gov.tr/tr/Upload/62643830/files/raporlar/genel_raporlar/kit_genel/Kamu%20%C4%B0%C5%9Fletmeleri%202013%20Y%C4%B1l%C4%B1%20Genel%20Raporu.pdf.

Chamber of Accounts. (2014). Kamu İşletmeleri Genel Raporu [Public Enterprises General Report]. Available at: https://www.sayistay.gov.tr/tr/Upload/62643830/files/raporlar/genel_raporlar/kit_genel/Kamu%20%C4%B0%C5%9Fletmeleri%202014%20Y%C4%B1l%C4%B1%20Genel%20Raporu.pdf.

Chamber of Accounts. (2015). Kamu İşletmeleri Genel Raporu [Public Enterprises General Report]. Available at: https://www.sayistay.gov.tr/tr/Upload/62643830/files/raporlar/genel_raporlar/kit_genel/2015_Ki2.pdf.

Chamber of Accounts. (2016). Kamu İşletmeleri Genel Raporu [Public Enterprises General Report]. Available at: https://www.sayistay.gov.tr/tr/Upload/62643830/files/raporlar/genel_raporlar/kit_genel/2016_ki.pdf.

Chamber of Accounts. (2017). Kamu İşletmeleri Genel Raporu [Public Enterprises General Report]. Available at: https://www.sayistay.gov.tr/tr/Upload/62643830/files/raporlar/genel_raporlar/kit_genel/Kamu%20%C4%B0%C5%9Fletmeleri%202017%20Y%C4%B1l%C4%B1%20Genel%20Raporu.pdf.

Chamber of Accounts. (2018). Kamu İşletmeleri Genel Raporu [Public Enterprises General Report]. Available at: https://www.sayistay.gov.tr/tr/Upload/62643830/files/raporlar/genel_raporlar/kit_genel/2018_Ki.pdf.

EMF Hypostat. (2013). A Review of Europe's Mortgage and Housing Markets. Available at: https://www.nuigalway.ie/media/housinglawrightsandpolicy/HYPOSTAT_2013.pdf.

EMF Hypostat. (2018).Unveiling Annual Statistics and Insights on European (and beyond) Housing and Mortgage Markets".Available at:https://hypo.org/ecbc/press -release/emf-hypostat-2018-unveiling-annual-statistics-insights-european-bey ond-housing-mortgage-markets/.

EMF Hypostat. (2019). A Review of Europe's Mortgage and Housing Markets. Available at: https://hypo.org/app/uploads/sites/3/2019/09/HYPOSTAT-2019_web.pdf.

EMLAK KONUT GYO. (2017). Faaliyet Raporu [Activity Report]. Available at: http: //www.emlakkonut.com.tr/_Assets/Upload/Images/file/Yatirimci/faaliyetraporl ari/RAPOR%20FINAL%202.pdf.

ENR. (2018). Top 250 International contractors. Available at: https://www.enr.com /toplists/2018-Top-250-International-Contractors-1.

GYODER. (2019). Türkiye Gayrimenkul Sektörü 2019 [Turkey Real Estate Sector in 2019]. Available at: https://www.gyoder.org.tr/uploads/GYODER%20Yay%C4% B1nlar%C4%B1/GOSTERGE-CEYREK4-2019-web.pdf.

IMF. (2011). Global Financial Stability Report, April 2011: Durable Financial Stability: Getting There from Here. Available at: https://www.imf.org/en/Publicati ons/GFSR/Issues/2016/12/31/Global-Financial-Stability-Report-April-2011-Dura ble-Financial-Stability-Getting-There-from-24324.

IMF. (2014). Turkey. Country Report No. 14/329, December. Available at: https://www .imf.org/external/pubs/ft/scr/2014/cr14329.pdf.

IMF. (2017). Turkey: Selected Issues.Country Report No. 17/33, February, 2017. Available at: https://www.imf.org/en/Publications/CR/Issues/2017/02/03/Turkey-Selected -Issues-44615.

IMF. (2018). Turkey. Country Report No. 18/110, April. Available at: https://www.imf.org /en/Publications/CR/Issues/2018/04/30/Turkey-2018-Article-IV-Consultation-Press -Release-Staff-Report-and-Statement-by-the-45822.

IMF. (2019). Turkey. Country Report No. 1/395, December. Available at: https://www .imf.org/en/Publications/CR/Issues/2019/12/26/Turkey-2019-Article-IV-Consultat ion-Press-Release-Staff-Report-and-Statement-by-the-48920.

IMO (İnşaat Mühendisleri Odası [Chamber of civil Engineers]). (2008). TOKI değer-lendirme raporu [TOKI assessment report]. Available at: http://www.imo.org.tr /genel/bizden_detay.php?kod=629&tipi=4&sube=0.

IMO (İnşaat Mühendisleri Odası [Chamber of civil Engineers]). (2011). Genel Seçime Giderken İnşaat Mühendisleri Odası'nın Talepleri [Demands of the Chamber of Civil Engineers While Going to the General Election], Available at: https://docpla yer.biz.tr/33158347-2011-genel-secime-giderken-insaat-muhendisleri-odasi-nin -talepleri.html.

INTES. (2014). İnşaat Sektörü Raporu [Construction Sector Report]. March, 2014. Available at: https://silo.tips/download/gr-ntes-naat-sektr-raporu-sayfa-1.

OECD. (2011). Economic Policy Reforms. Available at: https://www.oecd-ilibrary.org /economics/economic-policy-reforms-2011/housing-and-the-economy-policies-for -renovation_growth-2011-46-en.

SBB. (2018). İnşaat, Mühendislik — Mimarlık, Teknik Müşavirlik ve Müteahhitlik Hizmetleri Özel İhtisas Komisyonu Raporu [Construction, Engineering — Architecture, Technical Consultancy and Contracting Services Special Expertise Commission Report]. Available at: http://onbirinciplan.gov.tr/oik-ve-calisma-grubu -listeleri/insaat-muhendislik-mimarlik-teknik-musavirlik-ve-muteahhitlik-hiz metleri/.

TBB. (2013). Bankalarımız 2012. Available at: https://www.tbb.org.tr/Content/Upl oad/istatistikiraporlar/ekler/669/Bankalarimiz_2012.pdf.

TBB. (2019). 60. Yılında Türkiye Bankalar Birliği ve Türkiye Bankacılık Sistemi 1958-2018 [Banks Association of Turkey in the 60th Year and Turkey Banking System 1958-2018.]. Available at: https://www.tbb.org.tr/Content/Upload/Dokuman/7617/60 ._Yilinda_Turkiye_Bankalar_Birligi.pdf.

The Report: Turkey. (2012). Oxford Business Group. Available at: https://oxfordbusine ssgroup.com/turkey-2012.

TMB. (2014). 2013'ün Mirası: Belirsizlik ve Kaygılar ile Siyaset ve Ekonomide Yeni Bir Döneme Girerken Dünya — Türkiye — İnşaat Sektörü [2013 Heritage: Uncertainty and Concerns With A New Era in Politics and Economics at the onset of World — Turkey — Construction Sector]. January, 2014. Available at: https://www.tmb.org.tr /arastirma_yayinlar/tmb_bulten_ocak2014.pdf.

TMB. (2015). Gündem [Agenda].June, 2015. Ankara: Türkiye Müteahhitler Birliği. Available at: https://www.tmmmb.org.tr/images/basindan/demir_inozu_gundem _Haziran_2015.pdf.

TMB. (2019). Gündem [Agenda].Sırada Ekonomi Var [Time for the Economy]. July, 2019. Available at: https://www.tmb.org.tr/arastirma_yayinlar/tmb_bulten_tem muz2019.pdf.

TMB (2020). İnşaat Sektörü Analizi: Resesyon Endişelerinden Kırılgan Toparlanmaya [Construction Sector Analysis: From Recession Concerns to Vulnerable Recovery], January, 2020. Available at: https://www.tmb.org.tr/arastirma_yayinlar/tmb_bulten _ocak2020.pdf.

TOKI. (2011). Building Turkey of the future. Corporate profile 2010/2011. Available at: https://www.toki.gov.tr/content/images/main-page-slider/30102016224921-pdf.

TOKI. (2014). TOKI Housing Projects. Ankara: Toplu Konut İdaresi Başkanlığı Yayınları.

TOKI. (2016). Corporate profile. Available at: https://www.toki.gov.tr/content/ima ges/main-page-slider/16012017212815-pdf.

TOKI. (2018). Konut Üretim Raporu [Housing Production Report]. Available at: https: //www.toki.gov.tr/AppResources/UserFiles/files/FaaliyetOzeti/ozet.pdf.

TOKI. (2019). Toplu Konut İdaresi Başkanlığı, Kuruluş ve Tarihçe [Housing Development Administration, Establishment and History]. Available at: https://www.toki.gov.tr/.

TSKB. (2015). Büyüme Bağlamında İnşaat Sektörü [Construction Sector in Terms of Growth]. January, 2015. Available at: http://www.tskb.com.tr/i/content/2342_1 _TSKB_BuyumeBaglamindaInsaatSektoru_Ocak2015.pdf.

TURKSTAT.(2011). Population and Housing Survey Report. Available at: https://tuik web.tuik.gov.tr/PreHaberBultenleri.do?id=15843.

Undersecretariat of Treasury. (2005). Kamu İşletmeleri Raporu [Public Enterprise Report]. Available at: https://www.hmb.gov.tr/kamu-sermayeli-kurulus-ve-isletme ler-raporlari.

Undersecretariat of Treasury. (2006). Kamu İşletmeleri Raporu [Public Enterprise Report]. Available at: https://www.hmb.gov.tr/kamu-sermayeli-kurulus-ve-isletme ler-raporlari.

Undersecretariat of Treasury. (2007). Kamu İşletmeleri Raporu [Public Enterprise Report]. Available at: https://www.hmb.gov.tr/kamu-sermayeli-kurulus-ve-isletme ler-raporlari.

Undersecretariat of Treasury. (2008). Kamu İşletmeleri Raporu [Public Enterprise Report]. Available at: https://www.hmb.gov.tr/kamu-sermayeli-kurulus-ve-isletme ler-raporlari.

Undersecretariat of Treasury. (2009). Kamu İşletmeleri Raporu [Public Enterprise Report]. Available at: https://www.hmb.gov.tr/kamu-sermayeli-kurulus-ve-isletme ler-raporlari.

Undersecretariat of Treasury. (2010). Kamu İşletmeleri Raporu [Public Enterprise Report]. Available at: https://www.hmb.gov.tr/kamu-sermayeli-kurulus-ve-isletme ler-raporlari.

Undersecretariat of Treasury. (2011). Kamu İşletmeleri Raporu [Public Enterprise Report]. Available at: https://www.hmb.gov.tr/kamu-sermayeli-kurulus-ve-isletme ler-raporlari.

World Bank. (1993). Housing: Enabling Markets to Work/With Technical Supplements. Washington, DC: World Bank.

World Bank. (2001). Turkey: Public expenditure and institutional review, reforming budgetary institutions for effective government. Available at: https://openknowle dge.worldbank.org/handle/10986/15482?show=full.

World Bank. (2015)'.Rise of the Anatolian Tigers Turkey Urbanization Review'. April. Available at: https://www.worldbank.org/en/country/turkey/publication/turkey -urbanization-review.

World Bank (2018). 'Turkey Economic Monitor'. December, 2018. Available at: https: //elibrary.worldbank.org/doi/abs/10.1596/31129.

Daily Newspapers and News Portals (2002–2020)

Ajans Press. (2019). 'Türkiye'nin yüzde 12'si gecekonduda yaşıyor'. *Ajans Press.* 14 May [online]. Available at: https://www.iha.com.tr/haber-turkiyenin-yuzde-12si-gece konduda-yasiyor-780125/. [Accessed 1 Dec 2020].

Ant, O. & Koc, C. (2019). 'Turkey Resumes Push to Boost Budget With Central Bank's Cash'. *Bloomberg.* 27 June [online]. Available at: https://www.bloomberg.com/news /articles/2019-06-27/turkey-prepares-bill-to-transfer-central-bank-reserve-funds -bht?sref=pVYFKQyF. [Accessed 1 Dec 2020].

Bloomberg Businessweek. (2016). 'Special Report: Turkey'. *Bloomberg Businessweek.* [online]. Available at: https://issuu.com/umsinternational/docs/turkey. [Accessed 1 Dec 2020].

Cumhuriyet. (2019). 'Yüzde 118 arttı! İşte bankaların el koyduğu konut sayısı'. *Cumhuriyet.* 8 March [online]. Available at: https://www.cumhuriyet.com.tr/haber/yuzde-118 -artti-iste-bankalarin-el-koydugu-konut-sayisi-1285185. [Accessed 1 Dec 2020].

Cumhuriyet. (2020). 'Türkiye'de müteahhit sayısı: 453 bin 497 Almanya'da: 3 bin 550'. *Cumhuriyet.* 28 Jan [online]. Available at: https://www.cumhuriyet.com.tr/yazar lar/mustafa-balbay/turkiyede-muteahhit-sayisi-453-bin-497-almanyada-3-bin-550 -1716733. [Accessed 1 Dec 2020].

Daily Sabah. (2019). 'Financial restructuring for large-scale firms with debt over TL 25 million'. *Daily Sabah.* 14 Oct [online]. Available at: https://www.dailysabah.com /finance/2019/10/14/financial-restructuring-for-large-scale-firms-with-debt-over-tl -25-million. [Accessed 1 Dec 2020].

Daily Sabah. (2019). 'Reform package shows gov't will to address primary economic concerns'. *Daily Sabah.* 12 Apr [online]. Available at: https://www.dailysabah.com /economy/2019/04/12/reform-package-shows-govt-will-to-address-primary-econo mic-concerns. [Accessed 1 Dec 2020].

DISK. (2014). '"İş Sağlığı ve Güvenliği" toplantısında Başbakan Ahmet Davutoğlu'na sunulan rapor'. *DISK.* 19 Sep [online]. Available at: http://disk.org.tr/2014/09/is -sagligi-ve-guvenligi-toplantisinda-basbakan-ahmet-davutogluna-sunulan-rapor/. [Accessed 1 Dec 2020].

Emlakkulisi. (2018). 'İş dünyası tahsilat ve ödeme sorunuyla boğuşuyor!'. *Emlakkulisi.* 31 Dec [online]. Available at: https://emlakkulisi.com/is-dunyasi-tahsilat-ve-odeme -sorunuyla-bogusuyor/593819. [Accessed 1 Dec 2020].

Ersoy, E. & Kozok, F. (2020). 'Turkey to Add $3 Billion to Capital at Three State Banks'. *Bloomberg.* 11 May [online]. Available at: https://www.bloomberg.com/news /articles/2020-05-11/turkey-to-boost-state-banks-capital-by-3-billion-over-pande mic?sref=pVYFKQyF. [Accessed 1 Dec 2020].

Fortune. (2014). 'İnşaat sektörüne dur, sanayiye ilerle derseniz çöküntü başlar'. *Fortune*. 12 Dec [online]. Available at: https://www.fortuneturkey.com/insaat-sektorune-dur -sanayiye-ilerle-derseniz-cokuntu-baslar-4404. [Accessed 1 Dec 2020].

Gazete Duvar. (2018). 'İnşaatta İzmir rüyası'. *Gazete Duvar*. 29 May [online]. Available at: https://www.gazeteduvar.com.tr/ekonomi/2018/05/29/insaatta-izmir-ruyasi. [Accessed 1 Dec 2020].

Gazete Vatan. (2012). 'İstanbul'da bu semtlerden konut alan kazanıyor'. *Gazete Vatan*. 02 Feb [online]. Available at: https://www.gazetevatan.com/arsiv/istanbulda-bu -semtlerden-konut-alan-kazaniyor-425009. [Accessed 19 February 2023].

HaberTürk. (2013). 'Kredi kullananlar yaşadı!'. *HaberTürk*. 05 May [online]. Available at: https://www.haberturk.com/ekonomi/para/haber/841566-kredi-kullananlar-yas adi. [Accessed 19 February 2023].

Hürriyet. (2014). 'Sanayiden kaçıp konut yapıyoruz'. *Hürriyet*. 24 July [online]. Available at: https://www.hurriyet.com.tr/ekonomi/sanayiden-kacip-konut-yapiyoruz-26874 076. [Accessed 1 Dec 2020].

Hürriyet. (2016). 'Evde büyük faiz fırsatı'. Hürriyet. 8 November [online]. Available at: https://www.hurriyet.com.tr/ekonomi/evde-buyuk-faiz-firsati-40272307 [Accessed 19 February 2023].

Hürriyet. (2018). 'Bakan Kurum açıkladı: Hedefimiz 2030 yılına kadar 7.5 milyon konutu dönüştürmek'. *Hürriyet*. 19 Nov [online]. Available at: https://www.hurri yet.com.tr/ekonomi/bakan-kurum-acikladi-hedefimiz-2030-yilina-kadar-7-5-mil yon-konutu-donusturmek-41023930. [Accessed 1 Dec 2020].

Hürriyet. (2020). 'Ziraat Bankası konut kredisi faiz oranı: 0,64'den başlayan Vakıfbank Halkbank kredi oranları'. *Hürriyet*. 5 June [online]. Available at: https://www.hurri yet.com.tr/galeri-ziraat-bankasi-konut-kredisi-faiz-orani-0-64den-baslayan-vakifb ank-halkbank-kredi-oranlari-41533692/1. [Accessed 1 Dec 2020].

Milliyet. (2013). 'Konutun röntgenini çekti Ali Babacan'a rapor verdi'. 16 March [online]. Available at: https://www.milliyet.com.tr/ekonomi/konutun-rontgenini-cekti-ali -babacan-a-rapor-verdi-1681002. [Accessed 1 Dec 2020].

Milliyet. (2016). 'Cumhurbaşkanı: Yıllık faiz oranlarını yüzde 9'a çekin sürümden kazanın'. 4 Aug [online]. Available at: https://www.milliyet.com.tr/ekonomi /cumhurbaskani-yillik-faiz-oranlarini-yuzde-9a-cekin-surumden-kazanin-2289 460. [Accessed 1 Dec 2020].

Milliyet. (2017). 'Gayrimenkulde büyük güç birliği!'. *Milliyet*. 24 Feb [online]. Available at:https://www.milliyet.com.tr/ekonomi/gayrimenkulde-buyuk-guc-birligi-2402105. [Accessed 1 Dec 2020].

Milliyet. (2017). 'Gayrimenkul sertifikalarına talep patladı! Yetişen alacak'. *Milliyet*. 31 March [online]. Available at: https://www.milliyet.com.tr/ekonomi/gayrimen kul-sertifikalarina-talep-patladi-yetisen-alacak-2424000. [Accessed 1 Dec 2020].

NTV. (2012). '400 milyar dolar harekete geçecek'. *NTV*. 3 Oct [online]. Available at: https://www.ntv.com.tr/turkiye/400-milyar-dolar-harekete-gececek,CsbafQ2 SvUWJeRsr6vi4KQ. [Accessed 1 Dec 2020].

Sabah. (2007). 'Kentsel Dönüşüm ve Gayrimenkul Yatırım Konferansı'. *Sabah*. 13 Nov [online]. Available at: https://www.sabah.com.tr/yazarlar/yildirim/2007/11/13 /konut_kentsel_gayrimenkul_konferans. [Accessed 1 Dec 2020].

Sabah. (2012). 'Gayrimenkulde dev buluşma'. *Sabah*. 20 Jan [online]. Available at: https://www.sabah.com.tr/ekonomi/2012/01/20/gayrimenkulde-dev-bulu sma-ahmet-calik-turkuvaz-medya-grubu--calik-holding. [Accessed 1 Dec 2020].

Sabah. (2019). 'Dar gelirliye 20 yıl vadeli ucuz konut kredisi'. *Sabah*. 8 Nov [online]. Available at: https://www.sabah.com.tr/ekonomi/2019/11/08/dar-gelirliye-20-yil -vadeli-ucuz-konut-kredisi. [Accessed 1 Dec 2020].

Sigorta Dünyası. (2020). 'Bina tamamlama sigortası zorunlu ama yaptıran yok'. *Sigorta Dünyası*. 20 March [online]. Available at: https://www.sigortadunyasi.com.tr/2020 /03/20/servet-gurkan-bina-tamamlama-sigortasi-zorunlu-ama-yaptiran-yok/. [Accessed 1 Dec 2020].

Sözcü. (2018). 'Konutta indirim süresi uzatıldı'. *Sözcü*. 12 June [online]. Available at: https://www.sozcu.com.tr/2018/ekonomi/konutta-indirim-suresi-uzatildi-2464 231/. [Accessed 1 Dec 2020].

Sözcü. (2020). 'Konut kredisi şartları nelerdir?' *Sözcü*. 14 June [online]. Available at: https://www.sozcu.com.tr/2020/sigorta/konut-kredisi-sartlari-nelerdir-en-fazla -ne-kadar-konut-kredisi-kullanabilir-2szcu-5651604/. [Accessed 1 Dec 2020].

Takvim. (2020). 'Konut kredisi faiz oranları değişti!' *Takvim*. 6 Nov [online]. Available at: https://www.takvim.com.tr/ekonomi/2020/11/05/konut-kredisi-faiz-oranl ari-degisti-iste-kasim-ayi-tarifesi-099-uzerinden-120-ay-vade-son-dakika-konut -kredisi-faiz-depremi/3. [Accessed 1 Dec 2020].

Telegraph. (2019). 'Three family murder-suicides within ten days shock Turkey as the country faces record unemployment'. *Telegraph*. 17 Nov [online]. Available at: https://www.telegraph.co.uk/news/2019/11/17/three-family-murder-suicides-wit hin-ten-days-shock-turkey-country/. [Accessed 1 Dec 2020].

Index

Absolute rent   18, 21, 22, 22*n*7, 27, 28, 31, 31*n*9, 32, 33, 34, 41, 48

Absolute surplus-value   43, 43*n*17

Abstract labour   4, 5

Advanced-capitalist countries   69, 83, 84, 85, 85*n*14, 118, 122, 125, 131, 188, 191, 192, 216, 250, 251, 253

Affordable   38, 38*n*13, 39, 39*n*14, 40, 83, 86, 91, 92, 93, 129, 141, 144, 152, 157, 158, 159*n*7, 159*t*2, 160, 162, 163, 164, 165, 167, 195, 198, 217, 218*f*30, 219, 235, 240, 240*n*12, 240*n*13, 241, 242, 244, 248, 261, 267, 269, 270

Afghanistan   206

AKP   2, 95, 109, 113, 114, 115, 116, 117, 117*n*6, 125, 127, 128, 129, 129*n*11, 130, 131, 132, 133, 136, 149, 151, 155, 156, 162, 172, 178, 180, 181, 183, 185, 187, 188, 190, 191, 195, 195*n*2, 196, 197, 199, 199*n*6, 203, 208, 213, 214, 218, 222, 223, 228, 244, 246, 248, 249, 253, 254, 257, 260, 262, 267, 271

Algeria   246

Amnesty laws   137, 146, 176, 258*n*22

Analytical   1, 4, 6, 7, 10, 13, 15*n*1, 18, 54, 55, 57, 64, 72, 94, 95, 97, 229, 263, 264

ANAP   105, 107, 108, 109, 110, 114, 118, 141, 142, 145, 146, 149, 152

Anatolian   103, 107, 108, 109, 132, 157, 163, 176, 210, 240, 241

Anglo-Saxon   66, 68, 79*n*13, 88

Ankara   13, 138*n*4, 138*n*5, 145, 163, 181, 209, 210*f*26, 220

Artificial scarcities   34, 41, 52, 156, 207, 208, 219

Asset   1, 36, 44, 46, 49, 56, 63, 73, 75, 76, 82, 84, 87, 87*n*15, 89, 90, 111, 112, 114, 124, 127, 141, 147, 148, 168, 169, 169*f*9, 172, 174, 180, 185, 193, 194*f*17, 195*n*2, 200, 201, 212, 213, 236, 250, 252, 256, 262, 269

Austerity   66, 112, 114, 115, 163, 183

Australia   76*n*7, 78*n*9, 82

Authoritarian   2, 3, 7, 51, 68, 95, 96, 100, 101, 105, 106, 113, 115, 129, 130, 131, 133, 134, 141, 143, 147, 153, 154, 155, 156, 178, 183, 208, 222, 223, 247, 260, 262, 267, 270

Autonomy   2, 17, 61, 97, 99, 115, 118, 131, 143, 153, 160, 161*n*9

Bailout   256, 257

Balance of payments   66, 103, 112, 128

Balance of power   7, 45, 52, 68, 89, 98, 100, 102, 107, 130, 134, 152, 154, 183, 247, 262, 267

Banking   3, 56, 58, 104, 107, 108, 109, 111, 112, 113, 115, 117, 118, 119*f*2, 121, 122, 123, 123*f*7, 126, 143, 147, 149, 158, 188, 189, 190, 196, 201, 219, 231, 249, 256, 258, 269

Bankrupt   50, 79, 113, 121, 129, 148, 149, 185, 203, 227, 231, 237, 239, 242, 254, 257

Beneficiaries   102, 111, 131, 142, 143, 144, 145, 148, 158, 165, 178, 182, 214, 240, 244, 252, 270

Bond   62, 75, 76, 91, 122, 126, 148, 168, 174, 185, 186*t*7, 190, 247, 249, 250

Boom   2, 3, 39, 46, 49, 50, 52, 54, 77, 79, 88, 106, 110, 120, 123, 131, 184, 185, 188, 192, 195, 196, 197, 203, 208, 209, 211, 212, 214*n*9, 217, 219, 222, 224, 236, 258, 264, 266, 269

Borsa Istanbul   122, 172, 187, 250, 251

Bourgeoisie   98, 131, 154, 162

Brazil   38*n*13, 70, 76*n*7, 80, 82, 88, 93, 214*n*23

Bretton Woods   66, 104, 113, 116

Bubble   78*n*11, 87*n*15, 211, 211*n*16, 212, 257, 269

Budget   91, 106, 106*n*3, 112, 117, 119*f*3, 128, 131, 142, 143, 147, 148, 160, 163, 241

Builder   24, 30, 35, 40, 42*n*16, 44, 44*n*20, 45, 46, 46*n*21, 47, 48, 50, 51, 74, 75, 77, 139, 142, 144, 157, 160, 162, 167, 203, 228, 230, 232, 234, 236, 238, 242, 252, 264, 265

Building Permits   232, 233, 233*n*9, 239, 258, 259*f*36

Building process   157, 170, 230, 235, 241

Built environment   26, 28, 30, 35, 39, 152, 207, 223, 263, 267

Business associations   114*n*5, 130, 132, 231, 240*n*13, 243, 246

Business groups   102, 107, 109, 111, 114*n*5, 120, 129, 161, 222, 226, 234, 236, 247

Bust   2, 3, 49, 50, 52, 77, 78, 79n12, 123, 196,
    209, 211, 216, 219, 220, 237, 248, 258, 259,
    264, 266, 269
Buy-to-let   215
Buy-to-sell   213n18, 214, 216

Canada   82
Capital accumulation   2, 6, 13, 16, 17, 18, 26,
    28, 31, 33, 40, 42, 44, 48, 51, 56, 57, 58, 62,
    65, 69, 88, 95, 97, 99, 101, 103, 106, 107,
    110, 112, 120, 125, 133, 134, 148, 149, 152,
    223, 248, 257, 263, 264, 270
Capital flows   3, 19, 21, 32, 34, 51, 69, 78, 80,
    108, 110, 118, 120f4, 122, 125, 126, 127, 128,
    131, 135, 195n3, 223, 226, 246, 247, 249,
    251, 254, 258
Capital fractions   58, 100, 101, 107, 114, 127,
    129, 130, 131, 132, 133, 142, 185, 218, 224,
    240n13, 247, 248, 268, 270
Capital gains   3, 30, 30n8, 35, 36, 44, 45, 46,
    52, 75, 76, 77, 79, 82, 83, 85, 86, 90, 111,
    118, 121, 139, 147, 149n18, 163, 168, 170,
    171t6, 181, 182, 212, 213, 213n18, 214, 216,
    220, 224, 229, 242, 251, 265, 266, 269
Capital market   75, 76, 81, 82, 83, 91, 94, 117,
    125, 130n12, 147, 148, 150, 159, 163n10,
    168, 171, 172, 180, 183, 185, 186, 187, 188,
    197, 213, 250, 251, 252, 257, 265, 268
Capitalisation   62, 63, 71, 73, 76, 80, 123, 250,
    251, 265
CCFCC   72, 74, 80, 88, 265
Central Bank   13, 105, 115, 117, 125, 126n8, 128,
    151, 186, 195, 195n3, 209, 219, 258, 269
Centralisation   2, 51, 59, 101, 105, 132, 134, 143,
    145, 153, 155, 156, 179, 222, 223, 256, 264,
    268, 270
Certificates   59, 147, 148, 150, 172, 187, 225,
    230, 247, 258
Chile   65n3, 188, 214n23
China   43n18, 88, 93, 226, 246n17
Circuit of capital   42, 44, 47, 68, 98, 103
Circulation of capital   22, 28, 62, 64, 71, 229
Circulation of revenues   16, 22, 28, 29, 30, 31,
    35, 46, 48, 49, 52, 76, 162, 196, 213, 228,
    263, 264
Class contradictions   97, 99
Class fractions   7, 14, 26, 95, 98, 100, 102, 132,
    134, 256

Class struggle   10, 72, 97, 98, 99, 100, 223
Clientelism   131, 153, 246
Coercion   96, 133, 177, 178
Collateral   79, 84, 85, 91, 174, 186, 200, 201,
    236, 252, 266
Collateralised debt obligations   79, 82
Commercial banks   3, 81, 83, 88, 92, 118, 123,
    125, 140, 143, 148, 150, 168, 184, 186, 188,
    190, 192, 193, 195, 219, 252, 253, 268
Commercial capital   58, 61, 62, 98
Commercialisation   72, 118, 138, 139, 140, 141,
    146, 150, 177, 247
Commodification   3, 36, 53, 67, 70, 71, 72, 73,
    74, 86, 88, 89, 90, 91, 93, 95, 131, 133, 152,
    171, 187, 222, 224, 265, 266, 267
Commodity calculation   72, 73, 86, 160, 167,
    178, 187
Commodity form   43, 72, 73, 75, 80, 83, 92,
    120, 159, 167, 191, 219, 266, 268, 269
Commons   90, 91, 152, 240n11, 267
Compensation   175, 175n17, 176, 177
Competition   5, 16, 17, 19, 21, 24, 27, 41, 44, 45,
    47, 55, 61, 62, 65, 66n4, 72, 80, 100, 102,
    107, 111, 116, 146, 148, 151, 163, 170, 225,
    230, 233, 234, 235, 245
Concordat   128, 254, 254n20
Conglomerates   102, 103, 107, 122, 140,
    244, 246
Consent   114, 127, 175, 177, 178, 180, 233
Consolidation   2, 14, 67, 95, 96, 103, 106, 113,
    122, 129, 130, 133, 134, 135, 143, 152, 230,
    251, 267
Constitution   97, 105, 109, 128, 133
Construction boom   2, 3, 78, 88, 144, 212, 222,
    223, 224, 260, 266, 269, 270
Construction capital   116, 117, 130, 136, 146,
    148, 149, 161, 167, 169, 170, 178, 181, 182,
    183, 196, 199, 203, 224, 229, 232, 233,
    237, 240, 243, 246, 249, 257, 258, 260,
    262, 270
Construction companies   3, 13, 111, 130, 148,
    149n18, 155, 160, 167, 181, 200, 203, 206,
    225, 226, 226n3, 233, 234, 235, 236, 238,
    239, 240n12, 240n13, 242, 243, 245, 246,
    248, 250, 251, 252, 253, 253f35, 254, 256,
    257, 259, 271
Construction costs   15, 29, 147, 158,
    242n14

Construction firms   79, 93, 122, 138n6, 140,
     142, 149, 180, 231, 232, 234, 236, 240n12,
     245, 254, 256
Construction industry   32, 33n11, 34, 43, 88,
     92, 103, 103n1, 106, 109, 122, 127, 131, 142,
     149n18, 152, 153, 167, 185, 187, 188, 196,
     218, 222n1, 223, 225, 226, 228, 228n6,
     230, 234, 237, 244, 246, 253, 254, 256,
     257, 261, 262, 267, 268
Consumer loans   3, 73, 120, 121f5, 122, 123, 125,
     127, 129, 135, 184, 185, 192, 194f17, 195,
     195n4, 198, 198t8, 218, 268
Consumption   1, 3, 5, 7, 8, 9, 10, 11, 13, 14, 31,
     36, 37, 55, 56, 57, 70, 80, 83, 84, 85, 86,
     89, 94, 102, 118, 120, 124, 125, 127, 129, 143,
     151, 152, 183, 184, 187, 188, 190, 191, 195n2,
     196, 208, 213, 220, 224, 228, 240, 262,
     263, 266, 267, 269, 270, 271
Contingency   5, 9, 11, 17, 36, 41, 42, 51, 53, 64,
     102, 130
Contractors   44n20, 140n8, 157, 158, 160, 161,
     162, 167, 170, 213, 216, 225n3, 229, 235,
     237, 240, 241, 244, 246n17
Cooperatives   91, 116, 140, 140n8, 142, 143,
     144n13, 145, 145n14, 145n15, 146, 221, 270
Corporate loans   252, 256
Counter-cyclical   79n12, 93, 128, 191
Counter-tendencies   7, 22, 53, 72, 93, 264, 267
Coup d'état   104, 105, 127, 128, 134, 141, 189,
     195, 195n4, 211, 253
Credit Guarantee Fund   128, 253
Crisis   56, 64, 65, 78, 78n12, 83, 85, 87, 88, 92,
     99, 100, 103, 104, 106, 109, 112, 113, 114,
     115, 121, 123, 124n7, 125, 126, 128, 130, 133,
     148, 149, 150, 151, 163, 184, 188, 190, 195,
     203, 214, 216, 217, 220, 223, 227, 228n6,
     239, 241, 248, 253, 254, 255, 261, 264
Critical Accountants   56
Currency   69, 107, 111, 112, 113, 122, 125, 127,
     128, 130, 148, 189, 195, 201, 214, 228, 241,
     252, 254, 255, 256, 261
Cycle   2, 3, 42, 49, 52, 55, 77, 79, 79n12, 80, 110,
     123, 196, 212, 219, 232, 236, 257, 258n21,
     259, 266, 269, 270

De Soto   90, 162
Debt   3, 7, 59, 62, 62n1, 70, 73, 74, 75, 77, 79,
     82, 83, 85, 86, 87, 87n15, 107, 111, 112,

120, 121f6, 122, 123, 125, 125n7, 127, 128,
     129, 134, 135, 144, 147, 152, 158, 159, 175,
     176, 180, 184, 188, 190, 193, 194f17, 195,
     195n2, 197, 198, 200, 201, 203, 214, 218,
     219, 220, 228, 229, 238, 241, 249, 252,
     253, 253f35, 254, 254n20, 255t9, 256, 261,
     266, 268, 269
Decommodification   49, 53, 71, 72, 81, 87, 89,
     178, 205
Decrees   101, 105, 108, 117, 133, 152, 153, 153n2,
     179, 254
Default   85, 85n14, 128, 148, 197, 200, 201, 254
Demand   3, 5, 16, 22, 27, 31, 32, 34, 36, 37, 39,
     41, 43n18, 44, 46, 48, 49, 49n23, 50, 51,
     52, 59, 61, 74, 75, 77, 78, 79, 80, 84, 87,
     88, 92, 103, 114, 116, 120, 124, 130, 137, 142,
     144, 147, 148, 155, 174, 182, 184, 187, 188,
     191, 192, 195, 197, 201, 205, 206, 207, 208,
     211, 211n16, 212, 212n17, 214, 219, 228, 239,
     242n14, 248, 254, 257, 258, 262, 266, 269
Democratic   84, 100, 101, 106, 113, 114, 115, 247
Demographic   14, 136, 137n1, 175, 205
Depreciation   107, 111, 126, 127, 128, 131, 195,
     212, 215, 238, 241, 254
Deregulation   67, 81, 107, 150
Derivatives   79, 82, 91, 125n7, 171, 187,
     188, 268
Devaluation   79, 87, 107, 147, 148, 256
Developers   3, 13, 42n16, 45, 48, 75, 76, 77, 78,
     78n9, 79, 145, 163, 167, 174, 178, 179n22,
     180, 181, 182, 200, 201, 203, 208, 214, 221,
     222, 224, 225, 229, 231, 232, 233, 234, 235,
     236, 237, 238, 240, 242n14, 243, 244, 246,
     247, 248, 249, 250, 252, 253, 254, 256,
     257, 259, 262, 269, 270
Development finance   74, 75, 143, 221, 224,
     232, 249, 250, 251, 252, 257, 265, 270
Development Gains   26, 28, 30, 31, 34, 35, 37,
     41, 44, 45, 46, 48, 49, 50, 52, 77, 93, 139,
     146, 160, 161, 170, 224, 229, 232, 235, 236,
     237, 242, 243, 249, 254, 257, 262, 264
Differential Rent   18, 19, 20, 20n6, 21, 22, 25,
     27, 28, 29, 30, 31, 32, 35, 39, 40, 48
Discontent   109, 160, 161, 170, 243, 244
Dispossession   91, 177, 178, 199, 268
Distribution   5, 10, 17, 19, 20, 21, 22, 26, 27, 36,
     37, 45, 48, 49, 52, 61, 62, 64, 65, 68, 85,
     86, 131, 133, 135, 138, 139, 156, 163, 173f10,

Distribution (*cont.*)
  197n5, 199, 213, 216, 220, 229f32, 247, 261,
  262, 266
Dollarization   122, 196
Domestic capital   111, 116, 170
Dominant class   98, 99, 100, 113, 131
Down-payment   127, 142, 144, 158, 165, 191

Earthquake   49, 149, 179, 179n21, 181, 207, 208,
  219, 223, 233, 233n10, 248
Economic growth   56, 114, 120, 126, 127, 130,
  131, 162, 195n2, 196, 222, 261, 262
Economic reproduction   27, 58, 59, 71, 80,
  89, 93, 125, 152, 207, 267
Effective Demand   16, 29, 33, 36, 37, 38, 40,
  41, 44, 46, 47, 47n22, 48, 49, 50, 50n24,
  52, 74, 75, 77, 78, 78n9, 79, 80, 82, 88, 93,
  94, 123, 125, 133, 143, 144, 150, 156, 162,
  178, 181, 184, 187, 188, 191, 196, 200, 205,
  207, 208, 210, 212, 219, 224, 236, 247, 257,
  263, 266, 268, 269
Emergency Action Plan   151, 155, 174
Emlak Bank   140, 143, 148, 150, 168
Emlak Konut   13n1, 167, 168, 168n12, 168n13,
  168n14, 169, 169f9, 169n15, 170, 170t5, 171,
  171t6, 203, 236, 242, 243, 256, 268
Employment   39, 41, 61, 81, 88, 102, 129n11,
  133, 140, 152, 208, 217n25, 237, 256,
  261, 271
Enabling-markets approach   90, 92
Energy   71, 109, 117, 128, 131, 151n1, 224, 226,
  242n14, 250, 256
Equity withdrawal   85, 86, 216
Equity-sharing   139, 146, 232, 233, 238
Erdoğan   116, 129, 134, 151, 153, 153n2, 195n4,
  203, 223, 228n6, 249
Europe   68, 78n12, 79, 88, 91, 108, 114, 116,
  125n7, 127, 129, 158, 168, 186, 191, 206,
  210n15, 226
Eviction   91, 138n5, 176, 177, 182
Exceptional forms of state   100, 104, 134
Exchange rate   66, 66n4, 107, 110, 111, 112, 115,
  195n3, 242, 257
Exchange value   4, 6, 17, 20, 163, 167, 218,
  264, 270
Exclusion   3, 84, 86, 92, 101, 107, 117, 140,
  168n14, 182, 184, 192, 197, 198, 199, 200,
  219, 224, 266, 269

Executive   2, 99, 100, 101, 105, 106, 115, 133,
  143, 153, 155, 183, 222, 267
Export   66, 103, 103n1, 104, 106, 107, 108, 110,
  111, 123, 127, 130, 227, 246n17
Export-oriented industrialisation   66, 103,
  105, 106, 107, 110, 125, 141
Extensive   17, 21, 22, 34, 36, 48, 54, 57, 64, 70,
  71, 73, 74, 80, 87, 92, 94, 101, 117, 118, 143,
  212, 250, 261, 264, 265
External debt   103, 107, 122, 123f7, 128, 131, 185,
  191, 218, 228, 253, 255t9, 268
Extra-economic   96, 97, 247, 261

Family   11, 80, 81, 90, 92, 93, 96, 108, 129, 137,
  157, 176, 198, 200, 217, 220, 239
FED   66, 78n12, 126, 254
Fertility   20, 25
Fictitious capital   62, 63, 76, 79, 82, 111,
  121, 185
Financial capital   42n16, 56, 66, 72, 93, 98,
  108, 157, 260
Financial Inclusion   3, 73, 84, 127, 184, 187,
  197, 198, 200, 219, 269
Financial institutions   3, 26, 55, 59, 62, 76, 77,
  81, 83, 125n7, 128, 157, 159, 168, 200, 208,
  221, 229, 236, 252, 256, 264, 265, 266
Financialisation in the broad sense   80, 83,
  86, 88, 93, 117, 120, 159
Financialisation in the narrow sense   80, 82,
  83, 120, 150, 159, 249
Financialisation of banks   118
Financialisation of daily life   159
Financialisation of Housing   1, 2, 7, 11, 13, 55,
  56, 74, 78, 80, 84, 93, 94, 168, 187, 191,
  212, 218, 219, 220, 247, 248, 249, 252, 265,
  268, 269, 270
First-generation bourgeoisie   132, 133, 224,
  226, 230, 244, 248, 257, 258
Fiscal   66, 66n4, 67, 88, 103, 107, 110, 112, 115,
  117, 118, 123, 128, 147, 150, 152, 153, 163,
  163n11, 183, 196
Fixed capital   47, 47n22, 112, 228, 237
Foreign capital   3, 66, 66n4, 82, 104, 116,
  118, 122, 124, 208, 219, 224, 248, 252,
  270, 271
Foreign demand   205, 206, 206f24, 235, 249
Foreign direct investment   114, 118, 120f4, 124,
  201, 205, 207, 248

Foreign exchange   108, 110, 112, 122, 124, 124*t1*,
    125, 189, 191, 195, 195*n3*, 196, 203, 213,
    228, 238, 249, 250, 253, 254, 255
Fractionalisation   3, 132, 270
France   43*n18*, 46*n21*, 237, 252
Free market   97, 151, 245

Garanti Bank   186
GDP   83, 87, 119*f3*, 120, 120*f4*, 121*f6*, 129,
    144*n13*, 192, 193*f16*, 196, 213, 228*n7*,
    229*f32*, 230*f33*, 261
Gecekondu   137, 137*n2*, 138, 138*n5*, 139, 141,
    146, 146*n16*, 150, 151, 155, 174, 175, 175*n17*,
    176, 177, 199, 199*n6*, 208, 232, 248, 268
Gentrification   35, 39, 177, 199, 208, 232
Germany   43*n18*, 85*n14*, 237
Global Financial Crisis   1, 64, 88, 93, 118, 124,
    124*n7*, 130, 133, 135, 151, 182, 195, 197, 210,
    215, 251, 253, 258
Global North   65*n3*, 66, 68, 130*n12*, 237
Global South   66, 68, 69, 90, 237
Global tendencies   1, 9, 69
Government debt securities   111, 112, 118, 121,
    125, 135, 149*n18*, 184
Ground rent   4, 5, 6, 13, 15, 15*n1*, 16, 17, 18, 19,
    23, 24, 25, 26, 28, 30, 33, 36, 38, 39, 40,
    42, 43, 44, 44*n19*, 45, 51, 53, 74, 76, 85*n14*,
    91, 139, 140, 146, 156, 162, 176, 199, 205,
    211, 223, 247, 262, 263, 264, 265, 270
GYODER   182, 238, 244, 244*n16*, 257

Hedge funds   85*n14*, 252
Hegemonic   54, 71, 89, 98, 99, 100, 101, 102,
    103, 104, 107, 111, 113, 114, 115, 122, 130, 131,
    133, 135, 162, 185, 196, 199, 218, 223, 224,
    244, 248, 256, 260, 268, 270
High-income   44*n20*, 142, 197, 230, 240
Historical-systemic   1, 57, 64, 72, 94
Holding companies   102, 107, 108, 109, 111, 121,
    122, 128, 147, 225, 226, 245
Homeownership   49, 84, 86, 87, 92, 94, 142,
    144, 145, 146, 159, 184, 196, 197, 199, 213,
    214, 214*n20*, 218, 220, 244, 261, 266, 270
Hot money   125, 130, 251, 253
House prices   3, 7, 15, 28, 77, 77*n8*, 78, 78*n10*,
    79*n13*, 80, 82, 83, 84, 85, 86, 88, 92, 167,
    184, 187, 208, 209, 210, 210*f26*, 210*n15*,
    211, 211*f27*, 212, 213, 214, 214*n23*, 215, 216,

216*f29*, 217, 220, 224, 236, 242*n14*, 257,
    263, 266, 269
Housebuilder   8, 15, 31, 32, 33, 34, 35, 37, 40,
    41, 42, 44, 44*n19*, 44*n20*, 45, 47, 48, 50,
    51, 52, 53, 74, 75, 78, 93, 138, 138*n6*, 159,
    162, 167, 225, 229, 232, 235, 236, 237, 242,
    252, 254, 259, 264, 265
Housebuilding industry   1, 13, 16, 29, 30, 32,
    33, 33*n11*, 42, 43, 43*n18*, 47, 47*n22*, 48,
    49, 50, 52, 53, 75, 76*n7*, 77, 79, 80, 87,
    94, 106*n3*, 123, 126, 133, 140, 142, 144, 146,
    149, 167, 181, 182, 222*n1*, 225, 226, 227,
    233, 237, 246, 257, 262, 263, 264, 266
Housing deficit   137, 199, 260
Housing finance   44, 78, 79, 81, 83, 87, 140,
    142, 145, 148, 149, 157, 184, 185, 188, 190,
    197, 203, 221, 247
Housing ladder   86, 218, 261
Housing loans   3, 81, 82, 84, 123, 140, 148, 150,
    157, 184, 185, 188, 189, 191, 195, 197, 197*n5*,
    201, 203, 208, 217, 218, 219, 268
Housing Mobilisation   151, 156, 195, 203
Housing need   2, 36, 141, 142, 164, 193, 207,
    214*n20*, 218, 260, 262
Housing projects   76, 90, 93, 140, 147, 157,
    160, 162, 163, 164, 164*t3*, 187, 200, 203,
    234, 238, 239, 240, 240*n12*, 240*n13*, 241,
    242, 243, 244, 248, 251, 261, 270
Housing provision   1, 2, 3, 4, 6, 7, 8, 10, 14, 40,
    42*n16*, 49*n23*, 53, 55, 70, 81, 83, 86, 87,
    88, 89, 94, 136, 137, 139, 140, 150, 151, 154,
    156, 160, 163, 167, 178, 183, 184, 235, 247,
    263, 264, 266, 267
Housing stock   78, 91, 169*f9*, 185, 196, 212, 218,
    221, 256, 257, 259, 260*t10*, 268
Housing submarkets   16, 37, 38, 39, 40, 41, 48,
    52, 80, 92, 140, 207, 208*n14*, 263
Hybrid   62, 72, 109, 111, 251

Ideological   38, 51, 66, 67, 68, 71, 73, 76*n7*, 86,
    88, 89, 91, 93, 94, 95, 97, 98, 102, 109, 131,
    132, 138, 178, 184, 208, 231, 243, 266
Illegal   38, 109, 137, 137*n2*, 138*n3*, 177, 258*n22*
Iller Bank   155
IMF   104*n2*, 105, 112, 113, 114, 115, 116, 117, 118,
    123, 130, 151, 153, 185, 189, 191, 196, 200,
    209, 210*n15*, 213, 214*n23*, 238, 242*n14*,
    249, 256, 259, 261

Import dependency   103, 106, 110, 125

Import substitution industrialisation   66, 66n4, 102, 103, 105, 106, 132, 136, 137, 140, 150

Indonesia   181

Industrial capital   18, 28, 29, 30, 31, 44, 46, 50, 57, 58, 59, 60, 61, 62, 71, 100, 102, 103, 104, 111, 112, 137, 140, 226, 228, 235, 237, 263

Inflation   3, 65, 66, 77, 78, 78n10, 81, 85, 86, 87, 87n15, 110, 111, 113, 115, 123, 126, 126f8, 127, 128, 144n12, 147, 148, 150, 184, 185, 187, 195, 195n2, 196, 197, 209, 210, 212, 213, 215, 217, 220, 224, 242n14, 257, 262, 266, 269, 270

Informal   40, 40n15, 41, 43, 90, 108, 136, 137, 138, 138n5, 138n6, 140, 150, 165, 176, 199, 203, 230, 237, 247, 269

Infrastructure   3, 23, 28, 29, 33n11, 40, 42n16, 70, 88, 93, 109, 137, 139, 144n13, 145, 147, 151n1, 154, 157, 158, 162, 172, 178, 185, 224, 225, 225n3, 235, 245, 248, 250

Initial public offerings   75, 168, 168n14

Instalments   127, 144, 158, 161, 165, 175, 176, 197, 200

Institutional   2, 3, 7, 41, 50, 52, 64, 65, 67, 68, 69, 72, 75, 78, 80, 83, 85n14, 89, 93, 95, 96, 97, 98, 101, 102, 105, 113, 117, 134, 140, 141, 143, 145, 147, 152, 154, 156, 167, 172, 183, 185, 191, 193, 199n7, 201, 203, 219, 223, 224, 226, 231n8, 247, 251, 252, 257, 265, 267, 268, 270

Intensive   17, 22, 22n7, 31, 34, 43, 48, 57, 64, 70, 71, 73, 75, 87, 94, 108, 112, 135, 156, 212, 261, 264, 265

Interest rate   49, 61, 62, 63, 66, 66n4, 81, 84, 85, 87n15, 111, 112, 113, 120, 123, 125, 126, 126f8, 126n8, 127, 128, 139, 140, 144, 147, 182, 185, 189, 190, 191, 195n4, 196, 200, 201, 204f23, 213, 214n22, 217, 224, 248, 251, 252, 253, 256, 257, 271

Interest-bearing capital   4, 5, 57, 58, 59, 60, 61, 62, 63, 63n2, 64, 67, 70, 71, 72, 73, 74, 75, 76, 77, 80, 81, 82, 83, 87, 89, 91, 94, 111, 112, 121, 135, 187, 189, 207, 212, 216, 219, 250, 262, 264, 265, 266, 269

Internationalisation   67, 95, 101, 110, 116, 235, 265

Interview   12, 13, 13n1, 153, 153n2, 157, 158, 160, 161, 162, 165, 167, 169, 169n16, 170, 172, 174, 176, 177, 180, 181, 182, 197, 208n14, 223, 225, 226, 227, 231, 233, 233n9, 234, 235, 236, 237, 238, 239, 240, 241, 242, 243, 244, 248, 249, 252, 258

INTES   230, 231n8, 246, 257

Intra-class   2, 94, 100, 102, 109, 111, 116, 132, 133, 153

Investment tool   36, 182, 191, 208, 213, 220

Investors   3, 8, 71, 75, 77, 79, 82, 85n14, 90, 114, 126, 128, 130n12, 142, 155, 168, 172, 174, 187, 188, 191, 197, 206, 208, 210, 213, 216, 224, 229, 231, 244, 251, 252, 257, 262, 264, 271

Iran   206

Iraq   206, 246

Ireland   78n11, 79, 85n14, 87, 91, 216

Islamic   108, 109, 111, 113, 114, 114n5, 116, 130n12, 132, 240n13, 243

Istanbul   13, 103, 107, 108, 109, 111, 114, 130, 130n12, 132, 138n4, 138n5, 145, 147, 148, 149, 153, 160n8, 163, 165, 167, 172, 174, 176, 177, 180, 187, 205, 208n14, 209, 210, 210f26, 212, 214n19, 215, 217, 220, 225, 226, 227, 227n5, 231, 233, 242, 245, 248, 269

Italy   82

Izmir   138n4, 138n5, 145, 163, 209, 210f26, 220

Japan   76n7, 88, 127, 252

Kazakhstan   82, 246

Keynesian   54, 65, 88

KONUTDER   231, 244, 244n16

Labour cost   133, 235, 237

Labour theory of value   4, 5, 7, 42, 191, 195, 197, 200

Labour-intensive   43, 107, 110, 261

Labour-power   1, 4, 5, 6, 10, 39, 42, 57, 58, 71, 73, 80, 81, 97, 137, 138, 146, 152, 164, 165, 225, 267

Labour-time   5, 19, 20, 43, 44

Land bank   46, 50, 79, 93, 167, 200, 224, 247

Land development   2, 8, 37, 145, 152, 154, 158, 160, 222, 241, 242, 245, 247

Land Office   148, 154

Land prices   3, 41, 45, 77, 91, 175n17, 238, 246,
     262, 265, 269
Land quality   17, 20, 25, 27, 29, 30, 31, 34, 40,
     52, 207
Land regime   53, 76n7, 78, 137, 150
Land stock   154, 160, 168, 169, 224, 243,
     246, 268
Land title   25, 62, 63, 90, 91, 136, 137, 138,
     138n3, 139, 146, 175, 176, 196
Land values   52
Landed property   6, 11, 13, 15, 16, 17, 18, 20, 21,
     23, 24, 25, 26, 27, 31, 32, 33, 34, 42, 44n19,
     45, 51, 52, 74, 156, 263, 264
Land-for-flat   139
Landlord   23, 24, 26, 85n14, 140, 182
Landowner   3, 8, 11, 18, 20, 20n6, 21, 22, 23,
     24, 26, 28, 29, 30, 30n8, 31, 34, 35, 35n12,
     37, 40, 44, 45, 48, 50, 51, 52, 53, 74, 77,
     79, 139, 146, 154, 155, 160, 162, 167, 172,
     175n17, 176, 177, 178, 179, 221, 222, 224,
     229, 232, 233, 234, 236, 242, 262, 264,
     268, 269
Late-capitalist countries   69, 78n12, 90, 91,
     102, 112, 118, 124n7, 125, 188, 250, 253
Law   85n14, 116, 117, 141, 142, 145n14, 154, 155,
     160, 174, 178, 179, 185, 190, 238, 254
Law on the Transformation of Areas
     under Disaster Risk   178, 179, 181, 182,
     233, 238
Leasing   21, 22n7, 76, 85n14, 86, 138, 182, 185,
     199, 213, 251
Legal   3, 12, 38, 40, 61, 62, 63, 73, 76n7, 83, 90,
     92, 101, 116, 131, 133, 138, 140, 141, 145, 146,
     147, 154, 155, 156, 165, 174, 175, 175n17, 176,
     185, 191, 223, 230, 243, 250, 252, 268, 270
Legitimisation   97, 99, 101, 114, 138, 152, 153,
     162, 181, 183, 199, 233, 244, 267, 270
Leveraged   122, 184, 213, 218, 237, 241, 253,
     254, 258, 270
Liabilities   122, 125, 190, 193, 194f17, 197,
     241, 250
Libya   246
Liquid   3, 76, 79n12, 81, 82, 110, 114, 118, 122,
     124, 125, 127, 130, 172, 185, 186, 187, 218,
     224, 242, 257, 268, 270, 271
Loanable money capital   62, 71, 196, 212, 270
Loan-to-value   4, 5, 7, 42, 191, 195, 197,
     200, 203

Local governments   13, 109, 114, 116, 131, 140,
     145, 147, 151, 155, 174, 176, 178, 181, 233,
     233n9, 235
Location   10, 15, 24, 25, 28, 29, 30, 30n8, 31,
     37, 38, 39, 40, 41, 45, 47, 49, 51, 52, 68,
     69, 78n10, 81, 91, 98, 109, 132, 145, 156,
     162, 163, 176, 178, 181, 212n17, 232, 258,
     263, 270
Logical   1, 5, 6, 7, 16n1, 19, 25, 34, 50, 55, 57,
     60, 64, 67, 68, 94
Lower classes   38, 40, 159, 163, 167, 174, 178,
     178n18, 198, 199, 200, 203, 261, 268, 269
Low-income   88, 90, 92, 93, 158, 164, 165, 167,
     195, 197, 199, 218
Luxury housing   127, 130, 149, 157, 160, 161,
     163, 164, 167, 178, 191, 195, 196, 203,
     204f22, 226, 228, 236, 242, 245, 250,
     251, 259

M&A   80, 118
Macroeconomic   50, 52, 56, 66, 74, 81, 87,
     87n15, 112, 115, 120, 123, 148, 149, 193, 196,
     213, 219, 222n1, 223, 260, 262, 269, 271
Macroprudential   126, 195, 201
Malaysia   82, 88, 91, 188, 214n23
Malthus   16, 16n2
Market price   5, 17, 21, 24, 28, 32, 44, 61, 147,
     158, 263
Market value   19, 19n5, 20, 21, 29, 30n8, 32,
     50, 63, 84, 140, 168, 169, 169n15, 170, 172,
     175, 175n17, 179, 191, 215
Marketing   46, 162, 163, 168, 169, 236, 243
Marxist   1, 4, 5, 7, 8, 13, 15n1, 17, 19, 31, 35,
     38, 42n16, 54, 55, 57, 64, 65, 80, 96,
     263, 271
Mass Housing   2, 106, 117, 141, 142, 144, 147,
     150, 151, 157, 171, 172, 185, 241, 243, 245
Maturity   55, 129, 144, 148, 176, 180, 182, 189,
     191, 192, 196, 200, 217, 218f30, 256
Mercantile capital   44, 46, 47, 50, 58, 59, 60,
     61, 107, 121, 167, 232, 237, 238, 258
Metropolitan   13, 39, 40, 109, 145, 149, 156,
     162, 163, 168n12, 177, 178, 180, 181, 235,
     240, 247, 248, 257
Mexico   82, 91, 93, 214n23
Middle class   139, 139n7, 140, 145, 147, 198,
     199, 200, 208n14, 213, 219, 221, 244,
     269, 270

Middle East and North America   103, 149n17, 168, 168n13, 206, 235
Migrant   43, 108, 137, 138, 208n14, 211n16, 237
Migration   137, 139, 141, 205, 208, 209, 219
Ministry of Environment and Urbanisation   155, 156, 179, 231, 247
Money dealing capital   58, 61, 62, 212
Money form   44, 75, 80
Monopolistic   46, 55, 64, 167, 264
Monopoly price   16, 22, 25, 27, 28, 31, 32, 35, 39, 40, 44, 46, 74, 263
Monopoly rent   15, 18, 22, 27, 28, 29, 30, 31, 31n9, 32, 33, 34, 35, 35n12, 36, 37, 38, 39, 40, 41, 42, 44, 45, 46, 47, 47n22, 48, 49, 49n23, 50, 51, 52, 53, 61, 74, 75, 76, 77, 78n10, 79, 80, 82, 83, 86, 88, 94, 123, 133, 152, 156, 160, 162, 163, 178, 185, 187, 191, 207, 208, 212, 212n17, 213, 219, 220, 224, 228, 235, 242, 244, 249, 257, 262, 263, 265, 266, 267, 268, 269, 270
Monthly Review School   55
Mortgage loans   39, 62, 73, 74, 77, 80, 81, 82, 83, 84, 85, 88, 144, 147, 148, 157, 158, 159, 182, 184, 185, 186, 186n1, 188, 189, 190, 190f14, 191, 192, 192f15, 193, 193f16, 194f17, 194f18, 195n4, 196, 197, 198t8, 200, 201, 204f23, 214n19, 214n22, 217, 238, 248, 251, 252, 266
Mortgage market   3, 81, 82, 83, 84, 85, 89, 92, 95, 184, 185, 188, 189, 190, 191, 192, 193, 196, 197, 198, 200, 201, 203, 205, 219, 266, 268, 269
Mortgage rates   144n12, 176, 189, 191, 192, 195n4, 196, 200, 203, 210, 217, 224
Mortgage-Backed Securities   79, 82, 185, 186, 186n1, 188, 197
multi-storey   31, 34, 139, 146, 157
Municipality   13, 109, 131, 137, 145, 156, 162, 168n12, 174, 175, 177, 179, 180, 181, 232, 233, 247, 248, 257, 258
MUSIAD   114, 114n5, 132, 240n13
Mutual fund   75, 168

Neighbourhood   30n8, 37, 39, 49, 52, 162, 175, 176, 177, 178, 180, 181, 182, 208n14, 214n19
Neoclassical   8, 9, 16, 16n2, 17, 35, 41, 66, 211
Neoliberal   1, 2, 7, 13, 35, 51, 65n3, 66, 66n4, 67, 68, 71, 86, 87, 88, 89, 90, 92, 95, 96, 102, 104, 105, 106, 108, 113, 114, 115, 117, 126n8, 133, 134, 135, 136, 141, 142, 145, 149, 150, 154, 155, 163n11, 222, 223, 247, 248, 260, 262, 266, 268, 270
Neoliberalism   2, 6, 14, 51, 64, 65, 66, 67, 68, 69, 70, 71, 72, 88, 89, 90, 92, 94, 95, 96, 102, 105, 106, 110, 113, 114, 125, 134, 141, 143, 152, 183, 265, 267
Netherlands   78n9, 82, 87, 91
New Zealand   82
Non-financial companies   56, 71, 122, 123f7, 124t1, 125, 127, 128, 135, 195, 253, 255t9
Non-performing loans   197, 198t8, 253, 254, 256

Occupancy permits   258
Ollman   6, 7, 265
Oman   246
Organic composition of capital   19, 21, 22n7, 32, 33, 33n11, 34, 47
Owner-occupation   3, 84, 88, 90, 91, 95, 138, 140, 152, 184, 199, 217, 219, 251, 266, 268, 269
Özal   105, 142, 245

Pamuk Bank   143
Park Mavera   172
Pension funds   26
Periodisation   6, 7, 56, 57, 65, 110, 136, 150, 163, 203
Peripheral   2, 69, 90, 93, 107, 138, 145, 157, 176
Planning   2, 34, 51, 52, 76n7, 78, 78n9, 93, 138n5, 145, 152, 153n2, 154, 155, 156, 157, 180n22, 181, 183, 207, 208, 219, 222, 223, 247, 268
Poland   191, 214n23
Political manoeuvre   98, 132, 152, 153
Poor group   158, 164, 165
Population   16n2, 26, 49, 78, 91, 92, 136, 137n1, 138n4, 138n5, 140, 141n9, 146n16, 158, 164, 165, 175, 187, 197, 199, 199n7, 200, 205, 208, 214n20, 219
Portugal   82, 88, 91
Possession   177, 178, 199, 268
Post-Washington Consensus   67, 92
Poulantzas   133
Power bloc   96, 98, 99, 100, 101, 102, 103, 107, 109, 113, 114, 127, 129, 130, 131, 132, 133,

Power bloc (*cont.*)
   134, 152, 153, 231, 247, 248, 256, 260,
   267, 270
Presidential system   101, 129, 134, 179*n*20
Price-to-rent ratio   214
Private rental   85*n*14, 138, 184
Private sector   3, 92, 116, 122, 125, 127, 128, 129,
   131, 144*n*13, 147, 152, 153, 167, 168, 189,
   195, 201, 221, 228, 254, 267, 270
Privatisation   3, 39*n*14, 66*n*4, 67, 71, 72, 73,
   86, 88, 89, 90, 91, 114, 115, 117, 118, 131, 151,
   152, 155, 162, 167, 172, 183, 199, 222, 224,
   242, 245, 247, 265, 267
Production   1, 3, 4, 5, 6, 7, 8, 9, 10, 11, 13, 14,
   15, 15*n*1, 16, 17, 18, 18*n*4, 19, 20, 21, 22,
   22*n*7, 23, 24, 26, 27, 28, 29, 30, 31, 32,
   32*n*10, 33, 33*n*11, 34, 35, 36, 37, 38, 39,
   40, 40*n*15, 41, 42, 43*n*17, 43*n*18, 44, 46,
   47, 47*n*22, 48, 49, 50, 51, 52, 53, 55, 57,
   58, 59, 60, 61, 63, 64, 65, 66, 67, 70, 72,
   73, 74, 75, 77, 78*n*11, 79, 89, 92, 93, 94,
   96, 97, 98, 100, 102, 103, 106, 107, 108,
   112, 125, 132, 139, 140, 141, 142, 144*n*13,
   146, 149, 150, 151, 152, 158, 160, 163, 164,
   167, 175, 180, 183, 187, 203, 212, 214, 221,
   223, 224, 225, 226, 228, 229*f*32, 232, 233,
   234, 235, 236, 237, 238, 240, 240*n*12,
   240*n*13, 242, 242*n*14, 244, 245, 246, 247,
   249, 252, 257, 258, 260, 262, 263, 264,
   265, 266, 267, 270
Profit margins   46, 47, 77, 93, 235, 239, 244
Profit rates   19, 21, 33, 40, 61, 62, 66, 263
Property rights   76*n*7, 90, 91, 92, 136, 137, 140,
   143, 152, 158, 165, 175, 176, 247
Public procurement   116, 117*n*6, 157*n*5, 161*n*9,
   168, 168*n*14, 224, 225, 235, 243
Public sector borrowing
   requirement   118, 119*f*3

Qatar   245
Quantitative easing   78*n*12, 120, 122, 126, 127,
   131, 251, 254

Real estate   3, 42, 75, 76, 79, 88, 91, 123, 144,
   148, 158, 163, 163*n*10, 168, 168*n*12, 170, 172,
   174, 175, 179, 182, 183, 187, 203*n*9, 205,
   207, 208, 209, 213, 213*n*18, 214*n*19, 219,
   222*n*1, 223, 224, 225, 226, 228, 229*f*32,

   236, 244, 245, 246, 247, 249, 250, 251,
   252, 254, 255*t*9, 256, 261, 262, 265, 271
Real estate investment funds   3, 188, 249, 252
Real estate investment trusts   3, 13*n*1, 76,
   76*n*6, 85*n*14, 155, 167, 168, 168*n*12, 169,
   169*f*9, 169*n*15, 170, 170*t*5, 171, 185, 188,
   200, 203, 206, 222, 225, 226, 236, 240,
   242, 243, 247, 249, 250, 251, 251*f*34, 252,
   256, 268, 269, 271
Realisation   42*n*16, 59
Recession   49, 79, 124
Regeneration   155, 174, 175, 179, 233
Regulation School   56
Relative autonomy   63, 99, 100, 106
Relative surplus-value   5, 43, 43*n*17
Relocation   164, 174, 175, 178
Rent distribution   178, 244, 270
Rent-based accumulation   212, 216, 220
Rentier sectors   64, 229
Rent-seeker   177
Residential land   6, 13, 15, 26, 28, 31, 33, 34,
   37, 39, 40, 41, 42, 49, 52, 74, 156, 162, 184,
   207, 208, 209, 219, 262, 264
Resistance   45, 72, 99, 104, 105, 106, 175,
   177, 182
Restructuring of the banking sector   115, 117,
   118, 120, 185
Restructuring of the state   2, 14, 95, 104, 105,
   113, 117, 134, 141, 151, 163, 223, 247
Revenue-sharing   160, 160*n*8, 161, 161*n*9, 162,
   163, 164, 165, 167, 169, 172, 176, 178, 187,
   224, 236, 240*n*12, 242, 243
Ricardo   16, 17, 20, 21
Risk   46, 73, 79, 82, 84, 85, 87, 111, 125, 127,
   128, 129, 134, 155, 161, 167, 179, 179*n*20,
   179*n*21, 181, 182, 186*n*1, 187, 188, 190, 195,
   197, 200, 201, 207, 213, 214, 216, 228, 231,
   233*n*10, 237, 238, 241, 243, 254, 258
Rural   93, 103, 136, 137, 138, 205
Russia   149*n*17, 149*n*18, 246

Sales   12, 21, 28, 38, 45, 46, 47, 57, 74, 75, 82,
   90, 127, 139, 158, 160, 161, 162, 165, 169,
   172, 173*f*10, 174, 200, 201, 201*n*8, 202*f*20,
   202*f*21, 203, 203*n*9, 204*f*23, 206, 206*n*13,
   207*f*25, 209, 214, 214*n*22, 215*f*28, 216, 235,
   238, 242, 248, 249, 259
Saudi Arabia   245

Savings   49, 59, 62, 81, 85, 91, 92, 108, 112, 118, 129, 139, 141, 148, 150, 158, 174, 182, 187, 188, 195, 214, 242, 257

Scarcity   5, 16, 27, 29, 30, 31, 34, 35, 36, 37, 38, 39, 40, 41, 44, 48, 49, 74, 76, 78, 162, 208, 210, 233, 238, 247, 264

Secondary market   3, 63, 75, 84, 91, 150, 185, 186n1, 187, 188, 189, 193, 197, 218, 252, 268

Second-generation bourgeoisie   133, 135, 152, 178, 224, 231, 244, 247, 248, 252, 257, 260, 267, 270, 271

Second-hand housing   214, 214n22, 215f28, 216, 259

Securities   62, 84, 122, 147, 174, 186, 187, 190, 250

Securitisation   72, 73, 76, 82, 83, 84, 91, 157, 159, 168, 185, 188, 251, 265, 266

Sell-to-build   237

Shadow banking   184, 192, 200, 201, 201f19, 203, 205, 208, 219, 231, 238, 254

Shareholder   13, 75, 76, 76n7, 80, 94, 108, 122, 160, 162, 168, 169, 170t5, 179, 180, 222, 226, 233, 240, 242, 250, 252, 265

Sheltering   1, 6, 37, 81, 102, 137, 143, 146, 150, 165, 180, 198, 199, 203, 207, 218

Shock   66, 78, 79, 112, 127, 200, 205, 210, 241, 254, 266

Shortage   31, 33, 41, 49, 144, 156, 163, 164, 172, 223

Slum   2, 40, 90, 91, 152, 164, 174, 175

Small and medium-sized enterprises   12, 107, 108, 109, 114, 114n5, 116, 128, 129, 129n11, 130, 132, 225, 227, 231, 234, 235, 236, 240, 240n12, 246, 252, 256, 260

Social formation   6, 7, 38, 51, 68, 95, 98, 99, 104, 265

Social housing   39n14, 55, 75, 88, 89, 90, 91, 92, 93, 94, 136, 142n10, 145, 158, 162, 167, 180, 183, 221, 241, 247, 267, 268

Social Insurance Fund   140

Social relation   2, 4, 6, 8, 9, 15, 15n1, 17, 18, 23, 25, 26, 53, 67, 69, 81, 87, 94, 95, 263

Social reproduction   1, 3, 4, 5, 6, 15, 27, 35, 36, 38, 50, 51, 52, 64, 65, 67, 70, 71, 72, 73, 74, 80, 84, 87, 89, 93, 102, 113, 114, 118, 120, 123, 127, 131, 133, 134, 135, 152, 160, 176, 178, 217, 220, 261, 263, 265, 266, 267

Socialisation   84, 107, 129, 167

South Africa   82, 250

South Korea   43n18, 82, 87, 88, 93, 250

Spain   78n11, 79, 82, 84, 85n14, 87, 216

Specialisation   40, 58, 79, 80, 81, 101, 105, 108, 111, 115, 143, 155, 225, 260

Speculation   1, 28, 34, 35, 39, 44, 44n20, 45, 46n21, 47, 48, 50, 52, 53, 54, 55, 63, 71, 73, 74, 77, 79, 90, 91, 93, 110, 112, 128, 136, 139, 145, 150, 162, 212, 213, 214, 217, 220, 228, 232, 234, 237, 248, 265, 266

Sphere of circulation   22, 27, 56, 60

Squatter   137, 146, 164, 175, 175n17, 176, 177, 178, 199, 268

Stagflation   66

State apparatus   101, 104, 117, 143, 223

State capacity   2, 113, 115, 116, 136, 150, 183, 222

State intervention   92, 95, 97, 143, 156, 177, 247, 258, 261

State-owned banks   105, 118, 127, 127n9, 129, 143, 148, 150, 151, 186, 187, 188, 190, 196, 197, 214n22, 219, 248, 256, 269

State-owned enterprises   66n4, 105, 127n9, 154

Stock market   56, 65, 79, 80, 122, 250

Strategic field   98, 109, 132, 153

Structural adjustment   104, 112, 115, 141, 142, 146

Subcontracting   43, 43n18, 133, 157, 234, 235, 237, 241, 244

Subprime   84, 85, 92, 159, 187, 188, 197

Subsidy   81, 89, 91, 92, 93, 107, 110, 131, 137, 140, 141, 143, 144, 147, 152, 162, 163, 182, 191, 270

Superstructure   71, 154, 225, 245

Supply   5, 16, 27, 29, 36, 37, 41, 44, 49, 49n23, 51, 52, 61, 75, 77, 78, 78n11, 78n9, 125, 142, 146, 156, 201, 212, 212n17, 221, 222, 225, 237, 242n14, 266, 269

Surplus profit   17, 18, 19, 20, 20n6, 21, 22, 24, 25, 27, 30, 32, 33, 40

Surplus-value   4, 5, 6, 17, 18, 19, 20, 21, 22, 23, 26, 27, 28, 29, 31, 32, 39, 42, 42n16, 43n17, 44n19, 48, 57, 58, 59, 60, 61, 62, 63, 64, 80, 85, 96, 106, 207, 216, 220, 229, 262, 263, 264

Syria   205, 211n16, 237

System of accumulation   10, 49, 55, 66, 68, 69, 110, 111, 112, 126n8, 135, 262

Systems of Provision   8, 9, 10, 14, 94, 269

Technical composition of capital   32, 32*n*10, 33, 33*n*11
Technocratic authoritarianism   115, 133
Technological development   32, 33, 35, 43, 143, 146, 225
Tenant   8, 20*n*6, 21, 23, 40, 45, 91, 138*n*5, 176, 182, 198, 199
Tender   116, 131, 157, 160, 161, 167, 225*n*3, 240*n*13, 242, 243, 244, 245
Tenure   84, 87, 90, 94, 138, 143, 159, 184, 266
Timing   46, 47, 182
TMB   230, 231*n*8, 232, 241, 246, 257
Too big to fail   79, 129
Trade union   72, 104, 110, 237
Transition to Strong Economy Program   114, 117, 118, 120, 123, 130, 151, 154
Turkish Industrialists and Businessmen's Association   103, 104, 109, 114, 130, 132
Turkish Lira-dominated   189, 191
Turkmenistan   246
Turnover of capital   47, 50, 58, 61, 112, 139, 185, 196, 203, 206, 218, 257, 268

Unemployment   128, 134, 146, 165, 176, 195, 197, 217, 217*n*25, 220, 257
United Kingdom   49*n*23, 51, 65, 78*n*9, 80, 82, 83, 84, 87, 91, 240*n*11, 252
Unproductive   48, 98
Unsold housing   47, 79, 165, 185, 203, 212, 237, 256, 257, 259, 268
Upper class   38, 39, 40, 86, 169, 178*n*18, 199, 203, 214, 217
Upper-income   86, 144, 160, 164, 260
Urban land   13, 18, 22, 23, 24, 25, 26, 27, 28, 29, 34, 35, 35*n*12, 37, 45, 52, 139, 143, 156, 157, 160, 167, 181, 205, 207, 208, 210, 219, 233, 238, 242, 247
Urban poor   91, 114, 142, 146, 177, 198, 203, 218, 268

Urban transformation   2, 34, 56, 152, 154, 156, 174, 176, 177, 178, 179, 180, 181, 182, 183, 207, 228*n*6, 238, 243, 245, 257, 259
Urbanisation   14, 25, 35, 36, 67, 136, 139, 150, 221, 232
USA   65, 68, 76*n*7, 77*n*8, 78*n*11, 78*n*12, 79, 82, 83, 84, 85, 85*n*14, 87, 118, 120*f*4, 121*f*5, 121*f*6, 122, 124*n*7, 125, 126, 127, 142, 191, 192, 216, 250, 252, 254
Use-value   1, 4, 38, 39, 59, 81, 167, 208, 218, 264, 270

Vakıf Bank   143, 148, 185
Valorisation   37, 51, 60
Valuable land   9, 157, 165, 178, 243, 244, 268, 270
Value of labour-power   10, 39, 71, 80, 83, 217, 266
Value-added   43, 103, 261, 262
VAT   191, 196, 221, 248
Volatile   50, 52, 77, 78*n*10, 79*n*13, 123, 168, 172, 189, 191, 193, 195*n*3, 200, 212, 216, 250, 251, 266, 270

Wages   1, 4, 6, 18, 19, 22, 27, 39, 43, 49, 80, 81, 82, 84, 87, 94, 104, 105, 110, 120, 127, 129, 137, 146, 148, 195, 196, 229, 237, 263
Washington Consensus   66, 66*n*4, 67, 92
Wealth effect   74, 85, 214, 216, 217, 219
Wealth fund   79, 127, 127*n*9, 129, 256
Welfare   66, 84, 86, 88, 99, 109, 127, 151, 157, 168, 183, 266
Working-class   38, 38*m*13, 39, 51, 81, 99, 101, 104, 105, 115, 127, 137, 139, 150, 218
World Bank   67, 90, 92, 104*n*2, 116, 145, 213, 214*n*23, 235, 242*n*14, 259

Yapsatçıs   138, 139, 140

Zoning   34, 37, 51, 156, 157*n*5, 174, 177, 181, 207, 222, 223, 247

www.ingramcontent.com/pod-product-compliance
Lightning Source LLC
Chambersburg PA
CBHW070053030426
42335CB00016B/1878